# Baseball America
# HEAD
## OF THE CLASS

T0325514

BASEBALL AMERICA INC. · DURHAM, N.C.

# Baseball America

ESTABLISHED 1981
P.O. BOX 12877, DURHAM, NC 27709 • PHONE (919) 682-9635

**EDITOR AND PUBLISHER** B.J. Schecter *@bjschecter*
**EXECUTIVE EDITORS** J.J. Cooper *@jjcoop36*
Matt Eddy *@MattEddyBA*
**CHIEF REVENUE OFFICER** Don Hintze
**DIRECTOR OF BUSINESS DEVELOPMENT** Ben Leigh
**DIRECTOR OF DIGITAL STRATEGY** Mike Salerno

## *EDITORIAL*

**ASSOCIATE EDITORS** Kegan Lowe *@KeganLowe*
Josh Norris *@jnorris427*
Justin Coleman *@ElJayColes*
**SENIOR WRITER** Ben Badler *@benbadler*
**NATIONAL WRITERS** Teddy Cahill *@tedcahill*
Carlos Collazo *@CarlosACollazo*
Kyle Glaser *@KyleAGlaser*
**WEB EDITOR** Mark Chiarelli *@Mark_Chiarelli*
**SPECIAL CONTRIBUTOR** Tim Newcomb *@tdnewcomb*

## *PRODUCTION*

**DIRECTOR OF PRODUCTION** Linwood Webb
**DIRECTOR OF DESIGN** James Alworth

## *BUSINESS*

**TECHNOLOGY MANAGER** Brent Lewis
**ACCOUNT EXECUTIVE** Kellen Coleman
**OFFICE MANAGER & CUSTOMER SERVICE** Angela Lewis
**CUSTOMER SERVICE** Melissa Sunderman

## *STATISTICAL SERVICE*

MAJOR LEAGUE BASEBALL ADVANCED MEDIA

# *BASEBALL AMERICA ENTERPRISES*

**CHAIRMAN & CEO** Gary Green
**PRESIDENT** Larry Botel
**GENERAL COUNSEL** Matthew Pace
**DIRECTOR OF MARKETING** Amy Heart
**INVESTOR RELATIONS** Michele Balfour
**DIRECTOR OF OPERATIONS** Joan Disalvo
**PARTNERS** Jon Ashley
Stephen Alepa
Martie Cordaro
Brian Rothschild
Andrew Fox
Ian Ritchie
Dan Waldman
Sonny Kalsi
Glenn Isaacson
Robert Hernreich
Craig Amazeen
Peter Ruprecht
Beryl Snyder
Tom Steiglehner

# 3 S T≡P

**MANAGING PARTNER** David Geaslen
**CHIEF CONTENT OFFICER** Jonathan Segal
**CHIEF FINANCIAL OFFICER** Sue Murphy

**BASEBALL AMERICA** (ISSN 0745-5372/USPS 591-210) August 6, 2019, Vol. 39, No. 8 is published monthly, 12 issues per year, by Baseball America Enterprises, LLC, 4319 South Alston Ave, Suite 103, Durham, NC 27713. Subscription rate is $92.95 for one year; Canada $118.95 (U.S. funds); all other foreign $144.95 per year (U.S. funds). Periodicals postage paid at Durham, NC, & additional mailing offices. Occasionally our subscriber list is made available to reputable firms offering goods and services we believe would be of interest to our readers. If you prefer to be excluded, please send your current address label and a note requesting to be excluded from these promotions to Baseball America Enterprises, LLC, 4319 South Alston Ave, Suite 103, Durham, NC 27713, Attn: Privacy Coordinator. POSTMASTER: Send all UAA to CFS (See DMM 707.4.12.5); NON-POSTAL & MILITARY FACILITIES: send address corrections to Baseball America, P.O. Box 420235, Palm Coast, FL 32142-0235. CANADA POST: Return undeliverable Canadian addresses to IMEX Global Solutions, P.O. Box 25542, London, ON N6C 6B2. Please contact 1-800-381-1288 to start carrying Baseball America in your store.
©2019 by Baseball America Enterprises, LLC. All Rights Reserved. Printed in the USA.

# Baseball America
# HEAD
## OF THE
# CLASS

**Editor**
Matt Eddy

**Special Project Editor**
Allan Simpson

**BA College Beat Writers**
Jim Callis, John Manuel,
Will Kimmey, Aaron Fitt, Teddy Cahill

**Research Assistant**
Chris Hilburn-Trenkle

**Contributing Editors**
Kegan Lowe, J.J. Cooper, Josh Norris,
Jared McMasters, M'Lynn Dease

**Database and Application Development**
Brent Lewis

**Design & Production**
Linwood Webb, James Alworth

**Programming & Technical Development**
Brent Lewis

**Cover Photos**
Kris Bryant by Robert Gurganus
Buster Posey by Brian Westerholt
Stephen Strasburg by Stan Liu-Icon SMI-Corbis-Icon
Sportswire via Getty Images

For additional copies, visit our Website at
BaseballAmerica.com or call 1-800-845-2726 to order.

US $24.95 / CAN $36.95, plus shipping
and handling per order. Expedited shipping available.

Distributed by Simon & Schuster.
ISBN-13: 978-1-932391-88-6

Statistics provided by Major League Baseball Advanced
Media and compiled by Baseball America.

# INTRODUCTION

Baseball America published its first issue in February 1981. Known as All-America Baseball News at the time, the magazine's inaugural issue featured Arkansas' Kevin McReynolds on the cover and was branded as the College Baseball Preview.

While the magazine title would soon be shortened to Baseball America, and the issue theme to College Preview, the publication's mission has remained the same for the past four decades.

Baseball America delivers comprehensive coverage of the college game, from the College Preview issue each February to the College World Series in June. In more recent years, BA has expanded its offseason coverage to include prospect rankings of recruiting classes and the summer collegiate wood bat leagues.

But for the past 39 seasons, BA has demonstrated remarkable continuity. Each February, readers can look forward to a preseason All-America team, informed by major league scouting directors, and a preseason Top 25 ranking of teams to prepare them for the top storylines that year. At the conclusion of each season, BA selects its College Player of the Year and names its first, second and third All-America teams, while also delivering on-the-ground reporting from the College World Series in Omaha.

What gives Baseball America's coverage weight is the roster of baseball experts who have served as college beat writer. It began with Allan Simpson in the 1980s and continued with Jim Callis and John Manuel in the 1990s and then Will Kimmey and Aaron Fitt in 2000s. Today, Teddy Cahill skillfully extends the legacy of BA's industry-leading college baseball voices.

Now for the first time, "Head of the Class" presents an all-encompassing look at the best college reporting Baseball America has produced in its four decades on the beat, from 1981 to 2019. This book includes every contemporary College World Series game story, every Player of the Year feature, every postseason All-America team, every final Top 25 ranking and various other elements to add context to the game we love

"Head of the Class" also features exclusive new overview chapters for the 1980s, 1990s, 2000s and 2010s in which the top 25 programs, best players, top single-season teams and biggest storylines for each decade are identified. We relied on a modified scoring system (see table below) first devised by Jim Callis in 1997 to determine the top programs for each decade. Schools were rewarded for their postseason success, All-America representation, draft pedigree and the major league impact of their players.

But what excites me as much as anything about "Head of the Class" is its link to Baseball America history. Founding editor Allan Simpson contributes his singular perspective and expertise on the college game in the 1980s, 1990s and also the post-World War II growth period.

**TOP COLLEGE PROGRAM SCORING SYSTEM**

| Category | Explanation | Scoring |
|----------|-------------|---------|
| Regional | Regionals appearances | 5 points each |
| Super | Super regionals appearances | 7 points each |
| CWS | Reached College World Series | 10 points each |
| Title | National championships won | 20 points each |
| AA1 | BA first-team All-Americans | 5 points each |
| AA2 | BA second-team All-Americans | 3 points each |
| AA3 | BA third-team All-Americans | 2 points each |
| Top 10 | Players signed in top 10 rounds of draft | 1 point each |
| MLB | Players who reached major leagues | 1 point each |

**Matt Eddy**
**Executive Editor**

# *1981:* A WATERSHED YEAR FOR COLLEGE BASEBALL

Baseball America didn't invent college baseball coverage, but along with ESPN taking an early interest in the College World Series, it helped popularize and mainstream the college game.

As luck would have it, BA came along in 1981 at precisely the right time. Major league organizations were only just beginning to appreciate the value of college players. Nothing illustrates that point like an Allan Simpson report from the July 1981 issue.

In Simpson's report, he noted that 1981 was a watershed year for college baseball on many fronts. Attendance, led by Miami's record-setting 170,000 fans, established a new record. The College World Series shattered previous attendance records by 30 percent, and the event was broadcast on national TV for the first time by a fledgling ESPN network.

Paced by stars such as Arizona State's Reggie Jackson, college players made up a majority of all draft-eligible big leaguers (53.5 percent) by 1980.

But the biggest piece of evidence that the tide was turning came via the 1981 draft. For the first time, major league organizations emphasized collegians rather than high school players in the early rounds. As recently as 1971, no college players were taken in the first round, but the tables turned in 1981.

Simpson wrote: "This June, 34 of the first 50 players chosen (or a total of 36 in the first two rounds) were from the collegiate ranks. In other words, more than twice as many college players were claimed in the first 50 this year than ever before."

Reasons cited by scouts for the dramatic reversal included an unusually shallow high school class, particularly in California and Texas, and a robust group of college players.

In retrospect, the scouts were right. The top high school players who signed out of the 1981 draft were selected after the first round, including Mark Gubicza in the second round, David Cone and Sid Fernandez (third), Paul O'Neill (fourth), Devon White (sixth), Fred McGriff (ninth) and Lenny Dykstra (13th). Among them, only McGriff (Tampa) and Dykstra (Southern California) hailed from traditional talent hotbeds.

Irregular talent distribution told only half the story. Teams began to favor college players because of their major league proximity when compared with a teenager out of high school. The driving factor for this was the advent of free agency in the mid-to-late 1970s.

Simpson quoted one major league executive: "I don't think some teams can afford to take a high school player in the first round anymore, to spend four or five years developing him, then risk losing him to free agency when he gets to the big leagues.

"And by the same token, if a team has lost a player to free agency, they're often looking for a replacement right away. The way the game has changed, teams are looking for college players who can come quick and fill a void. With a college player, you're more sure of what you're getting. They are, obviously, farther along.

"As for college baseball, yes, there is no question that the major leagues are paying more attention. And with free agency having become such an issue, college baseball is going to have an even bigger impact." ∎

# TABLE OF CONTENTS

The cover of the Baseball America **College Preview** each February tells part of the story of college baseball. Here we present all 39 College Preview covers to introduce each season from 1981 to 2019 with the cover subject (top), the College World Series result (middle) and the BA College Player of the Year (bottom).

| Year | Page |
|------|------|

## 1981    20

**Kevin McReynolds**
Arkansas

**CWS FINAL SCORE**

| | |
|---|---|
| Arizona State | 7 |
| Oklahoma State | 4 |

**Player of the Year**
Mike Sodders, 3B
Arizona State

## 1982    26

An illustration depicting **Cal State Fullerton** and **Arizona State** players

**CWS FINAL SCORE**

| | |
|---|---|
| Miami | 9 |
| Wichita State | 3 |

**Player of the Year**
Jeff Ledbetter, OF/LHP
Florida State

## 1983    32

Texas pitchers, including **Roger Clemens** and **Calvin Schiraldi**

**CWS FINAL SCORE**

| | |
|---|---|
| Texas | 4 |
| Alabama | 3 |

**Player of the Year**
Dave Magadan, 1B
Alabama

## 1984    38

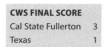

**Shane Mack**
UCLA

**CWS FINAL SCORE**

| | |
|---|---|
| Cal State Fullerton | 3 |
| Texas | 1 |

**Player of the Year**
Oddibe McDowell, OF
Arizona State

## 1985    44

**Rafael Palmeiro** and **Will Clark**
Mississippi State

**CWS FINAL SCORE**

| | |
|---|---|
| Miami | 10 |
| Texas | 6 |

**Player of the Year**
Pete Incaviglia, OF
Oklahoma State

## 1986    50

**Bo Jackson**
Auburn

**CWS FINAL SCORE**

| | |
|---|---|
| Arizona | 10 |
| Florida State | 2 |

**Player of the Year**
Casey Close, OF
Michigan

## 1987    56

Year of the Pitcher, including **Mike Harkey** and **Jack McDowell**

**CWS FINAL SCORE**

| | |
|---|---|
| Stanford | 9 |
| Oklahoma State | 5 |

**Player of the Year**
Robin Ventura, 3B
Oklahoma State

## 1988 | 62

Preseason All-Americans
**Robin Ventura** and
**Jim Abbott**

**CWS FINAL SCORE**

| | |
|---|---|
| Stanford | 9 |
| Arizona State | 4 |

**Player of the Year**
John Olerud, 1B/LHP
Washington State

## 1989 | 68

**Ben McDonald**
Louisiana State and
Team USA

**CWS FINAL SCORE**

| | |
|---|---|
| Wichita State | 5 |
| Texas | 3 |

**Player of the Year**
Ben McDonald, RHP
Louisiana State

## 1990 | 78

The Boones, including
**Bret Boone**
Southern California

**CWS FINAL SCORE**

| | |
|---|---|
| Georgia | 2 |
| Oklahoma State | 1 |

**Player of the Year**
Mike Kelly, OF
Arizona State

## 1991 | 84

Arizona State outfielders
**Jim Austin, Mike Kelly**
and **Tommy Adams**

**CWS FINAL SCORE**

| | |
|---|---|
| Louisiana State | 6 |
| Wichita State | 3 |

**Player of the Year**
David McCarty, 1B
Stanford

## 1992 | 90

**Jeffrey Hammonds**,
Stanford, and
**John Burke**, Florida

**CWS FINAL SCORE**

| | |
|---|---|
| Pepperdine | 3 |
| Cal State Fullerton | 2 |

**Player of the Year**
Phil Nevin, 3B
Cal State Fullerton

## 1993 | 96

Coach **Mark Marquess**
with Stanford recruits,
including **A.J. Hinch**

**CWS FINAL SCORE**

| | |
|---|---|
| Louisiana State | 8 |
| Wichita State | 0 |

**Player of the Year**
Brooks Kieschnick
DH/RHP, Texas

## 1994 | 102

**Jason Varitek**
Georgia Tech

**CWS FINAL SCORE**

| | |
|---|---|
| Oklahoma | 13 |
| Georgia Tech | 5 |

**Player of the Year**
Jason Varitek, C
Georgia Tech

## 1995 | 108

**A.J. Hinch**
Stanford

**CWS FINAL SCORE**

| | |
|---|---|
| Cal State Fullerton | 11 |
| Southern California | 5 |

**Player of the Year**
Todd Helton, 1B/LHP
Tennessee

# TABLE OF CONTENTS

**2004** 168

**Wade Townsend,
Philip Humber** and
**Jeff Niemann** of Rice

**CWS BEST-OF-THREE**

| | |
|---|---|
| Cal State Fullerton | 2 |
| Texas | 0 |

**Player of the Year**
Jered Weaver, RHP
Long Beach State

**2005** 172

**Micah Owings** and
**Brian Bogusevic**
Tulane

**CWS BEST-OF-THREE**

| | |
|---|---|
| Texas | 2 |
| Florida | 0 |

**Player of the Year**
Alex Gordon, 3B
Nebraska

**2006** 178

**Kyle McCulloch** and
**Drew Stubbs**
Texas

**CWS BEST-OF-THREE**

| | |
|---|---|
| Oregon State | 2 |
| North Carolina | 1 |

**Player of the Year**
Andrew Miller, LHP
North Carolina

**2007** 184

**Joe Savery** of Rice
and
**Huston Street** of Texas

**CWS BEST-OF-THREE**

| | |
|---|---|
| Oregon State | 2 |
| North Carolina | 0 |

**Player of the Year**
David Price, LHP
Vanderbilt

**2008** 190

**Jorge Reyes** and
**Mike Stutes**
Oregon State

**CWS BEST-OF-THREE**

| | |
|---|---|
| Fresno State | 2 |
| Georgia | 1 |

**Player of the Year**
Buster Posey, C/RHP
Florida State

**2009** 196

**Rosenblatt Stadium**
and The Road to Omaha

**CWS BEST-OF-THREE**

| | |
|---|---|
| Louisiana State | 2 |
| Texas | 1 |

**Player of the Year**
Stephen Strasburg, RHP
San Diego State

**2010** 206

**Rosenblatt Stadium**
in its final year hosting
the College World Series

**CWS BEST-OF-THREE**

| | |
|---|---|
| South Carolina | 2 |
| UCLA | 0 |

**Player of the Year**
Anthony Rendon, 3B
Rice

**2011** 212

**Anthony Rendon**
Rice

**CWS BEST-OF-THREE**

| | |
|---|---|
| South Carolina | 2 |
| Florida | 0 |

**Player of the Year**
Trevor Bauer, RHP
UCLA

# TABLE OF CONTENTS

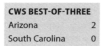

# College baseball enters new era post-WWII

By **ALLAN SIMPSON**

For nearly 100 years, college baseball was played in virtual anonymity—rightfully earning a reputation as the ugly stepsister in a sport that was otherwise thriving and had long secured its place as America's pastime. From 1859, when the first documented college game was played between two Massachusetts schools, Amherst and Williams, until the end of World War II, college baseball had little or no stature in the eyes of Major League Baseball—save for the odd Hall of Famer like Columbia's Lou Gehrig who had a college pedigree—and barely moved the needle among an apathetic sporting public much more attuned to the merits of campus endeavors like football and basketball.

As college baseball continued to plod along in relative obscurity through two of the darkest periods in America's history—the depression that gripped the 1930s and the global conflict that defined the 1940s—the post-war period signaled the beginning of a bold new era for baseball as interest in the game spread like wildfire, to the degree that baseball became the catalyst for a reinvigorated and newly enlightened society. Even college baseball began to matter.

The return of hundreds of players from the World War II effort sparked a renewed interest in MLB, and such a passion for the game developed overall that new minor league clubs popped up, almost at will, across the land. Integration came to the game during this period, but the demand for talent to meet the game's sudden wave of popularity was still at such a premium that even college players, largely an untapped resource to that point in the game's evolution, were recruited as never before. As the competition for talent intensified in the professional ranks, so did the financial incentives needed to lure players into pro ball—and bonus payments soon became prevalent. With a then-record $56,000 signing bonus from the Yankees in 1946, Tulane shortstop Bobby Brown was among the first wave of college players in high demand.

While baseball's new boom period was marked by a greater appreciation for college players, it wasn't the only consequential development in the mid-to-late '40s that brought increased attention to the college game. In 1945, the American Association of College Baseball Coaches (AACBC) was formed, and one of the organization's mandates was the pursuit of a national championship tournament. The AACBC settled initially for an all-star game involving the best college players from the East against those from the West, but in 1947, with the blessing of the NCAA, the first national tournament was staged. Eight teams were invited to participate, with the two victorious clubs from a pair of four-team, single-elimination regionals in Denver and New Haven, Conn., moving on to Kalamazoo, Mich., for a best-of-three series to determine college baseball's first recognized champion. California, featuring two-sport star Jackie Jensen, defeated Yale, led by team captain and first baseman George Bush, in two straight games. Jensen would later star for Cal in the Rose Bowl and become the American League MVP in 1958 as a member of the Red Sox, while Bush's rise to the presidency has been duly chronicled.

In 1948, Southern California won its first national title—the first of 11 over the next 30 years—by beating Yale 2-1 in the best-of-three finals, but the tournament struggled to make ends meet financially in Kalamazoo (conveniently chosen because it was the home of the national tournament chairman) and was relocated the next year to Wichita—home of the National Baseball Congress and its highly successful national semipro tournament. Texas was victorious in an expanded four-team field, but the tournament, plagued again by poor attendance, was another financial flop.

While its first three attempts at staging a national tournament fell far short of expectations—ironically, coming at a time when baseball's popularity was never greater—the NCAA still saw merit in a championship event and determined that a larger contest played in the right location would be the answer.

In 1950, the tournament was expanded to an ideal eight-team, double-elimination event, but the NCAA's real stroke of genius was in selecting Omaha as the host site. Though the newly-dubbed College World Series continued to lose money in its first two years at 7,500-seat Municipal Stadium, a foundation was established from the outset when three local colleges—Nebraska, Creighton and Omaha—agreed to co-sponsor the undertaking while various civic organizations in Omaha pitched in to sponsor the competing teams. By 1952, the CWS turned a profit for the first time by attracting a record 38,731 fans to Rosenblatt Stadium (newly renamed in honor of Omaha mayor Johnny Rosenblatt, who was instrumental in the series coming to his city). Not long after, as crowds continued to grow, the tournament became a fixture in Omaha and synonymous with the continued growth of college baseball.

Today, the CWS is a national institution with crowds upwards of 300,000 annually, while Omaha has earned its rightful place as the capital of the college baseball world.

In many respects, the growth and resulting popularity of the College World Series has mirrored the growth and accomplishments that college baseball as a whole has achieved over the last 70 years.

While the anonymity of the game and its players was the overriding theme through much of college baseball's first 100 years, the gradual evolution of the CWS into a successful sporting venture in the 20-year period after World War II happened at a time when a newfound respect and appreciation for the talent emanating from the college ranks was occurring. The early dominance displayed by Southern California also helped to define the growing impact of college baseball in the post-war era. Under longtime coach Rod Dedeaux, the Trojans won CWS titles in 1958, 1961 and 1963, but Dedeaux's influence on the college game extended well beyond his own team's success—and became even more pronounced over the next 20 years, when USC won five straight national championships from 1970-74 while producing dozens of future major leagues, including the likes of Tom Seaver, Dave Kingman, Fred Lynn, Steve Kemp, Mark McGwire and Randy Johnson.

In many regards, Dedeaux was a coach ahead of his time, especially as college baseball, for all its advances in the post-war era, was slow to gain a widespread foothold in the

1950s and early '60s. Dedeaux, a trucking magnate who coached the Trojans on the side for the princely sum of $1 a year, was not only able to go head to head with major league clubs in recruiting the best talent from prospect-rich California, but created a unique environment for his players that was roughly the equivalent to the experience they would have received in pro ball had they not decided to attend college. In addition to a full college season in the spring, Dedeaux astutely shipped his players to remote locations during the summer months—generally to western Canada in the 1950s, to Alaska in the 1960s—so they could play upwards of 60 more games with and against the best competition available in the semipro ranks. His program reaped the rewards when the players invariably returned to school in the fall bigger and better than ever.

Led by pitcher Tom Seaver (center) and coach Rod Dedeaux (right), Southern California emerged as the preeminent college power of the 1960s and '70s.

Dedeaux's influence transcended the game in a number of ways. He also was a pioneer in the development of baseball at the international level in the 1970s and was the driving force behind baseball achieving Olympic status. For his munificence, he was rewarded by being selected to coach the celebrated 1984 United States college all-star team—possibly the best amateur team ever assembled—in his hometown of Los Angeles.

Another bold new era in college baseball's steady growth began to occur in 1965, and coincided with the introduction of the draft and the emergence of a second national collegiate power, Arizona State, to rival USC. ASU had never previously appeared in the College World Series, but with a deep, talented lineup led by outfielder Rick Monday, the first pick in the draft, won its first national title that year while also becoming the first college team to eclipse the 50-win barrier. Between them, the Sun Devils and Trojans would win the CWS the staggering total of 11 times between 1965 and 1978.

Even as the two schools dominated college baseball through the 1970s, the intense rivalry between the Trojans and Sun Devils that was routinely on display in Omaha only stimulated greater interest in and appreciation for college baseball. Record crowds—both in Omaha and elsewhere—became commonplace throughout the decade. Major league clubs also continued to look to the colleges for talent with increasing regularity, and in 1977, more college players than high school players were drafted for the first time.

Changes in eligibility rules for college players in the late '60s also proved a boon—especially a draft rule in 1967 that forbid the selection, in most instances, of college sophomores; and a corresponding NCAA rule in 1968 that allowed for freshman eligibility. Almost overnight, the best college players were routinely playing three years of varsity ball, rather than only one—as occurred with Monday.

While it's appropriate when retrospectively viewing the history of college baseball through the lens of breakthrough developments or significant turning points that marked its evolution, there was nothing that transformed the game more than a landmark decision in 1974 that fundamentally changed the way college baseball was played. The introduction of aluminum bats that year was initially intended as more of a cost-cutting measure, but the impact was much more dramatic than envisioned and went so far as to give college baseball its own identity. The bats added a much-needed offensive punch to the game, and in kind greatly enhanced spectator appeal of the sport.

In the first six collegiate seasons after the aluminum bat was introduced, the NCAA single-season home run record was broken or tied five times—including 1978, when Arizona State slugger Bob Horner became the poster child for the rapidly growing influence of the aluminum bat in college baseball. Not only did Horner set NCAA season (25) and career records (56) for home runs on his way to becoming the No. 1 selection in that year's draft, but he brashly took his power-hitting act directly to the big leagues, where he homered in his first game for the Braves and didn't stop hitting home runs, even while switching to wood bats, on his improbable run to National League Rookie of the Year honors—an unprecedented achievement by a college player.

In 1979, UCLA's Jim Auten stretched the home run mark to 29, but an even more stunning development occurred in college baseball's evolution when Arizona State, along with state rival Arizona, joined forces with archrival USC and UCLA in an expanded Pacific-10 Conference—or Pac-6, as the Southern Division of the conference became better known. All the makings of a college baseball super conference were in play because USC had just beaten the Sun Devils in the 1978 CWS final, but it strangely never manifested. A year later, as conference rivals, the Trojans (15-15 in conference play) could do no better than finish fourth, while the Sun Devils (8-22) inexplicably brought up the rear. Neither school was even selected to that year's 34-team NCAA Tournament, and it proved to be foreshadowing of things to come. The two schools would combine to win just two national titles in the next 40 years—ASU in 1981, USC in 1998.

With newfound parity in the game, along with the promise of more of the crowd-pleasing offensive onslaught that became prevalent in the late '70s, the stage was set for the most revolutionary era yet in college baseball's continuing evolution. ∎

# ALL-AMERICA TEAM FOR 1965-80

| Pos, Player, School | Summary |
| --- | --- |
| C Danny Goodwin, Southern | Two-time No. 1 overall draft pick (1971, 1975) hit .394 with 20 HR, 166 RBIs |
| 1B Tim Wallach, Cal State Fullerton | As SR in 1979 led Titans to CWS title with 23 HR, NCAA record 102 RBIs |
| 2B Bob Horner, Arizona State | Capped brilliant career in 1978 by setting season (25), career (56) HR records |
| 3B Keith Moreland, Texas | Led Texas to CWS all three years (1973-75); hit .388 overall with 183 RBIs |
| SS Alan Bannister, Arizona State | Hit .381 in 1972 for 64-6 team; set NCAA records for H (101), TB (177), RBIs (90) |
| OF Fred Lynn, Southern Calif. | Key cog on 3 championship teams from 1971-73; hit career .320 with wood |
| OF Terry Francona, Arizona | 1980 Golden Spikes winner hit .401 with 9 HR, 81 RBIs; led club to CWS title |
| OF Tom Paciorek, Houston | Two-time All-American hit .435 with 10 HR in 1967; drafted by MLB/NFL in '68 |
| UT Dave Winfield, Minnesota | An ace (19-4, 169 IP, 229 SO) who broke out at plate as SR in 1973 (.385-8-33) |
| SP Steve Arlin, Ohio State | Won historic 1-0, 15-IP, 20-SO game in '66, worked all 5 wins for CWS champs |
| SP Eddie Bane, Arizona State | Crafty lefty went 40-4, 1.64, struck out 535 in 379 IP from 1971-73 |
| SP Floyd Bannister, Arizona State | Dominant arm in college game in 1975-76; No. 1 pick in '76 draft |
| SP Burt Hooton, Texas | 35-3 with school-record 1.14 ERA from 1969-71 with trademark knuckle-curve |
| SP Derek Tatsuno, Hawaii | 40-6, 2.04 from 1977-79, led nation in SO each year; set NCAA record with 234 |

**1** **PING!** Aluminum bats were introduced in 1974, mainly as a cost-cutting measure, but the bats had far greater implications than ever anticipated in helping college baseball achieve its own identity while substantially increasing the level of offensive productivity in the game.

**2** **THE ROAD TO OMAHA.** The inaugural College World Series was a two-team affair played in Kalamazoo, Mich., in 1947, but didn't begin to catch on as a viable athletic event until the tournament was moved to Omaha in 1950. After slow but steady growth, the tournament is now synonymous with the Omaha and has become one of the top sporting attractions in the U.S.

**3** **TOTAL DOMINATION.** Southern California dominated college baseball throughout the first three decades of the CWS era, winning 11 times from 1948 to 1978—all under the leadership of coach Rod Dedeaux, the most influential figure in the stunning growth of college and amateur baseball throughout his 45 years at USC.

**4** **REICHARDT BONUS TRIGGERS DRAFT.** Signing bonuses became commonplace after World War II to lure college and high school players to pro ball, but escalated in value through the years before peaking in 1964 when the Angels signed Wisconsin outfielder Rick Reichardt for $205,000. Reichardt's record deal triggered the implementation of the draft system a year later, and it had its intended effect when Arizona State outfielder Rick Monday received $100,000 from the Athletics as the first overall pick in 1965.

**5** **ARIZONA STATE INFLUENCE.** The 1965 season coincided with baseball's first draft, but it also marked the emergence of ASU as a budding power. The Sun Devils (54-8) not only had the first pick in the draft (Monday), but won their first CWS that year while becoming the first college team to eclipse the 50-win barrier. They won again in 1967 and '69 and won more games (416) and posted the best winning percentage (.776) of any college team in the '60s.

**6** **IN THE BEGINNING.** The first documented college baseball game was played on July 1, 1859, between two Massachusetts colleges, Amherst and Williams, with the contest predetermined to continue until the first team scored 65 runs. Williams won 73-32 in 25 innings—though an out, at the time, constituted an inning.

**7** **TITLE IX INTERVENTION.** One of the greatest challenges to the sustained growth of college baseball occurred as a result of a federal law passed in 1972, known as Title IX, that effectively prohibited gender discrimination in education. The amendment provided equal opportunity for men and women in collegiate sports, specifically in the way scholarships were allocated, and a number men's sports on college campuses either had their scholarship allotment trimmed or programs eliminated in order to become compliant. But the ruling also served to galvanize a number of schools into promoting their baseball programs to justify their existence.

**8** **STUNNING COMEBACK.** The most stunning development in a CWS game in the first 30 years of the event occurred in 1973, while Minnesota righthander Dave Winfield was in the process of dominating top-seeded USC and leading his team to a place in the championship game. Through eight innings, Winfield stymied the three-time defending champions on one scratch single while striking out 15. The Golden Gophers took a 7-0 lead to the bottom of the ninth inning, but a tiring Winfield was able to get only a single out while being touched for three singles before he was lifted with his team still leading 7-3. The Trojans went on to score five more runs in the inning off a pair of relievers to pull off a stunning 8-7 comeback.

**9** **HAWAIIAN DELIGHT.** Hawaii emerged as an unlikely national contender in the late '70s, mainly behind the dynamic pitching of native lefthander Derek Tatsuno, who won 40 games from 1977-79. He also led Division I pitchers in strikeouts all three seasons. As a junior, Tatsuno went 20-1 to become the first college pitcher to win 20 games, while his 234 strikeouts established a still-standing single-season record.

**10** **ORGANIZED STRUCTURE.** After the NCAA came into existence in 1910, all college baseball teams operated under one umbrella until 1957. At that point, the NCAA split teams into two divisions: university and college. The NCAA then split teams again in 1974 into the present-day format of Divisions I, II and III.

Robin Ventura, who authored a 58-game hitting streak, accepts the 1988 Golden Spikes Award with Joe DiMaggio.

THE

# 1980s

# TOP 25 PROGRAMS OF THE 1980s

Baseball America published its first issue in 1981, thus our sample covers the period of 1981 through 1989. See Introduction (Page 4) for a key to abbreviations and scoring. Category leaders in **bold**.

| No. | School | Regional | CWS | Title | AA1 | AA2 | AA3 | Top10 | MLB | Points |
|-----|--------|----------|-----|-------|-----|-----|-----|-------|-----|--------|
| 1. | Texas | **9** | **7** | 1 | **11** | 7 | 1 | 27 | 17 | 257 |
| 2. | Miami | **9** | **7** | 2 | 5 | 1 | 6 | 13 | 5 | 213 |
| 3. | Arizona State | 7 | 5 | 1 | 5 | 8 | 2 | **32** | 18 | 208 |
| 4. | Oklahoma State | **9** | **7** | 0 | 7 | 4 | 4 | 18 | 14 | 202 |
| 5. | Stanford | 8 | 5 | **2** | 0 | 6 | 4 | 20 | 15 | 191 |
| 6. | Wichita State | 7 | 3 | 1 | 7 | 6 | 4 | 14 | 10 | 170 |
| 7. | Cal State Fullerton | 6 | 3 | 1 | 2 | 7 | 3 | 23 | 15 | 155 |
| 8. | Florida State | **9** | 3 | 0 | 7 | 4 | 2 | 16 | 11 | 153 |
| 9. | Michigan | 8 | 3 | 0 | 5 | 3 | 1 | 18 | 10 | 134 |
| 10. | Fresno State | 7 | 1 | 0 | 6 | 3 | 3 | 18 | 11 | 119 |
| 11. | Arizona | 4 | 2 | 1 | 3 | 1 | 2 | 14 | 14 | 110 |
| 12. | Arkansas | 6 | 3 | 0 | 1 | 2 | 1 | 22 | 9 | 104 |
| 13. | Mississippi State | 7 | 2 | 0 | 4 | 4 | 0 | 10 | 5 | 102 |
| 14. | Louisiana State | 4 | 3 | 0 | 2 | 3 | 1 | 13 | 10 | 94 |
| 15. | Maine | 5 | 5 | 0 | 0 | 0 | 2 | 4 | 4 | 87 |
| 16. | South Carolina | 7 | 3 | 0 | 1 | 0 | 1 | 6 | 5 | 83 |
| 17. | New Orleans | 7 | 1 | 0 | 2 | 1 | 3 | 9 | 5 | 78 |
| 18. | Pepperdine | 6 | 0 | 0 | 4 | 1 | 0 | 12 | 7 | 72 |
| 19. | Brigham Young | 5 | 0 | 0 | 1 | 6 | 2 | 12 | 7 | 71 |
| 20. | Oklahoma | 7 | 0 | 0 | 0 | 3 | 3 | 12 | 7 | 69 |
| 21. | San Diego State | 5 | 0 | 0 | 2 | 2 | 2 | 15 | 7 | 67 |
| 22. | Texas A&M | 5 | 0 | 0 | 3 | 2 | 2 | 10 | 7 | 67 |
| 23. | Oral Roberts | 6 | 0 | 0 | 2 | 0 | 3 | 12 | 8 | 66 |
| 24. | North Carolina | 4 | 1 | 0 | 2 | 1 | 1 | 13 | 7 | 65 |
| 25. | UCLA | 2 | 0 | 0 | 3 | 1 | 1 | 18 | 15 | 63 |

# Rise of Texas, Miami signal change of guard

By **ALLAN SIMPSON**

The roots of college baseball can be traced to 1851—130 years before Baseball America was launched. But there is little mistaking that college baseball came of age in 1981, when a series of developments coalesced to transform the game in unimaginable ways and catapulted it into the national consciousness. By the time the '80s were over, the most revolutionary period in the game's history had transpired—and BA was there every step of the way to chronicle much of what happened.

From the advent of national TV coverage, to a dramatic swing toward college talent in the draft, to an unprecedented offensive explosion, to unparalleled national parity, to the growing popularity of the Omaha-based College World Series, college baseball can trace much of the popularity it now enjoys specifically to the landmark year of 1981.

While BA jumped on the bandwagon that year, a fledgling, two-year-old cable network was the media entity most responsible for the sudden and dramatic increase in the game's awareness. By televising five College World Series games in both 1980 and 1981, ESPN quickly discovered it had an untapped market at its disposal and soon made the CWS a staple of its coverage. Soon, major networks wanted a piece of the action and CWS officials obliged in altering the tournament format to accommodate TV coverage. Almost overnight, captivated audiences caught a glimpse of

## TOP 10 STORYLINES OF THE 1980s

**1** **FALL FROM GRACE.** Southern California dominated college baseball in the 1970s but failed to crack the nation's top 25 teams of the '80s, when the Trojans made no visits to Omaha.

**2** **DRAFT DEMOGRAPHICS.** Beginning in 1981, when a record 17 first-round picks came from the college ranks, the '80s saw teams make a dramatic shift toward college talent.

**3** **OFFENSIVE EXPLOSION.** Offensive levels using aluminum bats rose sharply in the '80s, peaking in 1985 when players hit a collective .306 and teams averaged 6.94 runs per game.

**4** **CHANGING OF THE GUARD.** Miami made the most CWS appearances in the '80s (eight) and Texas won the most games (587), signalling their rise to the top of the college heap.

**5** **SHOCKING DEVELOPMENT.** After an eight-year absence, baseball returned to Wichita State with a vengeance in 1978. By 1982, the Shockers had set an NCAA record with 73 wins.

**6** **HOME RUN DERBY.** With jacked-up aluminum bats and teams permitted to schedule 80 games or more, the greatest home run assault in college history took place in the '80s.

**7** **THUNDER AND LIGHTNING.** Mississippi State's Will Clark and Rafael Palmeiro were the most electrifying tandem in the college game during their tenure together from 1983-85.

**8** **RECORD STREAK.** Oklahoma State's Robin Ventura drew rare attention in 1987 when he hit safely in an NCAA record 58 straight games.

**9** **DIFFERENCE MAKER.** Louisiana State made the astute decision in 1984 to hire Miami pitching coach Skip Bertman as head coach. He almost immediately transformed LSU into a power after 90 undistinguished seasons.

**10** **SUDDEN DRAMA.** Stanford's Paul Carey earned his place in CWS lore in 1987 when he slugged a dramatic grand slam that propelled the Cardinal to a 6-5 win on their way to a title.

what college baseball offered as a potential spectator sport.

For years, Major League Baseball had largely paid only passing interest to college talent as a development source, but all that changed in 1981, when 34 of the first 50 players drafted—double the previous record—came from the collegiate ranks. The emphasis on college players only increased, and in 1985 it became so pronounced that 11 of the first 12 picks came from college. That year is generally acknowledged for producing the greatest draft crop ever, a class that included Barry Bonds, Barry Larkin and Randy Johnson.

College baseball had set itself apart from the professional game in 1974 when it adopted aluminum bats, mainly as a cost-cutting measure, but it wasn't until the early '80s that the real impact of the bats became evident when offensive records were set—even obliterated—as a matter of routine.

The single-season NCAA record of 17 home runs in the wood-bat era was escalated to 29 by 1979 with the introduction of aluminum. Florida State's Jeff Ledbetter shattered the mark two years later by going deep 42 times—in just 74 games—while driving in a record 124 runs. In 1985, Oklahoma State's Pete Incaviglia set new heights by smashing the improbable total of 48 homers, while also setting records for RBIs (143), total bases (285) and slugging (1.140)—all marks unlikely to ever be broken.

As extraordinary as Incaviglia's feats were, his place in the record book is no more prominent than Wichita State first baseman Phil Stephenson, who played for the Shockers from 1979-82 and still holds a slew of NCAA career records, including runs (420) hits (418), total bases (730), walks (300) and stolen bases (206).

The records set by Incaviglia, Stephenson and other players of that era have largely stood the test of time because there were no limits on the number of games college teams could play. With the NCAA largely turning a blind eye to college baseball—a traditional non-revenue sport—several free-wheeling coaches promoted their programs by liberally playing games, and in 1982, San Diego State participated in a record 91 contests. Others routinely topped 80. The NCAA soon became acutely aware of the rapidly growing impact of college baseball and some of the related problems it perceived were occurring, and in 1986 made a concerted effort to rein in the college game by, among other things, limiting

# ALL-AMERICA TEAM OF THE DECADE

| Pos | Player, School | Summary |
|-----|----------------|---------|
| C | B.J. Surhoff, North Carolina | No. 1 pick in '85 draft hit .392 with 32 HR, stole 84 of 99 bags, had 87 BB, 24 SO |
| 1B | Will Clark, Mississippi State | Hit .386-28-93, .420-25-77 in 1984 and '85; led '84 Olympic squad in AVG, HR |
| 2B | Ty Griffin, Georgia Tech | Excelled in college (.332, 22 HR, 127 SB); pro career fizzled as Cubs' top pick in '88 |
| 3B | Robin Ventura, Okla. State | Player of decade sizzled during 3-year career, hitting .428 with 68 HR, 301 RBIs |
| SS | Cory Snyder, Brigham Young | Began college career with HRs in first 3 ABs; ended it with .429 AVG, 73 HR |
| OF | Joe Carter, Wichita State | Unknown entering college, hit .430-58-312 in career on way to No. 2 pick in '81 |
| OF | Pete Incaviglia, Okla. State | Prolific power bat; NCAA leader in homers, both for season (48) and career (100) |
| OF | Rafael Palmeiro, Miss. State | Immediate sensation hit .406-18-78 as FR, .415-29-94 as SO, then tapered off |
| DH | Phil Stephenson, Wichita State | 4-year collegian established NCAA career records for runs, hits, total bases, steals |
| UT | John Olerud, Wash. State | Epic '88 season as hitter (.464-23-81), pitcher (15-0, 2.49); later felled by aneurysm |
| SP | Roger Clemens, Texas | Went 25-5, 2.63 in two seasons for Longhorns in 1982-83, led team to '83 title |
| SP | Neal Heaton, Miami | Set Miami records for wins (18 in '81, 42 career), strikeouts (172 in '81, 301 career) |
| SP | Ben McDonald, LSU | One of most acclaimed Ps of early draft era; 29-14, 3.24 with 373 SO in 308 IP |
| SP | Greg Swindell, Texas | Dominant in 3 seasons for Longhorns, went 43-8, 1.92 with 10 SV; 501 SO, 114 BB |
| RP | Gregg Olson, Auburn | Moved to closer as SO; two dominant seasons in role; went 18-4, 1.62 with 20 SV |

teams to 60 regular season games—a number that was later revised to 56.

From 1965-81, Arizona State and Southern California won a total of 12 College World Series titles. But in what amounted to an almost overnight changing of the guard, the Sun Devils and Trojans would combine to win only one more national title in the ensuing four decades. USC's fall from grace was particularly swift. It failed to even advance to postseason play in six of the next seven seasons after winning the national championship in 1978.

Led by Arizona State and USC, teams from Arizona or California won every CWS title but one from 1967-81—a graphic indicator of the regional nature of the sport at the dawn of the '80s. The one exception was Texas, in 1975, and the Longhorns not only quickly surpassed both ASU and USC to emerge as the dominant college team in the '80s, but they led the charge to broaden college baseball's national profile. Miami did its part, too, both on and off the field in elevating the game into a prime-time spectacle. In 1981, the Hurricanes drew 170,000 fans—shattering the existing national attendance record—and a year later broke through to become the first Florida team to win a national title.

With Miami and Texas leading the way, the balance of power shifted away from mainly West Coast schools to traditional Sun Belt colleges. Miami (1982, 1985) and Stanford (1987-88) each won two national titles in the '80s, but even upstart Wichita State, which won an NCAA-record 73 games in 1982, scored a major breakthrough in 1989 by becoming the first non-Sun Belt school in 23 years to hit pay dirt.

Through it all, reinvigorated college programs placed a renewed emphasis on promoting and marketing baseball as a viable collegiate sport, and the popularity of the game soared. Attendance records became commonplace, especially as lavish new ballparks began popping up on campus. It didn't happen a moment too soon, either, because baseball was being dropped at the time by an increasing number of colleges that were feeling a financial pinch while looking for easy budget-slashing targets.

The College World Series, meanwhile, remained the college game's shining beacon throughout the '80s. After witnessing an initial attendance spike of 26 percent from 1980 to 1981, new tournament records were set on almost an annual basis in the ensuing years, and TV ratings rose exponentially.

Nothing may have done more to popularize the college game in the '80s, though, than a watershed moment that occurred in 1984, when baseball gained demonstration status at the Los Angeles Olympics, and the host United States responded by fielding a team of college all-stars—a powerful entry that included the likes of future major league stars like Will Clark, Mark McGwire and Larkin, and a host of other current and future first-round draft picks. It was arguably the most talented amateur squad ever assembled in the U.S., and though that celebrated '84 Olympic team ended up with just a silver medal, the widespread attention that team generated throughout the summer generated a profound new appreciation for college baseball. ∎

Oral Roberts righthander Mike Moore went No. 1 overall to the Mariners in a watershed 1981 draft that saw more collegians than high school players selected for the first time.

**1981**

# Dukes, Holmes save best for last

By **ALLAN SIMPSON**

For Kevin Dukes and Stan Holmes, the 1981 College World Series was a chance to vindicate themselves.

Both players, Arizona State seniors, turned down offers to turn pro a year ago, electing to forego signing for an opportunity to return to ASU for their final years of eligibility, the hope being that they would have productive campaigns and ultimately improve on their draft status this season.

But until a few weeks ago, both Dukes and Holmes had done little to enhance their draft status over what it was as juniors, when both were selected by the Mariners.

Certainly they played instrumental roles in raising the Sun Devils to the No. 1 ranking in the country, but their performances were really no better than a year ago. In fact, both had fallen off to a degree.

**FROM THE ISSUE:**
JULY 1981

Then the CWS, where no two players stars shone so brightly.

Dukes, the hard-throwing lefthander, pitched spectacularly. In classic style, he won two games, including the championship game, as ASU rolled to its fifth national title, defeating Oklahoma State, 7-4. He was clearly the dominant pitcher in Omaha.

For Holmes, the Sun Devils powerfully built outfielder, it was a chance to muscle up and show his stuff. He merely led the tournament in hitting at .464 and established a new RBI record, with 17 in six games, actually breaking the old record of 11, set by former teammate Bob Horner, in his first three games.

In that the 1981 draft was held the same day as the championship game, both Dukes and Holmes couldn't have picked a more opportune time to shine.

Scouts had been divided on Dukes' potential the past couple of seasons.

He went in the sixth round of the draft a year ago and was originally ticketed for selection only slightly higher this year. But he became a premium pick based on his stellar performance in Omaha and was the first player selected in the second round.

Holmes went in the eighth round after speculation he wouldn't be claimed at all.

So there is little question that the 1981 CWS benefitted both players.

## TOP TEAMS
### 1981 COLLEGE WORLD SERIES STANDINGS

| School | Conference | Record | CWS | Head Coach |
|---|---|---|---|---|
| Arizona State | Pacific-10 | 55–13 | 5–1 | Jim Brock |
| Oklahoma State | Big Eight | 52–17 | 3–2 | Gary Ward |
| Texas | Southwest | 61–11–1 | 3–2 | Cliff Gustafson |
| South Carolina | Independent | 46–15 | 2–2 | June Raines |
| Miami | Independent | 61–10 | 1–2 | Ron Fraser |
| Mississippi State | Southeastern | 46–17 | 1–2 | Ron Polk |
| Maine | Eastern Collegiate | 32–14 | 0–2 | John Winkin |
| Michigan | Big Ten | 41–20 | 0–2 | Bud Middaugh |

## NATIONAL CHAMPION
### ARIZONA STATE

The Sun Devils defeated Oklahoma State 7-4 in the championship game, giving Arizona State its fifth national title in program history. Along with Southern California, ASU was a dominant force in the college game in the 1960s and '70s.

As deep and talented as the 1981 Sun Devils were—they ranked No. 1 from the outset—they would never have won without the sterling performances turned in by Dukes and Holmes, clearly the two outstanding players in the tournament.

In Dukes' case, all eyes in the tournament has been on Miami ace lefthander Neal Heaton, who came in 16-0 and led the nation in strikeouts.

But Dukes simply stole Heaton's thunder at Omaha.

The lefthander first attracted attention in a second-round encounter with Mississippi State, when he came on in the third inning with the Sun Devils trailing 3-1. He proceeded to no-hit the Bulldogs the remainder of the way, and the Devils pulled out a 4-3 win.

Combine that with the 3.1 hitless innings Dukes tossed against Texas in ASU's opening contest, when he entered to mop up a 11-2 romp against the Longhorns, and Dukes has a streak of 9.2 innings without allowing a hit to open the tournament.

That merely set the stage for the championship game against upstart Oklahoma State.

Well rested by then, the red-hot Dukes was a natural choice to go up against the Cowboys in the finale, even though he had pitched almost exclusively in relief.

A last-minute change of heart by head coach Jim Brock had Dukes in his familiar seat in the bullpen to start the game, but with the understanding that if freshman Kendall Carter, a 19-game winner but working on only a day's rest, should encounter any difficulties, Dukes would immediately get the call.

He didn't have to wait long.

Carter ran into trouble almost immediately and gave way to Dukes with one out in the first inning—and with two runners already in.

The 6-foot-2, 190-pound southpaw promptly slammed the door on the Cowboys, surrendering just two hits the rest of the way.

"Sure, starting Kendall was a gamble," Brock said. "But Kevin seems to psych himself out starting. Once he came in, he was in his element."

Doubtless it is a role he will continue as a pro. The Mariners certainly had no misgivings

# 1981 NEWSMAKERS

After starting the season 40-1, **Miami** went just 1-2 at the CWS. It was the fourth straight year that the Hurricanes fell short of expectations in Omaha, despite going a combined 225-45 over that stretch while being ranked No. 1 nationally over much of the 1980 and '81 seasons.

While first basemen **Bruce Castoria** of Mississippi State and **Franklin Stubbs** of Virginia Tech tied the NCAA single-season home run record of 29 in 1981, Florida State outfielder **Mike Fuentes** also hit 27, enabling him to break the existing career mark of 58, set in 1978 by Arizona State's Bob Horner.

St. John's lefthander **Frank Viola** outdueled Yale righthander **Ron Darling**, 1-0, over 12 innings in an NCAA Northeast regional game. Darling no-hit St. John's for 11 innings while striking out 16 but was a hard-luck loser when he allowed a flare single in the 12th and the runner stole second, third and home.

| FINAL TOP 20 FOR 1981 |
| --- |
| 1. #Arizona State* |
| 2. Miami* |
| 3. Texas* |
| 4. Oklahoma State* |
| 5. Oral Roberts |
| 6. South Carolina* |
| 7. Cal State Fullerton |
| 8. Mississippi State* |
| 9. San Diego State |
| 10. Stanford |
| 11. Wichita State |
| 12. Michigan* |
| 13. Florida |
| 14. Florida State |
| 15. Hawaii |
| 16. Missouri |
| 17. Alabama |
| 18. Memphis |
| 19. St. John's |
| 20. Virginia Tech |
| * Reached College World Series |
| # Preseason No. 1 |

# IN RETROSPECT: 1981 DRAFT

**Top 10 Draft Picks From College**
With overall selection number (Ov), drafting team (Team) and rank on Baseball America draft board (BA).

| Player | Pos | School | Ov | Team | BA |
|---|---|---|---|---|---|
| Mike Moore | RHP | Oral Roberts | 1 | Mariners | 1 |
| Joe Carter | OF | Wichita State | 2 | Cubs | 2 |
| Terry Blocker | OF | Tennessee State | 4 | Mets | 6 |
| Matt Williams | RHP | Rice | 5 | Blue Jays | 9 |
| Kevin McReynolds | OF | Arkansas | 6 | Padres | 3 |
| Bobby Meacham | SS | San Diego State | 8 | Cardinals | 7 |
| Ron Darling | RHP | Yale | 9 | Rangers | 4 |
| Mike Sodders | 3B | Arizona State | 11 | Twins | – |
| Jim Winn | RHP | John Brown (Ark.) | 14 | Pirates | – |
| Tim Pyznarski | 3B | Eastern Illinois | 15 | Athletics | – |

**Top 10 Major League Players From College Draft Class**
With draft round and Baseball-Reference.com total for wins above replacement (WAR) through 2019.

| Player | Pos | School | Rd | Ov | Team | WAR |
|---|---|---|---|---|---|---|
| Tony Gwynn | OF | San Diego State | 3 | 58 | Padres | 69.2 |
| Mark Langston | LHP | San Jose State | 2 | 35 | Mariners | 50.3 |
| Frank Viola | LHP | St. John's | 2 | 37 | Twins | 47.2 |
| Kevin McReynolds | OF | Arkansas | 1 | 6 | Padres | 30.1 |
| Mickey Tettleton | C | Oklahoma State | 5 | 118 | Athletics | 29.4 |
| Mike Moore | RHP | Oral Roberts | 1 | 1 | Mariners | 28.2 |
| John Franco | LHP | St. John's | 5 | 125 | Dodgers | 23.5 |
| Bob Tewksbury | RHP | St. Leo | 19 | 493 | Yankees | 20.9 |
| Ron Darling | RHP | Yale | 1 | 9 | Rangers | 19.7 |
| Joe Carter | OF | Wichita State | 1 | 2 | Cubs | 19.6 |

about taking him so high in the draft, considering his penchant for pitching in relief.

"We initially thought we could get him in the third round," Mariners farm director Hal Keller said. "But after he pitched all those hitless innings in Omaha, we felt we couldn't wait that long."

Scouts clocked Dukes' fastball at 91 mph, faster than what Heaton was timed at.

"Not only does Kevin have great velocity, but he has a major league curve right now," Brock said. "And there's not a better competitor in the country."

Considering the kind of tournament teammate Holmes had, it's surprising he wasn't snapped up earlier than he was.

In earning Most Outstanding Player honors, in addition to establishing a new tournament RBI record, Holmes also tied CWS records with 13 hits and 22 total bases.

In ASU's opening rout of Texas, Holmes went 5-for-5 with six RBIs. In the winner's bracket final against Oklahoma State, when the Sun Devils suffered their only setback, an 11-10 loss in 13 innings, the 6-foot, 205-pound left fielder drove in seven runs, three on a dramatic, game-tying home run in the ninth inning.

For Holmes, the series was an opportunity to make up for what he himself admits was an "off" senior year—and it was a chance to stick it to his critics.

Only junior colleges recruited Holmes out of high school four years ago. ASU didn't offer him a scholarship. Many thought he couldn't play at the major league level.

"I think I accomplished a lot at Omaha," Holmes said. "I was put down by a lot of junior college coaches who said I'd never play at ASU.

"I think I proved something to myself—and to them." ∎

# Sodders headlines All-America team

By **ALLAN SIMPSON**

**A**year ago, as a junior at Arizona State, Mike Sodders wasn't even so much as selected in the draft. In fact, he wasn't even guaranteed a regular job when he returned to ASU in the fall.

That was how grim Sodders' prospects were, not only as a potential major leaguer, but as a college baseball player.

Three years ago, as a senior in high school, Joe Carter didn't get so much as a nibble from scouts in the draft. He didn't even get a college scholarship offer.

That was how dim Carter's prospects were as he embarked on a college career at Wichita State, no mind being given at that time to a crack at professional baseball.

Yet here in 1981, the fortunes for both Sodders and Carter could never be brighter.

In Sodders' case, his turnaround is the result of a spectacular 1981 season, one which has earned him selection as the College Player of the Year. It wasn't that the 6-foot-3, 190-pound third baseman

Mike Sodders hit .424 with 22 home runs and 100 RBIs as an Arizona State senior. Drafted 11th overall by the Twins in 1981, his pro career began with a protracted holdout and ended after just four seasons. Sodders peaked at Triple-A.

couldn't hit the ball a year ago, that his career was such in doubt. Not at all.

After all, he had just completed a season in which he'd stroked the ball at a .349 clip with 14 home runs—figures generally good enough to warrant attention from scouts. But there was the matter of defense, and in that regard, Sodders built a bad reputation with 20 errors and a lowly .855 fielding percentage.

However, a sore throwing arm and damaged knee were contributing factors.

So it wasn't surprising then, in some ways, that Sodders was not regarded as a premium draft pick. But overlooked altogether?

This spring, though, Sodders enjoyed such a remarkable season, even showing dramatic improvement with his glove, that he was not only drafted, but was selected by the Twins as the 11th player overall.

For a player to improve his status so dramatically in the short period of a year is a testament to the outstanding season Sodders enjoyed in 1981 as he led the Sun Devils to a national title.

Sodders, part of the pipeline of talent between California's Orange Coast JC and ASU, hit .422 this season with 22 home runs and an even 100 RBIs. He was the heart of a team's offense that was considered the nation's best.

Joe Carter came to Wichita State on a football scholarship, and he became a starting wide receiver as a freshman. He went out for baseball, almost as an afterthought.

That makes it all the more remarkable that Carter, an All-American in each of his three seasons at Wichita State, should make shambles of the NCAA record book.

As a career .435 hitter, the 6-foot-3, 214-pound Carter, who signed a lucrative contract with the Cubs as the No. 2 overall pick in the draft, set six college baseball records, including career records for hits (344), total bases (634) and RBIs (312), and single-season marks for doubles (34, set in 1980), total bases (229, set in 1980) and RBIs (120).

From the day that Neal Heaton arrived at Miami, fresh from turning down a $35,000 bonus offer from the Mets, stardom was predicted for the hard-throwing lefthander.

The native of Holtsville, N.Y., has done nothing to disappoint in three years with the Hurricanes, for whom he turned in a lifetime record of 42-7 and an ERA a tick over 2.00.

This season, Heaton won his first 16 games before losing for the first time in Omaha in a contest in which knocked Miami out of the College World Series.

At 16-1, Heaton, who recently signed with the Indians, was one of the nation's leaders in victories and ERA (2.08). And he led the country with 172 strikeouts in 154 innings, an average of 10.1 per nine innings. He was certainly the dominating force in the remarkable season enjoyed by the Hurricanes.

Oddly enough, while both Sodders and Carter benefited dramatically from outstanding 1981 seasons, Heaton lost some of his value, becoming a second-round pick after being touted as a high first-round choice much of the season. ■

# TOP PLAYERS OF 1981

## ALL-AMERICA TEAM

| Pos | Player | School | Yr | AVG | AB | R | H | HR | RBI | BB | SO | SB |
|-----|--------|--------|-----|-----|-----|-----|-----|-----|-----|-----|-----|-----|
| C | Tommy Nieto | Oral Roberts | Jr | .354 | 189 | 47 | 67 | 14 | 52 | 16 | 17 | 0 |
| 1B | Phil Stephenson | Wichita State | Jr | .447 | 266 | 112 | 119 | 16 | 92 | 65 | 21 | 44 |
| 2B | Jeff Ronk | California | Jr | .389 | 244 | 58 | 95 | 5 | 49 | 49 | 25 | 7 |
| 3B | Mike Sodders | Arizona State | Sr | .424 | 269 | 93 | 114 | 22 | 100 | 51 | 33 | 14 |
| SS | Bobby Meacham | San Diego State | Jr | .375 | 260 | 90 | 97 | 7 | 51 | 38 | 32 | 44 |
| OF | Joe Carter | Wichita State | Jr | .411 | 287 | 88 | 118 | 24 | 120 | 32 | 22 | 24 |
| OF | Mike Fuentes | Florida State | Sr | .353 | 300 | 92 | 106 | 27 | 83 | 53 | 45 | 22 |
| OF | John Christensen | Cal State Fullerton | Jr | .362 | 246 | 83 | 89 | 23 | 78 | 47 | 37 | 11 |
| DH | Franklin Stubbs | Virginia Tech | So | .417 | 192 | 80 | 80 | 29 | 83 | 59 | 27 | 34 |

| Pos | Pitcher | School | Yr | W | L | ERA | G | CG | IP | H | BB | SO |
|-----|---------|--------|-----|-----|-----|-----|-----|-----|-----|-----|-----|-----|
| P | Neal Heaton | Miami | Jr | 16 | 1 | 2.16 | 20 | 9 | 154 | 102 | 56 | 172 |
| P | Kendall Carter | Arizona State | Fr | 19 | 1 | 2.86 | 28 | 1 | 110 | 114 | 25 | 40 |
| P | Tony Arnold | Texas | Jr | 17 | 1 | 2.84 | 21 | 13 | 146 | 131 | 21 | 72 |
| P | Frank Viola | St. John's | Jr | 10 | 0 | 0.87 | 10 | 5 | 83 | 41 | 32 | 43 |

## SECOND TEAM
C—Burk Goldthorn, Texas. 1B—Bruce Castoria, Mississippi State. 2B—Jimmy Thomas, Wichita State. 3B—Billy Max, Nevada-Las Vegas. SS—Dave Anderson, Memphis State. OF—Mark Gillaspie, Mississippi State; Kevin Romine, Arizona State; and Phil Bradley, Missouri. DH—Jeff Ledbetter, Florida State. P—Jeff Keener, Kentucky; Pete Kendrick, Brigham Young; Matt Williams, Rice; and Ron Darling, Yale.

## THIRD TEAM
C—Frank Castro, Miami. 1B—Mike Rubel, Cal State Fullerton. 2B—Bobby Doerrer, Southern Illinois. 3B—Darrell Baker, Georgia Southern. SS—Dan Davidsmeier, Southern California. OF—Tony Gwynn, San Diego State; Scott Parsons, Miami; and Mike Dotterer, Stanford. DH—Brick Smith, Wake Forest. P—Ray Hayward, Oklahoma; Mike Moore, Oral Roberts; Scott Tabor, Arkansas; and Bill Long, Miami (Ohio).

Wichita State produced four first-team All-Americans in a record-breaking season, but only catcher Charlie O'Brien, pictured here in 1994, impacted the majors.

1982

# Surprising Hurricanes turn back Wichita State

By **ALLAN SIMPSON**

I ronic, isn't it?

For four straight years, the Miami Hurricanes came to Omaha in search of their first College World Series title. Always they were among the favorites; always they went home disappointed.

But in a year the Hurricanes tied a club record for most losses in a season, and in a year that they insisted all along was for the purposes of rebuilding, they finally won the elusive national championship.

Lucky? Possibly. But certainly fitting, if not overdue for a baseball program that has become recognized in the past few years as one of the finest in the country.

"This is the greatest thrill of my life," said an excited Ron Fraser, who has coached the Hurricanes for 20 years.

"This team showed a lot of heart here. I didn't expect us to even get into a regional this year after losing all the players we did. And here we win it all."

Miami went through the eight-team, double-elimination field undefeated, becoming the first team other than Southern California to do so since 1957, and just the ninth over-all. The Trojans finished unbeaten in 1961, 1968, 1973 and 1978.

In the process, the Hurricanes became just the second club from a state other than Arizona or California to win college baseball's most coveted prize since 1966. Only Texas, in 1975, had previously interrupted the West's domination of the CWS prior to Miami's surprising win.

The Hurricanes took it all with a 9-3 victory over mighty Wichita State in a game they trailed 3-0 early and won on a three-run homer by third baseman Phil Lane.

Lane's big blow highlighted a six-run fifth inning outburst, and from there the Hurricanes relied on the clutch pitching of Mike Kasprzak and reliever Danny Smith, the CWS Most Outstanding Player.

Wichita State had jumped on Kasprzak for two runs in the first inning when Phil

**FROM THE ISSUE:**
JULY 10, 1982

## TOP TEAMS
### 1982 COLLEGE WORLD SERIES STANDINGS

| School | Conference | Record | CWS | Head Coach |
|---|---|---|---|---|
| Miami | Independent | 54–18–1 | 5–0 | Ron Fraser |
| Wichita State | Missouri Valley | 73–14 | 3–2 | Gene Stephenson |
| Maine | Eastern Collegiate | 34–14 | 2–2 | John Winkin |
| Texas | Southwest | 59–6 | 2–2 | Cliff Gustafson |
| Oklahoma State | Big Eight | 57–16 | 1–2 | Gary Ward |
| Stanford | Pacific-10 | 49–18–1 | 1–2 | Mark Marquess |
| Cal State Fullerton | SCBA | 51–23 | 0–2 | Augie Garrido |
| South Carolina | Independent | 45–13 | 0–2 | June Raines |

### NATIONAL CHAMPION
### MIAMI

The Hurricanes fell behind favored Wichita State 3-0 in the championship game but rallied for a 9-3 victory, securing the first title in Miami program history. In his 20th year at the helm, coach Ron Fraser finally had his first national title.

Stephenson doubled in one run and Russ Morman, with an NCAA record-breaking 129th RBI, singled home another.

Morman then led off the third inning with his 24th home run of the season, and third of the tournament, as the Shockers went ahead by three and seemed like they may put the game out of reach early.

Fraser even admitted concern at that point, but he was determined to stick with Kasprzak, a senior righthander who ended up 14-4 on the season.

"Mike is traditionally a slow starter," Fraser said. "And we had no one to bring in for long relief. So if the game were to get out of hand at that point, we would just have had to look at winning the next night."

But the "next night" never became an issue for the Hurricanes.

They exploded for six runs in the fifth off Wichita State's Don Heinkel, the NCAA's all-time winningest pitcher who ended up losing twice in the CWS to Miami.

Javier Velazquez led off the fifth inning for the Hurricanes with a single and moved to third on a double by Mitch Seoane.

Doug Shields then singled home both runners and advanced to third when Billy Wrona and Steve Lubsy walked to load the bases.

Sam Sorce's sacrifice fly scored Shields for the game-tying run before Lane, who with a late season onslaught lifted his homer total to 25, smashed his three-run shot.

The Hurricanes added an insurance run in the sixth and two more in the eighth to wrap up the championship.

Miami entered Omaha this year ranked No. 7 in the country—its lowest ranking ever for a team that qualified for the CWS—and some thought the Hurricanes even got a break in the first round when they were paired against lowly-regarded Maine, while the four top-ranked clubs were paired against each other.

But after disposing of the surprising Black Bears 7-2 in their opener, the Hurricanes used solo homers from Lane, Nelson Santovenia and Sorce to beat the No. 2-ranked Shockers 4-3 in a second-round game.

# 1982 NEWSMAKERS

The most famous baserunning escapade in CWS history, known as **The Grand Illusion**, occurred in a second round game between **Miami** and **Wichita State**. In a trick play devised by the Miami coaching staff, pitcher Mike Kasprzak made a series of token pickoff attempts at first base. He then faked an errant throw to first, hoping to deceive the baserunner, who was Phil Stephenson, the most prolific basestealer in college history. All the Hurricanes players acted as if the pickoff attempt had eluded the first baseman. Stephenson took off for second base and was easily tagged out when Kasprzak removed the ball from his glove and tossed it to awaiting shortstop Bill Wrona.

**Wichita State** rewrote the record book in 1982, winning an NCAA record 73 games while establishing new single-season marks for runs (858), hits (989), total bases (1,588) and stolen bases (333). The Shockers also led the nation with a 2.74 ERA.

**FINAL TOP 20 FOR 1982**

1. Wichita State*
2. Texas*
3. Arizona State
4. Miami*
5. Oklahoma State*
6. Stanford*
7. #Cal State Fullerton*
8. Fresno State
9. Virginia Tech
10. Nebraska
11. South Carolina*
12. Oral Roberts
13. Hawaii
14. Pepperdine
15. New Orleans
16. Florida State
17. Michigan
18. Maine*
19. Houston
20. South Florida

\* Reached College World Series
\# Preseason No. 1

# IN RETROSPECT: 1982 DRAFT

**Top 10 Draft Picks From College**

With overall selection number (Ov), drafting team (Team) and rank on Baseball America draft board (BA).

| Player | Pos | School | Ov | Team | BA |
|---|---|---|---|---|---|
| Augie Schmidt | SS | New Orleans | 2 | Blue Jays | 3 |
| Bryan Oelkers | LHP | Wichita State | 4 | Twins | – |
| Spike Owen | SS | Texas | 6 | Mariners | 5 |
| John Morris | OF | Seton Hall | 10 | Royals | – |
| Steve Stanicek | 1B | Nebraska | 11 | Giants | 7 |
| John Russell | C | Oklahoma | 13 | Phillies | – |
| Tony Woods | SS | Whittier (Calif.) | 17 | Cubs | – |
| Franklin Stubbs | 1B | Virginia Tech | 19 | Dodgers | 8 |
| Todd Worrell | RHP | Biola (Calif.) | 21 | Cardinals | – |
| Joe Kucharski | RHP | South Carolina | 24 | Orioles | – |

**Top 10 Major League Players From College Draft Class**

With draft round and Baseball-Reference.com total for wins above replacement (WAR) through 2019.

| Player | Pos | School | Rd | Ov | Team | WAR |
|---|---|---|---|---|---|---|
| Jimmy Key | LHP | Clemson | 3 | 56 | Blue Jays | 49.1 |
| Terry Pendleton | 3B | Fresno State | 7 | 179 | Cardinals | 28.5 |
| Zane Smith | LHP | Indiana State | 3 | 63 | Braves | 20.3 |
| Alvin Davis | 1B | Arizona State | 6 | 138 | Mariners | 20.0 |
| Tom Browning | LHP | Tenn. Wesleyan | 9 | 233 | Reds | 19.8 |
| Steve Buechele | 3B | Stanford | 5 | 122 | Rangers | 16.5 |
| Kirk McCaskill | RHP | Vermont | 4 | 88 | Angels | 14.3 |
| Vince Coleman | OF | Florida A&M | 10 | 257 | Cardinals | 12.5 |
| Spike Owen | SS | Texas | 1 | 6 | Mariners | 12.5 |
| Jim Deshaies | LHP | Le Moyne | 21 | 542 | Yankees | 12.0 |

Then, to prove they meant business, the Hurricanes promptly trimmed No. 1 Texas, 2-1, on the combined five-hit pitching of Sorce and Smith to guarantee themselves a spot in the finals and their best finish since they lost to USC in the 1974 championship game in their first-ever CWS appearance.

But, before meeting Wichita State again, first Miami had to dispose of upstart Maine, who were still alive.

After losing their opener to Miami, the Black Bears shockingly sent the two West representatives—Cal State Fullerton and Stanford—to the sidelines, marking the first time since 1954 that a team from the West had not advanced to the final four.

And it took all of a six-run ninth inning by the Hurricanes to finally subdue Maine, 10-4, reducing the field to two as Wichita State sent Texas packing with an 8-4 triumph.

On paper, the finale should have been no contest.

Wichita State, a team with a national-record 73 victories, three pitchers with 16 or more wins and an offense that made a mockery of the college baseball record book this season, versus Miami, a team with just two starting pitchers of any significance, no depth to their staff, and really only the ability to pop the long ball on occasion.

The Hurricanes didn't play it according to the book, though.

More than anything, they surprised themselves with their win.

"We had no dream we'd be in the finals," Fraser said. "The other teams we brought in were al highly ranked, had great pitching and played great defense. This was an entirely different type of club."

It sure was. It finally won. ∎

# Fiery Ledbetter has always been competitive

By **BILL McGROTHA**

J eff Ledbetter's temper had always been present.

It showed up when he thought an umpire was squeezing him in a playoff game.

Frustrated, he reared back and slammed the next pitch into the umpire's chest protector.

The umpire called time out and told Ledbetter that he would be ejected if it happened again.

"But it worked," Ledbetter said. "He started calling 'em right after that."

Ledbetter was 11 years old.

"I have never seen a more intense individual," Florida State head coach Mike Martin said. "He is certainly one of the biggest characters we've had in all the time I've been around here."

In his four-year career at Florida State, Ledbetter established college baseball's single-season (42) and career (97) home run records.

Florida State's Jeff Ledbetter established college records for home runs in a season (42) and a career (97). He fell short of expectations with a wood bat in pro ball and topped out at Double-A.

The lefthanded Ledbetter compiled a 10-1 record with Seminoles this season, but his bat was still his star attraction.

In perhaps the most incredible start this season by any college player, Ledbetter hit 12 home runs in his first 24 at-bats.

He quickly demolished the career record of 64 homers set in 1981 by teammate Mike Fuentes, then he cut to ribbons the single-season mark of 29.

With a .381 average, 42 homers and 10 wins as a pitcher, Ledbetter enjoyed a 1982 season as hot as his temperament and earned the College Player of the Year award.

Ledbetter, a communications major at Florida State, long ago received the message that the greatest victories often come against one's self.

"I'll have to look at it more maturely when I get to the pros," Ledbetter said just before coming to terms with the Red Sox. "Right now, I don't feel like there are any guys in college who are going to get me out consistently."

Ledbetter is usually the portrait of confidence at the plate, but not always.

"Sometimes I'm hitting and I'm King Kong up there—the beast in me comes out," he said. "Everything's falling into place, and I'm feeling very dominating up there.

"And sometimes up there I'm looking like Charlie Brown.

"Any time anyone is hitting like I was, you're going to hit a slump. Mechanically, you're going to start doing things wrong."

Drafted by the Yankees out of high school, drafted anew by the Expos last year, Ledbetter was naturally eager to begin his pro career in June, when the Red Sox tabbed him with the last pick in the first round.

Ledbetter said it doesn't matter where he plays in the pros, and there are some teams that would prefer he focus on hitting only.

For so long now, Ledbetter said, he has been hearing that he has all the ability in the world and it is a matter of him disciplining himself to do the things he must do to achieve his goals. He believes that, and he is trying hard to discipline himself.

Martin says Ledbetter has come an awfully long way from his freshman year.

"As different as day from night," he said. "He used to pout when things did not go right. He used to carry the bat on the field with him—worrying about his hitting when he should have been concentrating on his fielding. He has not always hustled out there the way he should.

"But all of that is behind him now. He has gained so much maturity. He has handled all of his current publicity so very well.

"Still, he is about as confident as he was when he was a freshman. He still does not think anybody can get him out, and he does not mind telling you." ∎

# TOP PLAYERS OF 1982

## ALL-AMERICA TEAM

| Pos | Player | School | Yr | AVG | AB | R | H | HR | RBI | BB | SO | SB |
|-----|--------|--------|----|-----|----|----|----|----|-----|----|----|----|
| C | Charlie O'Brien | Wichita State | Sr. | .359 | 340 | 87 | 122 | 25 | 116 | 23 | 10 | 6 |
| 1B | Steve Stanicek | Nebraska | Jr. | .449 | 185 | 73 | 83 | 20 | 70 | 44 | 20 | 7 |
| 2B | Mark Wasinger | Old Dominion | Jr. | .422 | 175 | 68 | 74 | 10 | 52 | 37 | 13 | 22 |
| 3B | Keith Mucha | Oral Roberts | Jr. | .364 | 206 | 68 | 75 | 18 | 65 | 54 | 19 | 22 |
| SS | Augie Schmidt | New Orleans | Jr. | .376 | 173 | 69 | 65 | 13 | 54 | 71 | 16 | 5 |
| OF | John Morris | Seton Hall | Jr. | .381 | 312 | 105 | 119 | 42 | 124 | 52 | 38 | 5 |
| OF | Jim Paciorek | Michigan | Sr. | .431 | 197 | 79 | 85 | 19 | 80 | 54 | 23 | 35 |
| OF | Jeff Ledbetter | Florida State | Sr. | .443 | 176 | 60 | 78 | 17 | 65 | 28 | 13 | 6 |
| DH | Phil Stephenson | Wichita State | Sr. | .399 | 293 | 123 | 117 | 23 | 115 | 97 | 24 | 87 |

| Pos | Pitcher | School | Yr | W | L | ERA | G | CG | SV | IP | H | BB | SO |
|-----|---------|--------|----|----|----|-----|----|----|----|----|----|----|----|
| SP | Don Heinkel | Wichita State | Sr. | 18 | 2 | 2.07 | 21 | 14 | 0 | 156 | 103 | 86 | 166 |
| SP | Bryan Oelkers | Wichita State | Jr. | 16 | 5 | 2.23 | 23 | 15 | 0 | 166 | 133 | 53 | 121 |
| SP | Jon Furman | Pepperdine | Sr. | 16 | 4 | 2.38 | 23 | 7 | 0 | 132 | 119 | 71 | 88 |
| SP | Randy Graham | Fresno State | Jr. | 14 | 0 | 2.82 | 17 | 12 | 0 | 137 | 131 | 29 | 82 |
| RP | Bryan Duquette | Hawaii | Jr. | 11 | 4 | 2.73 | 30 | 1 | 7 | 82 | 65 | 42 | 96 |

## SECOND TEAM

C—Robbie Wine Jr., Oklahoma State. 1B—Alvin Davis, Arizona State. 2B—Jeff Jacobsen, Michigan. 3B—Ronni Salcedo, Arizona State. SS—Spike Owen, Texas. OF—Kevin Romine, Arizona State; Jim Sherman, Delaware; and Mike Dotterer, Stanford. DH—Russ Morman, Wichita State. SP—Erik Sonberg, Wichita State; Rich Stoll, Michigan; Glenn Godwin, San Diego; and Roger Clemens, Texas. RP—Danny Smith, Miami.

## THIRD TEAM

C—Joe Szekely, Texas A&M. 1B—Bill White, The Citadel. 2B—Jimmy Thomas, Wichita State; and John Zelenka, Tulane. 3B—Jim Stewart, Virginia Tech; and Cory Snyder, Brigham Young. SS—Doug Gilcrease, Auburn; and Bill Merrifield, Wake Forest. OF—Tony Laurenzi, Long Beach State; John Russell, Oklahoma; and Terry Pendleton, Fresno State. DH—Jim Wilson, Oregon State. SP—Tony Mack, Lamar; Randy Conte, Illinois; Jeff Peterson, St. Mary's; and Joe Kucharski, South Carolina. RP—Mark Williamson, San Diego State; and Dennis Livingston, Oklahoma State.

Texas coach Cliff Gustafson won his second national title behind a Longhorns pitching staff headlined by All-Americans Roger Clemens and Calvin Schiraldi.

**1983**

# Longhorns capture fourth CWS title

By **STEVE PIVOVAR**

Cliff Gustafson admitted he couldn't take credit for the play that helped his Texas team win the College World Series with a 4-3 victory against Alabama, but it was Gus Ball at its best.

The play was Jose Tolentino's drag-bunt single with two outs in the seventh inning that scored Kirk Killingsworth with the Longhorns' fourth run.

"Jose did it on his own," Gustafson said. "I was just as surprised as they were."

No one in the final crowd of 14,957 figured Tolentino would bunt when he came to the plate in the seventh. Tolentino, although mired in a CWS slump, is Texas' cleanup hitter. He is also not the speediest Longhorn.

**FROM THE ISSUE:**
JULY 1, 1983

"He's their slowest runner, but he made a great bunt," said Alabama coach Barry Shollenberger, the College Coach of the Year.

Tolentino, who had just two hits in his first 17 at-bats in the CWS, figured he had nothing to lose by trying to bunt.

"You've got to make adjustments when you are pressing," said Tolentino, who was Texas' leading hitter throughout its 66-14 season.

"I was sure of my bat, but every time I'd swing I got too aggressive," Tolentino said. "I was swinging at bad pitches. I saw the runner on third and I saw both infielders staying back. I knew their pitcher was falling off to the right side. I knew if I put it past him I'd get on for sure."

Tolentino's bunt capped a four-run Texas rally in the sixth and seventh innings that helped erase a 2-0 Alabama lead. When the Longhorns survived a ninth-inning rally by the Crimson Tide, they walked away with their fourth NCAA championship.

It was Gustafson's second in the 16 years he's been coaching the Longhorns, and it provided him with one of his biggest thrills since he's been in Austin.

"I'm so proud of this bunch," Gustafson said. "Truthfully, the talent on this ball club

## TOP TEAMS
### 1983 COLLEGE WORLD SERIES STANDINGS

| School | Conference | Record | CWS | Head Coach |
|---|---|---|---|---|
| Texas | Southwest | 66–14 | 5–0 | Cliff Gustafson |
| Alabama | Southeastern | 46–11 | 3–2 | Barry Shollenberger |
| Arizona State | Pacific-10 | 44–24 | 2–2 | Jim Brock |
| Michigan | Big Ten | 50–9 | 2–2 | Bud Middaugh |
| Oklahoma State | Big Eight | 48–16 | 1–2 | Gary Ward |
| Stanford | Pacific-10 | 41–17–1 | 1–2 | Mark Marquess |
| James Madison | Eastern Collegiate | 37–13 | 0–2 | Brad Babcock |
| Maine | Eastern Collegiate | 29–16 | 0–2 | John Winkin |

## NATIONAL CHAMPION
### TEXAS

The Longhorns captured their fourth national title—their second under coach Cliff Gustafson—by winning five straight games. Texas defeated Alabama, 4-3, in the championship game. No team would go undefeated in Omaha again until 1991.

isn't as good as some of the talent we've had on other ball clubs. That's what makes this one so sweet.

"Our guys wanted this one badly. This is a bigger thrill than the 1975 club just because of our talent."

The Longhorns' talent had been knocked before. After being picked as the preseason No. 1 team, Texas lost games to teams such as Texas-Arlington, Texas Lutheran, Lubbock Christian, St. Mary's and Texas Wesleyan.

"People were down on us early in the season because we lost to clubs we hadn't lost to in millions of years," said Longhorns catcher Jeff Hearron, one of four Texas players who made the all-tournament team.

"But this year we started out the season saying we were going to win."

The Longhorns made good on their word. The title, however, didn't come easily.

Texas had to battle back from a second-game loss in the Central Regional to Mississippi State by winning four games just to earn the trip to Omaha.

Once at the CWS, the Longhorns had only one easy game. That came in the first round in a 12-0 victory against James Madison.

Texas' second game in the tournament was against No. 2-ranked Oklahoma State. The Longhorns were within one strike of posting a 5-4 victory before Scott Wade tied the game at 5-5 in the ninth inning with a run-scoring single.

Texas won in 11 innings when Jamie Doughty, a substitute third baseman who had played in only one-third of the Longhorns' games, doubled to score Mike Trent. Ironically, Texas had won a recruiting battle with Oklahoma State for Doughty's services.

Texas met Alabama for the first time in the tournament in a showdown of unbeaten teams. The Longhorns remained undefeated by scoring two runs in the 11th inning of a 6-4 triumph.

Calvin Schiraldi, the CWS Most Outstanding Player, picked up his second win in the tournament against Alabama by pitching 5.1 innings of relief. He struck out 11 hitters.

# 1983 NEWSMAKERS

Thirty years before **Mike Trout** became the best player in the major leagues, Trout's father **Jeff** earned his share of accolades as a collegian. A first-team All-American second baseman at Delaware, the 5-foot-9, switch-hitting Trout hit .519—second to Alabama's Dave Magadan, the national leader—while drilling 14 homers and driving in 63 runs as a senior.

Despite the availability of pitchers like Texas ace Roger Clemens in the 1983 draft, the **Twins** went off the board and selected little-known righthander **Tim Belcher** with the No. 1 pick. Belcher, from Mount Vernon Nazarene, an obscure NAIA school in Ohio, had surfaced as a legitimate pitching prospect in the final weeks before the draft, while the more established Clemens was in the process of leading the Longhorns to a national title. To the Twins' misfortune, they not only didn't draft Clemens but failed to even sign Belcher.

**FINAL TOP 20 FOR 1983**

1. #Texas*
2. Alabama*
3. Michigan*
4. Oklahoma State*
5. Stanford*
6. Brigham Young
7. Florida State
8. San Diego State
9. Arizona State*
10. Oral Roberts
11. Miami
12. Fresno State
13. Mississippi State
14. UC Santa Barbara
15. Cal State Fullerton
16. Wichita State
17. North Carolina
18. Tulane
19. Old Dominion
20. Maine*

\* Reached College World Series
\# Preseason No. 1

# IN RETROSPECT: 1983 DRAFT

**Top 10 Draft Picks From College**
With overall selection number (Ov), drafting team (Team) and rank on Baseball America draft board (BA).

| Player | Pos | School | Ov | Team | BA |
|---|---|---|---|---|---|
| Tim Belcher* | RHP | Mt. Vernon Nazarene | 1 | Twins | 1 |
| Jeff Kunkel | SS | Rider | 3 | Rangers | 5 |
| Stan Hilton | RHP | Baylor | 5 | Athletics | 8 |
| Darrel Akerfelds | RHP | Mesa (Colo.) | 7 | Mariners | 9 |
| Robbie Wine Jr. | C | Oklahoma State | 8 | Astros | 4 |
| Ray Hayward | LHP | Oklahoma | 10 | Padres | – |
| Dave Clark | OF | Jackson State | 11 | Indians | – |
| Rich Stoll | RHP | Michigan | 14 | Expos | – |
| Terry Bell | C | Old Dominion | 17 | Mariners | 20 |
| Erik Sonberg | LHP | Wichita State | 18 | Dodgers | 19 |

\* Did not sign

**Top 10 Major League Players From College Draft Class**
With draft round and Baseball-Reference.com total for wins above replacement (WAR) through 2019.

| Player | Pos | School | Rd | Ov | Team | WAR |
|---|---|---|---|---|---|---|
| Roger Clemens | RHP | Texas | 1 | 19 | Red Sox | 139.6 |
| Wally Joyner | 1B | Brigham Young | 3 | 67 | Angels | 35.8 |
| Doug Drabek | RHP | Houston | 11 | 279 | White Sox | 29.3 |
| Kevin Seitzer | 3B | Eastern Illinois | 11 | 283 | Royals | 28.9 |
| Terry Steinbach | C | Minnesota | 9 | 215 | Athletics | 28.0 |
| Rick Aguilera | RHP | Brigham Young | 3 | 58 | Mets | 21.9 |
| Dave Magadan | 1B | Alabama | 2 | 32 | Mets | 21.1 |
| Jeff Montgomery | RHP | Marshall | 9 | 212 | Reds | 20.6 |
| Glenn Davis | 1B | Georgia | 42 | 817 | Rangers | 19.7 |
| Dan Plesac | LHP | N.C. State | 1 | 26 | Brewers | 17.0 |

Texas ended Michigan's season with a 4-2 victory in the fourth round to set up a return meeting with Alabama. All of Texas' runs against the Wolverines came on Mike Brumley's grand slam in the fifth inning that erased a 2-0 Michigan lead.

"I was just looking to hit a fly ball or hit it hard somewhere to get us on the board," Brumley said after hitting Texas' first homer of the CWS.

In the championship game, Alabama jumped out to a 1-0 lead in the third inning on Bret Elbin's sacrifice fly. The Tide made it 2-0 in the fifth when Dee Smithey, a native of Austin who lives within a mile of Gustafson, hit a solo homer.

But the Longhorns tied the game in the sixth when they loaded the bases with none out. Losing pitcher Rick Browne then walked Steve Labay to force in one run, and the second scored on Johnny Sutton's infield out.

Brumley started Texas' winning rally in the seventh with a two-out single. He scored on Killingsworth's triple. Tolentino then caught everyone with their guard down with his gutty bunt.

"It was a big run," Gustafson said. "I was glad to see him do it when it got by their pitcher."

Alabama closed to within a run in the ninth before Roger Clemens got Frank Velleggia to fly out and Fermin Lake to pop out to end the game and start the Longhorns' celebration.

Added Tolentino: "Without any talent, we won this thing. It's too much for me. Everybody says we've got no talent. Everybody in the nation said this is the least talent we've ever had. We proved a point." ∎

# Alabama's Magadan selected '83 top player

By **ALLAN SIMPSON**

Alabama junior Dave Magadan led the nation in hitting with a .525 average. He went on to play 16 years in the majors as a high-average (.288) first baseman who never topped six homers in a season.

**D**ave Magadan knows about winning national player of the year awards.

Two years ago, following his freshman season at Alabama, Magadan was selected the American Legion player of the year after leading Tampa American Legion Post 248 to the national title.

Now, following one of the most remarkable seasons in college baseball history, the junior first baseman has been selected the College Player of the Year.

Magadan was a relatively clear-cut choice for the award after leading the nation in hitting with a .525 average and helping the Crimson Tide to a spot in the College World Series championship game.

He finished second in the country in hits (114), doubles (31) and RBIs (95).

After going 10-for-11 in the Southeastern Conference Tournament, he tied a College World Series record by going 5-for-5 in the opening game of the series. Overall, he batted .550 in Omaha.

Obviously, his most eye-catching statistic was his .525 average.

"I really don't feel like it's been a cheap .500," Magadan said. "I hit the ball hard pretty often."

Magadan's big season was particularly rewarding because he was not heavily recruited out of high school by area colleges. A number of pro scouts also downplayed his average this spring, choosing to dwell on his inability to hit the long ball with any consistency and his lack of running speed.

"They rapped my power, but I had three home runs in the SEC Tournament and two more in the World Series," Magadan said. "They say I'm not real fast, but I worked on it and knocked 0.8 seconds off my 60-yard dash time."

The Mets were obviously suitably impressed with Magadan's all-around game and drafted him in the second round.

Magadan encountered nothing but success during his amateur career, yet mysteriously was practically ignored by major schools in the Southeast after batting .500, going 13-2 as a pitcher and earning Tampa player of the year honors his senior year in high school.

The Red Sox thought highly enough of him to draft him in the 12th round, but Magadan gave little thought to the pros.

"I just didn't feel I was mentally ready for pro ball then," he said.

In his first two seasons at Alabama, Magadan hit .389 and .395 while playing third base. He already owned school career records for hits, doubles, total bases, RBIs and batting average prior to the season.

Magadan, a cousin of Yankees outfielder Lou Piniella, credits his improvement in 1983 to a number of factors, not the least of which was playing away from home for the first time last summer, when he played for Peninsula of the semipro Alaska League.

"I faced good pitching there, day in and day out," he said. "I learned the strike zone a little better, and I started hitting my pitch a little better."

Then, in the fall, he worked daily in the batting cage, spending hours learning the discipline to lay off bad pitches.

He later worked strictly on running and lifting weights—building up his speed and his ability to pop the long ball with more frequency.

The biggest adjustment for Magadan, though, came when Alabama coach Barry Shollenberger moved him from third base, where he had played throughout his career, to first base just prior to the '83 campaign. He handled the transition smoothly.

While his ability to hit the ball with more consistent power seems to be the one thing he has to work on for him to play in the big leagues, Magadan is just as content to rap a double as a homer. In fact, he downplays the value of the long ball.

"My doubles seem to be hit harder," he said.

"Most of my homers are really just fly balls." ■

# TOP PLAYERS OF 1983

## ALL-AMERICA TEAM

| Pos | Player | School | Yr | AVG | AB | R | H | HR | RBI | BB | SO | SB |
|-----|--------|--------|----|-----|----|----|----|-----|-----|----|----|----|
| C | Terry Bell | Old Dominion | Jr. | .400 | 164 | 37 | 66 | 7 | 63 | 29 | 43 | 1 |
| 1B | Dave Magadan | Alabama | Jr. | .525 | 217 | 67 | 114 | 9 | 95 | 42 | 12 | 1 |
| 2B | Jeff Trout | Delaware | Sr. | .519 | 189 | 86 | 98 | 14 | 63 | 45 | 16 | 17 |
| 3B | Chris Sabo | Michigan | Jr. | .368 | 209 | 58 | 77 | 16 | 56 | 26 | 11 | 19 |
| SS | Jeff Kunkel | Rider | Jr. | .399 | 143 | 48 | 57 | 6 | 37 | 20 | 13 | 12 |
| OF | Shane Mack | UCLA | So. | .419 | 210 | 54 | 88 | 11 | 60 | 18 | 26 | 20 |
| OF | Ben Abner | Georgia Southern | So. | .400 | 245 | 75 | 98 | 23 | 82 | 33 | 21 | 8 |
| OF | Rafael Palmeiro | Mississippi State | Fr. | .406 | 234 | 69 | 95 | 18 | 78 | 33 | 11 | 12 |
| DH | Russ Morman | Wichita State | Jr. | .439 | 255 | 99 | 112 | 23 | 105 | 61 | 26 | 40 |

| Pos | Pitcher | School | Yr | W | L | ERA | G | CG | SV | IP | H | BB | SO |
|-----|---------|--------|----|----|----|-----|----|----|----|----|----|----|----|
| P | Calvin Schiraldi | Texas | Jr. | 14 | 2 | 1.74 | 24 | 11 | 2 | 140 | 105 | 52 | 117 |
| P | Dennis Livingston | Oklahoma State | So. | 15 | 3 | 3.00 | 22 | 8 | 3 | 135 | 80 | 117 | 180 |
| P | Mike Cherry | The Citadel | Jr. | 12 | 0 | 3.11 | 14 | 8 | 0 | 88 | 62 | 45 | 132 |
| P | Jim Hickey | Pan American | Sr. | 16 | 2 | 1.66 | 18 | 16 | 1 | 130 | 103 | 29 | 109 |

## SECOND TEAM

C—Andy Allanson, Richmond. 1B—Wally Joyner, Brigham Young. 2B—Chris Cannizzaro, San Diego State. 3B—Don Montgomery, Creighton. SS—Cory Snyder, Brigham Young. OF—Oddibe McDowell, Arizona State; Stan Jefferson, Bethune-Cookman; and Glenn Edwards, Oklahoma State. DH—Eric Hardgrave, Stanford. P—Rayner Noble, Houston; Todd Simmons, Cal State Fullerton; Roger Clemens, Texas; and Rich Stoll, Michigan.

## THIRD TEAM

C—Ralph Antone, Western Kentucky. 1B—Mike Aldrete, Stanford. 2B—Robbie Cobb, Ohio State. 3B—Ron Henika, Oral Roberts. SS—Bill Merrifield, Wake Forest. OF—Dan Boever, Nebraska; Glenn Braggs, Hawaii; and Oriol Perez, Florida International. DH—Pete Incaviglia, Oklahoma State. P—Erik Sonberg, Wichita State; Dave Eichhorn, Miami; Scott Nielsen, Brigham Young; and Dan Yokubaitis, UC Santa Barbara.

Cal State Fullerton coach Augie Garrido won his second College World Series championship in 1984 and would claim a third with the Titans in 1995.

**1984**

# Cal State Fullerton trims Texas for '84 crown

By **MIKE BABCOCK**

I n the end, the most offensive College World Series in history came down to Cal State Fullerton's pitching and defense.

"It's offense, offense, offense, then it ends up being defense and a pitcher who hasn't started lately," Titans head coach Augie Garrido said, moments after his team had defeated defending national champion Texas, 3-1, in the finals of the 38th CWS before an audience of 13,487 at Rosenblatt Stadium.

Cal State Fullerton won its second national title in five years behind a 5-foot-8, 150-pound lefthander named Eddie Delzer, who was a lowly 21st-round pick of the Angels in the draft.

"Eddie pitched the biggest game of his life, the biggest game of our season, and he really cut 'em up," said Cal State Fullerton reliever Scott Wright, who pitched the final two innings to gain his 22nd save of the season.

Through seven innings, Delzer allowed just two hits, both first-inning singles, neither of which left the infield. For the next 6.1 innings he held Texas hitless.

Delzer's left leg cramped following his final warmup pitch in the top of the eighth, and he left the game to a standing ovation. "I hated coming out, but why stick with me if I had an injury," Delzer said. "Besides, Scotty (Wright) did a great job."

The other Longhorns went down quietly as Wright increased his NCAA-record total for saves to 22 and nailed down Cal State Fullerton's second national championship.

Even if the cramp hadn't put Delzer out of the last stages of the game, Garrido would have. The cramp "took the pressure off me," Garrido said. "Our decision was made. When Eddie got through their lefthanded batter, we were going with Scott. That's how we got here, and that's how we were going to end it."

Wright, a 6-foot, 180-pound senior drafted in the 14th round by the Phillies, didn't allow a run in his four appearances during the CWS. He was credited with a win against Michigan in the opening round and two saves for his 7.1 innings.

Lefthanded-hitting Dennis Cook, who was 5-for-19 in the College World Series, represented Texas' last hope.

**FROM THE ISSUE:**
JULY 1, 1984

## TOP TEAMS
### 1984 COLLEGE WORLD SERIES STANDINGS

| School | Conference | Record | CWS | Head Coach |
|--------|-----------|--------|-----|-----------|
| Cal State Fullerton | SCBA | 66–20 | 5–1 | Augie Garrido |
| Texas | Southwest | 60–14 | 3–2 | Cliff Gustafson |
| Oklahoma State | Big Eight | 61–15 | 3–2 | Gary Ward |
| Arizona State | Pacific-10 | 55–20 | 2–2 | Jim Brock |
| Miami | Independent | 48–28 | 1–2 | Ron Fraser |
| New Orleans | Independent | 46–26 | 1–2 | Ron Maestri |
| Maine | Eastern Collegiate | 33–20 | 0–2 | John Winkin |
| Michigan | Big Ten | 43–18 | 0–2 | Bud Middaugh |

## NATIONAL CHAMPION
### CAL STATE FULLERTON

Coach Augie Garrido captured his second national title in five years when his Titans defeated Texas 3-1 in the championship game. He won previously in 1979. Cal State Fullerton's victory denied the Longhorns a second straight CWS title.

Wright quickly got two strikes on Cook. Cook fouled off two pitches, then took two balls to even the count. Wright came sidearm, and Cook swung. The ball sailed to the opposite field, where John Fishel, the CWS Most Outstanding Player, took a couple of steps and cradled it for the national championship-clinching out. Then, the celebration began.

The junior from Brea, Calif., a 19th-round pick of the Athletics, tied a CWS record by getting 13 hits and finished with a .520 average in the tournament. Fishel hit home runs against Michigan and Oklahoma State and drove in 10 runs to tie Oklahoma State's Randy Whisler in that category.

"This is a great team," Garrido said. "It had to be a team because we don't match up physically with these other teams. I wouldn't think any differently had the outcome been different. We were the best balanced and most consistent team here."

Evidence of that was the major league draft, where 13 Titans were chosen through the first 28 rounds, beginning with Bob Caffrey, a first-round pick of the Expos.

Righthander Steve Rousey, a Mariners fourth-round pick, was Garrido's announced probable starter for the championship game.

Delzer didn't know he was going to start until 30 minutes before the game, even though Garrido and his pitching coach Dave Snow made the decision in the early morning hours on Sunday.

They didn't tell Delzer because "Eddie's real emotional," Garrido said. "We handled him like a reliever. We popped the ball in his hand and told him, 'Get 'em, youngster.' "

Delzer couldn't contain his emotions after the game. During Cal State Fullerton's celebration, he broke down and cried for his father, who was murdered two years ago.

"He was my No. 1 fan," Delzer said. "I wish he was here."

Texas got good pitching and defense in the championship game, but it wasn't good enough to support the lone run the Longhorns manufactured in the first inning.

From the first session of the CWS, the coaches kept saying pitching and defense would decide the champion.

Pitching and defense were rarely seen, except from the Titans.

# 1984 NEWSMAKERS

**San Diego State** has never qualified for the CWS but came closest in 1984, when it went 66-23 and finished second to eventual national champion Cal State Fullerton in the West I regional. The No. 5-ranked Aztecs tied the Titans (66-20) for the national lead in wins but lost to the Titans, 8-7, in the decisive game of a stacked regional field that also included No. 6 Fresno State and No. 9 Southern California, whose marquee player was Mark McGwire, the national leader with 32 homers.

With a No. 1 national ranking most of the season, a school attendance record of 163,374 and a nation-best 13 draft picks, **Arizona State** appeared primed to roll to its first national title in six years. But after winning its first two games at the CWS, including a wild, 23-12 victory over Oklahoma State, the Sun Devils inexplicably pulled up short, losing 8-4 to Texas and 6-1 to Cal State Fullerton, the eventual national champion.

**FINAL TOP 20 FOR 1984**

1. Cal State Fullerton*
2. #Arizona State*
3. Texas*
4. Oklahoma State*
5. San Diego State
6. Fresno State
7. Mississippi State
8. Hawaii
9. Southern California
10. New Orleans*
11. North Carolina
12. Florida
13. Oklahoma
14. South Alabama
15. Miami*
16. Maine*
17. Texas A&M
18. Stetson
19. Rice
20. Michigan*

\* Reached College World Series
\# Preseason No. 1

# IN RETROSPECT: 1984 DRAFT

**Top 10 Draft Picks From College**
With overall selection number (Ov), drafting team (Team) and rank on Baseball America draft board (BA).

| Player | Pos | School | Ov | Team | BA |
|---|---|---|---|---|---|
| Bill Swift | RHP | Maine | 2 | Mariners | 18 |
| Drew Hall | LHP | Morehead State | 3 | Cubs | 5 |
| Cory Snyder | SS | Brigham Young | 4 | Indians | 2 |
| Pat Pacillo | RHP | Seton Hall | 5 | Reds | 21 |
| Mike Dunne | RHP | Bradley | 7 | Cardinals | 4 |
| Alan Cockrell | OF | Tennessee | 9 | Giants | 23 |
| Mark McGwire | 1B | Southern California | 10 | Athletics | 10 |
| Shane Mack | OF | UCLA | 11 | Padres | 3 |
| Oddibe McDowell | OF | Arizona State | 12 | Rangers | 6 |
| Bob Caffrey | C | Cal State Fullerton | 13 | Expos | 29 |

**Top 10 Major League Players From College Draft Class**
With draft round and Baseball-Reference.com total for wins above replacement (WAR) through 2019.

| Player | Pos | School | Rd | Ov | Team | WAR |
|---|---|---|---|---|---|---|
| Mark McGwire | 1B | Southern Calif. | 1 | 10 | Athletics | 62.2 |
| Jamie Moyer | LHP | St. Joseph's | 6 | 135 | Cubs | 49.9 |
| Ken Caminiti | 3B | San Jose State | 3 | 71 | Astros | 33.5 |
| Lance Johnson | OF | South Alabama | 6 | 139 | Cardinals | 30.2 |
| Jeff Fassero | LHP | Mississippi | 22 | 554 | Cardinals | 23.8 |
| Shane Mack | OF | UCLA | 1 | 11 | Padres | 21.6 |
| Bill Swift | RHP | Maine | 1 | 2 | Mariners | 20.6 |
| Jody Reed | 2B | Florida State | 8 | 198 | Red Sox | 15.9 |
| Mike Henneman | RHP | Oklahoma State | 4 | 104 | Tigers | 12.9 |
| Scott Bankhead | RHP | North Carolina | 1 | 16 | Royals | 11.3 |

Cal State Fullerton's defense was consistent in a tournament that saw Miami commit eight errors in its opening-round loss to Arizona State and Texas tie a CWS single-game record by committing nine errors in an 18-13 loss to Oklahoma State.

Texas lefthander Greg Swindell, a freshman from Houston, provided some of the pitching. He allowed just three hits and two earned runs in 7.1 innings to gain credit for a 6-3 victory against New Orleans in the CWS opener, then came back to pitch an 8-4, complete game victory against Arizona State in a battle of the unbeatens.

But two days of rest weren't enough heading into the championship game. Swindell gave way to Eric Boudreaux with one out in the fifth. "I wasn't tired," said Swindell, who finished at 14-2. "Coach pulled me out because he was afraid I might hurt myself. My fastball wasn't as fast as it usually is, but everything else was fine.

"I really felt like we were going to do pretty well, but we just didn't hit the ball. It's hard to go out like this, but we'll be back next year."

Though Texas fell short of a second consecutive national championship, the 60-14 Longhorns surprised many people in what was figured to be a rebuilding year. "Maybe the youth was the difference at the end. We were just too tight," Gustafson said.

The Longhorns had taken two of three from Cal State Fullerton in Austin during the regular season and defeated the Titans 6-4 in a second round winners' bracket game. That first time, Texas collected eight hits off righthander Todd Simmons, who came back and went the distance against Oklahoma State to put Fullerton in the title game.

But Delzer was nearly untouchable in recording his eighth victory in 10 decisions.

"The game proved that good pitching can still get good hitters out," Gustafson said. ∎

# O-D-D-I-B-E selected Player of the Year

By **DANNY KNOBLER**

**A**t some point in the next couple of years, Oddibe McDowell will probably be playing center field for the Rangers. When he gets there, he has a mind to ask Texas to let him wear the letter "O" on the back of his uniform, rather than a more customary number.

It won't be without precedent.

For the last two years, McDowell—the Rangers' first-round pick in the 1984 draft—has worn a uniform with the letter "O" during a big career at Arizona State. And, of course, Al Oliver wore the same uniform several years ago when he played for the Rangers.

Head coach Jim Brock originally suggested to a shy and unassuming McDowell that he wear "O" at Arizona State—obviously as a take-off on Oddibe, but more as a publicity gimmick. That suggestion, along with Brock's long string of superlatives every time Oddibe's name came up, helped turn McDowell into one of college baseball's best-known players this year.

Oddibe McDowell starred for Arizona State and for the U.S. Olympic team in 1984, when the Rangers made him a first-round pick. He spent seven years in the majors as a league-average center fielder.

And while Brock was orchestrating McDowell's publicity campaign, Oddibe was quietly going out and convincing everybody that his coach was right.

In his first season at Arizona State after transferring from Miami Dade JC North, McDowell hit .352 with seven home runs, 50 RBIs and 36 stolen bases in 67 games. He wasn't satisfied, and the scouts weren't completely sold.

So after turning down the Twins' offer to skip his senior year and turn pro in 1983, McDowell returned to ASU in 1984 and made his previous numbers look rather ordinary.

In 74 games this season, Oddibe hit .405 with 23 homers, 74 RBIs, 101 runs, 117 hits, 18 doubles, eight triples, 66 walks and 36 stolen bases in 39 attempts.

In 30 Pacific-10 Conference games, he hit .431 with 15 homers, 33 RBIs and 15 steals in 16 tries. And in four games at the College World Series, he hit .500 with five more RBIs.

For his outstanding season, one of the best overall performances in college baseball history, the 5-foot-9, 165-pound McDowell has been named College Player of the Year.

One of college baseball's most exciting players ever because of his size, speed and power, McDowell delighted crowds who turned out to watch the 1984 Olympic team.

In 34 games of the Team USA tour, McDowell hit .275 in 138 at-bats. He led the team with nine triples, 10 steals and 35 runs, while hitting six homers and driving in 24 runs.

While his statistics make him a natural team leader, McDowell has been content to go back to his more comfortable role of being a quiet leader.

"Here, everybody's a leader," he said. "We've got a bunch of superstars on this team." McDowell might just be the biggest star of the lot.

Every time someone finds something they think he can't do, he goes out and does it.

Some people said McDowell didn't hit the ball hard enough or hit enough home runs. So this year, he hit 23, and his 15 in 30 Pac-10 games were three more than Southern California first baseman Mark McGwire, who was the overall national leader with 32.

McDowell batted leadoff most of the year at Arizona State, but he moved to third in the order for a game against Stanford, and he responded by hitting three home runs. No Sun Devils player had ever done that in Packard Stadium.

Olympic coach Rod Dedeaux is one of many baseball people who think McDowell could step right in and play in the major leagues as soon as the Olympics are over in early August. No one has gone straight from college to the big leagues since Bob Horner did it in 1978, but many scouts feel McDowell could do it if the Rangers give him a chance.

McDowell said he hopes to make it to the majors within a year and a half, and he hopes the Olympics experience will help.

"It's given me a chance to come out here and work with the wooden bat," he said. "It's also given me exposure, so people know who I am as a baseball player. Maybe if people remember me, the public pressure will help a major league team move me up faster." ■

# TOP PLAYERS OF 1984

## ALL-AMERICA TEAM

| Pos | Player | School | Yr | AVG | AB | R | H | HR | RBI | SB |
|-----|--------|--------|-----|-----|-----|-----|-----|-----|-----|-----|
| C | John Marzano | Temple | Jr. | .448 | 154 | 55 | 69 | 15 | 61 | 12 |
| 1B | Mark McGwire | Southern California | Jr. | .387 | 248 | 75 | 96 | 32 | 80 | 2 |
| 2B | Bob Ralston | Arizona | Sr. | .363 | 237 | 42 | 86 | 0 | 39 | 9 |
| 3B | David Denny | Texas | Jr. | .343 | 297 | 69 | 102 | 10 | 72 | 0 |
| SS | Cory Snyder | Brigham Young | Jr. | .450 | 231 | 81 | 104 | 27 | 85 | 11 |
| OF | Oddibe McDowell | Arizona State | Sr. | .405 | 289 | 101 | 117 | 23 | 74 | 36 |
| OF | Chris Gwynn | San Diego State | So. | .383 | 358 | 95 | 137 | 19 | 95 | 19 |
| OF | Rafael Palmeiro | Mississippi State | So. | .415 | 236 | 87 | 98 | 29 | 94 | 8 |
| DH | Pete Incaviglia | Oklahoma State | So. | .352 | 250 | 84 | 88 | 29 | 103 | 1 |

| Pos | Pitcher | School | Yr | W | L | ERA | G | SV | IP | H | BB | SO |
|-----|---------|--------|-----|-----|-----|-----|-----|-----|-----|-----|-----|-----|
| P | John Hoover | Fresno State | Sr. | 18 | 3 | 2.09 | 22 | 1 | 177 | 136 | 39 | 205 |
| P | Scott Bankhead | North Carolina | Jr. | 11 | 0 | 1.50 | 14 | 0 | 96 | 65 | 29 | 124 |
| P | Greg Swindell | Texas | Fr. | 14 | 2 | 2.05 | 25 | 3 | 132 | 89 | 43 | 117 |
| P | Scott Wright | Cal State Fullerton | Sr. | 6 | 1 | 2.67 | 47 | 22 | 87 | 70 | 42 | 55 |

## SECOND TEAM.

C—B.J. Surhoff, North Carolina. 1B—Will Clark, Mississippi State. 2B—Tim Dulin, Memphis State. 3B—Pete Coachman, South Alabama. SS—Flavio Alfaro, San Diego State. OF—Shane Mack, UCLA; John FIshel, Cal State Fullerton; and Ben Abner, Georgia Southern. DH—Tracy Woodson, North Carolina State. P—Drew Hall, Morehead State; Todd Simmons, Cal State Fullerton; Mike Dunne, Bradley; and Wally Whitehurst, New Orleans.

## THIRD TEAM

C—Bob Caffrey, Cal State Fullerton. 1B—Mark Higgins, New Orleans. 2B—Frank Mattox, California. 3B—Scott Raziano, New Orleans. SS—Gary Green, Oklahoma State. OF—Danny Wagner, Tulane; Todd Brown, Arizona State; Steve Iannini, Georgetown; and Lance Johnson, South Alabama. DH—Frank Fazzini, Florida State. P—Mike Christ, Jacksonville; Bill Mendek, Temple; Pete Hardee, Appalachian State; and Norm Charlton, Rice.

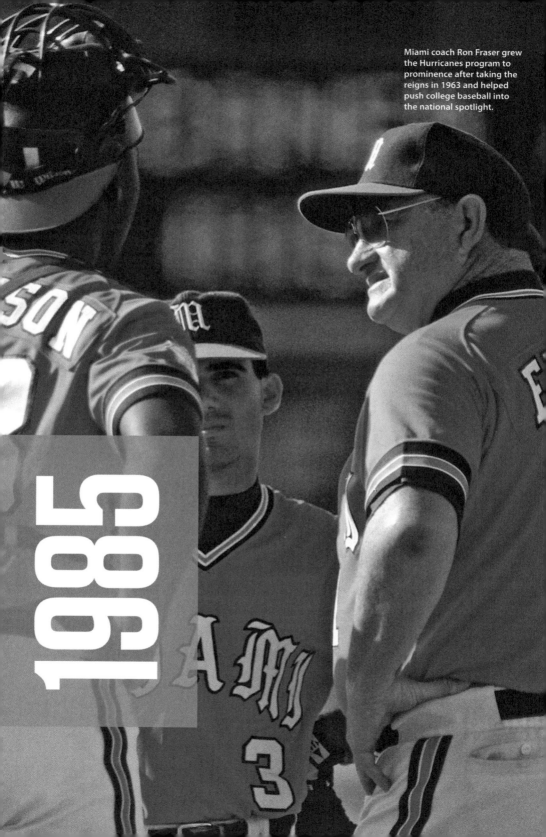

Miami coach Ron Fraser grew the Hurricanes program to prominence after taking the reigns in 1963 and helped push college baseball into the national spotlight.

1985

# Surprising Miami beats favored Texas twice

By **STEVE PIVOVAR**

**FROM THE ISSUE:**
JULY 10-24, 1985

**K**evin Sheary, a .500 pitcher during the season, won his third game at the College World Series to lead Miami to its second national championship with a 10-6 victory against Texas.

Sheary got relief help from Rick Raether in the championship game, played before a crowd of 9,830 at Rosenblatt Stadium. The tournament, twice delayed by rain, drew an all-time record attendance of 125,970.

Sheary, a 6-foot, 180-pound sophomore from Flanders, N.J., struggled throughout the 1985 season and was 4-4 when the Hurricanes began postseason play.

Pegged as Miami's No. 1 starter after a 10-2 freshman season, Sheary was plagued by academic and injury problems in 1985. He missed spring drills because of the academic problems, then ruptured a disc in his back shortly after he returned to action.

Sheary won Miami's first game against Stanford, then came back to keep the Hurricanes alive in elimination play with a 2-1 triumph against Oklahoma State.

The Hurricanes also got a big boost from DH Greg Ellena, who had four hits in the championship game and 12 for the tournament, one shy of the record. The CWS Most Outstanding Player hit two homers in the Hurricanes' win against Stanford and the game-winning homer in a 6-5 triumph against Mississippi State.

"This was a team of destiny," said Miami coach Ron Fraser, who has now won two national titles in the last four years. "This is a special team, unlike any other we've had. We've had better talent, but this team had the chemistry and that's what made the difference."

Texas contributed to its demise in the title game by committing five errors, four in the first three innings when Miami took a 6-0 lead.

The Hurricanes built their lead to 10-3 after six and a half innings, but Texas came back to score three times off Sheary in the seventh. Raether, who finished with two wins and a save in the CWS, then came in to shut off the Longhorns and clinch the title.

## TOP TEAMS

### 1985 COLLEGE WORLD SERIES STANDINGS

| School | Conference | Record | CWS | Head Coach |
|--------|-----------|--------|-----|-----------|
| Miami | Independent | 64–16 | 5–1 | Ron Fraser |
| Texas | Southwest | 64–14 | 4–2 | Cliff Gustafson |
| Arkansas | Southwest | 51–15 | 2–2 | Norm DeBriyn |
| Mississippi State | Southeastern | 50–15 | 2–2 | Ron Polk |
| Oklahoma State | Big Eight | 58–16 | 1–2 | Gary Ward |
| Stanford | Pacific-10 | 47–15 | 1–2 | Mark Marquess |
| Arizona | Pacific-10 | 47–22 | 0–2 | Jerry Kindall |
| South Carolina | Metro | 47–22 | 0–2 | June Raines |

## NATIONAL CHAMPION
### MIAMI

Texas played for a national title for the third straight season but was denied for a second straight year. Miami defeated the Longhorns, 10-6, in the championship game, giving coach Ron Fraser his second title in the last four years.

While Texas' appearance in the championship game came as no shocker—it was the Longhorns' third straight trip to the final—Miami emerged as the surprise of the 39th annual tournament.

Few gave the Hurricanes much chance. Fraser said his team lacked a superstar hitter, like Oklahoma State's Pete Incaviglia or Mississippi State's Will Clark, or a standout pitcher like Texas' Greg Swindell or Arizona's Joe Magrane.

The Hurricanes opened the tournament with a shocking 17-3 upset of Stanford. In that game, Ellena and Rusty DeBold, a 5-foot-9, 158-pound shortstop, each hit two home runs to tie a CWS record for homers in a game.

While Miami cruised to its first win, Texas struggled to get by Arizona. Magrane, a sturdy 6-foot-6, 225-pound lefthander, held Texas to four hits, but the Longhorns rallied for a 2-1 victory thanks to strong play by All-America second baseman Billy Bates.

The comeback was just the start of some late-inning drama for the Longhorns. Texas won its second game, defeating Miami 8-4 when Bates drove in five runs with two homers and a double. One of Bates' homers was an inside-the-park shot.

Texas picked up its third win of the tournament, clinching an automatic spot in the finals, by defeating Mississippi State 12-7. The Bulldogs were in control for the first five innings while Gene Morgan held the Longhorns to two hits.

The next night, Texas appeared to need its bye into the final. Arkansas held a 7-0 lead after five and a half innings.

Texas tied the game in the ninth against Razorback relief ace Tim Deitz, then won it 8-7 in the 10th when Bates opened the inning with a triple. After two intentional walks, Doug Hodo singled to score Bates and eliminate Arkansas.

"I can't recall winning two games in a row like this at Omaha," Gustafson said.

# 1985 NEWSMAKERS

Oklahoma State's **Pete Incaviglia** slugged the improbable total of 48 homers (in 75 games) to break the existing NCAA record of 42, set by Florida State's Jeff Ledbetter in 1982. Incaviglia also closed out his three-year career with the Cowboys by going deep 100 times—breaking Ledbetter's total of 97, achieved over four years.

Texas sophomore lefthander **Greg Swindell** was denied his bid to become just the second pitcher in NCAA history to win 20 games when he was beaten, 2-1, by Miami on a pair of unearned runs with the CWS title on the line. The loss was the first in the series by the Longhorns, and necessitated a second championship game, with Miami again prevailing, 10-6.

Notably absent from the NCAA Tournament field were three West Coast powers: five-time champion **Arizona State**, defending champion **Cal State Fullerton** and 11-time champion **Southern California**. ASU began the season ranked No. 3 but was almost immediately placed on probation by the Pacific-10 Conference for violations in its work-study program which caused several players to miss games at the start of the season.

## FINAL TOP 25 FOR 1985

1. Miami*
2. #Texas*
3. Mississippi State*
4. Arkansas*
5. Stanford*
6. Oklahoma State*
7. Oklahoma
8. Pepperdine
9. Michigan
10. Wichita State
11. Arizona*
12. Florida State
13. South Carolina*
14. Oral Roberts
15. Florida
16. Fresno State
17. Old Dominion
18. California
19. Nebraska
20. Louisiana State
21. Baylor
22. Houston
23. New Mexico
24. Virginia Tech
25. Indiana State

\* Reached College World Series
\# Preseason No. 1

# IN RETROSPECT: 1985 DRAFT

### Top 10 Draft Picks From College

With overall selection number (Ov), drafting team (Team) and rank on Baseball America draft board (BA).

| Player | Pos | School | Ov | Team | BA |
|---|---|---|---|---|---|
| B.J. Surhoff | C | North Carolina | 1 | Brewers | 1 |
| Will Clark | 1B | Mississippi State | 2 | Giants | 3 |
| Bobby Witt | RHP | Oklahoma | 3 | Rangers | 2 |
| Barry Larkin | SS | Michigan | 4 | Reds | 4 |
| Barry Bonds | OF | Arizona State | 6 | Pirates | 9 |
| Mike Campbell | RHP | Hawaii | 7 | Mariners | 7 |
| Pete Incaviglia | OF | Oklahoma State | 8 | Expos | 8 |
| Mike Poehl | RHP | Texas | 9 | Indians | 14 |
| Chris Gwynn | OF | San Diego State | 10 | Dodgers | 6 |
| Walt Weiss | SS | North Carolina | 11 | Athletics | 13 |

### Top 10 Major League Players From College Draft Class

With draft round and Baseball-Reference.com total for wins above replacement (WAR) through 2019.

| Player | Pos | School | Rd | Ov | Team | WAR |
|---|---|---|---|---|---|---|
| Barry Bonds | OF | Arizona State | 1 | 6 | Pirates | 162.8 |
| Randy Johnson | LHP | Southern Calif. | 2 | 36 | Expos | 101.1 |
| Rafael Palmeiro | 1B | Mississippi State | 1 | 22 | Cubs | 71.9 |
| Barry Larkin | SS | Michigan | 1 | 4 | Reds | 70.4 |
| Will Clark | 1B | Mississippi State | 1 | 2 | Giants | 56.5 |
| Mark Grace | 1B | San Diego State | 24 | 622 | Cubs | 46.4 |
| David Justice | OF | Thomas More (Ky.) | 4 | 94 | Braves | 40.6 |
| Brady Anderson | OF | UC Irvine | 10 | 257 | Red Sox | 35.0 |
| B.J. Surhoff | OF | North Carolina | 1 | 1 | Brewers | 34.4 |
| Randy Velarde | 2B | Lubbock Christian | 19 | 475 | White Sox | 24.9 |

Miami, meanwhile, was providing the tournament with an equal amount of drama. The Hurricanes remained in the tournament by eliminating Oklahoma State 2-1.

The Hurricanes then earned another shot at Texas by eliminating Mississippi State 6-5 on Ellena's two-run homer in the bottom of the ninth inning off Bulldogs reliever Bobby Thigpen.

Thigpen had put Mississippi State ahead 4-3 with a grand slam homer off Raether, who had entered the game with the bases full in the sixth.

The win over Mississippi State earned the Hurricanes a second shot at Swindell, bidding to join Hawaii's Derek Tatsuno as the only collegiate arm to win 20 games in one season.

The Hurricanes denied Swindell that honor, scoring a pair of unearned runs to take a 2-1 win and force a second championship game.

Raether, for the second straight night, pitched the final 3.1 innings to pick up the win. But the Hurricanes' real pitching hero was junior lefthander Dan Davies, who held Texas to four hits and an unearned run in the first 5.2 innings.

Davies, 15-1 coming into the tournament, had been bothered by a sore shoulder. He was ineffective against Texas in his first start, allowing four runs in three innings.

Fraser didn't decide to start Davies in the second meeting with the Longhorns until shortly before game time.

Afterward, Raether was asked what he thought about Swindell's rocky outing.

"You won't find many pitchers as good as Swindell," Raether said. "Except for Dan.

"I'm totally serious. He pitched with guts. Swindell is a heck of a pitcher, but he was out there with a fresh arm. Dan wasn't. He gave us everything he had." ∎

# Home run-hitting Incaviglia is tops in '85

By **DANNY KNOBLER**

T he numbers speak for themselves.
A .464 batting average. Forty-eight home runs. One hundred forty-three runs batted in.

No college player has ever had a season like that. Few major leaguers have approached any of those figures in a season more than twice as long.

But when Oklahoma State's season ended in early June at the College World Series, those were exactly the figures that earned Pete Incaviglia recognition as the College Player of the Year.

"The numbers seem humanly impossible," said Cowboys coach Gary Ward, who watched Incaviglia hit 100 home runs over three seasons at Oklahoma State. "It's a year like a Heisman Trophy winner might have in football. There was no three- or four-game stretch where he didn't hurt somebody."

Oklahoma State's Pete Incaviglia set NCAA single-season (48) and career (100) records for home runs that still stand. He reached the majors the next season and launched 30 of the 206 homers he would hit in a 12-season big league career.

As a freshman, Incaviglia hit .371 with 23 homers and 78 RBIs, earning Freshman All-America honors. In 1984, Incaviglia's average fell to .352, but he hit 29 homers and drove in a nation-high 103 runs—both Big Eight Conference records. This year, he shattered both of those marks—and the previous NCAA records of 42 home runs and 130 RBIs, set in 1982 by Florida State's Jeff Ledbetter and Wichita State's Russ Morman, respectively.

Despite the numbers, Incaviglia seems to be the object of as much criticism as praise.

He can't play defense, some say. The numbers are the result of the aluminum bat, others say. Finally, some major league scouting directors reportedly disliked Incaviglia's attitude so much that they refused to put him on their draft lists.

As it was, seven clubs passed on the chance to sign the player who this year set new NCAA records for home runs and RBIs; the player who, in three years, broke an NCAA career home run mark that took four years to set.

The Expos, drafting eighth overall, eventually selected Incaviglia.

While he was telling people he was ready to sign, reports circulated that he was demanding a major league contract and an unheard-of $300,000 signing bonus. By comparison, B.J. Surhoff, the first player picked in the draft, received a bonus of slightly more than $150,000.

Despite that, Expos vice president Jim Fanning had nothing but praise for Incaviglia.

"Of all the hitters available in the draft, I don't think there was any question in our minds that Pete had the most power and the most consistent power," Fanning said. "We wanted that kind of power."

Fanning and Ward agreed that Incaviglia's defense improved tremendously this year.

"Scouts who made many of those assumptions did not see him play late in the year," Fanning said. "He ran well, caught all the balls hit to him and threw well. He worked hard at being a good outfielder.

"However, he will improve in every phase as he moves up, as happened with Andre Dawson, Tim Raines and whoever."

Ward noticed in 1984 that Incaviglia had trouble with balls hit hard at him. So in the fall he spent many hours working with him, getting him to field balls off a live bat.

Fanning said he had never heard anyone question Incaviglia's attitude, though many scouts were reportedly turned off by incidents like the one during this year's Big Eight Tournament in which Incaviglia bowled over a Kansas State catcher and broke the catcher's leg, and another when he challenged the entire Texas team to a fight.

"He's been the focal point of opposing crowds and benches, and he's handled things well," Ward said. "Something all of us have enjoyed is that he's a sensitive guy who cares about other people's performances. If some guy had a bad game or a bad trip, Pete's over there showing compassion. He kept himself on our level as a leader.

"Maybe more than the numbers, that's what we'll remember about him." ■

# TOP PLAYERS OF 1985

## ALL-AMERICA TEAM

| Pos | Player | School | Yr | AVG | AB | R | H | HR | RBI | SB |
|-----|--------|--------|-----|-----|-----|-----|-----|-----|-----|-----|
| C | B.J. Surhoff | North Carolina | Jr. | .388 | 224 | 77 | 87 | 14 | 57 | 29 |
| 1B | Will Clark | Mississippi State | Jr. | .420 | 224 | 75 | 94 | 25 | 77 | 4 |
| 2B | Bill Bates | Texas | Jr. | .361 | 280 | 100 | 101 | 8 | 71 | 34 |
| 3B | Jeff King | Arkansas | So. | .366 | 254 | 64 | 93 | 17 | 83 | 10 |
| SS | Barry Larkin | Michigan | Jr. | .368 | 209 | 72 | 77 | 16 | 66 | 17 |
| OF | Pete Incaviglia | Oklahoma State | Jr. | .464 | 250 | 98 | 116 | 48 | 143 | 14 |
| OF | Brad Bierley | Pepperdine | Sr. | .354 | 263 | 69 | 93 | 27 | 76 | 29 |
| OF | Mike Watters | Michigan | Jr. | .417 | 218 | 81 | 91 | 17 | 61 | 20 |
| DH | Frank Fazzini | Florida State | Jr. | .413 | 332 | 109 | 147 | 33 | 118 | 19 |

| Pos | Pitcher | School | Yr | W | L | ERA | G | SV | IP | H | BB | SO |
|-----|---------|--------|-----|-----|-----|-----|-----|-----|-----|-----|-----|-----|
| P | Greg Swindell | Texas | So. | 19 | 2 | 1.47 | 26 | 3 | 172 | 118 | 41 | 189 |
| P | Mike Cook | South Carolina | Jr. | 16 | 2 | 1.91 | 19 | 0 | 141 | 99 | 60 | 168 |
| P | Jeff Brantley | Mississippi State | Sr. | 18 | 2 | 2.29 | 23 | 1 | 146 | 127 | 42 | 136 |
| P | Scott Marrett | Pepperdine | Jr. | 15 | 0 | 2.08 | 22 | 1 | 143 | 114 | 32 | 80 |
| P | Rick Raether | Miami | So. | 7 | 2 | 1.56 | 45 | 20 | 87 | 62 | 41 | 100 |

## SECOND TEAM

C—Doug Duke, Alabama. 1B—Rick Lundblade, Stanford. 2B—Jose Mota, Cal State Fullerton. 3B—Rob Tomberlin, Western Kentucky. SS—Jim Fregosi Jr., New Mexico. OF—Paul Meyers, Nebraska; Tim Barker, Central Florida; and Barry Bonds, Arizona State. DH—Mike Oglesbee, Nevada-Las Vegas. P—Doug Little, Florida State; Mark Gardner, Fresno State; Tim Burcham, Virginia; Steve Peters, Oklahoma; and Phil Cundari, Seton Hall.

## THIRD TEAM

C—Bill McGuire, Nebraska. 1B—Mike Duncan, Nebraska. 2B—Luis Alicea, Florida State. 3B—Bill Geivett, UC Santa Barbara. SS—Joey Cora, Vanderbilt. OF—Scott Jordan, Georgia Tech; Steve Iannini, Georgetown; Mike Prior, Illinois State; and Mario Monico, Hawaii. DH—Dave Otto, Missouri; and Winfred Johnson, East Carolina. P—Jeff Ballard, Stanford; Joe Magrane, Arizona; Kevin Bearse, Old Dominion; Mike Campbell, Hawaii; and Pat Heck, Evansville.

Arizona ace righthander Gil Heredia would go on to make the largest impact in the majors from the 1986 Wildcats. He got his first extended looks with the 1990s Expos.

1986

# Kindall wins third national crown

By **STEVE PIVOVAR**

**FROM THE ISSUE:**
JULY 10-24, 1986

**M**oments after his team had presented him with his third national championship, Arizona coach Jerry Kindall, his arm around his wife Georgia, stood in the outfield grass at Rosenblatt Stadium.

The Wildcats won the national championship for the Kindalls, who have been through some tough times in recent years. Georgia Kindall suffers from Lou Gehrig's disease.

She joined her husband in Omaha on June 5. Four days later, during one of his finest moments, she was at his side, smiling as Kindall talked about his players and their accomplishments.

"I'm so grateful for these guys," Jerry Kindall said.

The Wildcats, to a man, are equally grateful for the opportunity to play for one of the most respected men in the college game.

"In the back of our minds, we wanted to win this for coach Kindall," outfielder Gar Millay said. "There were times when he would come out to practice and we knew that he had other things on his mind. But every guy on this team loves him, and he loves every one of us."

Arizona finished in a tie for second in the Southern Division of the Pacific-10 Conference. It took a sweep of Arizona State in the final series of the season just to get the Wildcats, who came into the tournament with a 45-18 record, into postseason play.

"The Wildcats wanted to win. They wanted a chance to play in Omaha again," outfielder Mike Senne said. "We made up a thing called karma, and it became bigger and bigger with each game and each victory."

The Wildcats, erratic during the early season, put it all together in their late-season drive to the championship. Arizona won 12 of its last 13 games, including eight of nine under the pressure of tournament play.

The Wildcats swept the Central Regional in Austin to win a return trip to Omaha. Arizona qualified last year but lost its first two games and returned home.

"We got here last year, smelled it but didn't do much after that," first baseman Todd

## TOP TEAMS

### 1986 COLLEGE WORLD SERIES STANDINGS

| School | Conference | Record | CWS | Head Coach |
|---|---|---|---|---|
| Arizona | Pacific-10 | 49–19 | 4–1 | Jerry Kindall |
| Florida State | Metro | 61–13 | 4–2 | Mike Martin |
| Miami | Independent | 49–17 | 3–2 | Ron Fraser |
| Oklahoma State | Big Eight | 56–15 | 2–2 | Gary Ward |
| Louisiana State | Southeastern | 55–14 | 1–2 | Skip Bertman |
| Loyola Marymount | West Coast | 50–15 | 1–2 | Dave Snow |
| Indiana State | Missouri Valley | 48–21 | 0–2 | Bob Warn |
| Maine | Eastern Collegiate | 41–23 | 0–2 | John Winkin |

## NATIONAL CHAMPION
## ARIZONA

The Wildcats trounced Florida State 10-2 in the championship game, giving the Arizona program its third title team in 11 seasons, all helmed by coach Jerry Kindall. His Wildcats won the CWS previously in 1976 and 1980.

Trafton said. "But we knew what it was like."

After a disastrous 1984 season, Kindall brought in Senne, outfielder Chuck Johnson, second baseman Tommy Hinzo and shortstop Dave Rohde from junior colleges. They meshed with Trafton, Millay and third baseman Chip Hale to form the nucleus of this year's championship squad.

One of the players Kindall recruited after last year's trip to Omaha was pitcher/DH Gary Alexander. Against Florida State in the title game, he rose to the occasion.

The junior righthander, picked to start over ace Gil Heredia, held Florida State to just three hits in eight innings. By the time the Seminoles, who came into the game with a No. 1 ranking and a 61-12 record, pushed across their first run, Arizona held a 10-0 lead.

Florida State scored twice against Alexander in the ninth to prevent the Wildcats from claiming the most lopsided win in a championship game since 1956, when Minnesota, led by a young shortstop named Jerry Kindall, pounded Arizona 12-1.

The first half of the game had the makings of anything but a Wildcat romp. A heads-up defensive play by Rohde, who turned a hit-and-run into a double play to end the third inning, kept Florida State from scoring the first run.

With runners at first and third, the Seminoles sent Jose Marzan, who had singled Barry Blackwell to third. Paul Sorrento bounced a chopper up the middle that Rohde fielded and stepped on second. Rohde, playing with a sore arm, bounced a throw to Trafton that the Arizona first baseman dug out for the inning-ending out.

"That play picked me up big time," Alexander said. "That was the play of the game."

Arizona scored unearned runs off 20-game winner Mike Loynd in the fourth and fifth innings to take a 2-0 lead. Loynd, bidding to become the first Division I pitcher to win 21 games in a season, then surrendered his third hit, a double to Hale, to open the sixth.

# 1986 NEWSMAKERS

Preseason No. 1 **Texas** had won the 1983 CWS and advanced to the championship game in both 1984 and '85. The Longhorns hosted the six-team Central regional but lost 9-3 in the second round to Arizona and 2-0 to Pepperdine.

**Florida State** never won the CWS in coach **Mike Martin's** remarkable 40-year tenure, but it came closest in 1986 with a team that led the nation in wins (61) and featured five first- and second-team All-Americans. Unfortunately for the Seminoles, they lost twice to underdog Arizona in Omaha.

With a new limit on the number of games Division I teams could play, the national leader in home runs, Virginia Tech first baseman **George Canale**, hit just 29 (in 59 games).

The 1986 CWS marked the debut of **Louisiana State**, which would soon make a regular practice of returning to Omaha.

Historic Southern California coach **Rod Dedeaux**, 71, who led the Trojans to 11 NCAA titles and a then-record 1,334 wins over a 45-year coaching career, announced his retirement on June 3 after his 1986 team went just 26-29.

## FINAL TOP 25 FOR 1986

1. Arizona*
2. Florida State*
3. Miami*
4. Oklahoma State*
5. Louisiana State*
6. Loyola Marymount*
7. #Texas
8. UCLA
9. UC Santa Barbara
10. South Florida
11. Texas A&M
12. Stanford
13. Tulane
14. Pepperdine
15. Indiana State*
16. Michigan
17. Oklahoma
18. Georgia Tech
19. Arkansas
20. Maine*
21. Oregon State
22. Central Michigan
23. Nevada-Las Vegas
24. San Diego State
25. Alabama

* Reached College World Series
# Preseason No. 1

# IN RETROSPECT: 1986 DRAFT

**Top 10 Draft Picks From College**

With overall selection number (Ov), drafting team (Team) and rank on Baseball America draft board (BA).

| Player | Pos | School | Ov | Team | BA |
|---|---|---|---|---|---|
| Jeff King | 3B | Arkansas | 1 | Pirates | 1 |
| Greg Swindell | LHP | Texas | 2 | Indians | 2 |
| Matt Williams | SS | Nevada-Las Vegas | 3 | Giants | 3 |
| Kevin Brown | RHP | Georgia Tech | 4 | Rangers | 5 |
| Brad Brink | RHP | Southern California | 7 | Phillies | 14 |
| Thomas Howard | OF | Ball State | 11 | Padres | 15 |
| Scott Hemond | C | South Florida | 12 | Athletics | 4 |
| Roberto Hernandez | RHP | South Carolina-Aiken | 16 | Angels | 19 |
| Grady Hall | LHP | Northwestern | 20 | White Sox | 25 |
| Luis Alicea | 2B | Florida State | 23 | Cardinals | 30 |

**Top 10 Major League Players From College Draft Class**

With draft round and Baseball-Reference.com total for wins above replacement (WAR) through 2019.

| Player | Pos | School | Rd | Ov | Team | WAR |
|---|---|---|---|---|---|---|
| Kevin Brown | RHP | Georgia Tech | 1 | 4 | Rangers | 68.0 |
| Matt Williams | 3B | Nevada-Las Vegas | 1 | 3 | Giants | 46.6 |
| Greg Swindell | LHP | Texas | 1 | 2 | Indians | 30.7 |
| Kevin Tapani | RHP | Central Michigan | 2 | 40 | Athletics | 29.3 |
| Chris Hoiles | C | Eastern Michigan | 19 | 489 | Tigers | 23.5 |
| Erik Hanson | RHP | Wake Forest | 2 | 36 | Mariners | 22.2 |
| Rick Reed | RHP | Marshall | 26 | 644 | Pirates | 21.0 |
| Todd Zeile | 3B | UCLA | 2s | 55 | Cardinals | 19.4 |
| Roberto Hernandez | RHP | S. Carolina-Aiken | 1 | 16 | Angels | 18.5 |
| Jeff King | 3B | Arkansas | 1 | 1 | Pirates | 16.8 |

Florida State head coach Mike Martin elected to bring in Richie Lewis, the pitching star of the College World Series with two wins and two saves in his first four appearances, to pitch to Senne.

The strategy backfired when Senne drove a pitch to left field for his 11th homer of the season to make it 4-0. One walk and one out later, Millay delivered his second homer of the series to make it 6-0. The rout was on.

"I knew when we got 10 runs up that we were in good shape," said Kindall, whose team came from behind to post their first three wins of the CWS.

"We weren't so vulnerable after we won those first two games," said Kindall, whose 1976 and 1980 teams won titles by battling back through the losers' bracket after losing the first game of the series.

"But it didn't make it any easier. As far as we were concerned, everything tonight was grand, fresh, new."

With his players celebrating around him, Kindall stood on the outfield grass and talked about the thrill of returning to the championship throne.

"The thrill is as fresh and new as you can imagine," Kindall said. "But there's a Wildcat spirit that was born in this club and this program that comes from (former coach) Frank Sancet, and Pop McKale before him."

As he spoke, Kindall often glanced at his wife. Unable to speak, Georgia's response was apparent on her face.

For the Kindalls, these are not the easiest of times. But on June 9, thanks to a group of gutty Wildcats, they were just a little bit better. ■

# Outfielder Close made the right move

By **DANNY KNOBLER**

At the beginning of the 1986 season, Casey Close had a decision to make. The Michigan senior had doubled as a pitcher and outfielder the first three years of his Wolverines career, but he wanted to concentrate on one position in order to have a big final year and ultimately earn an opportunity to play pro ball.

As a junior, Close had been successful both at the plate (.388-16-58) and on the mound (6-1, 3.93). But the numbers didn't impress scouts, and he went undrafted.

In the end, Close told Michigan coach Bud Middaugh that he wanted to concentrate all his efforts on hitting and playing outfield.

The results he was looking for showed up immediately. On the Wolverines' season opening trip to Florida, Close batted .543 in nine games with five homers and 21 RBIs.

He kept up the sizzling pace the rest of the season, finishing the year with a .440 average, 19 homers and 72 RBIs—numbers that made him the College Player of the Year.

Drafted out of high school as a pitcher, Casey Close dropped pitching as a Michigan senior to focus on hitting. It worked. The Yankees chose the outfielder in the seventh round, but he peaked at Triple-A.

Apparently, Close also impressed professional scouts. The Yankees made him their seventh-round pick, assigning him to Oneonta of the New York-Penn League.

"I needed to have full concentration on hitting," said Close, a 20th-round draft pick as a pitcher four years ago out of high school "to know I was in the lineup, to know I was in the three-hole every day. I felt playing the outfield was my best shot at making it."

"In pro baseball, there are an awful lot of people in the outfield," said Middaugh, who still feels Close could have had a pro career as a pitcher. "He's not fleet of foot, so he'll have to hit a ton to survive. But he is capable of it.

"In the 20 years I've coached, I've never had a player have such a fantastic year—such a dominant year."

Close set school records for homers, RBIs and slugging percentage, and he was named the MVP in all four tournaments that Michigan played this year—with the exception of the Mideast Regional, when the Wolverines dropped two straight games. Still, he was the only Michigan player named to the regional all-tournament team.

The game-winners probably best told the story of Close's value. Three of them came on last-inning home runs, giving Michigan big wins against South Carolina, Miami and Indiana. Four of them came in Big Ten Conference competition, helping Close win league player of the week honors twice during the five-week conference season.

During his Michigan career, Close was always at his best in big games. As a freshman, his grand slam helped Michigan to an 11-4 win against Stanford in the College World Series. He was also the winning pitcher in that year's Big Ten Tournament championship game, and he homered against Central Michigan in the Mideast Regional.

The following year, Close pitched Michigan to the Big Ten title over Minnesota and yet again homered against Central Michigan in the Wolverines' regional championship game.

As a junior, he had eight hits and seven RBIs in Michigan's last three games in the South I Regionals.

This year, Close hit two homers in the Big Ten Tournament, and he picked up three hits in the championship game win against Minnesota. And in the final game of his career, trying to keep Michigan alive in the Midwest Regional, he went 3-for-4 and was on third base with the potential tying run before the Wolverines lost to Oral Roberts.

But Close's main goal this year was to find more consistency.

"Last year, I was more of a streaky hitter," said Close, who grew up in Worthington, Ohio, but now lists his hometown as Indianapolis. "This year, I worked hard on making hard contact to all fields. Being able to hit to right field helped."

Besides his on-field accomplishments, Close worked hard enough on his studies to earn Academic All-America honors this year, and he was also Michigan's winner of the Big Ten Medal of Honor for athletic and academic excellence. ■

# TOP PLAYERS OF 1986

## ALL-AMERICA TEAM

| Pos | Player | School | Yr | AVG | AB | R | H | HR | RBI | SB |
|-----|--------|--------|-----|-----|-----|-----|-----|-----|-----|-----|
| C | Doug Duke | Alabama | Jr. | .336 | 238 | 59 | 80 | 27 | 82 | 2 |
| 1B | George Canale | Virginia Tech | Jr. | .373 | 217 | 76 | 81 | 29 | 71 | 6 |
| 2B | Luis Alicea | Florida State | Jr. | .392 | 286 | 94 | 112 | 4 | 73 | 28 |
| 3B | Robin Ventura | Oklahoma State | Fr. | .469 | 241 | 107 | 113 | 21 | 96 | 9 |
| SS | Matt Williams | Nevada-Las Vegas | Jr. | .351 | 231 | 82 | 81 | 25 | 89 | 8 |
| OF | Casey Close | Michigan | Sr. | .440 | 191 | 68 | 84 | 19 | 72 | 15 |
| OF | Todd Azar | Old Dominion | Jr. | .486 | 210 | 58 | 102 | 12 | 87 | 5 |
| OF | Tom Howard | Ball State | Jr. | .448 | 210 | 70 | 94 | 23 | 67 | 22 |
| DH | Craig Cooper | Georgia Southern | Jr. | .446 | 213 | 78 | 95 | 26 | 94 | 7 |

| Pos | Pitcher | School | Yr. | W | L | ERA | G | SV | IP | H | BB | SO |
|-----|---------|--------|-----|-----|-----|-----|-----|-----|-----|-----|-----|-----|
| P | Mike Loynd | Florida State | Jr. | 20 | 3 | 2.45 | 25 | 1 | 165 | 136 | 57 | 223 |
| P | Greg Swindell | Texas | Jr. | 10 | 4 | 2.26 | 26 | 7 | 136 | 107 | 29 | 180 |
| P | Rick Raether | Miami | Sr. | 9 | 2 | 2.76 | 41 | 17 | 75 | 54 | 25 | 114 |
| P | Alex Sanchez | UCLA | So. | 16 | 3 | 4.06 | 23 | 0 | 139 | 130 | 71 | 142 |
| P | Richie Lewis | Florida State | So. | 14 | 2 | 3.59 | 28 | 4 | 128 | 105 | 72 | 202 |

## SECOND TEAM

C—John Eccles, Cal State Fullerton. 1B—Chuck Baldwin, Clemson. 2B—Kevin Burdick, Oklahoma. 3B—Jeff King, Arkansas. SS—Bien Figueroa, Florida State. OF—Albert Belle, Louisiana State; Mike Scanlin, Texas A&M; and Paul Sorrento, Florida State. DH—Jimmy Barragan, Oklahoma State. P—Grady Hall, Northwestern; Jack McDowell, Stanford; Tim Layana, Loyola Marymount; Mike Fetters, Pepperdine; and Barry Manuel, Louisiana State.

## THIRD TEAM

C—Scott Hemond, South Florida. 1B—Rick Bernardo, Maine. 2B—Greg Briley, North Carolina State. 3B—Chris Donnels, Loyola Marymount. SS—Kevin Pearson, Oklahoma. OF—Danny Wagner, Tulane; Rick Morris, Arizona State; and Billy Bean, Loyola Marymount. DH—Earl Sanders, Jackson State. P—Dale Barry, Texas A&M; Gil Heredia, Arizona; Scott Morse, Maine; Cris Carpenter, Georgia; and Randy Wilson, South Florida.

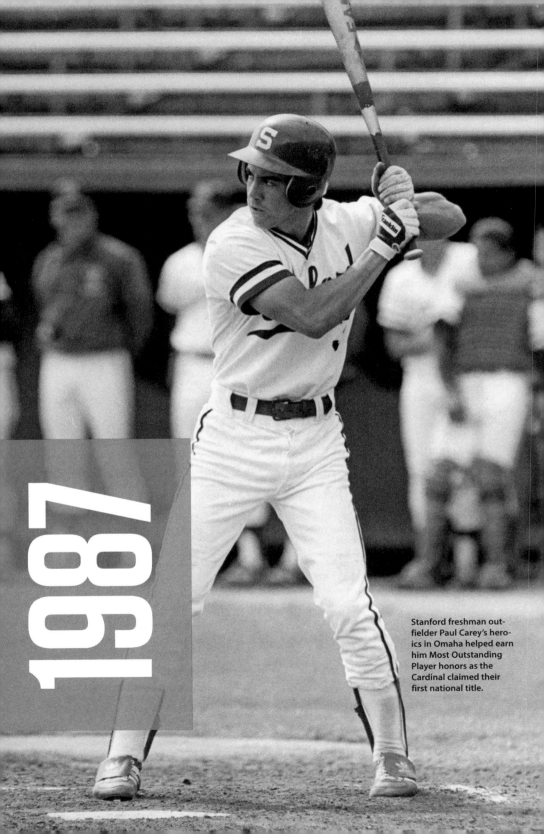

**1987**

Stanford freshman out-fielder Paul Carey's hero-ics in Omaha helped earn him Most Outstanding Player honors as the Cardinal claimed their first national title.

# Stanford pays a debt, wins first national title

By **DANNY KNOBLER**

**FROM THE ISSUE:**
JULY 10, 1987

**B**ack on Jan. 16, at Jack McDowell's 21st birthday party, the Stanford baseball team made a toast.

"To a national championship," said one player.

"Against Oklahoma State," responded another.

"That's no lie," McDowell insisted four and a half months later, standing on the field at Rosenblatt Stadium after Stanford had made good on both parts of the toast. McDowell, a 6-2 loser to the Cowboys earlier in the tournament, was the winning pitcher in the 9-5 victory that gave Stanford its first College World Series title.

The win repaid a debt dating back to last season, when the Cowboys eliminated Stanford in regional play. Comments by OSU assistant coach Tom Holliday on a postgame radio show stayed with the Stanford players through the 1987 season.

"Right now, it's good to beat anyone," third baseman Ed Sprague Jr. said after the final out. "But we played the team we wanted to play. All year, we wanted to beat them."

Stanford won the title game with its best offensive showing of the CWS. The Cardinal collected 15 hits, and three Stanford hitters contributed three hits apiece, including freshman right fielder Paul Carey, who was the CWS Most Outstanding Player.

It was the first time Stanford had reached double digits in hits since the West II Regional final against Oral Roberts almost two weeks earlier.

Stanford didn't do things the easy way in the CWS. Hitting .312 as a team coming into the College World Series—including .310 in the tough Pacific-10 Southern Division and .391 in regionals—the Cardinal were hitting just .234 in the CWS going into the finals.

Stanford also won without dominating performances from its top two pitchers. Lee Plemel stopped Texas 6-1 while scattering 12 hits in the second round, then McDowell wasn't sharp in the first meeting with OSU, in the winners' bracket final.

Plemel's return engagement with Texas lasted only one-third of an inning, and McDowell survived without particularly good command in the championship game.

## TOP TEAMS
### 1987 COLLEGE WORLD SERIES STANDINGS

| School | Conference | Record | CWS | Head Coach |
|--------|-----------|--------|-----|-----------|
| Stanford | Pacific-10 | 53–17 | 5–1 | Mark Marquess |
| Oklahoma State | Big Eight | 59–13 | 3–2 | Gary Ward |
| Texas | Southwest | 61–11 | 3–2 | Cliff Gustafson |
| Louisiana State | Southeastern | 49–19 | 2–2 | Skip Bertman |
| Arkansas | Southwest | 51–16–1 | 1–2 | Norm DeBriyn |
| Florida State | Metro | 55–18 | 1–2 | Mike Martin |
| Arizona State | Pacific-10 | 40–27 | 0–2 | Jim Brock |
| Georgia | Southeastern | 42–21 | 0–2 | Steve Webber |

## NATIONAL CHAMPION
### STANFORD

Stanford staved off elimination with a dramatic win against LSU in which they were down three runs with two outs in the 10th. The Cardinal then dispatched Texas, 9-3, and Oklahoma State, 9-5, to win its first national title.

The top Stanford pitching performances came from members of the staff who had been overlooked most of the year. Against Louisiana State in a losers' bracket game, Brian Keyser got a surprise start and allowed only one earned run in five innings. The Cardinal won that game in dramatic fashion, winning 6-5 in 10 innings on Carey's grand slam.

When Plemel faltered against Texas the following night, lefthander Al Osuna came in and shut out the Longhorns over the final 8.2 innings, winning 9-3.

The Cardinal defense, shaky for a good part of the CWS, came through with four double plays in each of the last two games.

The defense, pitching and timely hitting finally combined to give Stanford its most successful season. Four times previously Cardinal coach Mark Marquess had been to the College World Series—once as a player, three times as a coach—but Stanford had never had much success there. This time, things worked out.

They worked out especially well in the win against LSU. A loss in that game would have sent Stanford home with a 2-2 record—only marginally better than the 1-2 marks the last three Cardinal teams recorded in Omaha.

But after LSU scored three times in the top of the 10th inning to take a 5-2 lead, Stanford came rallying back.

When Carey came to the plate with the bases loaded, the confidence was there.

"I knew he (LSU freshman Ben McDonald) was coming fastball," Carey said. "All day long they threw me fastballs. They saw me against Georgia when I struck out three times against (Cris) Carpenter and (Derek) Lilliquist. But that's the high 80s.

"I just didn't know why they didn't throw anything offspeed to me."

Carey's home run left Stanford as one of the final three teams, and it gave the Cardinal momentum heading into the final two games.

# 1987 NEWSMAKERS

**Oklahoma State** (.789) ranked second, behind only Texas (.822), in winning percentage in the 1980s and also made seven CWS appearances in the decade. Yet the Cowboys could never quite get over the hurdle and win their first national title. They finished second twice, including in 1987, when they went 59-13 and led the nation in runs (823) and home runs (141).

After considerable debate on the future of the **CWS**, it was determined that the tournament would remain in Omaha—at least through 1989—but the format would change to better accommodate TV. In place of the traditional double-elimination tournament, the eight teams would be split into two brackets of four teams each, with the winners of each pool meeting in a single-game final televised by CBS. The NCAA regional field was also expanded from 40 to 48 teams.

**Seton Hall** fell short of a berth in the 1987 CWS, despite fielding one of the most talented Northeast teams ever. The Pirates (45-10) set numerous team and individual records with a roster that included junior catcher **Craig Biggio**, a 1987 first-rounder, and freshman first baseman **Mo Vaughn**, a 1989 first-rounder.

## FINAL TOP 25 FOR 1987

1. Stanford*
2. Oklahoma State*
3. #Texas*
4. Louisiana State*
5. Arkansas*
6. Florida State*
7. Cal State Fullerton
8. Pepperdine
9. Georgia*
10. Clemson
11. Arizona State*
12. Texas A&M
13. Georgia Tech
14. Auburn
15. Oklahoma
16. UCLA
17. Washington State
18. Wichita State
19. Michigan
20. Hawaii
21. New Orleans
22. Oral Roberts
23. Mississippi State
24. Seton Hall
25. Miami

\* Reached College World Series
\# Preseason No. 1

# IN RETROSPECT: 1987 DRAFT

## Top 10 Draft Picks From College
With overall selection number (Ov), drafting team (Team) and rank on Baseball America draft board (BA).

| Player | Pos | School | Ov | Team | BA |
|---|---|---|---|---|---|
| Mike Harkey | RHP | Cal State Fullerton | 4 | Cubs | 5 |
| Jack McDowell | RHP | Stanford | 5 | White Sox | 7 |
| Derek Lilliquist | LHP | Georgia | 6 | Braves | 9 |
| Kevin Garner | RHP | Texas | 10 | Padres | 19 |
| Bill Spiers | SS | Clemson | 13 | Brewers | 34 |
| Cris Carpenter | RHP | Georgia | 14 | Cardinals | 6 |
| Brad DuVall* | RHP | Virginia Tech | 15 | Orioles | 13 |
| Mike Remlinger | LHP | Dartmouth | 16 | Giants | 37 |
| Alex Sanchez | RHP | UCLA | 17 | Blue Jays | 27 |
| Jack Armstrong | RHP | Oklahoma | 18 | Reds | 21 |

\* Did not sign

## Top 10 Major League Players From College Draft Class
With draft round and Baseball-Reference.com total for wins above replacement (WAR) through 2019.

| Player | Pos | School | Rd | Ov | Team | WAR |
|---|---|---|---|---|---|---|
| Craig Biggio | 2B | Seton Hall | 1 | 22 | Astros | 65.5 |
| Steve Finley | OF | Southern Illinois | 13 | 325 | Orioles | 44.3 |
| Albert Belle | OF | Louisiana State | 2 | 47 | Indians | 40.1 |
| Jack McDowell | RHP | Stanford | 1 | 5 | White Sox | 28.0 |
| Jeff Conine | 1B | UCLA | 58 | 1226 | Royals | 19.5 |
| Mike Timlin | RHP | Southwestern (TX) | 5 | 127 | Blue Jays | 19.1 |
| Pete Harnisch | RHP | Fordham | 1s | 27 | Orioles | 18.0 |
| Dave Hollins | 3B | South Carolina | 6 | 146 | Padres | 17.8 |
| Dave Burba | RHP | Ohio State | 2 | 33 | Mariners | 16.4 |
| Scott Brosius | 3B | Linfield (Ore.) | 20 | 511 | Athletics | 15.7 |

Stanford's title was the culmination of 11 years of work for Marquess, called by his players and assistants the hardest working coach in the country.

"The thing is, I never have had a specific goal of winning a national championship," he said. "I really never said, 'I want to win a national championship.' Sure, you want to win a national championship, but I spent more time trying to get my team to play as hard as I want it to."

The Stanford team reflected Marquess' intensity and work ethic. Like their coach, the Stanford players sprint everywhere and stand in the dugout during the game.

That was in contrast to Oklahoma State, whose players sit quietly in the dugout, doing their job in a style more like that of a professional team.

"There's a definite contrast in styles," Sprague said. "They play laid back, wait for the big inning. We play aggressive, hard-nosed, keep the pressure on every minute. They didn't like the way we played. They thought we were rah-rah cheerleaders."

And so, a rivalry was born. During last year's regional tournament, Holliday made comments that would serve as inspiration for Stanford all year.

Holliday said the Stanford players were like cheerleaders, and that you could be sure they would have their "skirts" on for the rest of the tournament. The Cardinal players, in their cars driving back to the hotel, listened in disbelief.

"It really got us upset," McDowell said. "We sat in the parking lot and listened to their coach go off for 30 minutes with the radio guy trying to stop him."

"I don't give a damn what they think. It's a fact," Holliday responded before the championship game. "Their whole conference (Pac-10) is known for (cheerleading)." ∎

# A-plus: Ventura makes the grade

By **DANNY KNOBLER**

Oklahoma State coach Gary Ward can sometimes sound like that college professor whose class you really don't want to take. With his talk of "muscle memory" and his use of other complex terms, Ward has sent many an audience scrambling for a dictionary.

But even in such required courses, there's always one student who has a natural feel for the subject.

When Ward taught "The Science of Hitting" to his Oklahoma State team this year, the honors student was easy to spot. No one else in the class had a 58-game hitting streak.

But the streak, which shattered the existing record of 47 games, isn't the only reason Robin Ventura has been named College Player of the Year.

There was the .428 batting average, 21 home runs and 110 RBIs he amassed this spring. There were the 27 doubles, one short of his own school record. There is his .447 career batting average in two years at Oklahoma State. And his .483 career average in postseason games.

Oklahoma State's Robin Ventura attracted national attention with a 58-game hitting streak. He became a big league star, winning six Gold Gloves at third base and swatting 294 home runs in 16 seasons.

At a school where hitting has become a tradition, Ventura has become the textbook example.

"He's very aware," Ward said. "He's one of those guys who seems to consume everything you talk about."

Even Ventura, the star pupil, once found Ward's lessons confusing.

"When I got there it was like taking another class, with all the terms he uses," Ventura said. "But I'm still remembering the things he said last year during the fall. You're going in (to the Ward classroom) about an hour and a half. Sometimes it blew me away. Sometimes I was bored. But it helped me concentration-wise. He's just repeated it so much that in your mind you hear it."

Ventura came to Oklahoma State undrafted and not heavily recruited out of high school in Santa Maria, Calif. The pro scouts, who now consider him the best hitting prospect in college baseball, looked at his lack of speed and didn't consider him much of a prospect. For most, he wasn't worth the three-hour drive north from Los Angeles.

College recruiters didn't beat down his door, either. UCLA and UC Santa Barbara came in for a look, but neither was interested in offering much aid. Oklahoma State was the only school that offered him much hope of contributing as a freshman.

Ventura put together one of the top freshman seasons ever seen in Division I baseball, when he hit .469 with 21 homers and 96 RBIs. He made the All-America team and was an easy choice for Freshman of the Year.

Ventura knew it would be tough to match those numbers this year. It didn't matter that he still had Jimmy Barragan, Jim Ifland and Monty Fariss hitting behind him in the Cowboys' lineup. This year, no team wanted to let Ventura beat them.

Ventura walked 63 times—three more than last year, and he managed to stay disciplined enough to lead the team in virtually every statistical category.

And then there was "The Streak," which focused more attention on him than he really wanted.

"I felt like it took a lot away from what this team is doing," he said.

It began March 18 with a home run against Missouri Southern, three days after he had been held hitless by North Carolina. By the Big Eight Tournament, he passed the collegiate record, formerly held by Wichita State's Phil Stephenson. He extended it with an 11th-inning RBI single in the tournament final against Oklahoma.

And in the first game of the College World Series, against Arizona State, he evoked comparisons with Joe DiMaggio by recording a hit in his 57th consecutive game.

Ventura played in the Cape Cod League this summer, and he will enter 1988 with two of the most impressive college seasons ever already under his belt. ■

# TOP PLAYERS OF 1987

## ALL-AMERICA TEAM

| Pos | Player | School | Yr | AVG | AB | R | H | HR | RBI | SB |
|-----|--------|--------|-----|-----|-----|-----|-----|-----|-----|-----|
| C | Craig Biggio | Seton Hall | Jr | .407 | 214 | 97 | 87 | 14 | 68 | 30 |
| 1B | Marteese Robinson | Seton Hall | Jr | .529 | 238 | 89 | 126 | 16 | 90 | 58 |
| 2B | Torey Lovullo | UCLA | Sr | .350 | 237 | 83 | 83 | 24 | 73 | 7 |
| 3B | Robin Ventura | Oklahoma State | So | .428 | 271 | 97 | 116 | 21 | 110 | 16 |
| SS | Mike Benjamin | Arizona State | Sr | .327 | 263 | 83 | 86 | 18 | 55 | 30 |
| OF | Riccardo Ingram | Georgia Tech | Jr | .426 | 237 | 93 | 101 | 17 | 99 | 17 |
| OF | Ted Wood | New Orleans | So | .409 | 254 | 91 | 104 | 17 | 63 | 14 |
| OF | Brian Cisarik | Texas | Jr | .429 | 247 | 87 | 106 | 9 | 68 | 15 |
| DH | Scott Livingston | Texas A&M | Jr | .403 | 206 | 72 | 83 | 19 | 76 | 15 |

| Pos | Pitcher | School | Yr | W | L | ERA | G | SV | IP | H | BB | SO |
|-----|---------|--------|-----|-----|-----|-----|-----|-----|-----|-----|-----|-----|
| P | Derek Lilliquist | Georgia | Jr | 14 | 3 | 2.24 | 23 | 0 | 137 | 92 | 30 | 190 |
| P | Richie Lewis | Florida State | Jr | 15 | 4 | 3.06 | 23 | 2 | 150 | 107 | 88 | 196 |
| P | Anthony Telford | San Jose State | Jr | 10 | 7 | 2.57 | 23 | 1 | 133 | 102 | 49 | 161 |
| P | Curt Krippner | Texas | Jr | 14 | 2 | 2.80 | 21 | 1 | 151 | 108 | 78 | 147 |
| P | Gregg Olson | Auburn | So | 11 | 1 | 1.26 | 42 | 10 | 78 | 50 | 34 | 96 |

## SECOND TEAM

C—Andy Skeels, Arkansas. 1B—Jimmy Barragan, Oklahoma State. 2B—Terry Shumpert, Kentucky. 3B—Scott Coolbaugh, Texas. SS—Ken Bowen, Oregon State. OF—Mike Kelly, South Florida; Tim Raley, Wichita State; and Chris Ebright, Oklahoma. DH—Mike Willes, Brigham Young. P—Mike Remlinger, Dartmouth; Jody Supak, Houston; Larry Casian, Cal State Fullerton; Gregg Patterson, Louisiana State; and Cris Carpenter, Georgia.

## THIRD TEAM

C—Darrin Fletcher, Illinois. 1B—Adell Davenport, Southern. 2B—Steve Hecht, Oral Roberts. 3B—Chris Donnels, Loyola Marymount. SS—Dave Silvestri, Missouri. OF—Albert Belle, Louisiana State; Mike Fiore, Miami; and Tookie Spann, Tulane. DH—Mo Vaughn, Seton Hall. P—Jack McDowell, Stanford; Jim Abbott, Michigan; David Haas, Wichita State; Mike Harkey, Cal State Fullerton; and Brian Nichols, Southern California.

# 1988

Stanford senior righthander Lee Plemel claimed Most Outstanding Player honors with two College World Series wins for the back-to-back champions.

# Stanford bats wake up in time for second title

By **DANNY KNOBLER**

O n the next to last day of the College World Series, Stanford arrived at Rosenblatt Stadium just in time to watch Arizona State finish off a 19-1 rout of Wichita State.

"We were kind of laughing," first baseman Ron Witmeyer said. "We looked up at the scoreboard. They had 23 hits in the game, we had 25 in the whole (College World) Series."

Despite scoring just 19 runs on those 25 hits, Stanford had won three of its four games. Somehow, the Cardinal was two games from a second straight national championship.

Then, as suddenly as they had vanished, the Cardinal bats returned. Held to three hits in the first four innings of a semi-final game against Cal State Fullerton, Stanford scored six times on seven hits and won 9-5.

**FROM THE ISSUE:**
JULY 10, 1988

The next morning, the Cardinal was back on the field for the championship game—and the outburst continued. Two batters into the second inning, the Cardinal had already reached the third Arizona State pitcher of the game, and Stanford was well on its way to a 9-4 championship game win.

In the final two games a year ago, the Cardinal scored 18 runs on 24 hits. This time, it was 18 runs and 23 hits.

But this year's display was more of a surprise. All week, Cardinal coach Mark Marquess had told everyone who would listen that Stanford bats had been inconsistent all year.

"With this team, you don't know what you're going to get," he said over and over. "And it doesn't really matter who's pitching."

It certainly didn't matter in Stanford's final two games. In the semifinals against Cal State Fullerton's Mark Beck, who had held Stanford to four hits while striking out 13 in a 5-3 win four days earlier, the Cardinal scored nine runs on 10 hits.

That left a lefthanded obstacle from Arizona State named Rusty Kilgo. Kilgo didn't start a game all season before the CWS, but he had started and won twice in Omaha. In 17 CWS innings going into the final, Kilgo had allowed just three runs.

## TOP TEAMS
### 1988 COLLEGE WORLD SERIES STANDINGS

| School | Conference | Record | cWs | Head Coach |
|---|---|---|---|---|
| Stanford | Pacific-10 | 46–23 | 5–1 | Mark Marquess |
| Arizona State | Pacific-10 | 60–13 | 4–2 | Jim Brock |
| Cal State Fullerton | PCAA | 43–18 | 2–2 | Larry Cochell |
| Wichita State | Missouri Valley | 56–16–1 | 2–2 | Gene Stephenson |
| Florida | Southeastern | 48–19–1 | 1–2 | Joe Arnold |
| Miami | Independent | 51–14–1 | 1–2 | Ron Fraser |
| California | Pacific-10 | 40–25 | 0–2 | Bob Milano |
| Fresno State | PCAA | 56–12 | 0–2 | Bob Bennett |

## NATIONAL CHAMPION
### STANFORD

Stanford becomes the first team to repeat as College World Series champions since Southern California won five in a row from 1970-74. The Cardinal defeated Arizona State, 9-4, in the national championship game.

But against Stanford, Kilgo threw just 18 pitches and got one out in a five-run first inning. Three singles, a walk and an Ed Sprague Jr. home run ended his season and put the Sun Devils in a hole.

The next ASU pitcher, Blas Minor, threw one more pitch than Kilgo and got one more out. He also gave up three more hits and another run.

"We wanted to make them play from behind," said Sprague, whose inconsistent week was typical of the Stanford team. "We've played behind all year. They score so many runs, they don't play behind much."

The big cushion helped righthander Stan Spencer, Stanford's second freshman starter in as many days. He had worked out of a minor jam in the top of the first inning and later retired 10 of 11 hitters before tiring in the eighth.

The Cardinal won the CWS by defeating teams that had dominated them during the season.

Stanford started with a 10-3 win against Fresno State, which had beaten the Cardinal twice in as many tries before the CWS. After the 5-3 loss to Beck and Fullerton, in which Stanford made an uncharacteristic six errors, the Cardinal faced elimination against Miami, which a month earlier dominated Stanford in two games.

Spencer got Stanford into the seventh inning tied 1-1, but it wasn't until Miami's Jose Trujillo threw away a potential double-play ball in the ninth inning that the Cardinal advanced to face Fullerton.

Senior righthander Lee Plemel, who won the opener against Fresno State, forced a deciding game against Fullerton by scattering eight hits in a 4-1 win. Stanford scored its first three runs on one hit and had just four hits in the game against Longo Garcia.

Plemel's two tournament wins earned him Most Outstanding Player honors, even

# 1988 NEWSMAKERS

Just like in 1984, baseball held demonstration status for the **1988 Olympics** in Seoul, South Korea. But this time, the U.S. team of college all-stars responded by winning gold, turning the tables on defending champion Japan in the gold medal game when Michigan lefthander **Jim Abbott**, who was born without a right hand, pitched a complete-game seven-hitter.

**Oklahoma State** made seven straight CWS appearances from 1981-87 but failed to qualify in 1988 with what might have been their strongest club of the '80s. The Cowboys ranked No. 1 all but one week of the season with a lineup that featured third baseman **Robin Ventura** (.391-26-6) and shortstop **Monty Farris** (.397-30-114), two of the first 10 players drafted in 1988, but lost out to fierce rival Wichita State in a hard-fought Midwest regional.

After going just 11-11, 5.13 in his first two seasons at Evansville, righthander **Andy Benes** became somewhat of a surprise No. 1 overall pick in the 1988 draft by the Padres. But Benes had a breakout junior season, going 16-3, 1.42 while leading the nation with 188 strikeouts in 146 innings.

## FINAL TOP 25 FOR 1988

1. Stanford*
2. Arizona State*
3. Wichita State*
4. #Oklahoma State
5. Fresno State*
6. Cal State Fullerton*
7. Florida*
8. Miami*
9. California*
10. Texas
11. Texas A&M
12. Mississippi State
13. Loyola Marymount
14. Washington State
15. Clemson
16. Pepperdine
17. Florida State
18. Southern California
19. Kentucky
20. South Carolina
21. Santa Clara
22. Nevada-Las Vegas
23. Georgia Tech
24. Michigan
25. Central Michigan

\* Reached College World Series
\# Preseason No. 1

# IN RETROSPECT: 1988 DRAFT

## Top 10 Draft Picks From College
With overall selection number (Ov), drafting team (Team) and rank on Baseball America draft board (BA).

| Player | Pos | School | Ov | Team | BA |
|--------|-----|--------|-----|------|-----|
| Andy Benes | RHP | Evansville | 1 | Padres | 1 |
| Gregg Olson | RHP | Auburn | 4 | Orioles | 3 |
| Bill Bene | RHP | Cal State Los Angeles | 5 | Dodgers | 8 |
| Monty Fariss | SS | Oklahoma State | 6 | Rangers | 6 |
| Jim Abbott | LHP | Michigan | 8 | Angels | 26 |
| Ty Griffin | 2B | Georgia Tech | 9 | Cubs | 12 |
| Robin Ventura | 3B | Oklahoma State | 10 | White Sox | 5 |
| Pat Combs | LHP | Baylor | 11 | Phillies | 14 |
| Tom Fischer | LHP | Wisconsin | 12 | Red Sox | 33 |
| Tino Martinez | 1B | Tampa | 14 | Mariners | 7 |

## Top 10 Major League Players From College Draft Class
With draft round and Baseball-Reference.com total for wins above replacement (WAR) through 2019.

| Player | Pos | School | Rd | Ov | Team | WAR |
|--------|-----|--------|-----|-----|------|------|
| Kenny Lofton | OF | Arizona | 17 | 428 | Astros | 68.3 |
| Robin Ventura | 3B | Oklahoma State | 1 | 10 | White Sox | 56.1 |
| Luis Gonzalez | OF | South Alabama | 4 | 90 | Astros | 51.8 |
| Brian Jordan | OF | Richmond | 1s | 30 | Cardinals | 32.9 |
| John Valentin | SS | Seton Hall | 5 | 121 | Red Sox | 32.5 |
| Andy Benes | RHP | Evansville | 1 | 1 | Padres | 31.6 |
| Woody Williams | RHP | Houston | 28 | 732 | Blue Jays | 30.3 |
| Marquis Grissom | OF | Florida A&M | 3 | 76 | Expos | 29.6 |
| Tino Martinez | 1B | Tampa | 1 | 14 | Mariners | 29.0 |
| Charles Nagy | RHP | Connecticut | 1 | 17 | Indians | 24.9 |

though his contribution to the final two games was mostly as a cheerleader. But Plemel, a senior who rose to the occasion, represented one of the reasons Stanford kept winning.

Five of Stanford's everyday starters also played on last year's team.

Stanford's experience proved especially important in the Miami game. Against Fullerton the night before, the Cardinal held a 3-2 lead on Sprague's three-run homer, but three sixth-inning errors—two by Sprague—gave the Titans three unearned runs.

Arizona State, which advanced to the CWS last year but lost two straight games, faced similar adversity on its way to the final. Like Stanford, the Sun Devils lost their second game, falling 7-4 to Wichita State. Arizona State then needed a win over Florida and two against Wichita State to reach the final.

The Sun Devils pounded Florida 10-1 in one of the few lopsided games played early in the CWS. But in the second meeting against Wichita State, Arizona State trailed 3-1 and was down to one strike twice in the ninth inning.

With two out and Dan Rumsey on third, Ricky Candelari took two strikes, threw his bat to foul off a potential third one, then lined a 1-2 fastball into right field. Mike Burrola singled him to second, and he scored when Pat Listach singled to left on an 0-2 hanging curveball. Arizona State won the game in the 10th on Martin Peralta's single.

The defeat was crushing to Wichita State, which upset No. 1-ranked Oklahoma State in the Midwest Regional and looked like it would have two days before the championship.

"I'd have to say we had some carryover," Wichita State coach Gene Stephenson said after his team was beaten 19-1 the next night. "I had tried to come over very confident to our players, but the loss the other night was very difficult to take." ■

# 'Winfield Rule' makes Olerud top player

By **DANNY KNOBLER**

**W**hen college baseball considered adopting the DH rule in 1973, Washington State coach Bobo Brayton chaired the rules committee. During discussion, Minnesota's Dick Siebert convinced the committee to modify the rule so that it would cover a situation where the pitcher was also the DH.

The committee agreed, and Siebert's amendment became known as the "Winfield Rule." At the time, Dave Winfield was Minnesota's top pitcher, as well as one of the Gophers' leading hitters.

Brayton thought he was just helping out an old friend. He hadn't yet seen young John Olerud play.

Fifteen years later, after he arrived in Pullman, Wash., asking for a chance to pitch and hit for Brayton's Cougars, Olerud did both better than any college player ever—Winfield included. For his dynamic two-way performance, Olerud has been named the College Player of the Year.

**Washington State sophomore John Olerud won 14 games and slugged 22 homers as a two-way titan. In 17 big league seasons, he hit .295, won two World Series rings and three Gold Gloves.**

The 6-foot-4, 190-pound sophomore lefthander became the first collegian ever to reach double figures in wins and hit 20 or more home runs in the same year.

Olerud led the Pacific-10 Conference Northern Division in six of nine offensive categories, running away with the triple crown (.449 average, 22 homers, 75 RBIs). And he topped pitchers in wins (14), innings (122) and strikeouts (113), while finishing second in ERA (2.58).

He won seven of his eight Northern Division starts (one no-decision). In the first round of the conference tournament, he struck out 16 in a win against Eastern Washington. And in 22 league games, he batted .481 with 13 homers and 35 RBIs.

"It was definitely my year this year," Olerud said. "The hits were falling. I'd get breaks on the mound."

The talent was there, too.

"How good is he?" asked Gonzaga coach Steve Hertz, whose team lost to Olerud four times. "I think he might be the best player in the country. We've played both teams that have been ranked No. 1 in the country—Fresno State three times and Oklahoma State two times—and he's by far the best player we've seen."

But is Olerud a pitcher first, or a hitter?

"Coming out of high school, everybody was telling me I had to make a decision," Olerud said. "I was recruited by Stanford. They wanted me to pitch, and if I could prove I could hit, they might let me DH. Washington State and the University of Washington said I could pitch and hit. I went to Washington State because I wanted the chance to do both."

So what will he do next June, after he's an early-round draft pick?

"I'm not real sure about that," he said. "My freshman year, I felt real confident out there pitching. This year, I had a little trouble with my control, and I was hitting well. This year, I'd say hitting. It just depends on whichever I'm doing better at the time."

Olerud's father John E. could also hit, though Brayton said he didn't have the power his son exhibits. The Washington State coach should know, too, because the elder Olerud earned All-America honors under him in 1965, as a catcher.

Last summer, Olerud remained in Pullman and played for the local entry in the Alaska Summer League. He got a chance to play more first base than he had as a freshman, and he started to relax. He also earned himself a shot with Team USA, getting a chance to travel to Cuba for the Intercontinental Cup last fall.

He was strictly a pitcher, and he struggled some, finishing 2-0, 3.94 in 15 innings.

That may have cost him a chance to play in the Olympics. The versatile Olerud was not issued an invitation to try out for the U.S. team, even though his versatility would seem to be perfect for the 20-man roster.

"In another year, he'll really be something," Brayton said. ∎

# TOP PLAYERS OF 1988

## ALL-AMERICA TEAM

| Pos | Player | School | Yr | AVG | AB | R | H | HR | RBI | SB |
|---|---|---|---|---|---|---|---|---|---|---|
| C | Jim Campanis | Southern California | Jr. | .392 | 222 | 57 | 87 | 23 | 92 | 0 |
| 1B | Lance Shebelut | Fresno State | Sr. | .401 | 279 | 97 | 112 | 32 | 94 | 1 |
| 2B | Kevin Higgins | Arizona State | Jr. | .361 | 299 | 88 | 108 | 10 | 68 | 11 |
| 3B | Robin Ventura | Oklahoma State | Jr. | .391 | 230 | 89 | 90 | 24 | 88 | 2 |
| SS | Monty Fariss | Oklahoma State | Jr. | .397 | 242 | 95 | 96 | 30 | 114 | 6 |
| OF | Mike Fiore | Miami | Sr. | .397 | 224 | 81 | 89 | 15 | 83 | 30 |
| OF | Billy Masse | Wake Forest | Sr. | .422 | 223 | 83 | 94 | 24 | 77 | 35 |
| OF | Tom Goodwin | Fresno State | So. | .347 | 323 | 87 | 112 | 0 | 42 | 62 |
| DH | John Olerud | Washington State | So. | .464 | 233 | 83 | 108 | 23 | 81 | 1 |

| Pos | Pitcher | School | Yr | W | L | ERA | G | SV | IP | H | BB | SO |
|---|---|---|---|---|---|---|---|---|---|---|---|---|
| P | Andy Benes | Evansville | Jr. | 16 | 3 | 1.42 | 24 | 2 | 146 | 87 | 36 | 188 |
| P | Ben McDonald | Louisiana State | So. | 13 | 7 | 2.65 | 22 | 1 | 119 | 96 | 27 | 144 |
| P | Gregg Olson | Auburn | Jr. | 7 | 3 | 2.00 | 36 | 10 | 72 | 43 | 27 | 113 |
| P | John Olerud | Washington State | So. | 15 | 0 | 2.49 | 19 | 1 | 123 | 100 | 39 | 113 |
| P | Kirk Dressendorfer | Texas | Fr. | 15 | 2 | 2.26 | 23 | 2 | 136 | 103 | 36 | 134 |

## SECOND TEAM

C—Troy Buckley, Santa Clara. 1B—Turtle Zaun, North Carolina State. 2B—Mark Standiford, Wichita State. 3B—Ed Sprague Jr., Stanford. SS—Dave Silvestri, Missouri. OF—Tookie Spann, Tulane; Trey McCoy, Virginia Tech; and Ernie Carr, Jacksonville. DH—Mike Willes, Brigham Young. P—Eric Stone, Texas; Linty Ingram, Arizona State; John Salles, Fresno State; Brian Barnes, Clemson; and Tim McDonald, Central Michigan.

## THIRD TEAM

C—Brian Johnson, Texas. 1B—Eric Karros, UCLA. 2B—Ty Griffin, Georgia Tech. 3B—Don Sparks, Loyola Marymount. SS—Bret Barberie, Southern California. OF—Steve Hosey, Fresno State; Ted Wood, New Orleans; and Jay Knoblauh, Rice. DH—Oneri Fleita, Creighton. P—Rich Crane, Fresno State; Dana Allison, James Madison; Scott Erwin, Georgia Tech; Jeff Gidcumb, Florida; and Joe Grahe, Miami.

Wichita State coach Gene Stephenson guided the Shockers to the third-best winning percentage of the 1980s and capped the decade with a College World Series victory.

**1989**

# Wichita State beats injuries, Longhorns

By **JIM CALLIS**

**B**ryant Winslow limped toward the third-base dugout, his season ending weeks later than he wanted.

The Wichita State first baseman developed a stress fracture in his right shin in mid-April, yet stayed in the lineup. With the Shockers holding a 3-2 lead against Texas in the June 10 championship game of the 43rd College World Series, Longhorn center fielder Lance Jones led off the fifth inning by bunting.

Third baseman Mike Jones fielded the ball and threw wide to first, pulling Winslow into the runner's path. Lance Jones collided with Winslow, who hurt his leg more seriously. He refused to leave the game, but after one more pitch, realized he couldn't continue.

**FROM THE ISSUE:**
JULY 10, 1989

As he dragged himself across the infield, tears rolling down his cheeks, he yelled to pitcher Greg Brummett and catcher Eric Wedge:

"You guys better win this thing! Don't you dare lose this game!"

Like they had all postseason, the Shockers refused to quit. Shortstop Pat Meares hit a two-run home run in the bottom of the fifth to give Wichita State some breathing room, and Brummett pitched a complete game for a 5-3 win, his third of the Series and fourth of his CWS career, both tying records.

The fourth-seeded Shockers (68-16) looked like they belonged in a hospital instead of at Rosenblatt Stadium. Right fielder Jeff Bonacquista's season ended in April when a wild throw fractured his kneecap. Shortstop Mike Lansing's back and hamstring troubles kept him out of the regionals and CWS.

Winslow already was hobbled. Center fielder Jim Audley seriously sprained his ankle in his first game in the CWS, and Wedge and second baseman P.J. Forbes played with less serious bumps and bruises.

As a result, the Shockers offense sputtered early in the CWS. After averaging 10.1 runs per game before the CWS, Wichita State managed just five in its first two games, a 3-1 win by Brummett against Arkansas and a 4-2 loss to No. 1-seeded Florida State.

## TOP TEAMS
### 1989 COLLEGE WORLD SERIES STANDINGS

| School | Conference | Record | cWS | Head Coach |
|--------|-----------|--------|-----|-----------|
| Wichita State | Missouri Valley | 68–16 | 5–1 | Gene Stephenson |
| Texas | Southwest | 54–18 | 3–1 | Cliff Gustafson |
| Florida State | Metro | 54–18 | 2–2 | Mike Martin |
| Louisiana State | Southeastern | 55–17 | 2–2 | Skip Bertman |
| Arkansas | Southwest | 51–16 | 1–2 | Norm DeBriyn |
| Miami | Independent | 49–18 | 1–2 | Ron Fraser |
| Long Beach State | Big West | 50–15 | 0–2 | Dave Snow |
| North Carolina | Atlantic Coast | 41–18–1 | 0–2 | Mike Roberts |

### NATIONAL CHAMPION
### WICHITA STATE

One of the most consistently successful programs of the 1980s and '90s under coach Gene Stephenson, Wichita State made seven trips to Omaha but captured its lone national title in 1989, when they defeated Texas 5-3 in the championship game.

**69**

So Stephenson tinkered with his lineup before a rematch with Arkansas. He flip-flopped Wedge and left fielder Mike McDonald in the batting order, putting McDonald third and Wedge fourth, and moved Meares from ninth to sixth.

The move paid off immediately. Wedge blasted a three-run homer in the first inning, and the Shockers never looked back. McDonald later homered as Brummett won his second game 8-4.

Wichita State's tenacity was readily apparent. The Shockers lost the Missouri Valley Conference Tournament for the first time in three years and went into the West II Regional in Fresno with little confidence.

Doubts remained after the Shockers lost their third game 14-5 to Michigan. Wedge said the turning point was the next game, a 6-4 victory against host Fresno State, and they went on to beat Michigan twice for the regional title.

The win against Arkansas in their third game of the CWS raised the Shockers' record to 4-0 in elimination games. Their next step: find a way to beat Florida State twice.

For the second straight game, the answer was a Wedge shot. After a 56-minute rain delay in the eighth, he drove in two runs with a tie-breaking, bases-loaded bleeder up the middle against Seminole relief ace Ricky Kimball.

In the Bracket One final, Wichita State faced Florida State's unbeaten Clyde Keller, who had shut them down with his infuriating palmball in their first meeting.

The Seminoles scored four runs in the second for a 4-1 lead, but in the fourth, fifth-year senior Mike Wentworth hit a three-run homer to tie the game 4-4. The Shockers turned it into a rout from there, winning 12-9.

It was the fourth of Wentworth's career, his second this year. The first came in the elimination game against Fresno State, on his mother's birthday. No. 2 came on his

# 1989 NEWSMAKERS

Washington State's **John Olerud** missed the first half of the season after undergoing six hours of surgery in late February to remove an aneurysm near the base of his brain. He returned in the second half, but his uncertain status caused him to drop to the third round of the draft. He ended up signing a three-year deal with the Blue Jays in late August that provided a $575,000 signing bonus—the largest ever given a draft pick—and less than a week later singled in his first major league at-bat.

**Long Beach State** turned to former Loyola Marymount coach **Dave Snow** to reverse its fortunes after one winning season in nine years. The 49ers not only won their first 18 games under Snow, but as co-champions of the Big West Conference they swept aside host and No. 1 ranked Arizona in the West I regional to reach the CWS for the first time in program history.

**Texas**, the winningest team of the '80s, lost more games than any Longhorn team ever and failed to win the Southwest Conference title for the first time in 11 years, but still made a valiant run towards its second CWS title of the decade before finally falling to Wichita State, 5-3, in the championship game.

## FINAL TOP 25 FOR 1989

1. Wichita State*
2. Texas A&M
3. Texas*
4. Florida State*
5. Miami*
6. #Mississippi State
7. Louisiana State*
8. Long Beach State*
9. Arizona
10. Arkansas*
11. Arizona State
12. Fresno State
13. North Carolina*
14. Clemson
15. Oklahoma State
16. Loyola Marymount
17. Auburn
18. Southern California
19. Michigan
20. South Florida
21. Florida
22. Pepperdine
23. Nevada-Las Vegas
24. Jacksonville
25. Villanova

\* Reached College World Series
\# Preseason No. 1

# IN RETROSPECT: 1989 DRAFT

**Top 10 Draft Picks From College**
With overall selection number (Ov), drafting team (Team) and rank on Baseball America draft board (BA).

| Player | Pos | School | Ov | Team | BA |
|---|---|---|---|---|---|
| Ben McDonald | RHP | Louisiana State | 1 | Orioles | 1 |
| Donald Harris | OF | Texas Tech | 5 | Rangers | 61 |
| Frank Thomas | 1B | Auburn | 7 | White Sox | 7 |
| Kyle Abbott | LHP | Long Beach State | 9 | Angels | 9 |
| Brent Mayne | C | Cal State Fullerton | 13 | Royals | 33 |
| Steve Hosey | OF | Fresno State | 14 | Giants | 40 |
| Cal Eldred | RHP | Iowa | 17 | Brewers | 14 |
| Eddie Zosky | SS | Fresno State | 19 | Blue Jays | 8 |
| Scott Bryant | OF | Texas | 20 | Reds | 35 |
| Greg Gohr | RHP | Santa Clara | 21 | Tigers | 12 |

**Top 10 Major League Players From College Draft Class**
With draft round and Baseball-Reference.com total for wins above replacement (WAR) through 2019.

| Player | Pos | School | Rd | Ov | Team | WAR |
|---|---|---|---|---|---|---|
| Jeff Bagwell | 1B | Hartford | 4 | 110 | Red Sox | 79.9 |
| Frank Thomas | 1B | Auburn | 1 | 7 | White Sox | 73.9 |
| John Olerud | 1B | Washington State | 3 | 79 | Blue Jays | 58.2 |
| Jeff Kent | 2B | California | 20 | 523 | Blue Jays | 55.4 |
| Chuck Knoblauch | 2B | Texas A&M | 1 | 25 | Twins | 44.8 |
| Tim Salmon | OF | Grand Canyon | 3 | 69 | Angels | 40.6 |
| Trevor Hoffman | RHP | Arizona | 11 | 290 | Reds | 28.0 |
| Mo Vaughn | 1B | Seton Hall | 1 | 23 | Red Sox | 27.2 |
| Scott Erickson | RHP | Arizona | 4 | 112 | Twins | 25.0 |
| Denny Neagle | LHP | Minnesota | 3 | 85 | Twins | 22.5 |

father's birthday.

Before the game, he opened a bubble-gum wrapper with a fortune. It read: "Something magical will happen today." He put it in his pocket for good luck.

The Shockers knocked Keller out in the sixth and handed him his first loss since the 1988 regionals. Wichita State advanced to the championship game as Jim Newlin tied CWS records with his third save and fifth appearance.

Conversely, No. 2-seeded Texas (54-18) cake-walked to the title game.

If you had listened to Longhorns coach Cliff Gustafson, who tied former Southern California great Rod Dedeaux by taking his 15th team to Omaha, you wouldn't have thought it was possible.

Gustafson has been coaching seemingly forever, but in truth it has been 21 years. Louisiana State probably won't want to play his team again for a while after a 12-7 setback, which eliminated the Tigers. Ben McDonald, the College Player of the Year, lost his fourth career CWS game and gave up 11 earned runs, both records.

Texas starter Kirk Dressendorfer lasted six innings despite back problems, and Gustafson called it the gutsiest performance he had ever seen. Behind Dressendorfer, though, Gustafson's cupboard was unusually bare.

Scott Bryant started the championship game after pitching 16 innings all season. He has a strong arm, but his inexperience showed when he walked four batters in two-thirds of an inning.

Wichita State cruised from that point, and for once, Wedge was satisfied. "It's the ultimate state of Nirvana," he said. "Nothing is better than this." ∎

# Top college player no longer a goat

By **JIM CALLIS**

The worst moment of his career turned out to be the best thing that ever happened to Ben McDonald.

In a memorable 1987 College World Series game, McDonald served up a 10th-inning grand slam to Stanford's Paul Carey, turning a 5-2 lead into a 6-5 loss. The Cardinal went on to the first of two straight CWS titles. Louisiana State went home.

"I learned a lot from it," said McDonald, tagged with both of LSU's losses at the CWS, "and it probably made me a better person and a better ballplayer. It helped me because I started to work a lot harder. I wasn't too serious at the time about baseball."

He's serious now, and it shows. Last summer, McDonald won an Olympic gold medal with Team USA. This year the Major League Scouting Bureau gave him the highest pitching rating in its history, and he's perhaps the most predetermined No. 1 overall draft pick of all time.

One of the top prospects in draft history to that point, Louisiana State ace Ben McDonald went No. 1 overall to the Orioles and reached the majors quickly. He was a rotation fixture for eight seasons.

McDonald, a junior righthander, edged another righty, Miami freshman Alex Fernandez, to become the first pitcher ever to win College Player of the Year.

"He's the best pitcher I've coached in 28 years," said Tigers coach Skip Bertman, who has worked with Stan Jakubowski and Neal Heaton at Miami, and Clay Parker and Eric Hetzel at LSU.

McDonald won his first nine decisions this season, and fashioned a 44.2 inning scoreless streak to break a Southeastern Conference record. He won outstanding player of the year honors at the Central Regional. On the year he went 14-4, 3.49 with 202 strikeouts in 152 innings, allowing just 124 hits and 40 walks.

"At the juncture he's at now, he's very comparable and a little further along than Frank Viola, Calvin Schiraldi, Roger Clemens and Mike Moore, all of whom I saw pitch in the College World Series," Bertman said. "To get where those guys are today, he just needs more experience, professional baseball experience."

Even bad luck has turned into good for McDonald. At midseason, he pulled tendons in the middle finger of his pitching hand and couldn't cut loose on his fastball. But he said it might have been a blessing in disguise because it reduced his workload for a month.

The Carey grand slam definitely was. After recovering from the initial shock, McDonald dedicated himself completely to baseball. That meant long hours of running and weight-lifting. And that meant no basketball.

The 6-foot-7 McDonald declined a $67,000 offer from the Braves out of high school to accept a basketball scholarship at LSU. As a freshman forward, he averaged 2.3 points and started six times.

Telling LSU basketball coach Dale Brown that you don't want to play for him is tough. Brown could charm the habit off a nun.

"He was a really good prospect," Brown said. "He's the best athlete I've ever seen in the state of Louisiana, and that's overall—basketball, football, baseball. There's been no one to compare to him."

Said McDonald, who would have started full-time for Brown this year: "I definitely miss basketball. I wish I could still play it. But basketball runs into baseball, and obviously my career is in baseball."

McDonald remembered something Bertman had told him during recruiting.

"He told me if I went to college, I would be a first-round pick in three years," McDonald said. "He knew more of my abilities than I did."

After his first taste of failure, he had to confront and defeat it.

And now he's the best player in college baseball, with a chance to jump directly to the major leagues.

"He's a winner, he's just a winner," Brown said. "He's got it." ■

# TOP PLAYERS OF 1989

## ALL-AMERICA TEAM

| Pos | Player | School | Yr | AVG | AB | R | H | HR | RBI | SB |
|-----|--------|--------|----|-----|----|----|----|----|-----|----|
| C | Alan Zinter | Arizona | Jr. | .352 | 247 | 56 | 87 | 18 | 81 | 9 |
| 1B | Frank Thomas | Auburn | Jr. | .403 | 206 | 62 | 83 | 19 | 83 | 0 |
| 2B | Terry Taylor | Texas A&M | Jr. | .335 | 236 | 82 | 79 | 17 | 71 | 8 |
| 3B | John Blyington | Texas A&M | Jr. | .442 | 199 | 76 | 88 | 15 | 89 | 12 |
| SS | Eddie Zosky | Fresno State | Jr. | .370 | 273 | 55 | 101 | 3 | 51 | 1 |
| OF | Tom Goodwin | Fresno State | Jr. | .369 | 295 | 68 | 109 | 4 | 38 | 61 |
| OF | Dan Peltier | Notre Dame | Jr. | .446 | 258 | 81 | 115 | 15 | 93 | 12 |
| OF | Rick Hirtensteiner | Pepperdine | Sr. | .366 | 216 | 68 | 79 | 12 | 41 | 13 |
| DH | Scott Bryant | Texas | Jr. | .386 | 277 | 83 | 107 | 18 | 112 | 3 |

| Pos | Pitcher | School | Yr | W | L | ERA | G | SV | IP | H | BB | SO |
|-----|---------|--------|----|----|----|-----|----|----|----|----|----|----|
| P | Ben McDonald | Louisiana State | Jr. | 14 | 4 | 3.49 | 26 | 4 | 152 | 124 | 40 | 202 |
| P | Alex Fernandez | Miami | Fr. | 15 | 2 | 2.01 | 20 | 0 | 148 | 98 | 36 | 177 |
| P | Scott Erickson | Arizona | Jr. | 18 | 3 | 3.49 | 23 | 1 | 173 | 183 | 50 | 116 |
| P | Kyle Abbott | Long Beach State | Jr. | 15 | 3 | 2.73 | 21 | 0 | 135 | 109 | 73 | 140 |
| P | Brian Barnes | Clemson | Sr. | 16 | 3 | 2.22 | 23 | 1 | 146 | 87 | 66 | 208 |

## SECOND TEAM.

C—Eric Wedge, Wichita State. 1B—Tommy Raffo, Mississippi State. 2B—Ed Giovanola, Santa Clara. 3B—Gary Scott, Villanova. SS—Chuck Knoblauch, Texas A&M. OF—Mike Kelly, Arizona State; Paul Cary, Stanford; and Kevin Long, Arizona. DH—Dave Staton, Cal State Fullerton. P—Kirk Dressendorfer, Texas; John DeSilva, Brigham Young; Dave Fleming, Georgia; Rich Crane, Fresno State; and Donovan Osborne, Nevada-Las Vegas.

## THIRD TEAM

C—Miah Bradbury, Loyola Marymount. 1B—Steve O'Donnell, La Salle. 2B—Mitch Hannahs, Indiana State. 3B—Fred Cooley, Southern Mississippi. SS—Tim Costo, Iowa. OF—Chris Hatcher, Iowa; Matt Mieske, Western Michigan; and Greg Rideau, Grambling State. DH—Ray Ortiz, Oklahoma State. P—John Thoden, North Carolina; Greg Gohr, Santa Clara; Joe Grahe, Miami; Greg Brummett, Wichita State; and Tom Hickox, Stetson.

Louisiana State coach Skip Bertman guided the Tigers to an incredible four national championships in the 1990s.

THE **1990s**

# TOP 25 PROGRAMS OF THE 1990s

Georgia, the surprising 1990 CWS champions, accumulated 50 points in the decade to rank No. 33. See Introduction (Page 4) for a key to abbreviations and scoring. Category leaders in **bold**.

| No. | School | Regional | Super | CWS | Title | AA1 | AA2 | AA3 | Top 10 | MLB | Points |
|-----|--------|----------|-------|-----|-------|-----|-----|-----|--------|-----|--------|
| 1. | Louisiana State | **10** | 1 | **7** | **4** | **9** | 5 | 2 | 23 | 15 | 309 |
| 2. | Miami | **10** | 1 | **7** | 1 | 7 | 1 | 6 | 22 | 14 | 233 |
| 3. | Florida State | **10** | 1 | **7** | 0 | 7 | 6 | 5 | 23 | 17 | 230 |
| 4. | Southern California | 9 | 1 | 2 | 1 | 4 | 7 | 6 | **32** | 21 | 198 |
| 5. | Stanford | 9 | 1 | 4 | 0 | 8 | 4 | 1 | 31 | 19 | 196 |
| 6. | Cal State Fullerton | 9 | 1 | 5 | 1 | 4 | 2 | 4 | 16 | 15 | 187 |
| 7. | Wichita State | **10** | 0 | 4 | 0 | 4 | 8 | 5 | 19 | 13 | 176 |
| 8. | Clemson | **10** | 1 | 3 | 0 | 3 | 8 | 2 | 23 | 11 | 164 |
| 9. | Arizona State | 6 | 0 | 3 | 0 | 8 | 2 | 3 | 31 | 12 | 155 |
| 10. | Long Beach State | 9 | 0 | 3 | 0 | 3 | 4 | 2 | 20 | 12 | 138 |
| 11. | Oklahoma State | **10** | 1 | 4 | 0 | 2 | 0 | 5 | 11 | 8 | 136 |
| 12. | Oklahoma | 6 | 0 | 3 | 1 | 2 | 2 | 1 | 17 | 15 | 130 |
| 13. | Texas A&M | 7 | 1 | 2 | 0 | 2 | 1 | 7 | 22 | 12 | 123 |
| 14. | Georgia Tech | 9 | 0 | 1 | 0 | 5 | 4 | 3 | 15 | 9 | 122 |
| 15. | Texas | 8 | 0 | 2 | 0 | 3 | 4 | 1 | 22 | 10 | 121 |
| 16. | Pepperdine | 5 | 0 | 1 | 1 | 3 | 4 | 4 | 16 | 12 | 118 |
| 17. | UCLA | 6 | 0 | 1 | 0 | 5 | 1 | 4 | 23 | 11 | 110 |
| 18. | Rice | 5 | 1 | 2 | 0 | 6 | 2 | 0 | 12 | 8 | 108 |
| 19. | Florida | 6 | 0 | 3 | 0 | 4 | 0 | 1 | 11 | 12 | 105 |
| 20. | Mississippi State | 8 | 0 | 3 | 0 | 1 | 2 | 0 | 14 | 7 | 102 |
| 21. | Auburn | 6 | 1 | 2 | 0 | 3 | 2 | 1 | 15 | 5 | 100 |
| 22. | Alabama | 6 | 1 | 3 | 0 | 1 | 0 | 2 | 13 | 6 | 95 |
| 23. | Fresno State | 8 | 0 | 1 | 0 | 2 | 3 | 0 | 12 | 7 | 88 |
| 24. | Texas Tech | 5 | 0 | 0 | 0 | 2 | 7 | 2 | 14 | 11 | 85 |
| 25. | Tennessee | 5 | 0 | 1 | 0 | 4 | 1 | 3 | 7 | 9 | 80 |

# Louisiana State ushers in era of SEC dominance

By **ALLAN SIMPSON**

College baseball enjoyed a wave of unprecedented popularity in the 1980s. Among the factors contributing to its rapidly growing public acceptance over the course of the decade were the advent of national TV coverage, an offensive explosion facilitated by the use of aluminum bats, the increased emphasis on college talent in the draft and a growing number of colleges around the country, particularly in the Sun Belt states, that began emphasizing college baseball as a viable revenue sport.

The 1990s emphasized more of the same, and the game only continued to grow as it tapped into more of a mainstream audience—particularly as it related to the unparalleled popularity of its showcase event, the College World Series. But a crossroads moment in the game's continuing evolution came to light late in the decade when almost everyone connected with college baseball began asking the question:

When does more of a good thing become too much?

That sentiment percolated in 1997, and became a rhetorical question a year later when the aluminum bats that were designed to bring a wave of offensive excitement to the college game soon began to be viewed instead as lethal weapons because they were producing a level of offense that was exacting fundamental change in the way the college game was being played—or, at least, the way it was intended to be played.

## TOP 10 STORYLINES OF THE 1990s

**1** **TIGER BY THE TAIL.** Louisiana State won four CWS titles in the '90s and carried the torch for Southeastern Conference dominance.

**2** **STORYBOOK BLAST**. LSU's Warren Morris hit a dramatic, two-out, walk-off home run in the 1997 CWS championship game.

**3** **GORILLA BALL.** LSU coach Skip Bertman coined the term "gorilla ball" to describe the power-hitting style that characterized his teams in the 1990s.

**4** **USC 21, ARIZONA STATE 14.** A decade of unchecked offense reached its zenith on June 5, 1998, when USC defeated Arizona State 21-14 in the CWS championship game.

**5** **GAME OF A LIFETIME.** On May 9, 1999, Florida State's Marshall McDougall shattered NCAA records when he hit six home runs and had 16 RBIs in a 28-2 rout of Maryland.

**6** **SCHOLARSHIP LIMITS.** The NCAA slashed scholarships 10 percent across the board in 1991. For baseball, that meant a drop in scholarships from 13 to the current limit of 11.7.

**7** **CONTENTIOUS NEGOTIATIONS.** In an era of bonus hyperinflation, the Phillies failed to come to terms with Florida State's J.D. Drew, whom they drafted second overall in 1997.

**8** **OPTICAL ILLUSION.** A Rangers team physician detected trouble when he saw a Baseball America cover depicting 1996 first-rounder R.A. Dickey's arm hanging at an odd angle. Dickey was born without a UCL in his elbow.

**9** **COMING UP EMPTY.** Wichita State won the 1989 CWS but subsequently failed to win another in the '90s—despite winning more games (543) than any program in the decade.

**10** **CHANGING TIMES.** The NCAA Tournament underwent radical changes in 1999, moving from a 48-team field to 64 teams. The revised structure resulted in 16 four-team regionals, with the winners advancing to super regionals that pitted two clubs in a best-of-3 series.

No program symbolized the juxtaposition the college game began encountering more than Louisiana State, which came to national prominence in the mid-to-late 1980s, or shortly after the hiring of innovative Skip Bertman as its coach. Tangible results came to the Tigers in 1991 when they won their first College World Series crown, and it wasn't long before LSU began making its mark on the game and exerting its sphere of influence—especially after winning three more national titles in the next six years.

No one was more attuned to the growing emphasis the college game was placing on offense in the '90s than Bertman, and he began structuring his teams accordingly. He recruited big, unusually strong players who specialized in driving balls out of the park. After winning the 1997 College World Series with a largely one-dimensional club that slugged 188 home runs, an astounding total that shattered the previous NCAA single-season record, he admitted as much.

"The game's changed a lot in the last five or six years," Bertman said. "Next year, you better get on the power train if you want to compete, at least until they change the alloy in the aluminum bats."

True to his word, offense continued to run amok in 1998 with a host of new records set for batting average, runs scored and home runs, and everything came to a climax at that year's College World Series with Southern California beating Arizona State in the deciding game by the outlandish score of 21-14. The reverberations from that offensive onslaught were swift and immediate—especially with college baseball's image, which had been on a positive upswing for the better part of two decades, now hanging in the balance. The recognition finally hit home that the aluminum bats being used in the college game were out of control, and steps needed to be taken to rectify the situation.

Ironically, it took a high-scoring game between USC and ASU, two revered programs, to draw national attention to the travesty that was occurring, just as it was a series of low-scoring, pitching-dominated games between the same schools 25 years earlier that set the wheels in motion to spice up the college game by introducing aluminum bats. The two teams met in the championship game of the 1972 College World Series, with USC

# ALL-AMERICA TEAM OF THE DECADE

| Pos, Player, School | Summary |
| --- | --- |
| **C** Jason Varitek, Georgia Tech | Two-time first-rounder, future MLB all-star hit .384 with 57 HR in 4-year career |
| **1B** Todd Helton, Tennessee | Had stellar Vols career as hitter (.370-38-238) and pitcher (19-5, 2.24) |
| **2B** Todd Walker, Louisiana State | Hitting machine began career at .400; overall: .396, 52 HR, 246 RBIs |
| **3B** Troy Glaus, UCLA | No. 3 pick in '97 gets nod over Phil Nevin on strength of 34 HR as JR, 62 career |
| **SS** Nomar Garciaparra, Ga. Tech | Became best college SS of '90s by hitting .427 with 16 HR and 33 SB as JR |
| **OF** Lance Berkman, Rice | Breakout JR year with .431 AVG and national-best 41 HR and 134 RBIs |
| **OF** J.D. Drew, Florida State | Draft saga overshadowed stellar college career: .391 AVG, 69 HR and 257 RBIs |
| **OF** Mark Kotsay, CS Fullerton | Led Titans to '95 CWS as hitter (.422-21-90) and reliever (0.31 ERA, 11 SV) |
| **DH** Pat Burrell, Miami | Hit NCAA-best .484 as FR; taken No. 1 in '98 after .441 career mark, 61 HR |
| **UT** Brooks Kieschnick, Texas | Excelled as both hitter (.360-43-215) and pitcher (34-8, 3.05) for Longhorns |
| **SP** Kris Benson, Clemson | Top pick in '96 draft after breakout JR year (14-2, 2.02, 156 IP, 27 BB/202 SO) |
| **SP** Jeff Granger, Texas A&M | Led A&M to No. 2 rank in '93 with 15-3, 2.62 season; became No. 5 pick in draft |
| **SP** Bobby Jones, Fresno State | Gets nod over fellow Bulldog Jeff Weaver with 32-9, 2.45 career mark |
| **SP** John Powell, Auburn | Undersized righty had limited pro appeal, but holds NCAA strikeout record (604) |
| **RP** Darren Dreifort, Wichita State | Unconventional relief role, responded with 26-5, 2.24 record; No. 2 pick in '93 |

winning 1-0. They also squared off on two other occasions in that series, with the teams trading a pair of low-scoring decisions. The Sun Devils, with a pitching staff that posted an overall 1.76 ERA on the season, also won two other CWS games by 1-0 scores. When the two teams met a year later, USC prevailed again, winning 4-3, with the 1973 championship on the line.

The level of offense in college baseball generally was at a low ebb at the time, but it took a series of low-scoring College World Series games between the nation's two marquee programs to drive home the point that changes needed to be made to reinvigorate the game. A year later, aluminum bats were introduced to college baseball.

The high-scoring contest between the same two schools in 1998 was also the catalyst to change, and less than two months later the NCAA baseball rules committee recommended the most drastic change to the sport since the aluminum bat itself was introduced. The NCAA executive committee quickly ratified the plan, but while structural changes to the bat were set in motion—with bat manufacturers mandated to produce an aluminum bat that performed more like wood—little could be done to modify them for the 1999 season. It wasn't until 2000 that the new bats took effect, and a noticeable dip in offensive production occurred.

The debate over aluminum bats was the most far-reaching topic to impact college baseball in the 1990s, but the decade was also marked by the continued popularity of the College World Series. From a record attendance of 132,865 in 1989, new attendance marks were set seven times in the next 10 years, peaking at 206,639 in 1999, as Omaha's Rosenblatt Stadium, which served as the home of the College World Series from 1950-2010, was routinely expanded to meet the increased demand. The all-time single session record of 24,859 was set, too, in 1999.

Major League Baseball also continued to rely on college talent with increasing frequency in the 1990s—and showed little reluctance to pay for premium talent. As a result, signing bonuses rose exponentially through the decade. With so much money at stake, it was only inevitable that controversy would permeate some of the negotiations between clubs and players, and the high-profile dispute between the Phillies and their first-round pick, Florida State outfielder J.D. Drew, in 1997 was so contentious that the sides would never came close to reaching an agreement.

Drew not only did not sign with the Phillies but decided to relinquish his senior year of eligibility at FSU for the precedent-setting step of signing with an independent league. Drafted again in 1998, Drew ended up signing with the Cardinals for $3 million—an amount that was far below the figure San Diego State first baseman Travis Lee signed for in 1996, when a loophole in the existing draft rules enabled him to become a free agent and offer his services to the highest bidder. Lee subsequently signed a windfall, $10 million deal with the Diamondbacks—a lavish sum that spoke to the growing value of college talent and the growing relevance of college baseball. ■

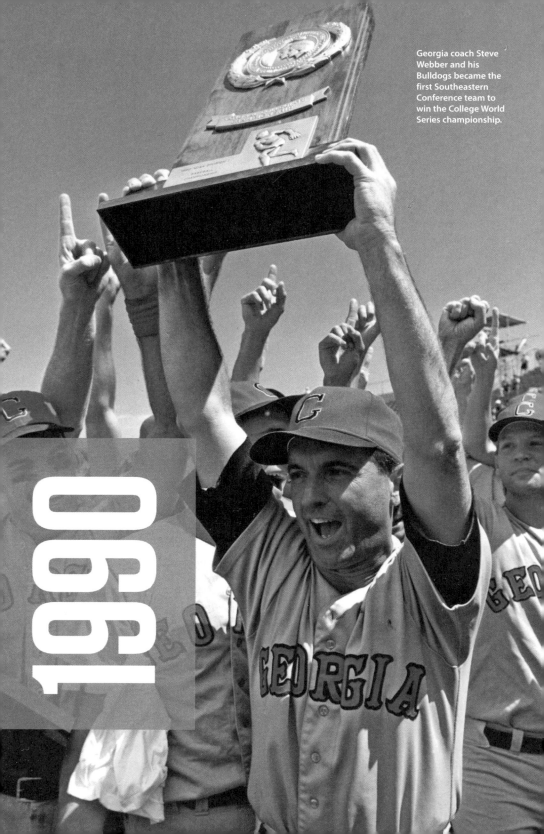

Georgia coach Steve Webber and his Bulldogs became the first Southeastern Conference team to win the College World Series championship.

1990

# Georgia wins CWS with great pitching

By **JIM CALLIS**

**FROM THE ISSUE:**
JULY 10, 1990

**T**he night before the College World Series championship game, Georgia coach Steve Webber said freshman pitcher Stan Payne wouldn't be rattled by his starting assignment.

"Knowing Stan, I wouldn't think so," Webber said. "He's very confident. He loves to pitch."

But Payne's roommate, first baseman Doug Radziewicz, said he spent a difficult night.

"He didn't sleep," Radziewicz said. "He kept me up. He was rolling, tossing and turning until 3 a.m., and that's when I fell asleep.

"But then we got up in the morning and watched 'The Smurfs,' and everything was OK."

Was it ever. Payne allowed only one run in six innings as the Bulldogs won their first ever CWS title with a 2-1 win against Oklahoma State.

"I was so excited about pitching," Payne said, "it didn't even hit me it was a national championship game."

Payne's effort capped an improbable title run by Georgia. The Bulldogs ended their regular season by losing three games at Louisiana State to blow the Southeastern Conference title, then lost two straight games in the SEC Tournament.

The Bulldogs entered the Northeast Regional in Waterbury, Conn., with seven losses in their last eight games. But they were wiser for the experience.

"We learned something against LSU," Webber said. "We went in thinking we were going to win the conference championship, and we forgot to play LSU. After that, we emphasized that you can't win a championship unless you play one pitch at a time."

The Bulldogs had five seniors who had been to Omaha before—though none had played in the 1987 CWS—and they knew what to expect. Georgia followed the same script throughout the CWS: excellent pitching (1.40 ERA), good defense (six double plays versus five errors) and adequate hitting (.261).

In Georgia's opener, Dave Flemming moved the ball in-and-out and up-and-down for

# TOP TEAMS

## 1990 COLLEGE WORLD SERIES STANDINGS

| School | Conference | Record | CWS | Head Coach |
|---|---|---|---|---|
| Georgia | Southeastern | 52–19 | 4–1 | Steve Webber |
| Oklahoma State | Big Eight | 56–17 | 3–1 | Gary Ward |
| Stanford | Pacific-10 | 59–12 | 3–2 | Mark Marquess |
| Louisiana State | Southeastern | 54–19 | 2–2 | Skip Bertman |
| Mississippi State | Southeastern | 50–21 | 1–2 | Ron Polk |
| The Citadel | Southern | 46–14 | 1–2 | Chal Port |
| Cal State Fullerton | Big West | 36–23 | 0–2 | Larry Cochell |
| Georgia Southern | TAAC | 50–19 | 0–2 | Jack Stallings |

## NATIONAL CHAMPION
### GEORGIA

The Southeastern Conference sent three teams to Omaha—which tied for the record at the time—and emerged with its first national champion: Georgia. The Bulldogs edged Oklahoma State 2-1 in the championship game.

the first of four Bulldogs complete games, a 3-0 victory against Mississippi State that was the first CWS shutout since 1987. It wasn't much of a surprise because Flemming had ended the Bulldogs' streak of 177 games without being shut out during the regular season.

Georgia's second win, though, was a real shocker. The Bulldogs sent Mike Rebhan against No. 1 Stanford and Mike Mussina, fresh off an MVP performance in the West I Regional.

After four innings, the Cardinal led 2-0 and Mussina had eight strikeouts. Georgia scored a record 11 runs in the sixth en route to a 16-2 laughter. Stanford had lost only one of the 58 games in which it had led all season.

"I was in high school in 1987," Bulldogs right fielder Bruce Chick said, "and I watched Paul Carey hit an opposite-field home run to beat Ben McDonald. I really believed this was Stanford, this was supposed to be a close game. You're not supposed to score 16 runs."

Stanford won the second game 4-2, and seemed primed to win its third game. Mussina hadn't lost to the same opponent twice all year. Again, Rebhan and Georgia spotted Stanford a lead, 1-0 through three innings. Then the Bulldogs scored four in the fourth to knock out Mussina, and Rebhan outdid his previous outing with a 5-1 victory.

In the other bracket, Oklahoma State laid waste to any team that dared cross its path.

The Cowboys beat Cal State Fullerton 14-4 and Louisiana State 7-1 and 14-3. In the three games, they batted .390, well ahead of the record .347 compiled by 1977 national champion Arizona State. LSU coach Skip Bertman said the Cowboys were the best team he had seen in years.

"They remind me of the Southern California and the Arizona State teams of the late '70s," Bertman said. "They're very geared to win, and they're playing the best baseball a

# 1990 NEWSMAKERS

Not only did **Georgia** become the first **Southeastern Conference** school to win a CWS, but 1990 marked the beginning of the SEC's dominance, with Louisiana State and Mississippi State also represented in Omaha. The only other conference to send as many as three teams to the CWS was in 1988, when Arizona State, California and champion Stanford came from the Southern Division of the Pacific-10 Conference.

For the first time since the **CWS** adopted its eight-team format in 1948, no representatives from the states of Arizona, Florida or Texas was present. Georgia's unexpected win further pointed out the parity that existed in college baseball.

After a three-year sojourn to Illinois, **Augie Garrido** returned home to California after the 1990 season to retake the coaching reins at **Cal State Fullerton**, where he had coached from 1973-87 while leading the school to CWS championships in 1979 and 1984. Garrido would win another national title at Fullerton in 1995, before leaving for Texas in 1997, where he won two more titles on his way to becoming college baseball's all-time winningest coach.

### FINAL TOP 25 FOR 1990

1. Georgia*
2. Oklahoma State*
3. Stanford*
4. Louisiana State*
5. Arizona State
6. #Southern California
7. Florida State
8. Mississippi State*
9. Cal State Fullerton*
10. Texas
11. Georgia Southern*
12. Arkansas
13. Miami
14. Southern Illinois
15. North Carolina
16. Illinois
17. San Diego State
18. Washington State
19. Wichita State
20. The Citadel*
21. Houston
22. Loyola Marymount
23. South Alabama
24. UCLA
25. Creighton

\* Reached College World Series
\# Preseason No. 1

# IN RETROSPECT: 1990 DRAFT

**Top 10 Draft Picks From College**
With overall selection number (Ov), drafting team (Team) and rank on Baseball America draft board (BA).

| Player | Pos | School | Ov | Team | BA |
|---|---|---|---|---|---|
| Dan Wilson | C | Minnesota | 7 | Reds | 12 |
| Tim Costo | SS | Iowa | 8 | Indians | 3 |
| Donovan Osborne | LHP | Nevada-Las Vegas | 13 | Cardinals | 11 |
| Dan Smith | LHP | Creighton | 16 | Rangers | 30 |
| Jeromy Burnitz | OF | Oklahoma State | 17 | Mets | 66 |
| Eric Christopherson | C | San Diego State | 19 | Giants | 23 |
| Mike Mussina | RHP | Stanford | 20 | Orioles | 26 |
| Lance Dickson | LHP | Arizona | 23 | Cubs | 44 |
| Don Peters | RHP | St. Francis (Ill.) | 26 | Athletics | 31 |
| Mike Zimmerman | RHP | South Alabama | 27 | Pirates | 55 |

**Top 10 Major League Players From College Draft Class**
With draft round and Baseball-Reference.com total for wins above replacement (WAR) through 2019.

| Player | Pos | School | Rd | Ov | Team | WAR |
|---|---|---|---|---|---|---|
| Mike Mussina | RHP | Stanford | 1 | 20 | Orioles | 83.0 |
| Bret Boone | 2B | Southern Calif. | 5 | 134 | Mariners | 22.8 |
| Rusty Greer | OF | Montevallo (Ala.) | 10 | 279 | Rangers | 22.4 |
| Jeromy Burnitz | OF | Oklahoma State | 1 | 17 | Mets | 19.8 |
| Troy Percival | RHP | UC Riverside | 6 | 179 | Angels | 17.1 |
| Bob Wickman | RHP | Wis.-Whitewater | 2 | 44 | White Sox | 16.9 |
| Dan Wilson | C | Minnesota | 1 | 7 | Reds | 12.9 |
| Fernando Viña | 2B | Arizona State | 9 | 253 | Mets | 12.3 |
| Mike Lansing | 2B | Wichita State | 6 | 155 | Miami (FSL) | 9.9 |
| Damian Miller | C | Viterbo (Wis.) | 20 | 544 | Twins | 9.0 |

team can play."

Few expected Payne and Georgia to stand up to Oklahoma State's offense, and no one thought they could win with just two runs. For the fifth time in five games, the Omaha World-Herald picked the Bulldogs to lose.

But Payne kept the Cowboys off balance with his fastball and curveball, and Jeff Cooper scored the first run and drove in the second to put Georgia ahead 2-0 after five innings. Oklahoma State closed to 2-1 in the sixth, and a leadoff double by DH Brian Kelly in the seventh drove Payne from the game. Enter Flemming, who escaped when Kelly was nailed at the plate one out later on a grounder to shortstop J.R. Showalter. Showalter threw a perfect peg to catcher Terry Childers, who withstood a violent collision.

"I promised myself they were going to have to kill me to get me to drop it," said Childers, who suffered a concussion and dropped the ball on a similar play in a regional game against Rutgers.

Fleming enticed Michael Daniel to hit into a double play to end the eighth. He said he threw harder than he had all season in the ninth, when he struck out the side.

"I was just smiling out there," said Fleming, who was at the bottom of a pile of Bulldogs, "with my head buried in the grass."

The loss was the record fifth for Oklahoma State in the championship game, its third under Gary Ward.

"How can you compare knife wounds?" Ward said when asked how much it hurt. "By how deep it goes? Three inches? Four inches? Five inches?"

Georgia's title was the first ever for an SEC team. ■

# Kelly's magical talent makes believers of all

By **BOG EGER**

The ballpark was nearly deserted. The game had been over for half an hour, and most of the fans had gone off into the night.

In front of the visitors dugout, a young man in a baseball uniform was surrounded by youthful admirers. He signed his name on their programs, their gloves, their T-shirts.

Nothing strange here. It happens every day in ballparks around the nation.

Except the ballpark was Arizona's Frank Sancet Field, and the player was Mike Kelly, who just happens to play for the home team's most bitter rival, Arizona State.

They usually hurl insults, or worse, at the Sun Devils in Tucson. They definitely don't ask for autographs. But that's the kind of impact Kelly, the College Player of the Year, is having.

Kelly has decided a lot of baseball games the past two years. If he doesn't do it with his glove, he's likely to do it with his bat. If he can't do it with his bat, he might use his legs.

Arizona State sophomore Mike Kelly hit .376 with 21 home runs and 20 stolen bases. While he failed to impact the major leagues, he served as a semi-regular for the expansion 1998 Devil Rays.

The day he was mobbed by young Wildcats fans, Kelly made a catch for the ages to rob Arizona's Jack Johnson of a three-run homer. He glided to the fence at the 400-foot mark, leaped and snared the ball well beyond the fence, making the difference in a 6-4 Arizona State victory.

"Almost every night I dream about making a play like that," Kelly said. "It's by far the best play I've ever made. It was a once-in-a-lifetime thing."

Said Sun Devils coach Jim Brock: "College, pro, any form of baseball—it was the best."

"He's the best I've had," said Brock, who has coached two previous Players of the Year—Mike Sodders (1981) and Oddibe McDowell (1984)—and sent 41 players to the major leagues. "And he's the best I ever hope to have."

At 6-foot-4 and 195 pounds, with 4.0-second speed from home plate to first base, Kelly is perhaps the most physically imposing player in ASU history. And his statistics rank with anyone in Arizona State's galaxy of stars.

On the season, Kelly hit .376 with 21 home runs, 20 stolen bases, 83 runs and 82 RBIs. Only one other Pacific-10 Southern Division player ever pulled off the 20 homer-20 steal season: McDowell in 1984.

Perhaps Kelly's most astounding feat didn't even take place during a game. In mid-

March, he smoked a batting practice offering so hard that the ball landed 480 feet away—with a clear "A" tattooed on it from his Easton bat.

If Kelly were eligible for this year's draft, he would be a good bet to be the No. 1 overall pick. He will likely have that honor next year. As a freshman, Kelly batted .300 with 10 home runs, 16 stolen bases, 48 runs and 56 RBIs, though he struggled toward the end.

"I let myself get caught up in some things, like chasing some of Barry Bonds' (Arizona State) freshman records," Kelly said. "I'm trying to keep those kinds of thoughts in the back of my head this year."

Arizona State hitting coach Jeff Pentland credits Kelly's big sophomore season to experience.

"His ability to hit the offspeed pitch has improved, and his confidence level is a lot higher," Pentland said. "Plus, he's much stronger physically than he was last year. He's becoming a man."

Of all the major leaguers he has coached, Brock said Kelly probably is most like Alvin Davis.

"McDowell was a great college player, but you knew his ceiling was somewhat limited by his size," Brock said. "Bonds had exceptional talent, but there were some minuses.

"Kelly has all the intangibles that made Davis such a great player, plus he runs much better. Davis was not strong defensively at first base. Kelly is the best center fielder I've ever seen in college." ■

# TOP PLAYERS OF 1990

## ALL-AMERICA TEAM

| Pos | Player | School | Yr | AVG | AB | R | H | HR | RBI | SB |
|-----|--------|--------|-----|-----|-----|-----|-----|-----|-----|-----|
| C | Dan Wilson | Minnesota | Jr | .370 | 181 | 43 | 67 | 8 | 49 | 10 |
| 1B | Don Barbara | Long Beach State | Sr | .474 | 215 | 69 | 102 | 7 | 61 | 9 |
| 2B | Anthony Manahan | Arizona State | Jr | .366 | 284 | 66 | 104 | 10 | 81 | 9 |
| 3B | Greg D'Alexander | Arkansas | Sr | .387 | 212 | 51 | 82 | 14 | 65 | 10 |
| SS | Tim Costo | Iowa | Jr | .372 | 196 | 59 | 73 | 16 | 64 | 5 |
| OF | Mike Kelly | Arizona State | So | .376 | 258 | 83 | 97 | 21 | 82 | 20 |
| OF | Jeffrey Hammonds | Stanford | Fr | .355 | 301 | 83 | 107 | 7 | 44 | 48 |
| OF | Wes Grisham | Louisiana State | Sr | .360 | 278 | 65 | 100 | 11 | 72 | 5 |
| DH | Paul Ellis | UCLA | Jr | .360 | 247 | 61 | 89 | 29 | 83 | 3 |

| Pos | Pitcher | School | Yr | W | L | ERA | G | SV | IP | H | BB | SO |
|-----|---------|--------|-----|-----|-----|-----|-----|-----|-----|-----|-----|-----|
| P | Sean Rees | Arizona State | So | 13 | 3 | 2.67 | 22 | 0 | 138 | 98 | 54 | 162 |
| P | Stan Spencer | Stanford | Jr | 14 | 1 | 2.73 | 20 | 0 | 142 | 126 | 28 | 145 |
| P | Dan Smith | Creighton | Jr | 14 | 3 | 1.96 | 17 | 0 | 120 | 84 | 48 | 134 |
| P | Oscar Munoz | Miami | Jr | 15 | 2 | 2.39 | 20 | 1 | 128 | 98 | 57 | 115 |
| P | Kirk Dressendorfer | Texas | Jr | 12 | 4 | 3.16 | 22 | 2 | 125 | 98 | 33 | 152 |

## SECOND TEAM

**C**—Mike Harrison, California. **1B**—Steve Estroff, North Carolina. **2B**—David Tollison, Texas. **3B**—Tim Griffin, Stanford. **SS**—Chris Martin, Pepperdine. **OF**—Paul Cary, Stanford; Marc Ronan, Florida State; and Brian Kowitz, Clemson. **DH**—Mark Dalesandro, Illinois. **P**—Joey Hamilton, Georgia Southern; Randy Powers, Southern California; Mike Zimmerman, South Alabama; Gar Finnvold, Florida State; and Paul Byrd, Louisiana State.

## THIRD TEAM

**C**—Eric Christopherson, San Diego State. **1B**—Chris Pritchett, UCLA. **2B**—Kevin Jordan, Nebraska. **3B**—Jeff Ball, San Jose State. **SS**—Robert Eenhoorn, Davidson. **OF**—Todd Greene, Georgia Southern; Doug Shields, Southern Illinois; and Darren Bragg, Georgia Tech. **DH**—Gary Daniels, Brigham Young. **P**—Mike Hostetler, Georgia Tech; Phil Stidham, Arkansas; Aaron Sele, Washington State; Rich Robertson, Texas A&M; and Dave Fleming, Georgia.

Louisiana State catcher Gary Hymel helped power the Tigers to a national title with four home runs and 10 RBIs to win Most Outstanding Player honors.

1991

# Tigers pummel World Series field

By **JIM CALLIS**

Known for churning out pitchers, Louisiana State changed tactics and bludgeoned its way to its first national championship.

The Tigers won the 45th College World Series with a 6-3 victory against Wichita State June 8 at Rosenblatt Stadium. LSU, the first team to go undefeated in the CWS since Texas in 1983, averaged a record 12 runs in its four games, and hit a record-tying nine home runs.

"The offense is usually overshadowed by a Ben McDonald-type pitcher," Tigers coach Skip Bertman said. "But the kids have hit well for two months now, and they kept getting better."

Leading the way for LSU were roommates Gary Hymel and Lyle Mouton, who drove in 10 runs apiece. Hymel, named the CWS Most Outstanding Player, hit four home runs and Mouton added three. Hymel tied the record for home runs in a CWS, and both tied the CWS career record of four.

**FROM THE ISSUE:**
JULY 10, 1991

"This is a business trip for us," Mouton said two days before the final. "It doesn't become a fun trip until we play in the national championship game and win it."

The Tigers took care of business, becoming the third straight No. 4 seed and second straight Southeastern Conference team to win the championship.

For the first time since the CWS switched to a two-bracket system to accommodate CBS in 1988, two teams advanced unbeaten to the final. That made the Friday before the championship game an off day, and the hype started flying.

Most of the attention focused on Shockers righthander Tyler Green, who would start the final game. Earlier in the week, on the same day the Phillies made him the 10th overall pick in the draft, Green struck out 14 and held Creighton to two unearned runs in nine innings. He received no decision as Wichita State won the best game of the series 3-2 in 12 innings.

Green throws a major league fastball and changeup, but it's his unique knuckle-curveball that sets him apart from other pitchers. He taught himself the pitch, which comes to the plate at 85 mph before suddenly darting down, and reporters wondered how LSU

---

## TOP TEAMS
### 1991 COLLEGE WORLD SERIES STANDINGS

| School | Conference | Record | CWS | Head Coach |
|---|---|---|---|---|
| Louisiana State | Southeastern | 55–18 | 4–0 | Skip Bertman |
| Wichita State | Missouri Valley | 66–13 | 3–1 | Gene Stephenson |
| Creighton | Missouri Valley | 51–22 | 2–2 | Jim Hendry |
| Florida | Southeastern | 51–21 | 2–2 | Joe Arnold |
| Fresno State | Big West | 42–23 | 1–2 | Bob Bennett |
| Long Beach State | Big West | 45–22 | 1–2 | Dave Snow |
| Clemson | Atlantic Coast | 60–10 | 0–2 | Bill Wilhelm |
| Florida State | Metro | 57–14 | 0–2 | Mike Martin |

### NATIONAL CHAMPION
### LOUISIANA STATE

Louisiana State coach Skip Bertman wins the first of five national titles as  the Tigers sweep through Omaha and defeat Wichita State 6-3 in the championship game. LSU tied a CWS record with nine home runs while averaging 12 runs per game.

could possibly hit it.

But LSU avoided Green's changeup and knuckle-curve whenever possible, and teed off on his fastball. Green lasted just three innings, allowing four runs on five hits and three walks.

"All the attention he got made us concentrate harder," second baseman Tookie Johnson said. "We knew the knuckle-curve was going to be a tough pitch to lay off. If there wasn't as much said about it, we probably would have been fooled by it."

The Tigers led 4-1 after two innings, scored two more in the fourth and cruised from there. The biggest blows weren't struck by Hymel or Mouton, but by Armando Rios and Rich Cordani.

Rios, a center fielder who transferred from UNC Charlotte after last season, hit a two-run home run, his fourth of the year, in the second inning to break a 1-for-13 CWS slump. Cordani, 3-for-28 in his CWS career when he faced reliever Darren Dreifort in the fourth, tripled in two runs.

The Tigers' Chad Ogea pitched into the eighth inning for his 14th victory before Rick Greene relieved him and earned his 14th save. Ogea said he was happy the pregame hoopla focused on Green.

Bertman, who has brought LSU to Omaha in five of the last six seasons, said this was the most talented team he has coached. It also was his most vexing.

Though the Tigers won a school-record 55 games, they couldn't get all the facets of their game—hitting, pitching and defense—in sync early in the year. They also made many more mistakes than Bertman expected from a team with five seniors.

"We made a lot of mental mistakes. We couldn't execute pickoff plays and bunt defense, which is unlike us," Bertman said. "It was very frustrating."

# 1991 NEWSMAKERS

Omaha-based **Creighton**, technically the host institution for the CWS, became the first Nebraska school to appear in the tournament. While the Bluejays went 0-8 against Missouri Valley Conference rival Wichita State, they still won a school-record 52 games while coach **Jim Hendry**, the Cubs' future general manager, was named Coach of the Year.

Fresno State righthander **Bobby Jones** was the nation's premier pitcher in 1991, leading the Bulldogs to a fifth-place finish at the CWS by going 16-2 1.88. He was second in the country in wins, first in complete games (18) and tied for the lead in innings (172) and strikeouts (166).

At No. 7, **Southern California** was the highest-ranked team in the Top 25 to not reach the CWS. The Trojans (46-17) ran away with the Pacific-10 Conference South, beating Stanford by six games, but the Trojans stumbled as the host team in the West I regional. The Pac-10 had dominated for years but did not have a representative in Omaha in 1991. California and Stanford also lost in regional play, and Arizona State, the preseason No. 1, struggled to a 12-18 conference record and 35-27 overall.

## FINAL TOP 25 FOR 1991

1. Louisiana State*
2. Wichita State*
3. Florida*
4. Clemson*
5. Florida State*
6. Creighton*
7. Southern California
8. Long Beach State*
9. Fresno State*
10. Texas
11. Cal State Northridge
12. Oklahoma State
13. Ohio State
14. Hawaii
15. Stanford
16. Miami
17. Pepperdine
18. Southwestern Louisiana
19. Texas A&M
20. Maine
21. North Carolina State
22. Notre Dame
23. California
24. Alabama
25. Southern Mississippi

\* Reached College World Series
\# Arizona State preseason No. 1

# IN RETROSPECT: 1991 DRAFT

**Top 10 Draft Picks From College**
With overall selection number (Ov), drafting team (Team) and rank on Baseball America draft board (BA).

| Player | Pos | School | Ov | Team | BA |
|---|---|---|---|---|---|
| Mike Kelly | OF | Arizona State | 2 | Braves | 2 |
| David McCarty | 1B | Stanford | 3 | Twins | 15 |
| John Burke* | RHP | Florida | 6 | Astros | 5 |
| Joe Vitiello | 1B | Alabama | 7 | Royals | 20 |
| Joey Hamilton | RHP | Georgia Southern | 8 | Padres | 4 |
| Mark Smith | OF | Southern California | 9 | Orioles | 3 |
| Tyler Green | RHP | Wichita State | 10 | Phillies | 10 |
| Doug Glanville | OF | Pennsylvania | 12 | Cubs | 22 |
| Eduardo Perez | 1B | Florida State | 17 | Angels | 18 |
| Allen Watson | LHP | New York Tech | 21 | Cardinals | 29 |

\* Did not sign

**Top 10 Major League Players From College Draft Class**
With draft round and Baseball-Reference.com total for wins above replacement (WAR) through 2019.

| Player | Pos | School | Rd | Ov | Team | WAR |
|---|---|---|---|---|---|---|
| Jeff Cirillo | 3B | Southern Calif. | 11 | 286 | Brewers | 34.6 |
| Steve Trachsel | RHP | Long Beach State | 8 | 215 | Cubs | 25.2 |
| Joe Randa | 3B | Tennessee | 11 | 288 | Royals | 21.4 |
| Aaron Sele | RHP | Washington State | 1 | 23 | Red Sox | 20.3 |
| Kirk Rueter | LHP | Murray State | 18 | 477 | Expos | 16.4 |
| Paul Byrd | RHP | Louisiana State | 4 | 112 | Indians | 16.2 |
| Joey Hamilton | RHP | Georgia Southern | 1 | 8 | Padres | 14.4 |
| Doug Glanville | OF | Pennsylvania | 1 | 12 | Cubs | 10.9 |
| Scott Hatteberg | 1B | Washington State | 1s | 43 | Red Sox | 10.1 |
| Darren Bragg | OF | Georgia Tech | 22 | 578 | Mariners | 8.9 |

So Bertman and assistant coaches Beetle Bailey and Smoke Laval junked a lot of the pickoff plays and bunt defenses.

"They told us to just go out and win, that this team had a lot of talent and we should take advantage of it," Ogea said. "They found a way to make us play in the system without realizing it."

The turning point of LSU's season may have come after an April 2 loss to McNeese State. Bertman gathered the team in right field and asked to lead the prayer the Tigers say together after each game. Bertman prayed that his players would stop chasing bad pitches, stop falling behind hitters, stop failing to advance runners, stop missing the cutoff man. The Tigers realized he was being facetious, but they got the message.

LSU survived a three-game sweep at the hands of Kentucky and won the SEC regular season title. The Tigers lost the SEC Tournament to Florida, but breezed through the South Regional and arrived at the CWS playing their best baseball of the year.

Omaha had treated the Tigers cruelly in the past. The first year they made it to the CWS was 1986, when both their losses were by one run. The same was true in 1987, and ESPN still shows the 10th-inning grand slam Stanford's Paul Carey hit off McDonald. In 1989, LSU lost to Miami's Joe Grahe and Texas' Kirk Dressendorfer, who now have major league addresses.

Last season, the Tigers were steamrolled by an Oklahoma State juggernaut that was upset by Georgia in the final. This time, destiny was with the Tigers.

"The last two years were like eating a cake with no icing," Johnson said. "This was like eating a cake with the icing." ∎

# Stanford's McCarty named top collegian

By **CASEY TEFERTILLER**

For David McCarty, being smart didn't just get him a ride to Stanford. It helped him learn from his one big mistake.

As a senior at Houston's Sharpstown High, McCarty put too much pressure on himself. After hitting .508 as a junior, he attempted to do too much as a senior. It cost him. He wasn't even drafted.

"I hit .397, and it was kind of disappointing," he said. "The year before, we were ranked second in the country and I was the only non-senior starter. I came back my senior year and tried to carry the team, and it just really screwed me up."

He learned his lesson. He entered 1991 as the first baseman on the preseason All-America team, but had no illusion of becoming a one-man band. Fittingly, McCarty enjoyed a superb season, hitting .420 with 24 home runs and 66 RBIs.

Not only did he carry his team, but he carried himself to the College Player of the Year award. This despite not becoming a top POY candidate until the second half.

Stanford's David McCarty doubled his home run output as a junior, and the Twins drafted him No. 3 overall. Though he played in parts of 11 big league seasons, McCarty never secured a regular role.

"I learned from my mistakes in high school. I matured as a ballplayer," McCarty said. "I learned to go up and swing for a home run every time, it's not going to happen. What I have to do is just go up and try to hit the ball hard. If I do that, the home runs are going to come."

McCarty makes it sound so simple. But with the draft looming and high expectations, performance pressure has done in more than a few juniors. McCarty is different.

"My approach toward the draft has been it's something out of my control," he said. "I didn't set any number goals. Sometimes you can set them too high, but you can also set them too low, and they limit you. My goal was just to make it back to Omaha and win (the College World Series). Unfortunately, we couldn't do that."

Stanford finished third at the West II Regional.

McCarty, who bats right and throws left, did make one major adjustment this year—he became a power hitter. After hitting 12 home runs in 1990, he doubled his output in '91.

"The big question mark on me was power," McCarty said. "I can kind of understand why, because I didn't put up the home run numbers, but I knew I could. I kind of questioned how the scouts doubted my power when my 12 home runs last year, none of them were cheap.

"Coming into this season, I knew that's what the scouts wanted to see. I knew that's what we needed, too. All I did was adjust my swing to get the ball in the air a little more—that and I started pulling the ball a little more."

Home runs were flying, not barely over fences but far into the distance. McCarty hit one into the soccer field beyond the left-field fence at Stanford's Sunken Diamond. His last of the year, in the regional at Fresno State, traveled an estimated at 450 feet.

At 6-foot-5, 210 pounds, McCarty has the lanky build of a power prodigy. He just had to wait for his time, when maturity and experience would enhance his ability.

"I think this last summer helped. I got used to seeing guys throwing in the upper 80s and into the 90s," McCarty said, referring to his experience with Team USA. "Coming back to school this year, it was almost like a step below."

Fresno State coach Bob Bennett saw the changes.

"The first time we saw him, I thought you could get him out with breaking balls," Bennett said. "And like most hitters, if you really pitched to him, you can get him. But if you really pitch to him now, he can still hit the ball."

McCarty hit .445 with Team USA last summer against the best pitching he had faced. That is what McCarty is all about, and in 1991 he played his best under pressure.

McCarty was smart enough to learn from his mistakes, and good enough to profit by his knowledge. For McCarty, a Stanford education came both in the classroom and on the field. ■

# TOP PLAYERS OF 1991

## ALL-AMERICA TEAM

| Pos | Player | School | Yr | AVG | AB | R | H | HR | RBI | SB |
|-----|--------|--------|----|-----|-----|---|---|----|-----|-----|
| C | Pedro Grifol | Florida State | Jr | .344 | 276 | 58 | 95 | 16 | 80 | 10 |
| 1B | David McCarty | Stanford | Jr | .420 | 238 | 71 | 100 | 24 | 66 | 4 |
| 2B | Steve Rodriguez | Pepperdine | So | .419 | 248 | 64 | 104 | 7 | 49 | 32 |
| 3B | Scott Stahoviak | Creighton | Jr | .449 | 267 | 87 | 120 | 13 | 74 | 16 |
| SS | Brent Gates | Minnesota | Jr | .412 | 221 | 53 | 91 | 8 | 60 | 10 |
| OF | Mark Smith | Southern California | Jr | .336 | 241 | 72 | 81 | 16 | 80 | 18 |
| OF | Mike Kelly | Arizona State | Jr | .373 | 233 | 66 | 87 | 15 | 56 | 23 |
| OF | Joe Vitiello | Alabama | Jr | .395 | 220 | 55 | 87 | 15 | 67 | 3 |
| DH | Mike Daniel | Oklahoma State | Sr | .350 | 226 | 67 | 79 | 27 | 107 | 4 |

| Pos | Pitcher | School | Yr | W | L | ERA | G | SV | IP | H | BB | SO |
|-----|---------|--------|----|---|---|-----|---|----|----|---|----|----|
| P | Bobby Jones | Fresno State | Jr | 16 | 2 | 1.88 | 21 | 0 | 172 | 112 | 36 | 166 |
| P | Kennie Steenstra | Wichita State | So | 17 | 0 | 2.17 | 20 | 0 | 141 | 129 | 31 | 82 |
| P | Craig Clayton | Cal State Northridge | Jr | 14 | 5 | 2.25 | 21 | 0 | 160 | 114 | 50 | 166 |
| P | Steve Whitaker | Long Beach State | Jr | 11 | 3 | 2.83 | 18 | 0 | 124 | 99 | 63 | 99 |
| P | John Burke | Florida | So | 9 | 5 | 2.25 | 18 | 0 | 104 | 69 | 47 | 135 |

## SECOND TEAM

**C**—Mike Durant, Ohio State. **1B**—Joe Ciccarella, Loyola Marymount. **2B**—Jimmy Crowley, Clemson. **3B**—Mike Edwards, Utah. **SS**—Chris Wimmer, Wichita State. **OF**—Mark Sweeney, Maine; Marty Neff, Oklahoma; and Damon Mashore, Arizona. **DH**—Andy Bruce, Georgia Tech. **P**—Jason Angel, Clemson; Bill Blanchette, Hawaii; Dave Tuttle, Santa Clara; Steve Trachsel, Long Beach State; and Chad Ogea, Louisiana State.

## THIRD TEAM

**C**—Doug Mirabelli, Wichita State. **1B**—Eduardo Perez, Florida State. **2B**—Brett Jenkins, Southern California. **3B**—Dan Cholowsky, California. **SS**—Craig Wilson, Kansas State. **OF**—Chris Roberts, Florida State; Jerrold Rountree, UC Santa Barbara; and Gene Schall, Villanova. **DH**—Greg Thomas, Vanderbilt. **P**—Ivan Zweig, Tulane; Jeff Granger, Texas A&M; Ken Kendrena, Cal State Northridge; John MacCauley, Evansville; and Tony Phillips, Southern Mississippi.

Pepperdine coach Andy Lopez poses with the College World Series championship trophy. The Waves won the title on their second ever trip to Omaha.

**1992**

# Pepperdine wins first CWS crown

By **JIM CALLIS**

Dan Melendez, Chris Sheff and Derek Wallace styled them-selves as the big men on campus when they arrived at Pepperdine in the fall of 1989.

All three had just helped the U.S. junior team win the world championship, and they had similar dreams of college glory. Pepperdine's veterans didn't know what to make of the guys who wore their Team USA jackets and boasted of one day winning the College World Series.

"When we first arrived at Pepperdine as freshmen, we were labeled as cocky, arrogant type of people," said Melendez, an All-America first baseman. "We said, 'Wait until we're juniors and see what we do.' People laughed at us, guys like Chris Martin and Jalal Leach. They'd say, 'You don't know college baseball yet. You're so naive.'

"We were. So many of us had never experienced failure."

Melendez and Co. would learn the taste of defeat. As freshman, they didn't get an NCAA Tournament bid. As sophomores, they fell apart in May, losing seven of their last nine games and going 0-2 at the West I Regional.

"Wait until we're juniors . . ."

That's what those arrogant, cocky freshmen said, and they backed it up. They won the national title June 6 by beating Cal State Fullerton 3-2 before a final game-record crowd of 17,962 at Rosenblatt Stadium.

It was the first CWS championship for Pepperdine, which had been to Omaha only once before, in 1979. By winning the title, the Waves proved something to themselves and to the NCAA baseball committee.

This year's team had basically the same personnel as the one that collapsed last season. The difference, Pepperdine coach Andy Lopez said, was the players realized how good they were. It's one thing to boast, another to believe.

"I really don't think they were self-confident last year," Lopez said. "They were a tal-ented team, but the intangible every great team has is self-confidence."

**FROM THE ISSUE:**
JULY 10, 1992

---

## TOP TEAMS
### 1992 COLLEGE WORLD SERIES STANDINGS

| School | Conference | Record | CWS | Head Coach |
|---|---|---|---|---|
| Pepperdine | West Coast | 48–11–1 | 4–0 | Andy Lopez |
| Cal State Fullerton | Big West | 46–17 | 4–2 | Augie Garrido |
| Miami | Independent | 55–10 | 2–2 | Ron Fraser |
| Texas | Southwest | 48–17 | 2–2 | Cliff Gustafson |
| Florida State | Atlantic Coast | 49–21 | 1–2 | Mike Martin |
| Oklahoma | Big Eight | 43–24 | 1–2 | Larry Cochell |
| California | Pacific-10 | 35–28 | 0–2 | Bob Milano |
| Wichita State | Missouri Valley | 56–11 | 0–2 | Gene Stephenson |

### NATIONAL CHAMPION
**PEPPERDINE**

Pepperdine claimed its first national title in its second-ever trip to Omaha. The Waves defeated Cal State Fullerton 3-2 in the championship game, the first ever featuring two teams from the same state. This was the last CWS with-out SEC representation.

"I think the minute we stepped on the field in September, from that point on we knew we were going to do something special this year," Melendez said. "We didn't know it was going to end like this, though."

As Pepperdine swept through the CWS undefeated in four games, Lopez and his players dodged discussion about why the team was ranked No. 3 in the nation but seeded seventh among the eight teams in Omaha by the baseball committee. After the victory, Lopez admitted his team was inspired by what it perceived as a lack of respect for Pepperdine and the West Coast Conference.

"I think we were looked upon as, 'They had a great season, but . . . ' " Lopez said. "We came in here as a seventh seed, and I'll say it now, our guys took it as a slap in the face."

No lower seed ever has won the CWS. Stanford was seeded seventh in 1988, the first year the current two-bracket format was used.

The championship game also was historic as the first to feature two teams from the same state. The Pepperdine and Fullerton campuses sit just 60 miles apart in Southern California. Scheduling difficulties prevented the traditional rivals from playing during the regular season, but they staged a game worth the wait.

Against Fullerton, the Waves used the same formula that worked against Wichita State once and Texas twice: outstanding pitching, outstanding fielding and timely hitting.

Pepperdine scored a pair of two-out runs in the top of the first inning, then turned over the lead to All-American Patrick Ahearne. Ahearne, the Orel Hershiser clone who kicked off the Waves' record 24-inning scoreless streak at the start of the tournament, gave up only an unearned run in the bottom of the fourth.

The Waves extended their lead to 3-1 in the fifth in most unexpected fashion. Shortstop Eric Ekdahl, a .227 hitter who hadn't hit a home run all season and was 1-for-12 in the

# 1992 NEWSMAKERS

After successful tournaments as a demonstration sport at both the 1984 and '88 Olympics, baseball was awarded full-medal status for the **1992 Olympics** in Barcelona. As in the past two events, the U.S. fielded a college all-star squad Cuba, which had boycotted the two previous Olympics, stormed to the gold medal; Team USA placed fourth.

Coach **Ron Fraser**, who built **Miami** into a national power and did more than anyone to elevate the national profile of college baseball through its innovative tactics and promotional flair, retired after the 1992 CWS. Fraser coached Miami for 30 seasons and finished with 1,271 victories, second only to USC's Rod Dedeaux. Fraser subsequently led Team USA to a disappointing fourth-place finish in the 1992 Barcelona Olympics.

Indiana shortstop **Mike Smith** became the first Division I player to win a triple crown since the NCAA began tracking statistics in 1965. Smith, a senior, hit .490—finishing .0004 percentage points ahead of Maryland's Derek Hacopian—while slamming 27 homers and driving in 95 runs..

## FINAL TOP 25 FOR 1992

1. Pepperdine*
2. Cal State Fullerton*
3. #Miami*
4. Texas*
5. Wichita State*
6. Louisiana State
7. Clemson
8. Oklahoma State
9. Florida State*
10. Oklahoma*
11. Stanford
12. Hawaii
13. Arizona
14. California*
15. Notre Dame
16. Florida
17. Long Beach State
18. South Carolina
19. Texas A&M
20. North Carolina State
21. UCLA
22. Georgia Tech
23. Western Carolina
24. Virginia Commonwealth
25. South Alabama

* Reached College World Series
# Preseason No. 1

# IN RETROSPECT: 1992 DRAFT

**Top 10 Draft Picks From College**
With overall selection number (Ov), drafting team (Team) and rank on Baseball America draft board (BA).

| Player | Pos | School | Ov | Team | BA |
|---|---|---|---|---|---|
| Phil Nevin | 3B | Cal State Fullerton | 1 | Astros | 1 |
| Paul Shuey | RHP | North Carolina | 2 | Indians | 2 |
| B.J. Wallace | LHP | Mississippi State | 3 | Expos | 10 |
| Jeffrey Hammonds | OF | Stanford | 4 | Orioles | 4 |
| Chad Mottola | OF | Central Florida | 5 | Reds | 13 |
| Calvin Murray | OF | Texas | 7 | Giants | 22 |
| Pete Janicki | RHP | UCLA | 8 | Angels | 14 |
| Michael Tucker | SS | Longwood (Va.) | 10 | Royals | 3 |
| Derek Wallace | RHP | Pepperdine | 11 | Cubs | 8 |
| Kenny Felder | OF | Florida State | 12 | Brewers | 28 |

**Top 10 Major League Players From College Draft Class**
With draft round and Baseball-Reference.com total for wins above replacement (WAR) through 2019.

| Player | Pos | School | Rd | Ov | Team | WAR |
|---|---|---|---|---|---|---|
| Jason Giambi | 1B | Long Beach State | 2 | 58 | Athletics | 50.5 |
| Jon Lieber | RHP | South Alabama | 2 | 44 | Royals | 24.3 |
| Bobby Higginson | OF | Temple | 12 | 336 | Tigers | 23.1 |
| Charles Johnson | C | Miami | 1 | 28 | Marlins | 22.6 |
| Craig Counsell | 2B | Notre Dame | 11 | 319 | Rockies | 22.4 |
| Rick Helling | RHP | Stanford | 1 | 22 | Rangers | 20.3 |
| Rich Aurilia | SS | St. John's | 24 | 678 | Rangers | 18.2 |
| Phil Nevin | 3B | Cal State Fullerton | 1 | 1 | Astros | 15.9 |
| Scott Karl | LHP | Hawaii | 6 | 164 | Brewers | 8.7 |
| Jeffrey Hammonds | OF | Stanford | 1 | 4 | Orioles | 8.6 |

College World Series, lined a Paco Chavez pitch through a stiff wind and into the left field bleachers.

"What a great time to have it," Ekdahl said. "I had an almost numb feeling, I hit it so well. Just trotting around the bases, I was numb."

After Wallace relieved Ahearne and quelled a Fullerton rally in the seventh, the Titans made another run in the eighth. All-America closer Steve Montgomery hit Nate Rodriguez and Jeremy Carr to lead off the inning before Chris Powell bunted the tying runs into scoring position.

Montgomery intentionally walked Phil Nevin, the first CWS Most Outstanding Player in from a losing team since Minnesota's Dave Winfield in 1973, to load the bases. Jason Moler hit a sacrifice fly to cut the lead to 3-2 as Carr went to third base.

Tony Banks then smashed a fastball between first and second base that seemed destined to tie the game.

"Off the bat, I thought it was a routine ground ball," Montgomery said. "Then I turned around and saw Steve leave his feet, and it was pretty shocking."

But destiny favored the Waves. All-America second baseman Steve Rodriguez dived to his left, caught the ball cleanly on a true hop and threw Banks out.

"There's no better feeling," Rodriguez said. "When I caught the ground ball, I said, 'Oh, my God!' Then I saw everybody jumping for joy in the dugout."

One inning later, Rodriguez squeezed a Bret Hemphill pop-up to end the game and empty the Pepperdine dugout onto the field. Somewhere, Chris Martin and Jalal Leach must have been smiling. ∎

# Nevin matures into top talent

By **JIM CALLIS**

Phil Nevin suffered an identity crisis in 1991.

"Sometimes he tried to be the coach, sometimes he tried to be the general manager, sometimes he tried to be the chief of umpires," said Augie Garrido, Nevin's coach at Cal State Fullerton. "But it was always for all the right reasons. We just wanted to put him in the framework of who he wanted to be."

This season, Nevin concentrated on just being the Titans' third baseman, and it showed. He hit .402 with 22 home runs and 86 RBIs, was named the College Player of the Year and was the No. 1 pick in the draft by the Astros.

The main thing Nevin needed was maturity. Last season, he slumped to .335-3-46 after batting .358-14-52 as a Freshman All-American in 1990. Nevin said he tried to do too much, and as a result did too little. He became frustrated that both he

Phil Nevin matured as a Cal State Fullerton junior, hitting .390 with 22 homers and went No. 1 overall in the draft. He didn't find big league success until he was 28 but went on to mash 208 home runs.

and the Titans were underachieving, and left a trail of thrown helmets and harsh words for umpires in his wake.

He hit bottom during the summer. After Team USA featured him on the cover of its media guide, Nevin hit .179. He sparred with U.S. head coach Ron Polk and didn't make the cut for the Pan American Games.

"I don't dislike Phil Nevin," said Polk, the coach at Mississippi State. "But he wasn't a team player when he wasn't playing. I'm glad to hear Phil has had an attitude adjustment. He's a great talent."

When Nevin returned to Fullerton in the fall, he had a talk with Titans catcher Jason Moler. Moler has tossed a few batting helmets of his own.

"We had a problem letting our temper get to us," said Moler, who like Nevin was invited to try out for the U.S. Olympic team this summer. "We talked about those things, and we made a commitment to not let each other do it. He's been 100 percent better. I haven't seen him go off all year, and he's had the opportunity."

Nevin rededicated himself during the offseason, adding 15 pounds with a weightlifting program. The added bulk and his controlled intensity produced a Big West Conference triple crown season.

"What really turned it around for him in my mind is that he accepted baseball as a trade," Garrido said. " 'Baseball is my trade, and I have to serve an apprenticeship and learn my skills.' That is where he found the sanctuary to block out the pressure."

Teams stopped challenging Nevin at midseason, and except for one series against Long Beach State, he didn't let it bother him. Teams at the South I Regional in Baton Rouge adopted the same strategy, and he was content to serve as a tablesetter.

Once arriving in Omaha, Nevin continued to show patience. He was confronted with a lot more than the College World Series.

As the College Player of the Year and the projected No. 1 overall draft pick, he conducted as many print, radio and television interviews in one weekend as anyone on the presidential campaign trail.

Pressure? Nevin scoffed at the word.

"A big reason why I've had success this year is that I stayed focused on playing baseball," he said. "The other things that come with it, I've been able to put aside when I stepped on the field. There's more going on now, but I came to college wanting to win a College World Series and that's why I'm here."

If there was any question where Nevin's concentration was, he answered it with a grand slam and six RBIs in a 7-2 win against Florida State in Fullerton's first game.

Growing up was all Nevin had to do.

Once he stopped trying to fulfill all the other roles, he found one he could excel at and enjoy: himself. ■

# TOP PLAYERS OF 1992

## ALL-AMERICA TEAM

| Pos | Player | School | Yr | AVG | AB | R | H | HR | RBI | SB |
|-----|--------|--------|----|----|----|----|----|----|----|----|
| C | Jason Varitek | Georgia Tech | So | .406 | 212 | 54 | 86 | 11 | 52 | 2 |
| 1B | Doug Hecker | Tennessee | Jr | .351 | 174 | 41 | 61 | 12 | 55 | 5 |
| 2B | Brian Eldridge | Oklahoma | Sr | .382 | 225 | 65 | 86 | 23 | 77 | 13 |
| 3B | Phil Nevin | Cal State Fullerton | Jr | .402 | 219 | 73 | 88 | 22 | 86 | 7 |
| SS | Craig Wilson | Kansas State | Sr | .416 | 209 | 54 | 87 | 8 | 62 | 5 |
| OF | Jeffrey Hammonds | Stanford | Jr | .370 | 184 | 40 | 70 | 6 | 33 | 33 |
| OF | Chad McConnell | Creighton | Jr | .400 | 220 | 68 | 88 | 14 | 73 | 29 |
| OF | Calvin Murray | Texas | Jr | .351 | 268 | 74 | 94 | 4 | 42 | 47 |
| DH | Troy Penix | California | Jr | .360 | 247 | 55 | 89 | 22 | 79 | 0 |

| Pos | Pitcher | School | Yr | W | L | ERA | G | SV | IP | H | BB | SO |
|-----|---------|--------|----|----|----|----|----|----|----|----|----|----|
| P | Patrick Ahearne | Pepperdine | Sr | 15 | 2 | 2.40 | 21 | 0 | 143 | 103 | 32 | 127 |
| P | Jeff Alkire | Miami | Sr | 14 | 3 | 2.62 | 20 | 0 | 131 | 106 | 42 | 121 |
| P | Darren Dreifort | Wichita State | So | 6 | 2 | 1.76 | 24 | 12 | 81 | 52 | 22 | 92 |
| P | Lloyd Peever | Louisiana State | Jr | 14 | 0 | 1.98 | 17 | 0 | 105 | 67 | 20 | 116 |
| P | Mike Romano | Tulane | So | 17 | 4 | 2.40 | 23 | 1 | 165 | 134 | 70 | 174 |

## SECOND TEAM

C—Bobby Hughes, Southern California. 1B—Dan Melendez, Pepperdine. 2B—Todd Walker, Louisiana State. 3B—Mike Gulan, Kent State. SS—Chris Wimmer, Wichita State. OF—Todd Dreifort, Wichita State; John LaMar, Indiana State; and Kevin Northrup, Clemson. DH—Derek Hacopian, Maryland. P—Roger Bailey, Florida State; Matt Donahue, North Carolina State; Benji Grigsby, San Diego State; Scott Karl, Hawaii; and B.J. Wallace, Mississippi State.

## THIRD TEAM

C—Doug Mirabelli, Wichita State. 1B—Ryan McGuire, UCLA. 2B—Steve Rodriguez, Pepperdine. 3B—Chris Snopek, Mississippi. SS—Mike Smith, Indiana. OF—Chad Mottola, Central Florida; Papo Ramos, Southwestern Louisiana; and Chris Roberts, Florida State. DH—Dan Kopriva, Louisville. P—Alan Benes, Creighton; Javi DeJesus, Southwestern Louisiana; Pete Janicki, UCLA; Jon Lieber, South Alabama; and Steve Montgomery, Pepperdine.

**1993**

Louisiana State sophomore second baseman Todd Walker delivered a series of big hits to win Most Outstanding Player honors at the College World Series.

# LSU prevails in breathtaking CWS

By **JIM CALLIS**

College World Series? No, this was the Cardiac World Series.

"If I have a heart attack before I get home," Louisiana State second baseman Todd Walker said, "I wouldn't be surprised."

Walker made those comments before his heart endured the exhilaration of the Tigers' second national title in three seasons. LSU beat Wichita State 8-0 in a June 12 championship game rematch of the 1991 CWS final, when the Tigers beat the Shockers 6-3.

What the finale lacked in drama, the rest of the 1993 CWS more than made up for. There were so many comebacks. Just twice in 14 games did a team score first and hold its lead throughout the game.

**FROM THE ISSUE:**
JULY 12-25, 1993

"This has been the greatest comeback Series I can ever recall all the times I've been here," said Skip Bertman, who has made 11 trips to Omaha. "Especially the low percentage types of comebacks."

There were two game-winning rallies in the seventh inning, four in the eighth, two in the ninth and one in the 11th, all against some of college baseball's best pitchers. All-Americans Marc Barcelo, Daniel Choi and Brooks Kieschnick would have felt right at home, because CWS relievers blew all five save opportunities they were handed.

All in all, there were more resurrections than a George Romero film festival. Except Hollywood wouldn't buy these scripts.

LSU rose from the dead twice after scoring seven runs in its last three innings to beat Long Beach State 7-1 and snap Choi's 14-game winning streak in its opener. Two players provided clutch hits throughout: center fielder Armando Rios and Walker.

Besides batting lefthanded, they share little in common. Rios is a senior who wasn't drafted this year. But he rebounded from a .239 junior season to hit .319-9-61 with 20 stolen bases, and he's a flashy player who can win a game in several ways.

Walker will be one of the top college players drafted next year. More reserved than Rios, he doesn't leave much of an impression until he steps in the batter's box. And oh, what an

---

## TOP TEAMS
### 1993 COLLEGE WORLD SERIES STANDINGS

| School | Conference | Record | CWS | Head Coach |
|---|---|---|---|---|
| Louisiana State | Southeastern | 53–17–1 | 4–1 | Skip Bertman |
| Wichita State | Missouri Valley | 58–17 | 3–1 | Gene Stephenson |
| Long Beach State | Big West | 46–19 | 3–2 | Dave Snow |
| Oklahoma State | Big Eight | 45–17 | 2–2 | Gary Ward |
| Texas | Southwest | 51–16 | 1–2 | Cliff Gustafson |
| Texas A&M | Southwest | 53–11 | 1–2 | Mark Johnson |
| Arizona State | Pacific-10 | 46–20 | 0–2 | Jim Brock |
| Kansas | Big Eight | 45–18 | 0–2 | Dave Bingham |

## NATIONAL CHAMPION
### LOUISIANA STATE

The Tigers downed Wichita State for the second time in three years to capture the CWS title. Louisiana State blanked the Shockers 8-0 in the championship game, punctuating both their dominance in Omaha and in the rugged Southeastern Conference.

impression that is.

Walker hit .400-12-76 to earn Freshman of the Year honors in 1992 and batted .395-22-102 this season. His RBI total established LSU and Southeastern Conference marks and helped him break Albert Belle's school record for career RBIs in just his second season.

In LSU's second game, Rios and Walker had the big hits in a sudden six-run rally in the bottom of the eighth that toppled top seed Texas A&M 13-8. Rios singled in the go-ahead run and Walker iced the game with a grand slam, his first hit in eight CWS at-bats.

In the next contest, Rios tied the game with an RBI single and scored the go-ahead run in a six-run sixth inning that gave LSU an 8-5 lead and pushed Long Beach State to the brink of elimination. But the 49ers answered with a four-run counterpunch in the bottom of the eighth, setting up a third showdown.

Long Beach State scored two unearned runs in the top of the ninth to take a 5-3 lead, and ace reliever Gabe Gonzalez needed just three outs for the 49ers to maker their final championship-game appearance. But no lead was safe in this CWS.

With one out, Rios doubled to left-center to plate the tying runs, and two batters later Walker hit a smash off first baseman John Swanson's glove to complete a 6-5 miracle. Walker's single completed a 4-for-5 day that also included a homer and muffled talk of his 1-for-11 CWS start.

The differences between LSU's two clutch hitters were evident again on the game's final play. As Walker raced intently to first, Rios trotted home, arms outstretched, then hurled his batting helmet onto the home plate screen.

Rios, a hero in the 1991 CWS when he homered, scored two runs and drove in two in the finale. Walker and Rios continued to hit in the championship game. While standing in the batter's box in the bottom of the first, Walker tried to call time. Umpire Jim Garman

## 1993 NEWSMAKERS

Led by Wichita State righthander **Darren Dreifort**, who went 10-1, 2.23 in 93 innings in a unique role as a long reliever, college pitchers dominated the 1993 draft like never before. Dreifort went No. 2 overall to the Dodgers, and 14 of the first 28 picks were college arms, including five of the first six.

Traditional power **Miami** had a difficult adjustment in its first season after the retirement of coach **Ron Fraser**. It went just 36-22 and was eliminated in two straight games in the South regional. Moreover, the Hurricanes had to deal with the lingering aftereffects of Hurricane Andrew, which devastated the Miami area in the fall of 1992, and the emergence of the Marlins as a major league expansion franchise. Miami's attendance fell drastically in the wake of all those developments. First-year coach Brad Kelley, Fraser's pitching coach for eight years, resigned under fire after a three-month investigation determined he was seen drinking in public with one of his players. **Jim Morris** took over the Miami coaching reins in 1994, leaving a Georgia Tech club that would be ranked No. 1 nationally to begin that season.

### FINAL TOP 25 FOR 1993

1. #Louisiana State*
2. Texas A&M*
3. Arizona State*
4. Wichita State*
5. Long Beach State*
6. Oklahoma State*
7. Texas*
8. Georgia Tech
9. Arizona
10. Kansas*
11. North Carolina State
12. Pepperdine
13. Cal State Fullerton
14. Fresno State
15. Florida State
16. Notre Dame
17. Clemson
18. Tennessee
19. Southern California
20. UCLA
21. North Carolina
22. Ohio State
23. Baylor
24. Auburn
25. South Carolina

* Reached College World Series
# Preseason No. 1

# IN RETROSPECT: 1993 DRAFT

## Top 10 Draft Picks From College
With overall selection number (Ov), drafting team (Team) and rank on Baseball America draft board (BA).

| Player | Pos | School | Ov | Team | BA |
|---|---|---|---|---|---|
| Darren Dreifort | RHP | Wichita State | 2 | Dodgers | 1 |
| Brian Anderson | LHP | Wright State | 3 | Angels | 3 |
| Wayne Gomes | RHP | Old Dominion | 4 | Phillies | 4 |
| Jeff Granger | LHP | Texas A&M | 5 | Royals | 5 |
| Steve Soderstrom | RHP | Fresno State | 6 | Giants | 6 |
| Brooks Kieschnick | OF | Texas | 10 | Cubs | 30 |
| Daron Kirkreit | RHP | UC Riverside | 11 | Indians | 16 |
| Billy Wagner | LHP | Ferrum (Va.) | 12 | Astros | 11 |
| Alan Benes | RHP | Creighton | 16 | Cardinals | 10 |
| Scott Christman | LHP | Oregon State | 17 | White Sox | 17 |

## Top 10 Major League Players From College Draft Class
With draft round and Baseball-Reference.com total for wins above replacement (WAR) through 2019.

| Player | Pos | School | Rd | Ov | Team | WAR |
|---|---|---|---|---|---|---|
| Billy Wagner | LHP | Ferrum (Va.) | 1 | 12 | Astros | 27.7 |
| Bill Mueller | 3B | Missouri State | 15 | 414 | Giants | 23.9 |
| Mark Loretta | 2B | Northwestern | 7 | 207 | Brewers | 19.4 |
| Paul Lo Duca | C | Arizona State | 25 | 690 | Dodgers | 17.9 |
| Brian Moehler | RHP | UNC Greensboro | 6 | 165 | Tigers | 10.8 |
| Brian Anderson | LHP | Wright State | 1 | 3 | Angels | 10.0 |
| Steve Kline | LHP | West Virginia | 8 | 223 | Indians | 9.9 |
| Mike Sirotka | LHP | Louisiana State | 15 | 425 | White Sox | 9.9 |
| Chris Singleton | OF | Nevada | 2 | 48 | Giants | 9.7 |
| Scott Spiezio | 1B | Illinois | 6 | 181 | Athletics | 8.8 |

denied the request, so Walker swung away and hit a two-run homer on his way to a 2-for-4, three-RBI day and Most Outstanding Player honors. Rios contributed four RBIs.

Though LSU has ridden offense to two national titles—the Tigers scored 42 runs in five CWS games this year, and 48 in four games two years ago—and produced Albert Belle, the school still is known primarily for its pitchers. Bertman has sent six pitchers from Baton Rouge to the major leagues, most notably Ben McDonald, and a slew of former Tigers are working their way through the minors.

That tradition isn't dead at LSU, as Mike Sirotka and Brett Laxton showed in Omaha. Sirotka, a senior lefthander who went 11-0 for the 1991 champions, beat Long Beach State twice in two starts, though he did give up the game-winning homer in the 49ers' come-back victory. In the dramatic 6-5 Tigers win, Sirotka threw 152 pitches while battling through five LSU errors and stranding 13 runners, 11 in scoring position.

Bertman called it the gutsiest pitching performance he had seen in 30 years and, after LSU won the championship, the biggest victory in 100 years of Tigers baseball.

Bertman hoped to use Sirotka in the championship game but had to pitch him in the West Bracket finale. So Bertman handed the ball to Laxton, the Freshman of the Year. Overpowering the Shockers mainly with fastballs, he provided the only drama in an otherwise ho-hum finale that saw the Tigers grab a 7-0 lead after three innings.

Laxton fanned pinch-hitter Tony Mills in the ninth inning for his 16th strikeout, breaking the championship-game record set by Arizona State's Tom Burgess in 1967. He became the first pitcher to spin a shutout in the finale since Southern California's Jim Withers in 1961. ∎

# Kieschnick wins top college honor

By **JIM CALLIS**

Thanks to a bad-hop double, some clutch hitting and the usual dose of Brooks Kieschnick, the Texas Longhorns had just disposed of Southern California to win the Central II Regional.

As is the custom, a microphone was placed at home plate for Texas coach Cliff Gustafson. After his usual routine of saluting his team and the Disch-Falk Stadium fans, Gustafson broke from tradition.

"I don't usually do this," Gustafson said, "but one of the truly great players to ever wear a Longhorn uniform probably played his last game at Disch-Falk today, and I'd like him to come up here."

Kieschnick, the College Player of the Year, needed no introduction. In typical fashion, he had saved the USC clincher with an inning of perfect relief, the day after shutting down the Trojans for 7.1 innings in the key game of the regional.

Brooks Kieschnick set a Texas program record for home runs but was equally celebrated as a pitcher. He resumed pitching in 2003 as he tried to prolong an undistinguished six-year big league career.

His bat was somewhat silent, only because going 6-for-16 with four doubles and four RBIs was slightly below his lofty standards.

But the Central II Regional finally may have revealed a Kieschnick weakness. He wavered as he approached the microphone, and all he could say was, "You're the best fans I've ever played in front of."

He concluded by giving the 7,401 Longhorns diehards a Hook-'em Horns sign with his right hand, and was in tears by the time he returned to the Texas dugout.

Unfortunately for Longhorns opponents, the 6-foot-4, 219-pound Kieschnick doesn't have to say much on the field. His results speak for themselves.

Kieschnick batted .374, primarily as a DH, with 19 home runs, 27 doubles and 81 RBIs. A righthander, he also went 16-4, 3.25 with 126 strikeouts in 155 innings. Considering what Kieschnick has done in three seasons, he's one of the best college players ever. He has been named Southwest Conference player of the year three times in three seasons.

Rice coach Wayne Graham said Kieschnick and Frank Thomas are the best college hitters he has ever seen. Baylor coach Mickey Sullivan said Kieschnick was the best hitter he had seen in the last 40 years, then revised that appraisal after watching Kieschnick smack a ball 470 feet for the longest homer in Ferrell Field history.

"He may be the best in the last 50 years," said Sullivan, who still holds the SWC record with a .519 batting average in 1954.

Texas has produced 72 major league players, and Gustafson has had his share of greats. None better, he said, than Kieschnick.

"I wouldn't call him the best pure hitter, but I'd call him the best power hitter, and I think the record shows that," Gustafson says. "I won't call him the best pitcher, but he's among the best. But in terms of doing both, he's the best we've had."

Sports information director/historian/radio broadcaster Bill Little also arrived at Texas in 1968. He said the only two-way player who compared to Kieschnick was Dave Winfield.

"The difference between Brooks and Winfield was that Winfield was the epitome of the athlete," Little said. "Brooks is almost a throwback to the ballplayer of another era."

Kieschnick is John Wayne in burnt orange. A man of few words, concerned about getting the job done and not caring if he looks pretty doing it. His intensity is on a par with that of former Longhorn Roger Clemens. But where Clemens only pitched every few days, Kieschnick maintains a burning desire each game.

He has been known to curse umpires, and even opposing pitchers if they refuse to challenge him. He once got kicked off a Little League team temporarily after he punched an opponent.

"I've always been real intense in any sport I've played," Kieschnick said. "It comes from the love of the game. I don't want to lose. If I'm playing chess, I want to win because I hate to lose. Show me a good loser, and I'll show you a loser." ■

# TOP PLAYERS OF 1993

## ALL-AMERICA TEAM

| Pos | Player | School | Yr | AVG | AB | R | H | HR | RBI | SB |
|-----|--------|--------|----|-----|----|----|----|----|-----|----|
| C | Jason Varitek | Georgia Tech | Jr | .404 | 228 | 78 | 92 | 22 | 72 | 5 |
| 1B | Ryan McGuire | UCLA | Jr | .376 | 221 | 71 | 83 | 26 | 91 | 14 |
| 2B | Todd Walker | Louisiana State | So | .395 | 276 | 85 | 109 | 22 | 102 | 14 |
| 3B | Antone Williamson | Arizona State | So | .378 | 275 | 71 | 104 | 14 | 85 | 2 |
| SS | Mark Loretta | Northwestern | Sr | .408 | 184 | 38 | 75 | 3 | 34 | 20 |
| OF | Eric Danapillis | Notre Dame | Sr | .438 | 219 | 71 | 96 | 13 | 85 | 13 |
| OF | Brooks Kieschnick | Texas | Jr | .374 | 257 | 76 | 96 | 19 | 81 | 3 |
| OF | Pat Watkins | East Carolina | Jr | .445 | 220 | 63 | 98 | 19 | 57 | 29 |
| DH | Paul Lo Duca | Arizona State | Jr | .446 | 289 | 63 | 129 | 14 | 88 | 0 |

| Pos | Pitcher | School | Yr | W | L | ERA | G | SV | IP | H | BB | SO |
|-----|---------|--------|----|----|----|-----|----|----|----|----|----|----|
| P | Brian Anderson | Wright State | Jr | 10 | 1 | 1.14 | 14 | 1 | 95 | 62 | 6 | 98 |
| P | Daniel Choi | Long Beach State | So | 17 | 2 | 2.57 | 20 | 0 | 147 | 116 | 52 | 116 |
| P | Darren Dreifort | Wichita State | Jr | 11 | 1 | 2.48 | 30 | 4 | 102 | 67 | 34 | 120 |
| P | Jeff Granger | Texas A&M | Jr | 15 | 3 | 2.62 | 20 | 0 | 127 | 87 | 54 | 150 |
| P | John Powell | Auburn | Jr | 15 | 5 | 2.81 | 24 | 0 | 141 | 102 | 41 | 191 |

## SECOND TEAM

C—Casey Burrill, Southern California. 1B—Braxton Hickman, Texas. 2B—Mark Merila, Minnesota. 3B—George Arias, Arizona. SS—Gabe Alvarez, Southern California. OF—Brian Banks, Brigham Young; Vee Hightower, Vanderbilt; and Dante Powell, Cal State Fullerton. DH—Jason Thompson, Arizona. P—Scott Christman, Oregon State; Steve Duda, Pepperdine; Brooks Kieschnick, Texas; Brett Laxton, Louisiana State; and Brad Rigby, Georgia Tech.

## THIRD TEAM

C—Willie Morales, Arizona. 1B—Todd Helton, Tennessee. 2B—Jeff Berblinger, Kansas. 3B—Gerad Cawhorn, San Jose State. SS—David Smith, Le Moyne. OF—Todd Greene, Georgia Southern; Marc Sagmoen, Nebraska; and Brian Thomas, Texas A&M. DH—Pat Clougherty, North Carolina State. P—Marc Barcelo, Arizona State; Troy Brohawn, Nebraska; Dan Hubbs, Southern California; Trey Moore, Texas A&M; and Jimmy Walker, Kansas

Oklahoma coach Larry Cochell guided a deep, fundamentally-sound Sooners team that was short on starpower all the way to a College World Series championship.

**1994**

# Sooners win Series
# as a team

By **JIM CALLIS**

It's a fact of life at the College World Series that the best team doesn't always win the championship.

Just ask Arizona State, which lost the 1988 championship game to Stanford, a team they had beaten five times in six regular season meetings. Or ask the Cardinal, who entered the 1990 CWS ranked No. 1 with a team featuring four future first-round draft picks, and then watched Mike Mussina lose twice to Georgia's Mike Rebhan, who never played pro ball.

But 1994 was the exception that proves the rule. Oklahoma was the best team in Omaha, and won its first national title since 1951 by crushing Georgia Tech 13-5 in the championship game on June 11.

**FROM THE ISSUE:**
JULY 11-24, 1994

On paper, the Sooners didn't appear very daunting. They weren't ranked in any pre-season poll, and entered Omaha ranked No. 10 by Baseball America. They didn't win the Big Eight Conference regular season or tournament championships.

Twelve CWS players made one of BA's three All-America teams chosen before the tournament, none from Oklahoma. Counting supplemental picks, nine CWS players were first-round choices in the draft, and again not one was a Sooner.

The other seven teams in Omaha might have had more recognizable stars, but none of them could match Oklahoma's depth.

The Sooners had a lineup with eight tough outs, a defense that routinely made difficult plays look easy and a pitching staff with a quality ace, a quality closer and quality middle relief. They were the one team that almost flawlessly executed bunts, bunt defenses, steals, hit-and-runs and double plays in a CWS marred by 49 errors in 13 games. As a result, Oklahoma won all four of its games, trailing for a grand total of one inning.

Now they have the acclaim they felt they deserved all along. Sooners coach Larry Cochell and his staff used the preseason rankings to motivate their team, hanging signs in each player's locker.

Here's a quick look at some of the players who delivered the national championship:

## TOP TEAMS
### 1994 COLLEGE WORLD SERIES STANDINGS

| School | Conference | Record | cWS | Head Coach |
|--------|-----------|--------|-----|-----------|
| Oklahoma | Big Eight | 50–17 | 4–0 | Larry Cochell |
| Georgia Tech | Atlantic Coast | 50–17 | 3–1 | Danny Hall |
| Arizona State | Pacific-10 | 45–18 | 2–2 | Jim Brock |
| Cal State Fullerton | Big West | 47–16 | 2–2 | Augie Garrido |
| Florida State | Atlantic Coast | 53–22 | 1–2 | Mike Martin |
| Miami | Independent | 49–14 | 1–2 | Jim Morris |
| Auburn | Southeastern | 44–21 | 0–2 | Hal Baird |
| Louisiana State | Southeastern | 46–20 | 0–2 | Skip Bertman |

### NATIONAL CHAMPION
### OKLAHOMA

The Sooners romped Georgia Tech 13-5 in the championship game despite an unassuming résumé. Oklahoma didn't rank in the preseason top 25, they ranked 10th heading into Omaha and didn't win the Big Eight regular season or tournament.

Sophomore lefthander Mark Redman. Coming out of high school, the deeply religious Redman spent his freshman year at The Master's College, a private Christian NAIA school in Newhall, Calif. Last summer he pitched for the National Baseball Congress World Series champion Kenai Peninsula Oilers.

He added another championship by winning two games in the Central Regional and two more in Omaha, beating Auburn 5-4 in the opener and Arizona State 6-1 in the game that put the Sooners in the final.

Redman tied for second in Division I in victories by finishing 14-3, 2.71 with 136 strike-outs in 135 innings. He was shocked to not get an invitation to try out for Team USA this summer, after participating in a preliminary camp last November and then posting his big numbers this season. If the United States has better lefthanders than Redman, this will be a big summer for Team USA.

Junior closer Bucky Buckles. His name prompted jokes in Omaha, but the laugh-ing stopped when he took the mound. He saved Oklahoma's first and last victories, and picked up a victory with three innings of scoreless relief in a pivotal 4-3, 11-inning win against Arizona State in the second round.

Buckles had hoped to play for the Sun Devils after spending two seasons at San Diego City Community College, but he didn't make the necessary grades last fall at Mesa (Ariz.) Community College. His dad originally wanted him to go to Oklahoma to go work with pitching coach Vern Ruhle, so Buckles joined the Sooners.

The Sun Devils had the same success most teams did against Buckles. His 14 saves this year set a Big Eight career record.

Senior center fielder Chip Glass. Nicknamed "Pop-Up Chip" by the Oklahoma coaching staff because of his tendency to swing for the fences, Glass choked up on the bat during

# 1994 NEWSMAKERS

No team impacted the 1994 draft like **Georgia Tech**, which had four of the first 38 selections—led by shortstop **Nomar Garciaparra**, who was drafted by the Red Sox at No. 12. Catcher **Jason Varitek** went 14th to the Mariners, outfielder **Jay Payton** went 29th to the Mets and righthander **Brad Rigby** (14-4, 3.46, national-high 184 strikeouts) went in the second round to the Athletics. Ranked No. 1 in the preseason, the Yellow Jackets placed second in Omaha.

Despite his undersized 5-foot-10, 185-pound frame, righthand-er **John Powell** set one of the most significant records for a col-lege pitcher in 1994 by striking out 604 hitters (in 477 innings), achieved over a four-year career at Auburn.

**Jim Brock**, who went 1,110-440 in 23 years as the coach at **Arizona State** and led the school to national titles in 1977 and 1981, was forced to step down from his position immediately after leading his team to a first-round win over Miami at the CWS. Eight days later, Brock was dead, having lost his year-long battle with colon and liver cancer. Notre Dame's **Pat Murphy** was subsequently hired to coach the Sun Devils.

## FINAL TOP 25 FOR 1994

1. Oklahoma*
2. #Georgia Tech*
3. Cal State Fullerton*
4. Clemson
5. Arizona State*
6. Miami*
7. Florida State*
8. Tennessee
9. Oklahoma State
10. Louisiana State*
11. Southern California
12. Ohio State
13. Auburn*
14. Texas
15. Stanford
16. Washington
17. Nevada
18. Long Beach State
19. Wichita State
20. Notre Dame
21. Texas Tech
22. Texas Christian
23. Memphis
24. Kansas
25. Minnesota

* Reached College World Series
# Preseason No. 1

# IN RETROSPECT: 1994 DRAFT

## Top 10 Draft Picks From College

With overall selection number (Ov), drafting team (Team) and rank on Baseball America draft board (BA).

| Player | Pos | School | Ov | Team | BA |
|---|---|---|---|---|---|
| Paul Wilson | RHP | Florida State | 1 | Mets | 1 |
| Dustin Hermanson | RHP | Kent State | 3 | Padres | 2 |
| Antone Williamson | 3B | Arizona State | 4 | Brewers | 4 |
| Todd Walker | 2B | Louisiana State | 8 | Twins | 17 |
| C.J. Nitkowski | LHP | St. John's | 9 | Reds | 8 |
| Nomar Garciaparra | SS | Georgia Tech | 12 | Red Sox | 16 |
| Jason Varitek | C | Georgia Tech | 14 | Mariners | 10 |
| Cade Gaspar | RHP | Pepperdine | 18 | Tigers | 6 |
| Bret Wagner | LHP | Wake Forest | 19 | Cardinals | 13 |
| Dante Powell | OF | Cal State Fullerton | 22 | Giants | 32 |

## Top 10 Major League Players From College Draft Class

With draft round and Baseball-Reference.com total for wins above replacement (WAR) through 2019.

| Player | Pos | School | Rd | Ov | Team | WAR |
|---|---|---|---|---|---|---|
| Nomar Garciaparra | SS | Georgia Tech | 1 | 12 | Red Sox | 44.2 |
| Jason Varitek | C | Georgia Tech | 1 | 14 | Mariners | 24.2 |
| Keith Foulke | RHP | Lewis-Clark State | 9 | 256 | Giants | 20.7 |
| Jay Payton | OF | Georgia Tech | 1s | 29 | Mets | 15.4 |
| Aaron Boone | 3B | Southern Calif. | 3 | 72 | Reds | 13.5 |
| Dustin Hermanson | RHP | Kent State | 1 | 3 | Padres | 11.3 |
| Bob Howry | RHP | McNeese State | 5 | 144 | Giants | 10.8 |
| Todd Walker | 2B | Louisiana State | 1 | 8 | Twins | 10.5 |
| Dave Roberts | OF | UCLA | 28 | 781 | Tigers | 9.0 |
| John Halama | LHP | St. Francis (N.Y.) | 23 | 640 | Astros | 5.6 |

the CWS in order to keep the ball on the ground and better utilize his speed.

So of course, Glass led all players with three home runs, and batted .389 with four stolen bases to win Most Outstanding Player honors. Defensively, he saved the first win against Arizona State with a spectacular diving catch in the gap to end the sixth inning with the bases loaded.

Rick Gutierrez. Last summer, he started telling just about anyone who would listen that Oklahoma would make it to Omaha. Once he got there, he batted .563 to lead all players and played solid up-the-middle defense with double-play partner Rich Hills.

The only coach to bring three different schools to Omaha, Cochell picked up his recruiting philosophy while playing for the legendary Bobby Winkles at Arizona State: pursue athletes at key positions.

So like Cochell's 1990 CWS team at Cal State Fullerton, this Oklahoma team featured an infield with four former shortstops. Even catcher Javier Flores is a former shortstop who will replace the graduating Hills next year. The Sooners' athleticism translates into speed on the basepaths and devastating range on defense.

The other characteristic Cochell covets besides athleticism is mental toughness. Oklahoma's tenacity showed most during the Central Regional in Austin, where the temperature on the artificial turf reached 117 degrees and Texas fans rode the archrival Sooners unmercifully. Oklahoma responded by winning four straight games in which they never trailed.

The Sooners' title was surprising to those who looked at their lack of individual stars. But not to those who saw them play as a team. ■

# Varitek earns respect, top honor

By **JIM CALLIS**

Jason Varitek commands more respect than Aretha Franklin.

Two years ago, his Georgia Tech teammates voted him the first sophomore captain in school history. That summer at the Olympics, the champion Cubans considered Varitek Team USA's best catcher, both offensively and defensively, even though he was backup to Miami's Charles Johnson.

When Jim Morris left the Yellow Jackets to take the Miami coaching job last November, Georgia Tech's search committee joked that all it had to do was hire Varitek.

On the day before this year's College World Series began, the Mariners made Varitek the 14th overall pick in the draft. The 21st overall selection last June by the Twins, Varitek is one of 10 two-time first-round June picks in draft history.

Baseball America has selected Varitek as the greatest catcher in college baseball history. His is also the College Player of the Year.

One of the best catchers in college baseball history, Varitek lived up to his billing in pro ball. He captained the 2004 and '07 Red Sox to World Series titles and made three all-star teams in 15 seasons.

An impressive résumé, for sure. But the best example of the high regard in which college baseball observers hold Varitek comes from Morris.

While discussing the possibility of a CWS matchup between his past and present teams, Morris was asked what he would do if he faced Varitek with the bases loaded, two outs in the ninth inning, down by two runs and the national title on the line.

Morris barely hesitated.

"I'd walk him," he said.

As a senior, Varitek hit .426 with 17 home runs and 86 RBIs. He also drew 76 walks, even with the nation's top run-producer, 102-RBI man Jay Payton, batting directly behind him in the Yellow Jackets' lineup.

Florida State coach Mike Martin said the last player who intimidated him as much as Varitek was Auburn's Frank Thomas. The Seminoles joined the Atlantic Coast Conference in 1992, just in time for the first of Varitek's three consecutive .400 seasons.

Martin figured he was safe when the Twins drafted Varitek last year.

"My first reaction was, 'You got to be kidding me,' " Martin said of when he learned Varitek had returned to school. "I refused to believe it for so much time, until he came into Howser Stadium live and in living color."

Varitek left Howser Stadium with an eighth-inning, three-run homer in his final at-bat, giving Georgia Tech a series win. Martin was relieved when the Seminoles avoided the Yellow Jackets in the ACC Tournament, but then the two teams won their CWS openers to set up a second-round matchup in Omaha.

Varitek hit a three-run homer and the game-winning RBI single in the 10th inning of Georgia Tech's 12-4 victory. He also threw out three basestealers.

Though the Yellow Jackets have other All-Americans in Payton, shortstop Nomar Garciaparra and righthander Brad Rigby, Georgia Tech coach Danny Hall said the player his team could least afford to lose is Varitek.

"It's the leadership he brings to the club, the leadership he brings by being the catcher," said Hall, who said during the pre-CWS press conference that he believes Varitek could have coached Georgia Tech to Omaha. "All the pitchers have a tremendous amount of confidence in him calling pitches and throwing to him. He makes the pitchers better, and he makes the other players better because of how hard he works."

Hall said his lasting memory of Varitek will come from February. Varitek had gone 7-for-10 with six RBIs against Minnesota. That would be enough to satisfy most players, but Varitek was unhappy with his swing and showed up early for practice to work on his hitting every day for a week.

This season, Varitek was the best player in college baseball. And he has the respect to prove it. ■

# TOP PLAYERS OF 1994

## ALL-AMERICA TEAM

| Pos | Player | School | Yr | AVG | AB | R | H | HR | RBI | SB |
|-----|--------|--------|-----|-----|-----|-----|-----|-----|-----|-----|
| C | Jason Varitek | Georgia Tech | Sr | .426 | 249 | 87 | 106 | 17 | 86 | 5 |
| 1B | Tommy Davis | Southern Mississippi | Jr | .409 | 252 | 81 | 103 | 19 | 82 | 16 |
| 2B | Todd Walker | Louisiana State | Jr | .393 | 257 | 77 | 101 | 18 | 68 | 19 |
| 3B | Antone Williamson | Arizona State | Jr | .371 | 248 | 56 | 92 | 15 | 74 | 4 |
| SS | Nomar Garciaparra | Georgia Tech | Jr | .427 | 274 | 92 | 117 | 16 | 73 | 33 |
| OF | Jose Cruz Jr. | Rice | So | .401 | 182 | 72 | 73 | 14 | 68 | 29 |
| OF | Shane Monahan | Clemson | So | .415 | 330 | 97 | 137 | 11 | 53 | 23 |
| OF | Jay Payton | Georgia Tech | Jr | .434 | 297 | 78 | 129 | 20 | 102 | 8 |
| DH | Brian Buchanan | Virginia | Jr | .396 | 197 | 57 | 78 | 22 | 66 | 11 |

| Pos | Pitcher | School | Yr | W | L | ERA | G | SV | IP | H | BB | SO |
|-----|---------|--------|-----|-----|-----|-----|-----|-----|-----|-----|-----|-----|
| P | Jason Bell | Oklahoma State | So | 14 | 2 | 3.30 | 19 | 0 | 128 | 102 | 46 | 140 |
| P | R.A. Dickey | Tennessee | Fr | 15 | 2 | 3.00 | 21 | 0 | 147 | 129 | 39 | 87 |
| P | Danny Graves | Miami | Jr | 1 | 1 | 0.89 | 39 | 21 | 61 | 31 | 17 | 70 |
| P | Gary Rath | Mississippi State | Jr | 10 | 3 | 1.71 | 16 | 0 | 116 | 80 | 42 | 141 |
| P | Paul Wilson | Florida State | Jr | 13 | 5 | 2.08 | 19 | 0 | 143 | 106 | 32 | 161 |

## SECOND TEAM

**C**—Karl Thompson, Santa Clara. **1B**—Todd Helton, Tennessee. **2B**—Jeff Ferguson, Cal State Fullerton. **3B**—Mike Hampton, Clemson. **SS**—Russ Johnson, Louisiana State. **OF**—Jeff Abbott, Kentucky; Jacob Cruz, Arizona State; and Mark Little, Memphis. **DH**—Ryan Jackson, Duke. **P**—Jason Beverlin, Western Carolina; Mark Guerra, Jacksonville; Ryan Nye, Texas Tech; Brad Rigby, Georgia Tech; and Scott Rivette, Long Beach State.

## THIRD TEAM

**C**—A.J. Hinch, Stanford. **1B**—Sean Hugo, Oklahoma State. **2B**—Mark Merila, Minnesota. **3B**—Kevin Young, Central Michigan. **SS**—Mark Lewis, Nevada. **OF**—Kevin Gibbs, Old Dominion; Geoff Jenkins, Southern California; and Paul Ottavinia, Seton Hall. **DH**—Mike Kinkade, Washington State. **P**—Shane Dennis, Wichita State; Jonathan Johnson, Florida State; Brett Merrick, Washington; Randy Flores, Southern California; and Mason Smith, Oregon State.

**1995**

Cal State Fullerton's Mark Kotsay turned in one of the most epic College World Series performances for one of most epic CWS champions of all time.

# Titans assure their place in history

By **JIM CALLIS**

College World Series champion, yes. Threat to Jeane Dixon, the famous psychic and syndicated astrology columnist, no.

When Cal State Fullerton gathered for three weeks of offseason workouts last fall, the mood was one of gloom, even with lighthearted Augie Garrido at the helm. Four of the five full-time position players and all four starting pitchers had departed from the Titans' 1994 third-place CWS team.

The future looked grim.

"I got on both recruiters when I saw the first three weeks," Garrido said. "I said, 'This isn't good enough.' "

Garrido wasn't merely trying to motivate his team.

"We were very pessimistic, almost apologetic around campus, about what might lie ahead," associate head coach George Horton said. Even the players didn't sense anything special.

"When we first started in the fall, we didn't expect to go even as far as the regionals," said senior first baseman D.C. Olsen, who had made trips to Omaha in 1992 and 1994.

Seven months later, Fullerton could stop apologizing. The Titans breezed through four games in Omaha, capping a 57-9 season and their national championship on June 10 with an 11-5 dispatching of Southern California.

"We rebuild fast," Garrido said. "You sit around trying to build a house forever, and then you get it done in a hurry. Hell, I don't know how it happened."

What happened was this: Fullerton was led by the greatest CWS performer ever and played such fundamentally solid baseball that the Titans can make a case for being the best college baseball team of all time.

It's a lot easier to explain what sophomore center fielder/lefthander Mark Kotsay didn't accomplish this season. "He didn't drive the bus," Garrido said.

Kotsay batted .422-18-75 and went 2-1, 0.38 with nine saves during the regular season, then drove in five runs and picked up a save as the Titans won the South Regional in Baton Rogue. All that was nothing compared to the show he put on in Omaha.

**FROM THE ISSUE:**
JULY 10-23, 1995

## TOP TEAMS
### 1995 COLLEGE WORLD SERIES STANDINGS

| School | Conference | Record | CWS | Head Coach |
| --- | --- | --- | --- | --- |
| Cal State Fullerton | Big West | 57–9 | 4–0 | Augie Garrido |
| Southern California | Pacific-10 | 49–21 | 4–2 | Mike Gillespie |
| Miami | Independent | 48–17 | 2–2 | Jim Morris |
| Tennessee | Southeastern | 54–16 | 2–2 | Rod Delmonico |
| Florida State | Atlantic Coast | 53–16 | 1–2 | Mike Martin |
| Stanford | Pacific-10 | 40–25 | 1–2 | Mark Marquess |
| Clemson | Atlantic Coast | 54–14 | 0–2 | Jack Leggett |
| Oklahoma | Big Eight | 42–16 | 0–2 | Larry Cochell |

### NATIONAL CHAMPION
### CAL STATE FULLERTON

The fundamentally-sound 1995 Titans have a case as the best college baseball team ever after trouncing USC 13-5 in the championship game. Fullerton two-way star Mark Kotsay set CWS records for career average (.517) and slugging (1.103).

**109**

In an opening-round 6-5 win against Stanford, Kotsay doubled and scored the tying run, sacrificed to set up the go-ahead run and got the last five outs for his 11th save.

In an 11-1 demolition of Tennessee in round two, he sacrificed to set up the first run, hit a grand slam in the second inning to put the game out of reach and added three more singles.

In an 11-0 drubbing of the Volunteers in a semifinal rematch, he walked during a seven-run first inning and added an RBI double in the fifth. Proving that he's mortal, Kotsay grounded into a double play in the seventh inning.

In the championship game, Kotsay essentially decided the outcome with his first two swings. He hit a three-run home run over the 26-foot center field wall in the first inning, then added a two-run bomb to right to snap a 3-3 tie in the second. And when starter Ted Silva's back stiffened, Kotsay came on to record the last five outs.

Afterward, USC coach Mike Gillespie called Kotsay "The Messiah." Kotsay was named CWS Most Outstanding Player in the biggest landslide since Reagan '84.

If there's a CWS record Kotsay doesn't own, he probably doesn't want it. He holds the marks for career batting average (.517), slugging percentage (1.103) and grand slams (two). He tied standards for career home runs (four) and championship game homers (two) and RBIs (five).

Much like Kotsay, the Titans rarely dazzle beyond their box scores. Their highest draft pick, righthander Jon Ward, went in the eighth round to the Cardinals. But few teams have been as relentlessly efficient.

Ranked No. 15 in the preseason, Fullerton beat then top-ranked Stanford in its first series of 1995, ascended to No. 1 by the end of February and stayed there for 13 of the season's last 15 weeks. The Titans closed the year with 18 consecutive wins, sweeping the Big

# 1995 NEWSMAKERS

**Cal State Fullerton** dominated the CWS like few teams before it, winning the title in four straight games while hitting .372 and slugging 11 home runs—the highest figures ever by a championship team. The offensive outburst by the Titans was in keeping with the highest-scoring CWS on record as the eight-team field hit a collective .303 and slugged 48 home runs, easily eclipsing the previous high of 29, set in 1994. Those records would last just three more years.

**Southern California**, with a record 11 CWS championships to its credit, made its first return trip to Omaha in 17 years, or since winning its last title in 1978. With a 21-9 record, the Trojans (49-21) finished first in the Pac-10 South standings for just the second time in that period, and they cemented an appearance in Omaha by capturing the West regional. USC also finished first in the Pac-10 South in 1991, but In a 16-year stretch from 1979-94 was an overall 14 games below .500 in conference play. Outfielder **Geoff Jenkins**, who led the Pac-10 South with a .399 average, 23 homers and 78 RBIs and was selected eighth overall in the 1995 draft, led USC's resurgence.

| FINAL TOP 25 FOR 1995 |
| --- |
| 1. Cal State Fullerton* |
| 2. Southern California* |
| 3. Florida State* |
| 4. Miami* |
| 5. Tennessee* |
| 6. Clemson* |
| 7. Oklahoma* |
| 8. Texas Tech |
| 9. Auburn |
| 10. #Stanford* |
| 11. Oklahoma State |
| 12. Rice |
| 13. Wichita State |
| 14. Alabama |
| 15. Louisiana State |
| 16. Texas A&M |
| 17. Long Beach State |
| 18. Mississippi |
| 19. Central Florida |
| 20. Pepperdine |
| 21. Texas |
| 22. Florida International |
| 23. Fresno State |
| 24. Lamar |
| 25. North Carolina |
| * Reached College World Series |
| # Preseason No. 1 |

# IN RETROSPECT: 1995 DRAFT

## Top 10 Draft Picks From College
With overall selection number (Ov), drafting team (Team) and rank on Baseball America draft board (BA).

| Player | Pos | School | Ov | Team | BA |
|---|---|---|---|---|---|
| Darin Erstad | OF | Nebraska | 1 | Angels | 1 |
| Jose Cruz Jr. | OF | Rice | 3 | Mariners | 3 |
| Jonathan Johnson | RHP | Florida State | 7 | Rangers | 13 |
| Todd Helton | 1B | Tennessee | 8 | Rockies | 5 |
| Geoff Jenkins | OF | Southern California | 9 | Brewers | 9 |
| Mike Drumright | RHP | Wichita State | 11 | Tigers | 8 |
| Matt Morris | RHP | Seton Hall | 12 | Cardinals | 4 |
| Mark Redman | LHP | Oklahoma | 13 | Twins | 20 |
| David Yocum | LHP | Florida State | 20 | Dodgers | 14 |
| Alvie Shepherd | RHP | Nebraska | 21 | Orioles | 25 |

## Top 10 Major League Players From College Draft Class
With draft round and Baseball-Reference.com total for wins above replacement (WAR) through 2019.

| Player | Pos | School | Rd | Ov | Team | WAR |
|---|---|---|---|---|---|---|
| Todd Helton | 1B | Tennessee | 1 | 8 | Rockies | 61.2 |
| Darin Erstad | OF | Nebraska | 1 | 1 | Angels | 32.4 |
| Jarrod Washburn | LHP | Wis.-Oshkosh | 2 | 31 | Angels | 28.2 |
| Randy Winn | OF | Santa Clara | 3 | 65 | Marlins | 27.6 |
| Joe Nathan | RHP | Stony Brook | 6 | 159 | Giants | 26.7 |
| Mike Lowell | 3B | Fla. International | 20 | 562 | Yankees | 24.9 |
| Geoff Jenkins | OF | Southern Calif. | 1 | 9 | Brewers | 21.9 |
| Matt Morris | RHP | Seton Hall | 1 | 12 | Cardinals | 20.5 |
| Jose Cruz Jr. | OF | Rice | 1 | 3 | Mariners | 19.5 |
| Sean Casey | 1B | Richmond | 2 | 53 | Indians | 16.5 |

West Conference tournament, the South Regional and the CWS.

"I have to admit I felt a little bit like David and Goliath out there," Tennessee coach Rod Delmonico said after Fullerton twice brushed off the Volunteers like lint on its shoulder. "They're an outstanding team, an unbelievable team. I kind of wonder why they lost nine games."

The last team to exceed Fullerton's .864 winning percentage was Texas A&M, which went 58-9 (.866) in 1989 but failed to advance to Omaha. Only three CWS champions have better marks: Holy Cross (21-3, .875) in 1952, Arizona State (54-8, .871) in 1965 and Texas (56-6, .903) in 1975.

Of Fullerton's nine losses, only one was to a team unranked at the time: San Jose State on March 26. Silva struck out 15 but was victimized by five Titans errors in a 6-3 loss.

Fullerton's place in history doesn't concern Garrido. "It's not about other teams, other people," he said. "It's all about your own team. I think history limits our thinking. You look back to learn to be more efficient."

Though he has known enough to win 1,107 games, 10th all-time among Division I coaches, Garrido declared he had deciphered the secret to coaching this season.

"We started out eliminating some things like goals," Garrido said. "We didn't have any goals. Then we dropped that down to where we didn't expect anything. You operate without objectives, it's a lot softer. You're not slammed against the wall as hard with your failures."

The bad news for Garrido is that expectations will follow his team next season. The good news is that Mark Kotsay and "Augieball" will be there to meet him. ■

# Tennessee's Helton resists icon label

By **JIM CALLIS**

Todd Helton is as accommodating as a player can be.

As the first baseman and No. 3 hitter in Tennessee's lineup, Helton smacks home runs to all fields, rifles doubles into the gaps and drives in clutch runs. As a closer, he has nailed down several of the most important wins in Volunteers history.

Need him to start on the mound? Tennessee has asked Helton to do so four times this season, and he has responded with a complete game victory each time.

About the only thing he hasn't done in three years with the Volunteers is lay down a sacrifice, and that's only because he never has been given a bunt sign.

Todd Helton, the College Player of the Year and Tennessee's best player ever, is willing and able to do it all. Just don't ask him to admit that he has become an icon in Knoxville.

Todd Helton shined at the plate and on the mound at Tennessee before embarking on 17-year big league career in which he blasted 369 home runs and made five all-star teams for the Rockies.

"People know who I am," said Helton, who was born and raised in Knoxville. "But I'm definitely not a celebrity or anything. It's just because I've been in town so long."

He hasn't quite reached (Vols quarterback) Health Shuler status, and there hasn't been an explosion of No. 3 baseball tops in the stands at Lindsey Nelson Stadium. But whether he's willing to admit it or not, Helton's legacy will extend beyond his 20 school records.

"I think I'll be proud of playing at Tennessee," Helton said. "I'll be proud to be a part of everything we accomplished. I'm just one of many people who has done a lot for this program."

No one has done more to establish the Volunteers as a national baseball power, though Helton said, "I don't see myself that way." But Rod Delmonico, the coach who has presided over the rise of Tennessee baseball, certainly does.

"Look at the programs around the country," Delmonico said. "Mississippi State had Rafael Palmeiro and Will Clark. Louisiana State had Albert Belle and Ben McDonald. Our two guys have been R.A. Dickey and Todd Helton.

"They've taken the program to where it is now."

The Volunteers almost didn't get Helton after his senior year of high school in 1992. Not only did they have to contend with the Padres, who had drafted him in the second round and offered him $450,000, but they also had to contend with Alabama's football program, which wanted Helton as a quarterback.

Wherever Helton went that summer, he usually was followed by cries of "Go Vols!" He said he didn't feel any pressure to stay at home to play for Tennessee because deep down he knew early that would be his decision.

The local scrutiny never has abated, but it has yet to bother him.

"A lot of times I feel like I've been under a microscope. There's nothing wrong with that," Helton said. "It keeps you in line, one thing which everyone needs."

For the third straight year, Helton was named an All-American and was named MVP of the Southeastern Conference Eastern Division Tournament.

This was his best season—he hit .407 with 20 homers and 92 RBIs—of a banner career that included a 47.2-inning scoreless streak in 1994 that erased McDonald's SEC record.

Helton has accomplished everything he could have dreamed of at Tennessee, except perhaps winning the Sugar Bowl. Helton got a chance to start at quarterback last fall and had modest success before spraining his knee against Mississippi State.

The only thing left for Helton to prove entering his junior season was whether he had enough power to be a big league first baseman. He hit 18 homers in his first two years and didn't go deep last summer with wood bats in the Cape Cod League, though he did win the home run contest at the Cape all-star game.

Suffice it to say that Helton passed the test. If he continues to improve, just imagine what he might do in Coors Field, now that the Rockies have drafted him eighth overall. ■

# TOP PLAYERS OF 1995

## ALL-AMERICA TEAM

| Pos | Player | School | Yr | AVG | AB | R | H | HR | RBI | SB |
|-----|--------|--------|----|----|----|----|----|----|----|----|
| C | A.J. Hinch | Stanford | Jr | .366 | 238 | 61 | 87 | 9 | 58 | 13 |
| 1B | Todd Helton | Tennessee | Jr | .407 | 258 | 86 | 105 | 20 | 92 | 11 |
| 2B | Marlon Anderson | South Alabama | Jr | .362 | 246 | 60 | 89 | 7 | 46 | 31 |
| 3B | Clint Bryant | Texas Tech | Jr | .422 | 258 | 91 | 109 | 16 | 93 | 25 |
| SS | Mark Bellhorn | Auburn | Jr | .342 | 243 | 66 | 83 | 12 | 60 | 11 |
| OF | Jose Cruz Jr. | Rice | Jr | .377 | 223 | 77 | 84 | 16 | 76 | 19 |
| OF | Darin Erstad | Nebraska | Jr | .410 | 251 | 84 | 103 | 19 | 76 | 11 |
| OF | Geoff Jenkins | Southern California | Jr | .399 | 258 | 75 | 103 | 23 | 78 | 14 |
| DH | Mark Kotsay | Cal State Fullerton | So | .422 | 263 | 85 | 111 | 21 | 90 | 15 |

| Pos | Pitcher | School | Yr | W | L | ERA | G | SV | IP | H | BB | SO |
|-----|---------|--------|----|----|----|----|----|----|----|----|----|----|
| P | Jonathan Johnson | Florida State | Jr | 12 | 3 | 2.89 | 19 | 0 | 134 | 98 | 53 | 130 |
| P | Matt Morris | Seton Hall | Jr | 10 | 3 | 2.68 | 14 | 0 | 94 | 64 | 54 | 104 |
| P | Kyle Peterson | Stanford | Fr | 14 | 1 | 2.96 | 20 | 1 | 143 | 129 | 35 | 112 |
| P | Mark Redman | Oklahoma | Jr | 15 | 3 | 2.22 | 20 | 0 | 142 | 109 | 35 | 158 |
| P | Ted Silva | Cal State Fullerton | Jr | 18 | 1 | 2.83 | 29 | 6 | 153 | 140 | 35 | 142 |

## SECOND TEAM

C—Javier Flores, Oklahoma. 1B—Sean Casey, Richmond. 2B—Jason Totman, Texas Tech. 3B—Jeff Liefer, Long Beach State. SS—Jason Adams, Wichita State. OF—David Delluci, Mississippi; Shane Monahan, Clemson; and Mark Wulfert, New Mexico. DH—Steve Hacker, Southwest Missouri State. P—Darin Blood, Gonzaga; Jamey Price, Mississippi; Evan Thomas, Florida International; Scott Winchester, Clemson; and David Yocum, Florida State.

## THIRD TEAM

C—Brian Lloyd, Cal State Fullerton. 1B—David Miller, Clemson. 2B—Tom Sergio, North Carolina State. 3B—Casey Blake, Wichita State. SS—Gabe Alvarez, Southern California. OF—Chad Alexander, Texas A&M; Ryan Christensen, Pepperdine; and Tony Ellison, North Carolina State. DH—Tal Light, Oklahoma State. P—R.A. Dickey, Tennessee; Mike Drumright, Wichita State; Ryan Halla, Auburn; Bryan Link, Winthrop; and Scott Schultz, Louisiana State.

Louisiana State's Warren Morris delivered the most dramatic moment in College World Series history with a two-out, title-clinching home run against Miami.

1996

# Morris returns to win CWS for LSU

By **JIM CALLIS**

Warren Morris is the poster boy for everything good about college baseball.

Morris came to Louisiana State in 1992 on a full academic scholarship. He was 5-foot-11, 150 pounds when he attended his first team meeting as an unrecruited walk-on.

"I looked around," Morris said, "and the only person I was bigger than was the equipment manager."

He spent a season as a redshirt behind Tigers great Todd Walker before becoming a three-year starter. He worked hard to add 20 pounds and put just as much effort in the classroom, carrying a 3.57 GPA with a zoology (pre-med) major.

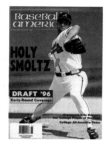

**FROM THE ISSUE:**
JULY 8-21, 1996

The quintessential college player, Morris is a self-made star who wasn't a top prospect coming out of high school. Despite this humble beginnings, he will probably be the starting second baseman on the U.S. Olympic team this summer.

That background is why Skip Bertman calls what happened to Morris earlier this year the saddest thing he's seen at Louisiana State in his 13 seasons as head coach. Morris was bothered by wrist problems that limited him to 14 regular season starts before doctors finally found a broken hamate bone in his right hand.

He had surgery to remove the bone April 24, jeopardizing his prospects for the postseason and possibly the Olympics. Yet Morris missed just 28 days—if you're counting, that's 65 fewer than Jose Canseco required after similar surgery—before returning to earn all-tournament honors at the South II Regional.

As Morris strode to the plate in the bottom of the ninth on June 8, someone in the Tigers dugout said loud enough for all to hear, "Warren hasn't hit a home run all season." Miami freshman closer Robbie Morrison had just struck out Tim Lanier, stranding Brad Wilson at third base to preserve an 8-7 lead and bring the Hurricanes within one out of the College World Series championship.

CWS history is chock full of dramatic hits, but it took 50 years for a home run to end a game and determine the national champion. Morris did it, lining Morrison's first pitch,

## TOP TEAMS
### 1996 COLLEGE WORLD SERIES STANDINGS

| School | Conference | Record | CWS | Head Coach |
|--------|-----------|--------|-----|-----------|
| Louisiana State | Southeastern | 52–15 | 4–0 | Skip Bertman |
| Miami | Independent | 50–14 | 3–1 | Jim Morris |
| Clemson | Atlantic Coast | 51–17 | 2–2 | Jack Leggett |
| Florida | Southeastern | 50–18 | 2–2 | Andy Lopez |
| Alabama | Southeastern | 50–19 | 1–2 | Jim Wells |
| Florida State | Atlantic Coast | 52–17 | 1–2 | Mike Martin |
| Oklahoma State | Big Eight | 45–21 | 0–2 | Gary Ward |
| Wichita State | Missouri Valley | 54–11 | 0–2 | Gene Stephenson |

### NATIONAL CHAMPION
### LOUISIANA STATE

The Tigers claimed their third national title of the '90s and did so in dramatic fashion. LSU walked off Miami 9-8 in the championship game when Warren Morris, homerless during the season, hit a two-out, two-run homer in the bottom of the ninth.

a curveball, just over the right field fence, screaming as he rounded first base and realizing that he had just led LSU to a heart-stopping 9-8 victory and the national title. Miami players lay prone on the infield as if they had been shot.

"I hadn't hit a home run in so long, I didn't know what one looked like," Morris said. "It's been a tough year, but it's all worth it now."

There hasn't been a more clutch home run in World Series history, be it college or the major leagues.

Bill Mazeroski? The game was tied. Kirk Gibson? It came in the first game of the World Series. Joe Carter? If he doesn't take Mitch Williams deep, the Blue Jays come back the next day with another chance to win the championship.

"Isn't it ironic that Warren Morris would be there to hit his first home run of the year?" Bertman said. "That shows you that the kids who are the greatest always come through."

The CWS finished as it began. Alabama first baseman Chris Moller ended the opener with a three-run homer off Oklahoma State reliever Heath Askew, leading the Crimson Tide to a 7-5 win. That set the tone for a tournament in which offense was king despite the presence of six of Division I's top 13 pitching staffs.

Teams combined to hit .299 with 35 homers in Omaha this June, each the second-highest figure in CWS history, as was the 13.5 runs per game. The average game lasted three hours, 20 minutes, a record that all who were there hope never will be broken,

Miami set another mark with a team batting average of .377, slugging its way to the championship game behind third baseman Pat Burrell, the Freshman of the Year.

The second player in the last 23 years to win the CWS Most Outstanding Player award despite not playing for the national champion, Burrell went 7-for-14 in Omaha with a pair of majestic homers and eight RBIs. He finished the season hitting .484, becoming the

# 1996 NEWSMAKERS

Miami third baseman **Pat Burrell** batted .484 to become the first freshman to lead Division I in hitting. He also led the nation with a .948 slugging percentage, while setting school freshman records with 23 home runs and 64 RBIs. Burrell was particularly hot in postseason play. He went 13-for-18 with four doubles and four homers to earn MVP honors while leading Miami to victory at the Central I regional, then won the Most Outstanding Player at the CWS, where he went 7-for-14 with two more homers. Burrell easily claimed Freshman of the Year.

Some of biggest names in the college coaching annals stepped aside after the 1996 season. Among them: Texas' **Cliff Gustafson**, the winningest coach in Division I history, and Arizona's **Jerry Kindall**, who won three CWS titles in 24 seasons. Gustafson, 65, was undone by a scandal involving his summer baseball camps and elected to retire hours before the university detailed how he had broken rules by diverting funds from his camps into an unauthorized back account. He was replaced by another coaching giant, **Augie Garrido**, who one day would become the winningest coach in college history.

## FINAL TOP 25 FOR 1996

1. #Louisiana State*
2. Miami*
3. Florida*
4. Alabama*
5. Clemson*
6. Florida State*
7. Southern California
8. Wichita State*
9. Stanford
10. Cal State Northridge
11. Oklahoma State*
12. Cal State Fullerton
13. Tennessee
14. Virginia
15. Texas Tech
16. South Florida
17. Rice
18. Texas
19. Massachusetts
20. Tulane
21. UCLA
22. Georgia Tech
23. Nevada-Las Vegas
24. Georgia Southern
25. Arizona State

* Reached College World Series
# Preseason No. 1

# IN RETROSPECT: 1996 DRAFT

**Top 10 Draft Picks From College**
With overall selection number (Ov), drafting team (Team) and rank on Baseball America draft board (BA).

| Player | Pos | School | Ov | Team | BA |
|---|---|---|---|---|---|
| Kris Benson | RHP | Clemson | 1 | Pirates | 1 |
| Travis Lee* | 1B | San Diego State | 2 | Twins | 2 |
| Braden Looper | RHP | Wichita State | 3 | Cardinals | 3 |
| Billy Koch | RHP | Clemson | 4 | Blue Jays | 5 |
| Seth Greisinger | RHP | Virginia | 6 | Tigers | 12 |
| Chad Green | OF | Kentucky | 8 | Brewers | 8 |
| Mark Kotsay | OF | Cal State Fullerton | 9 | Marlins | 9 |
| R.A. Dickey | RHP | Tennessee | 18 | Rangers | 10 |
| Mark Johnson | RHP | Hawaii | 19 | Astros | 19 |
| Eric Milton | LHP | Maryland | 20 | Yankees | 20 |

* Did not sign; later signed with D-backs as "loophole" free agent

**Top 10 Major League Players From College Draft Class**
With draft round and Baseball-Reference.com total for wins above replacement (WAR) through 2019.

| Player | Pos | School | Rd | Ov | Team | WAR |
|---|---|---|---|---|---|---|
| Casey Blake | 3B | Wichita State | 7 | 189 | Blue Jays | 24.9 |
| R.A. Dickey | RHP | Tennessee | 1 | 18 | Rangers | 23.6 |
| Mark Kotsay | OF | Cal State Fullerton | 1 | 9 | Marlins | 21.3 |
| Jamey Carroll | 2B | Evansville | 14 | 400 | Expos | 16.6 |
| Eric Milton | LHP | Maryland | 1 | 20 | Yankees | 16.5 |
| Kris Benson | RHP | Clemson | 1 | 1 | Pirates | 12.9 |
| Jacque Jones | OF | Southern Calif. | 2 | 37 | Twins | 11.6 |
| Chad Bradford | RHP | Southern Miss. | 13 | 377 | White Sox | 10.1 |
| Mark DeRosa | 3B | Pennsylvania | 7 | 212 | Braves | 9.9 |
| Braden Looper | RHP | Wichita State | 1 | 3 | Cardinals | 8.2 |

first freshman ever to capture the D-I batting title.

While the Hurricanes had an easy time disposing of Alabama and Clemson twice, LSU struggled in each of its three victories on the way to the final. But the Tigers' dangerous power—they led D-I with 131 homers—helped them overcome other deficiencies.

"We're about as dependent on the home run as the United States is on foreign oil," Bertman said at the outset of the CWS. "We can get by without it for a couple of innings, but then we have to have it."

Louisiana State's championship left no doubt about the premier program in college baseball. The Tigers, who went 52-15 this year, also won the CWS in 1991 and 1993, and are just the fourth team to win three titles in six years.

The others were Southern California (1958, '61 and '63), Arizona State (1965, '67 and '69) and USC again (1970, '71, '72, '73 and '74).

Nothing can compare with the Trojans' five straight titles, but LSU is dominating in an era of increased parity, scholarship reductions and greater competition with professional baseball for players. The Tigers have made nine trips to Omaha in the last 11 years, and they have played in 13 regional and CWS championship games in those years—winning every one of them.

"Personally, this is the greatest championship I've ever been associated with," said Bertman, who also was an assistant on Miami's 1982 CWS winner and the 1988 U.S. Olympic team that won the gold medal.

"This is the most competitive team I've ever had. We had every opportunity not to win." ■

# Clemson's Benson wins top honor

By **JIM CALLIS**

Last June, Kris Benson sat in the outfield at USA Stadium in Millington, Tenn., trying to figure out why he wasn't good enough to make the U.S. national team.

He had never been cut from a team before, and he thought he had pitched well during the tryout camp. That night, he called home to suburban Atlanta and told his parents, "I'm outta here."

"He felt pretty bad," Benson's father Paul said. "He vowed at the time to make it a positive experience. I think he was as motivated as at any time in his life."

U.S. Olympic coach Skip Bertman portrays the decision to make Benson the final cut in 1995 as doing him a favor. Bertman said Benson wanted to take classes at Clemson and work on weightlifting.

Benson, of course, would have preferred to spend his summer pitching for Team USA. A year later, he realizes Bertman did do him a favor.

Clemson's Kris Benson surged as a junior, leading the Pirates to draft him No. 1 overall in June. He had his moments in a nine-year big league career but finished 70-75 with a 4.42 ERA.

"Once I realized what they were doing, they were right," Benson said. "It gave me time off to go work out in the weight room. That's probably my main point of success this year. It gave me 15 pounds of muscle, and I'm a lot more aggressive this year."

And a lot more effective. Benson, the College Player of the Year, went 14-2, 2.02 and ranked second with 204 strikeouts and fourth in wins. In 156 innings, the junior right-hander walked just 27 batters.

Benson was much happier this June than he was a year ago. He was chosen as the No. 1 overall pick in the draft by the Pirates. He was scheduled to leave for Millington and another Team USA camp after Clemson finished in Omaha.

Benson's metamorphosis into a 6-foot-4, 190-pound uber-pitcher was revealed last October at the U.S. Olympic combine in Homestead, Fla. Benson blew hitters away as coaches and pro scouts watched in awe.

"My eyes jumped," Team USA assistant Ray Tanner said. "Every pitch had a little bit extra, a little something more than what he had before, which was pretty good. That was the first indication that he was on the way."

Benson opened the 1996 season with a three-hit shutout of South Florida, striking out 14 and walking none. It was one of six times in 1996 that he would reach double digits in strikeouts without a walk, including a 17-whiff two-hitter against Virginia Tech.

Benson's package of stuff, command and makeup was so dominant that by March, the Pirates pretty much knew they would select him with the first overall pick, even if they wouldn't tip their hand.

The last two players who were such certain No. 1 overall picks also were college right-handers, Louisiana State's Ben McDonald (1989) and Florida State's Paul Wilson (1994).

Bertman said Benson may be better than McDonald, whom he coached with LSU.

"He has a much better curveball than Ben had," Bertman said. "He has a little more command than Ben had with different pitches. He throws about the same—92 (mph) for the whole game."

Florida State coach Mike Martin said he never has seen a pitcher improve as much in one year as Benson.

Benson loves to read and re-read books on pitching, and he keeps a detailed journal of his outings, noting such things as diet, game time and weather.

"We've always stressed that he's a student first and an athlete second," Paul Benson said. "He's kind of pushed that into being a student of the game. He's had some of those books since junior high. He's picked up a nice little library on pitching."

"He's just the very best that I've ever seen in terms of consistency, focus and concentration," Clemson coach Jack Leggett said. "He has tremendous mental attributes that separate him from any other pitcher who I've ever seen at the college level.

"I know that's strong, but that's the way he is." ■

# TOP PLAYERS OF 1996

## ALL-AMERICA TEAM

| Pos | Player | School | Yr | AVG | AB | R | H | HR | RBI | SB |
|-----|--------|--------|-----|-----|-----|-----|-----|-----|-----|-----|
| C | Robert Fick | Cal State Northridge | Jr | .420 | 283 | 79 | 119 | 25 | 96 | 22 |
| 1B | Travis Lee | San Diego State | Jr | .355 | 220 | 57 | 78 | 14 | 60 | 33 |
| 2B | Josh Kliner | Kansas | Sr | .438 | 208 | 66 | 91 | 10 | 85 | 7 |
| 3B | Pat Burrell | Miami | Fr | .484 | 192 | 76 | 93 | 23 | 64 | 8 |
| SS | Josh Klimek | Illinois | Jr | .400 | 215 | 86 | 73 | 26 | 94 | 1 |
| OF | J.D. Drew | Florida State | So | .386 | 241 | 90 | 93 | 21 | 94 | 10 |
| OF | Chad Green | Kentucky | Jr | .352 | 256 | 71 | 90 | 12 | 44 | 55 |
| OF | Mark Kotsay | Cal State Fullerton | Jr | .402 | 243 | 78 | 97 | 20 | 91 | 20 |
| DH | Eddy Furniss | Louisiana State | So | .374 | 238 | 68 | 89 | 26 | 103 | 1 |

| Pos | Pitcher | School | Yr | W | L | ERA | G | SV | IP | H | BB | SO |
|-----|---------|--------|-----|-----|-----|-----|-----|-----|-----|-----|-----|-----|
| P | Kris Benson | Clemson | Jr | 14 | 2 | 2.02 | 19 | 0 | 156 | 109 | 27 | 204 |
| P | Seth Greisinger | Virginia | Jr | 12 | 2 | 1.76 | 16 | 0 | 123 | 78 | 36 | 141 |
| P | Braden Looper | Wichita State | Jr | 4 | 1 | 2.09 | 26 | 12 | 56 | 37 | 15 | 64 |
| P | Evan Thomas | Florida International | Sr | 10 | 3 | 1.78 | 20 | 1 | 147 | 102 | 58 | 220 |
| P | Ed Yarnall | Louisiana State | Jr | 11 | 1 | 2.38 | 19 | 0 | 125 | 89 | 52 | 156 |

## SECOND TEAM
**C**—A.J. Hinch, Stanford. **1B**—Lance Berkman, Rice. **2B**—Travis Young, New Mexico. **3B**—Clint Bryant, Texas Tech. **SS**—Kip Harkrider, Texas. **OF**—Kevin Barker, Virginia Tech; Matt Kastellic, Texas Tech; and Jeremy Morris, Florida State. **DH**—Casey Blake, Wichita State. **P**—Brian Carmody, Santa Clara; Eric DuBose, Mississippi State; Seth Etherton, Southern California; Robbie Morrison, Miami; and Jeff Weaver, Fresno State.

## THIRD TEAM
**C**—Brian Loyd, Cal State Fullerton. **1B**—Danny Peoples, Texas. **2B**—Rudy Gomez, Miami. **3B**—Chris Heintz, South Florida. **SS**—Jason Grabowski, Connecticut. **OF**—Jeff Guiel, Oklahoma State; Jacque Jones, Southern California; and Brad Wilkerson, Florida. **DH**—Aaron Jaworowski, Missouri. **P**—Julio Ayala, Georgia Southern; Ryan Brannan, Long Beach State; Randy Choate, Florida State; R.A. Dickey, Tennessee; and Ken Vining, Clemson.

Louisiana State's Brandon Larson launched 40 homers to help the Tigers set a still-standing team record of 188, then won Most Outstanding Player honors in Omaha.

1997

# Powerful LSU repeats as national champion

By **JIM CALLIS**

If you can't beat 'em, beat 'em to death.

As an assistant at Miami and in his first years as head coach at Louisiana State, Skip Bertman won with pitching and defense. But as the Tigers kept coming up agonizingly short in the College World Series, he realized it was time for a change in philosophy.

**FROM THE ISSUE:**
JULY 7-20, 1997

In an era when he said shutouts are about as rare as finding a disco in Bunkie, La., Bertman began thinking offense first.

"At Miami and early at LSU, I looked for guys who could run and play defense, then figured out how we were going to score runs," he said. "I had to change. The only way to win in the regionals and Omaha is to hit, because no one has got four front-liners and two relief pitchers to dominate the opposition."

The results have been dramatic in Baton Rouge. LSU averaged 12 runs a game to win the 1991 CWS. The Tigers haven't stopped slugging since. They rode their bats to another CWS title in 1993, and hit a Southeastern Conference-record 131 home runs while winning a third last year.

All that was a mere prelude to 1997. Louisiana State homered in each of its 70 games, believed to be an unprecedented feat, and went deep 188 times, obliterating the NCAA record of 161 set by Brigham Young in 1988.

The payoff was a repeat CWS championship, the first since Stanford in 1987 and '88. The Tigers steamrolled SEC rival Alabama 13-6 on June 7 to become the second school to capture four titles in a decade. Southern California won six series in the 1970s, and only Trojans coach Rod Dedeaux (10) has more crowns than Bertman's four.

The four championships match the number of sacrifice bunts LSU executed this season. Bertman enjoys the success that comes with playing long ball, but he still finds that style hard to accept.

"It's a lot tougher to change than what you think," he said. "It's tough on an old coach like me when you live and die with the home run. You chase bad pitches, you can't bunt,

## TOP TEAMS

### 1997 COLLEGE WORLD SERIES STANDINGS

| School | Conference | Record | CWS | Head Coach |
|---|---|---|---|---|
| Louisiana State | Southeastern | 57–13 | 4–0 | Skip Bertman |
| Alabama | Southeastern | 56–14 | 4–2 | Jim Wells |
| Miami | Independent | 51–18 | 2–2 | Jim Morris |
| Stanford | Pacific-10 | 45–20 | 2–2 | Mark Marquess |
| Auburn | Southeastern | 50–17 | 1–2 | Hal Baird |
| Mississippi State | Southeastern | 47–21 | 1–2 | Ron Polk |
| Rice | Western Athletic | 47–16 | 0–2 | Wayne Graham |
| UCLA | Pacific-10 | 45–21–1 | 0–2 | Gary Adams |

### NATIONAL CHAMPION
### LOUISIANA STATE

LSU is the first team to win back-to-back CWS titles since Stanford in 1987-88. In Omaha, the Tigers narrowly defeated Rice before romping Stanford twice and winning the championship game against Alabama with a 13-6 score.

you can't steal. Your defense isn't great but only adequate. It's difficult when you grew up in your coaching career with pitching and defense."

This year's Tigers were expected to be little more than adequate, at least by LSU standards. They lost seven of their nine starters from their 1996 lineup, plus ace lefthander Eddie Yarnall.

When told his team was ranked No. 11 in the Baseball America preseason Top 25 ranking, Bertman said, "I think we're a year away. I think a year from now you will be calling me about being on top."

The Tigers moved up the timetable by winning their first 19 games, running their two-season winning streak to an SEC-record 27. Their power allowed them to rally time and again, because they trailed at some point in 30 of their 57 victories.

Once the Tigers arrived in Omaha, they were challenged seriously only in their opener, when they trailed Rice 4-2 in the bottom of the eighth. Then junior shortstop Brandon Larson stunned All-America righthander Matt Anderson, who had allowed one homer all year, with a two-run blast to tie it. Freshman right fielder Jeremy Witten won the game moments later with a sacrifice fly.

Anderson, the No. 1 overall pick in the draft four days later, was the first of three first-round picks savaged by Louisiana State.

Stanford junior righthander Kyle Peterson took his worst loss of the year when the Tigers touched him for three homers and seven runs in five innings of a 10-5 rout the day before the Brewers selected him in the first round. Then they ripped Cardinal sophomore righthander Chad Hutchinson, the Braves' top choice in 1995, for six runs in two innings en route to a 13-9 victory.

The championship game featured a renewal of what quickly has become college base-

# 1997 NEWSMAKERS

The level of offense took a notable uptick in 1997, with batting averages in **Division I** climbing from a collective .294 to .304 and home runs taking a pronounced leap from 0.77 per game in 1996 to a record 0.96. National champion Louisiana State set the tone for much of the offensive onslaught by hitting an NCAA single-season record 188 homers.

After making its first NCAA Tournament appearance in 1995 with the talented freshman tandem of righthander **Matt Anderson** and outfielder **Lance Berkman** contributing, **Rice** made its first trip to the CWS in 1997 behind the exhilarating performances of Anderson, who became the top pick in the 1997 draft on the strength of his 100 mph fastball, and Berkman, whose breakout power display led to his being taken by the hometown Astros with the 16th pick overall. Anderson pitched only in relief as a junior, but led the Owls with 10 wins, nine saves, a 2.05 ERA and 105 strikeouts (in 79 innings), while Berkman hit a team-best .431 and topped the nation with 41 homers and 134 RBIs—after homering just six times as a freshman and going deep on 20 occasions as a sophomore. .

**FINAL TOP 25 FOR 1997**

1. Louisiana State*
2. Alabama*
3. Miami*
4. #Stanford*
5. UCLA*
6. Auburn*
7. Mississippi State*
8. Rice*
9. Florida State
10. Southern California
11. Arizona State
12. Texas Tech
13. Washington
14. Oklahoma State
15. South Alabama
16. Florida
17. Georgia Tech
18. Long Beach State
19. Oklahoma
20. Southwestern Louisiana
21. North Carolina State
22. Santa Clara
23. Fresno State
24. Cal State Fullerton
25. Tennessee

* Reached College World Series
# Preseason No. 1

# IN RETROSPECT: 1997 DRAFT

**Top 10 Draft Picks From College**
With overall selection number (Ov), drafting team (Team) and rank on Baseball America draft board (BA).

| Player | Pos | School | Ov | Team | BA |
|---|---|---|---|---|---|
| Matt Anderson | RHP | Rice | 1 | Tigers | 4 |
| J.D. Drew* | OF | Florida State | 2 | Phillies | 2 |
| Troy Glaus | 3B | UCLA | 3 | Angels | 3 |
| Jason Grilli | RHP | Seton Hall | 4 | Giants | 6 |
| Dan Reichert | RHP | Pacific | 7 | Royals | 35 |
| Chris Enochs | RHP | West Virginia | 11 | Athletics | 11 |
| Kyle Peterson | RHP | Stanford | 13 | Brewers | 26 |
| Brandon Larson | SS | Louisiana State | 14 | Reds | 92 |
| Jason Dellaero | SS | South Florida | 15 | White Sox | 13 |
| Lance Berkman | 1B | Rice | 16 | Astros | 19 |

\* Did not sign

**Top 10 Major League Players From College Draft Class**
With draft round and Baseball-Reference.com total for wins above replacement (WAR) through 2019.

| Player | Pos | School | Rd | Ov | Team | WAR |
|---|---|---|---|---|---|---|
| Tim Hudson | RHP | Auburn | 6 | 185 | Athletics | 58.2 |
| Lance Berkman | OF | Rice | 1 | 16 | Astros | 52.1 |
| Troy Glaus | 3B | UCLA | 1 | 3 | Angels | 38.0 |
| Michael Young | SS | UC Santa Barbara | 5 | 149 | Blue Jays | 24.6 |
| Randy Wolf | LHP | Pepperdine | 2 | 54 | Phillies | 22.8 |
| Adam Kennedy | 2B | Cal State Northridge | 1 | 20 | Cardinals | 21.0 |
| David Eckstein | SS | Florida | 19 | 581 | Red Sox | 20.9 |
| Jerry Hairston | 2B | Southern Illinois | 11 | 345 | Orioles | 13.1 |
| Scot Shields | RHP | Lincoln Memorial | 38 | 1137 | Angels | 12.1 |
| Scott Downs | LHP | Kentucky | 3 | 94 | Cubs | 10.9 |

ball's best rivalry against Alabama.

They had met five times before and all were high-stakes matchups. In the final week of the regular season, Alabama won twice, including a 28-2 blowout that was the worst loss in Tigers history, before Louisiana State took the third game to earn the SEC regular season title. The Crimson Tide lost to the Tigers in the third round of the SEC Tournament, then rebounded to win the rematch in the finale for its third straight SEC postseason title.

After Alabama won the SEC championship game, little-used junior righthander Mike Daniel was pummeled in the CWS finale. Louisiana State junior DH Danny Higgins led off the bottom of the first with a homer, setting the tone for a six-run outburst that he capped with a two-run single. Daniel recorded only two outs and surrendered five runs and LSU stretched the lead to 9-0 after two innings.

Alabama cut the lead to 9-4 and had the bases loaded in the fifth before junior righthander Doug Thompson entered the game and squelched the rally. Larson, the CWS Most Outstanding Player, sealed the Tide's fate with a two-run single in the sixth.

Louisiana State will return most of its lineup and should contend for a three-peat in 1998. The Tigers will lose some key pitchers, but they have shown that championships aren't won on the mound.

"It's changed a lot in the last five or six years," Bertman said. "Next year you better get on the power train if you want to compete, at least until they change the alloy in the aluminum bats."

Bertman has had no problem adapting in the past. The rest of college baseball still is trying to catch up. ∎

# Drew tops off career as top college player

By **JIM CALLIS**

Mike Martin relishes the question about as much as pitchers relished facing his superstar center fielder.

Is J.D. Drew the best player ever at Florida State?

"J.D. Drew is the best hitter I've seen at FSU, and I've been there half the years they've had baseball," said Martin, a Seminoles center fielder in the mid-1960s and their head coach since 1980.

"There's been only one guy who could run better than him, and he's playing defensive back for the Dallas Cowboys," he said, referring to Deion Sanders. "He has as strong an arm as anybody we've had in the program from the outfield.

"He's obviously the total package."

Press Martin, and he'll concede that he doesn't want to answer the question directly. FSU has produced 22 first-team All-Americans and 13 first-round draft picks. He doesn't want to slight anybody.

Florida State's J.D. Drew hit 31 homers and stole 32 bags to become college baseball's first 30-30 player. In a quietly consistent 14-year big league career, he hit .278/.384/.489 with 242 homers.

But it's Martin's own fault. Drew had not played a game for the Seminoles before his coach said he had the potential to be the best player in program history. Martin reiterated that point after Drew, as a freshman, became the first player to hit three home runs in a College World Series game.

Drew has done nothing to hurt his case in three years at Tallahassee. He has batted .391-69-257 with 53 steals in 200 games, setting nine school and eight Atlantic Coast Conference records.

He furthered his cause in 1997, winning the College Player of the Year award. Drew hit .455-31-100 with 32 steals, led Division I with 110 runs and 84 walks and even put together a 34-game hitting streak.

The 30-30 season was unprecedented in college baseball. Only Virginia Tech first baseman Franklin Stubbs, who had 29 homers and 34 steals in 1981, and Utah outfielder Casey Child, who had 31 homers and 27 steals this year, ever approached the feat.

Drew, who would much rather hunt or fish than talk about himself, isn't one to worry about personal accomplishments. But he did want to become college baseball's first 30-30 man.

"People asked me at the beginning of the year what my goals were, and I told them I just wanted to have quality at-bats," Drew said. "But once I found out the mark could be accomplished, I wanted to do it. As I got closer, the home runs were a little tougher to come by. I started to press a little bit."

Martin noticed Drew at his baseball camp. Martin couldn't believe such a skinny kid could have so much power, and he told his assistants not to bother recruiting Drew because there was no way major league teams would let him get away.

But they did. The Giants took him in the 20th round of the 1994 draft and tried to sway him with a late $100,000 offer. When Drew declined, saying he wanted to go to college to get bigger and stronger, the Giants' area scout asked, "How much bigger and stronger can you get?"

The answer was plenty. Drew has cut his time in the 60-yard dash from 6.77 to 6.4 seconds. He spent last offseason lifting weights and bulked up to 6-foot-1, 195 pounds. He also made himself into the consensus best prospect in the 1997 draft class.

"I've never seen anybody have a better year than J.D. Drew had," Martin said. "Consistency is paramount, and this is a guy who hits .455, scores 110 runs. That's mind-boggling to go with 100 RBIs, 31 home runs and 32 steals. That's something that may not ever really happen again."

Florida State may not ever really see another player like Drew. Just don't ask Mike Martin to admit it. ■

# TOP PLAYERS OF 1997

## ALL-AMERICA TEAM

| Pos | Player | School | Yr | AVG | AB | R | H | HR | RBI | SB |
|-----|--------|--------|----|----|----|----|----|----|----|----|
| C | Matt LeCroy | Clemson | Jr | .359 | 237 | 62 | 85 | 24 | 79 | 5 |
| 1B | Lance Berkman | Rice | Jr | .431 | 255 | 109 | 110 | 41 | 134 | 8 |
| 2B | Tom Sergio | North Carolina State | Sr | .412 | 243 | 85 | 100 | 16 | 68 | 18 |
| 3B | Troy Glaus | UCLA | Jr | .409 | 264 | 100 | 108 | 34 | 91 | 10 |
| SS | Brandon Larson | Louisiana State | Jr | .381 | 289 | 82 | 110 | 40 | 118 | 9 |
| OF | J.D. Drew | Florida State | Jr | .455 | 233 | 110 | 106 | 31 | 100 | 32 |
| OF | Jeremy Morris | Florida State | Sr | .356 | 250 | 73 | 89 | 25 | 116 | 25 |
| OF | Brad Wilkerson | Florida | So | .386 | 236 | 82 | 91 | 23 | 76 | 11 |
| DH | Pat Burrell | Miami | So | .409 | 215 | 79 | 88 | 21 | 76 | 12 |
| UT | Tim Hudson | Auburn | Sr | .396 | 273 | 71 | 108 | 18 | 95 | 2 |

| Pos | Pitcher | School | Yr | W | L | ERA | G | SV | IP | H | BB | SO |
|-----|---------|--------|----|----|----|----|----|----|----|----|----|----|
| P | Matt Anderson | Rice | Jr | 10 | 2 | 2.05 | 30 | 9 | 79 | 48 | 29 | 105 |
| P | Jim Parque | UCLA | Jr | 13 | 2 | 3.08 | 19 | 0 | 120 | 117 | 63 | 119 |
| P | Kyle Peterson | Stanford | Jr | 11 | 3 | 4.19 | 20 | 0 | 144 | 134 | 38 | 156 |
| P | Dan Reichert | Pacific | Jr | 13 | 4 | 2.30 | 20 | 0 | 133 | 96 | 51 | 169 |
| P | Jeff Weaver | Fresno State | So | 11 | 5 | 3.63 | 21 | 2 | 141 | 130 | 25 | 181 |
| UT | Tim Hudson | Auburn | Sr | 15 | 2 | 2.97 | 22 | 0 | 118 | 87 | 50 | 165 |

## SECOND TEAM

**C**—Giuseppe Chiaramonte, Fresno State. **1B**—Joe Dillon, Texas Tech. **2B**—Keith Ginter, Texas Tech. **3B**—Andy Dominique, Nevada. **SS**—Kevin Nicholson, Stetson. **OF**—Mark Fischer, Georgia Tech; Mike Marchiano, Fordham; and Dan McKinley, Arizona State. **DH**—Adam Kennedy, Cal State Northridge. **UT**—Mike Frank, Santa Clara. **P**—Randy Choate, Florida State; Chris Enochs, West Virginia; Jason Gooding, Texas Tech; Jason Navarro, Tulane; and Randy Wolf, Pepperdine.

## THIRD TEAM

**C**—Jason Grabowski, Connecticut. **1B**—Ross Gload, South Florida. **2B**—Harvey Hargrove, Sacramento State. **3B**—Rusty McNamara, Oklahoma State. **SS**—Kevin Miller, Washington. **OF**—Casey Child, Utah; Jason Fitzgerald, Tulane; and Geofrey Tomlinson, Houston. **DH**—Jon Heinrichs, UCLA. **UT**—Roberto Vaz, Alabama. **P**—Patrick Coogan, Louisiana State; Robbie Morrison, Miami; Jason Parsons, UNC Greensboro; Trey Poland, Southwestern Louisiana; and Kris Wilson, Georgia Tech.

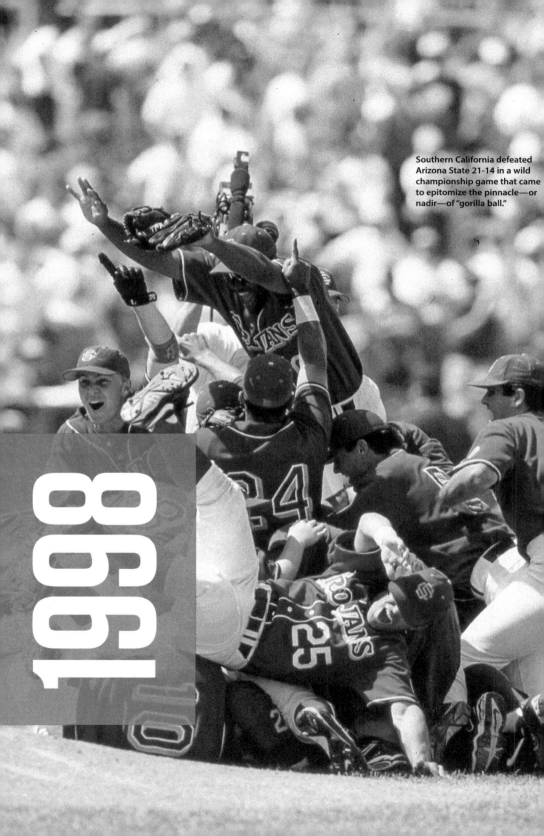

Southern California defeated Arizona State 21-14 in a wild championship game that came to epitomize the pinnacle—or nadir—of "gorilla ball."

1998

# Southern California restores old order

By **JOHN MANUEL**

Only at the College World Series could the old and new worlds of college baseball come together so perfectly.

In the new world, players get juiced up on weightlifting and creatine, swing juiced bats at a tightly wound, juiced ball and produce juiced scores. Hitters turned Rosenblatt Stadium into Rosenblast this year, with 56 offensive records tied or broken in the CWS and 35 runs scored in the championship game alone.

In the old world, teams from the Pacific-10 Conference South were king. Current Six-Pac members claimed 23 championships in the first 42 years of the CWS, including 11 by Southern California and longtime coach Rod Dedeaux, the most of any school. Arizona State was second with five.

**FROM THE ISSUE:**
JULY 6-19, 1998

Worlds collided in the championship game this year between the Trojans and Sun Devils, guaranteeing the Six-Pac its first title since Stanford repeated as champion in 1988. Southern California pounded out 23 hits, five of them by tournament Most Outstanding Player Wes Rachels, for a 21-14 victory. It was the first championship for the Trojans since 1978, when they had also defeated Arizona State.

"If you had told me 20 years ago that it would be 20 years before Southern California won a national championship, no, I would not have believed it," Trojans coach Mike Gillespie said.

"And I would not have believed you if you had told me 10 years ago it would be 10 years before another team from our conference would win the national championship.

Perhaps it took that long for the old world to catch up to college baseball's brave new one. The epitome of that new order is Southeastern Conference powerhouse Louisiana State, which had won the last two championships and four of the last seven. Coach Skip Bertman's Tigers were seeded fifth behind USC, and the two teams locked up in three of the tournament's best games.

In the first matchup, the Tigers looked like they would prevail again. With the wind blowing out at up to 20 mph, they pounded Trojans senior ace Seth Etherton for six home

## TOP TEAMS
### 1998 COLLEGE WORLD SERIES STANDINGS

| School | Conference | Record | CWS | Head coach |
| --- | --- | --- | --- | --- |
| Southern California | Pacific-10 | 49–17 | 5–1 | Mike Gillespie |
| Arizona State | Pacific-10 | 41–23 | 3–1 | Pat Murphy |
| Long Beach State | Big West | 44–23–1 | 2–2 | Dave Snow |
| Louisiana State | Southeastern | 48–19 | 2–2 | Skip Bertman |
| Miami | Independent | 51–12 | 1–2 | Jim Morris |
| Mississippi State | Southeastern | 42–23 | 1–2 | Pat McMahon |
| Florida | Southeastern | 46–18 | 0–2 | Andy Lopez |
| Florida State | Atlantic Coast | 53–20 | 0–2 | Mike Martin |

### NATIONAL CHAMPION
### SOUTHERN CALIFORNIA

The Trojans claimed their record 12th national title, but it was their first since 1978 and it remains the program's last through 2019. USC defeated Arizona State 21-14 in the championship game, epitomizing the college game's "gorilla ball" period.

runs and seven runs in six innings. LSU hit eight homers in the game, smashing the CWS single-game record of five, and got a two-run bloop single by Trey McClure in the eighth for a 12-10 victory.

No team had lost its first game and won the championship since Arizona in 1980. The Trojans came close in 1995, when they lost their opener and advanced to the championship game before losing to Cal State Fullerton.

Five members of this year's team were on that club, including Etherton, Rachels, closer Jack Krawczyk and starting third baseman Morgan Ensberg. They knew what it would take to recover from the opening loss.

USC rebounded from its loss to LSU with a wild, 12-10 win against top-seeded Florida. The Gators became the second No. 1 seed to go 0-2 in Omaha.

The Trojans then got the tournament's best pitching performance from freshman righthander Rik Currier. He fanned 12 in eight innings while allowing four hits as USC eliminated Mississippi State to reach the bracket championship against LSU. Four days after he was hammered by the Tigers, Etherton struck out 10 in a 5-4 win. That ended LSU's 10-game Omaha winning streak.

LSU's season ended the next day when junior righthander Mike Penney outdueled Tigers ace Doug Thompson. Penney shut out the Tigers over the first seven innings in a 7-3 triumph. Louisiana State hit just three home runs in the two losses.

Arizona State hit fewer homers than any team in the CWS, but the Sun Devils came to the brink of a national championship with opportunistic offense and strong pitching. Pat Murphy's club used six Florida State errors and stellar relief pitching by freshman right-hander Chad Pennington to win its opener. The Sun Devils then dominated Miami and Long Beach State, giving them two days off before meeting Southern California for the

# 1998 NEWSMAKERS

Offensive records tumbled in 1998 in the highest-scoring sea-son in college history. **Division I** teams combined to hit .306 (tying a record set in 1985), and established marks for runs per game (7.12) and home runs per game (1.06). Appropriately, the collective ERA of pitchers rose to 6.12—easily the highest ever.

**Wichita State** became the highest-scoring team on record by scoring 760 runs in 63 games—an average of 12.06 runs per game, which eclipsed the old mark of 11.43, set in 1987 by Oklahoma State. All that production enabled the Shockers to post a sterling 56-7 record (.889), for the best winning percent-age of the '90s. In one of the biggest upsets of the decade, the Shockers failed to advance out of regional play—going just 1-2 as the host team in the Midwest Regional.

With a save in **Southern California's** wild 21-14 win over Arizona State, senior closer **Jack Krawczyk** not only set the NCAA single-season mark of 23, but also the career record of 49. Krawczyk's season record lasted until 2013, when it was broken by UCLA's David Berg, with 24, and the career mark until 2003, when UC Irvine's Blair Erickson finished with 53.

**FINAL TOP 25 FOR 1998**

1. Southern California*
2. Arizona State*
3. Miami*
4. Louisiana State*
5. Florida*
6. #Stanford
7. Florida State*
8. Wichita State
9. Auburn
10. Long Beach State*
11. Texas A&M
12. Alabama
13. Cal State Fullerton
14. Mississippi State*
15. Rice
16. South Carolina
17. Washington
18. South Alabama
19. Georgia Tech
20. Tulane
21. Clemson
22. Baylor
23. Illinois
24. North Carolina
25. Texas Tech

\* Reached College World Series
\# Preseason No. 1

# IN RETROSPECT: 1998 DRAFT

## Top 10 Draft Picks From College
With overall selection number (Ov), drafting team (Team) and rank on Baseball America draft board (BA).

| Player | Pos | School | Ov | Team | BA |
|---|---|---|---|---|---|
| Pat Burrell | 3B | Miami | 1 | Phillies | 1 |
| Mark Mulder | LHP | Michigan State | 2 | Athletics | 2 |
| Jeff Austin | RHP | Stanford | 4 | Royals | 4 |
| Ryan Mills | LHP | Arizona State | 6 | Twins | 3 |
| Carlos Pena | 1B | Northeastern | 10 | Rangers | 10 |
| Adam Everett | SS | South Carolina | 12 | Red Sox | 18 |
| Jeff Weaver | RHP | Fresno State | 14 | Tigers | 13 |
| Clint Johnston | LHP | Vanderbilt | 15 | Pirates | 54 |
| Kip Wells | RHP | Baylor | 16 | White Sox | 7 |
| Brad Lidge | RHP | Notre Dame | 17 | Astros | 16 |

## Top 10 Major League Players From College Draft Class
With draft round and Baseball-Reference.com total for wins above replacement (WAR) through 2019.

| Player | Pos | School | Rd | Ov | Team | WAR |
|---|---|---|---|---|---|---|
| J.D. Drew | OF | Florida State | 1 | 5 | Cardinals | 44.9 |
| Carlos Peña | 1B | Northeastern | 1 | 10 | Rangers | 25.1 |
| Aaron Rowand | OF | Cal State Fullerton | 1s | 35 | White Sox | 20.9 |
| Aubrey Huff | 1B | Miami | 5 | 162 | Devil Rays | 20.4 |
| Mark Mulder | LHP | Michigan State | 1 | 2 | Athletics | 20.1 |
| Brandon Inge | 3B | Va. Commonwealth | 2 | 57 | Tigers | 19.2 |
| Pat Burrell | OF | Miami | 1 | 1 | Phillies | 18.9 |
| Juan Pierre | OF | South Alabama | 13 | 390 | Rockies | 17.1 |
| Jeff Weaver | RHP | Fresno State | 1 | 14 | Tigers | 15.2 |
| Morgan Ensberg | 3B | Southern Calif. | 9 | 272 | Astros | 13.8 |

seventh time this season. They had split their first six meetings.

Lefthander Ryan Mills was on the mound with five days of rest for Arizona State, facing Currier and a Trojans team playing its sixth game in seven days. The Sun Devils should have been favored coming in, but Murphy wasn't so sure.

Mills had thrown 150 pitches in the Midwest Regional final against Georgia Tech and he wasn't at his best against Miami. All he had left for the Trojans was one trip through the order. "I think he's just run out of gas," Murphy said.

Mills gave up six runs in one-plus inning. After eight hits, two homers by Robb Gorr and one by Rachels, the Trojans led 8-0.

But Currier and three USC relievers barely held the lead. With a grand slam by Michael Collins and two-run homers by Jeff Phelps and Andrew Beinbrink, the Sun Devils twice clawed back within a run at 9-8 and 14-13. It took the 75 mph changeup of Krawczyk to silence the bats, as he retired two batters who represented the tying run in the bottom of the eighth.

In the top of the ninth, the Trojans put it away. With a run in, the Sun Devils intentionally walked Brad Ticehurst to get to junior DH Jason Lane. Lane, who was credited with the win in relief of Currier, blasted a 1-1 pitch from Chuck Crumpton for a grand slam and a 21-14 cushion.

Krawczyk retired the last three batters, setting off the obligatory celebration. It could have been a celebration of college baseball's old world as well. With the elimination of the baseball program at Portland State, Pac-10 coaches were discussing a move to a nine-team, one-division league that would end the Six-Pac on an unmatched high note. ∎

# Top player Austin avoids mistakes

By **JOHN MANUEL**

Just 962 fans attended the April 3 matchup of No. 1 Stanford at No. 2 Southern California at Dedeaux Field.

As the years pass, though thousands of college baseball fans, scouts, scouting directors and players probably will claim to have been among the crowd.

What those 962 fans witnessed was a cut above the average baseball game, whatever the level. They saw two pitchers at the top of their games, dueling pitch for pitch. One mistake was all it took to lose.

Senior righthander Seth Etherton had his best performance as a Trojan. He yielded just four hits, walked one batter and struck out 15 while throwing 130 pitches.

But he made one mistake. He hung a curveball to Cardinal center fielder Jody Gerut, who deposited the pitch over the right field wall.

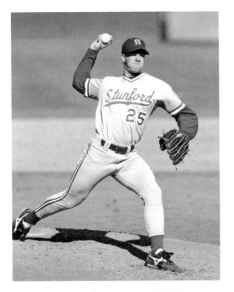

In an epic year for offense, Stanford's Jeff Austin kept opposing bats at bay by going 12-4, 3.11. He never made an impact in the big leagues, logging a 6.75 ERA in 65 innings in three cups of coffee.

Stanford righthander Jeff Austin scattered six hits across his nine innings. In the bottom of the ninth, clinging to the one-run lead, Austin did what he does best. He made the pitches he had to make. After a leadoff double to Eric Munson and a sacrifice bunt, Austin got a strikeout and a pop out to seal the shutout and win the year's best game.

Austin didn't make a mistake that night, and he made precious few during a splendid junior season. For that, he is the College Player of the Year.

One game isn't all that separates Austin from Etherton or other candidates. Austin's consistency and leading role on what was the nation's best team for most of the season put him at the forefront.

Austin's 12-4, 3.11 record put him among the national leaders in wins and ERA. And every Friday night, Austin faced off with the Pacific-10 Conference's top starters.

That was a major goal of Austin's coming into the season. He wanted to be the one to replace two-time All-American Kyle Peterson at the front of the Stanford rotation.

Austin won his first nine decisions, losing the week after his showdown with Etherton. Both pitchers admitted to a letdown after that game. It was just too good to match.

"There was a lot of hype, and I had not had anything like that," Etherton said. "All I could think about the whole week was playing Stanford, the No. 1 team, and facing Jeff."

"I was exactly the same way," Austin said.

"The second my game ended the week before, I was looking forward to USC. If I hadn't thought that way, I probably would have lost. It takes that kind of concentration and effort to go against those guys."

Austin says he emulates Etherton in some respects, such as knowing when to stay out of the middle of the strike zone. He also picked up pointers while pitching for Team USA last summer.

"I started pitching and learning I don't have to overpower every hitter, not always max out," Austin said. "There were a lot of older guys, guys like Pedro Lazo for Cuba. Here's this guy who can throw in the upper 90s, but he only does it 20 percent of the time.

"Watching him hit the black time after time, I took a little of that and put it in my own bag."

Austin's improved bag of pitches helped Stanford win 41 games. Austin won the rematch with Southern California, a 4-2 victory that clinched the Pac-10 South title.

But Stanford won only one more game, losing six of its last seven.

Austin has plenty of pitching ahead of him after the Royals drafted him fourth overall. But he knows he may never again pitch a game as unique and as special as the one he pitched April 3.

"I think Seth outpitched me that night," Austin said. "He made one mistake and they hit some hard balls right at our guys. But we got the win." ∎

# TOP PLAYERS OF 1998

## ALL-AMERICA TEAM

| Pos | Player | School | Yr | AVG | AB | R | H | HR | RBI | SB |
|-----|--------|--------|-----|-----|-----|-----|-----|-----|-----|-----|
| C | Sammy Serrano | Stetson | Jr | .457 | 245 | 71 | 112 | 13 | 68 | 8 |
| 1B | Eddy Furniss | Louisiana State | Sr | .403 | 236 | 85 | 95 | 28 | 76 | 0 |
| 2B | Jeff Pickler | Tennessee | Sr | .445 | 245 | 79 | 109 | 7 | 61 | 25 |
| 3B | Aubrey Huff | Miami | Jr | .412 | 233 | 71 | 96 | 21 | 95 | 4 |
| SS | Adam Everett | South Carolina | Jr | .375 | 267 | 71 | 100 | 13 | 63 | 15 |
| OF | Bubba Crosby | Rice | Jr | .394 | 221 | 73 | 87 | 25 | 91 | 2 |
| OF | Mike Curry | South Carolina | Jr | .400 | 260 | 102 | 104 | 16 | 46 | 60 |
| OF | Eric Valent | UCLA | Jr | .336 | 220 | 69 | 74 | 30 | 73 | 4 |
| DH | Damon Thames | Rice | Jr | .424 | 283 | 88 | 120 | 26 | 115 | 4 |
| UT | Brad Wilkerson | Florida | Jr | .347 | 222 | 86 | 77 | 23 | 70 | 20 |

| Pos | Pitcher | School | Yr | W | L | ERA | G | SV | IP | H | BB | SO |
|-----|---------|--------|-----|-----|-----|-----|-----|-----|-----|-----|-----|-----|
| SP | Jeff Austin | Stanford | Jr | 12 | 4 | 3.11 | 18 | 0 | 133 | 118 | 32 | 136 |
| SP | Seth Etherton | Southern California | Sr | 13 | 3 | 3.23 | 18 | 0 | 137 | 113 | 29 | 182 |
| SP | Mike Fischer | South Alabama | Jr | 11 | 1 | 2.31 | 20 | 1 | 125 | 91 | 23 | 120 |
| SP | Alex Santos | Miami | So | 15 | 1 | 2.54 | 18 | 0 | 110 | 85 | 28 | 142 |
| RP | Josh Fogg | Florida | Jr | 7 | 2 | 2.03 | 40 | 13 | 84 | 63 | 30 | 114 |
| UT | Brad Wilkerson | Florida | Jr | 10 | 5 | 5.05 | 18 | 0 | 118 | 134 | 69 | 136 |

## SECOND TEAM

C—Eric Munson, Southern California. 1B—Jason Hart, Southwest Missouri State. 2B—Xavier Nady, California. 3B—Paul Day, Long Beach State. SS—Zach Sorensen, Wichita State. OF—Clinton Johnston, Vanderbilt; Kevin Mench, Delaware; and Jeff Ryan, Wichita State. DH—Pat Magness, Wichita State. UT—Brandon Inge, Virginia Commonwealth. SP—Matt Burch, Virginia Commonwealth; Ryan Rupe, Texas A&M; Jeff Weaver, Fresno State; and Kip Wells, Baylor. RP—Jack Krawczyk, Southern California.

## THIRD TEAM

C—Josh Bard, Texas Tech. 1B—Casey Bookout, Oklahoma. 2B—Willie Bloomquist, Arizona State. 3B—Brant Ust, Notre Dame. SS—Bobby Hill, Miami. OF—Chris Magruder, Washington; Terrmel Sledge, Long Beach State; and Jason Tyner, Texas A&M. DH—Pat Burrell, Miami. UT—Jason Jennings, Baylor. SP—Nate Bump, Penn State; Benito Flores, Cal State Fullerton; John Hendricks, Wake Forest; and Shane Wright, Texas Tech. RP—Robbie Morrison, Miami.

**1999**

Miami coach Jim Morris, pictured here in 2010, took over in 1994 and guided the Hurricanes to regionals for 23 straight seasons, winning titles in 1999 and 2001.

# Miami uses plan to perfection

By **JOHN MANUEL**

Runners on first and second, no outs.

Miami coach Jim Morris never hesitated in that situation this season. Whether it was the first inning or later, whether it was the No. 9 hitter in the lineup or his No. 3 hitter, outfielder Manny Crespo, Morris often called for the sacrifice bunt.

"I like to bunt and I like the running part of the game," Morris said. "That was part of the game before we got gorillas at the plate, with both aluminum and wood. We've gotta go with what's best for us and our team, and that's putting pressure on the other guys. When you do that, a lot of times they make mistakes. We've worked very hard on bunting this year, probably more than ever. I like this type of game; it's more fun to coach.

**FROM THE ISSUE:**
JULY 12-25, 1999

"We focus on getting a lead and getting the game to our bullpen. I believe in our setup guy and our closer. I feel like if we go into the seventh inning with a lead, we've got a great shot at getting a win."

Miami didn't deviate from that blueprint for victory all year, even at Rosenblatt Stadium, site of some of baseball's most offensive games. The 1998 championship game, won 21-14 by Southern California, was college baseball's ultimate offensive orgy, the cap of a prolific Omaha tournament that saw 56 offensive records broken or tied.

Facing Florida State—its biggest rival—in the 1999 championship game, Miami used some gorilla ball itself. Sophomore first baseman Kevin Brown was the offensive hero, driving in four runs with a mammoth solo home run and a three-run double in the Hurricanes' 6-5 victory.

But when he had first and second with no one out in the championship game's first inning, Morris didn't hesitate. He called on Crespo, his best hitter, to bunt.

Miami didn't score in the inning thanks to Florida State outfielder Matt Diaz, who gunned down Bobby Hill at the plate on a fly ball to end the inning. But Diaz couldn't keep Hill off base—he was on four times in the title game, stole a base, scored a run and generally kept the pressure on Florida State.

## TOP TEAMS
### 1999 COLLEGE WORLD SERIES STANDINGS

| School | Conference | Record | CWS | Head Coach |
|---|---|---|---|---|
| Miami | Independent | 50–13 | 4–0 | Jim Morris |
| Florida State | Atlantic Coast | 57–14 | 4–2 | Mike Martin |
| Alabama | Southeastern | 53–16 | 2–2 | Jim Wells |
| Stanford | Pacific-10 | 50–15 | 2–2 | Mark Marquess |
| Cal State Fullerton | Big West | 50–14 | 1–2 | George Horton |
| Rice | Western Athletic | 59–15 | 1–2 | Wayne Graham |
| Oklahoma State | Big 12 | 46–21 | 0–2 | Tom Holliday |
| Texas A&M | Big 12 | 52–18 | 0–2 | Mark Johnson |

### NATIONAL CHAMPION
### MIAMI

The NCAA Tournament expanded to 64 teams, but the championship game came down to Sunshine State rivals. Miami defeated Florida State 6-5 to claim the program's third national title and first under coach Jim Morris. Kevin Brown drove in four.

All according to Jim Morris' plan.

Those blueprints for victory propelled Miami through the regular season and earned it the No. 1 seed in the nation entering regional play. The Hurricanes backed up the ranking by streamrolling through the postseason, winning nine consecutive games and their third national championship, the first since 1985.

They capped the season by defeating the No. 2-seeded Seminoles for the sixth consecutive time out of their seven meetings. Five of the six wins were decided by one run, with Miami's bullpen always preserving a tight game.

"That's the way we had to play," said Hill, the junior shortstop who ignited Miami's lineup for three seasons. "We had to do the little things to win. Last year, we'd make mistakes and we still won. We just mashed our way through mistakes until we got to Omaha. This year, we couldn't afford to make mistakes, and we had to do all the little things like bunt, steal bases, hit the cutoff man, just to win games."

Miami could throw a pair of solid junior righthanders, David Gil and Alex Santos, to give them quality starts. And the Hurricanes had little trouble once they got to their bullpen.

Morris never hesitated to use freshman righthander Vince Vazquez, his setup man who regularly got the game to closer Mike Neu with a lead.

After giving up a game-winning home run in his first save opportunity of the season, Neu blew only one other save. He finished the year with 16 saves, registering three in the CWS, and led the nation in strikeout rate with 14.6 per nine innings.

Out of fresh arms for the championship game, Florida State sent freshman righthander Blair Varnes to the mound for the championship game, despite Varnes' damaged left knee. A Sam Scott solo homer staked Varnes to a 2-1 lead, but the Hurricanes rallied

# 1999 NEWSMAKERS

The overriding storyline was an attempt by the NCAA to regulate **aluminum bats**, which contributed to record offensive numbers in 1998. Until a new set of regulations were put in place for the 2000 season, most aluminum bats used in 1999 were a little heavier and narrower—and a little less nuclear. Home runs dipped by 10 percent across the board.

A revised **NCAA Tournament** format in 1999 made it doubly difficult for teams to advance to Omaha. The regional field expanded from 48 to 64 teams, and now teams were required to compete in one of 16 four-team regionals, with the survivors then squaring off in eight best-of-three series, or super regionals. The 64-team arrangement eliminated the old grinding, pitching-depleting six-team regional format

Florida State's **Marshall McDougall** led the nation in runs (104), hits (126), total bases (242), RBIs (106) and slugging (.804). His May 9 barrage in his team's 26-2 win over Maryland helped lead the way. McDougall went 7-for-7 in the encounter, while hitting six home runs, driving in 16 runs and piling up 25 total bases—all NCAA single-game records.

## FINAL TOP 25 FOR 1999

1. Miami*
2. Florida State*
3. Stanford*
4. Alabama*
5. Rice*
6. Cal State Fullerton*
7. Texas A&M*
8. Baylor
9. Oklahoma State*
10. #Southern California
11. Wake Forest
12. Ohio State
13. Auburn
14. Wichita State
15. Tulane
16. Louisiana State
17. Clemson
18. Pepperdine
19. East Carolina
20. Southwestern Louisiana
21. Florida Atlantic
22. Providence
23. Arkansas
24. Houston
25. Nebraska

\* Reached College World Series
\# Preseason No. 1

# IN RETROSPECT: 1999 DRAFT

## Top 10 Draft Picks From College
With overall selection number (Ov), drafting team (Team) and rank on Baseball America draft board (BA).

| Player | Pos | School | Ov | Team | BA |
|---|---|---|---|---|---|
| Eric Munson | C | Southern California | 3 | Tigers | 3 |
| Kyle Snyder | RHP | North Carolina | 7 | Royals | 9 |
| Barry Zito | LHP | Southern California | 9 | Athletics | 32 |
| Ben Sheets | RHP | Northeast Louisiana | 10 | Brewers | 4 |
| Mike Paradis | RHP | Clemson | 13 | Orioles | 17 |
| Jason Jennings | RHP | Baylor | 16 | Rockies | 24 |
| Larry Bigbie | OF | Ball State | 21 | Orioles | 37 |
| Matt Ginter | RHP | Mississippi State | 22 | White Sox | 21 |
| Keith Reed | OF | Providence | 23 | Orioles | 8 |
| Kurt Ainsworth | RHP | Louisiana State | 24 | Giants | 43 |

## Top 10 Major League Players From College Draft Class
With draft round and Baseball-Reference.com total for wins above replacement (WAR) through 2019.

| Player | Pos | School | Rd | Ov | Team | WAR |
|---|---|---|---|---|---|---|
| Mark Ellis | 2B | Florida | 9 | 271 | Royals | 33.6 |
| Barry Zito | LHP | Southern Calif. | 1 | 9 | Athletics | 32.0 |
| Brian Roberts | 2B | South Carolina | 1s | 50 | Orioles | 30.4 |
| Ben Sheets | RHP | Louisiana-Monroe | 1 | 10 | Brewers | 23.3 |
| Aaron Harang | RHP | San Diego State | 6 | 195 | Rangers | 20.1 |
| Lyle Overbay | 1B | Nevada | 18 | 538 | D-backs | 16.8 |
| J.J. Putz | RHP | Michigan | 6 | 185 | Mariners | 13.1 |
| Jason Jennings | RHP | Baylor | 1 | 16 | Rockies | 11.2 |
| Ryan Ludwick | OF | Nevada-Las Vegas | 2 | 60 | Athletics | 11.2 |
| Reed Johnson | OF | Cal State Fullerton | 17 | 523 | Blue Jays | 10.3 |

behind Brown's powerful bat. Morris handed the game to his bullpen with a 6-2 lead.

"That's been their role all year," Morris said, "and they got it done. When we got up after Brown's double, I thought we were going to win because of our bullpen. I didn't think anybody could catch us with a four-run lead."

Florida State almost proved him wrong. Vazquez gave up two runs in two innings, and Neu wobbled when he entered the game in the eighth. He gave up a leadoff triple to Ryan Barthelemy and a sacrifice fly to John-Ford Griffin as the Seminoles crept within a run.

But Neu had too much for them. He struck out Scott to start the ninth inning, forced Jeremiah Klosterman to pop out, and had a full count to Kevin Cash with the national championship on the line.

"That last pitch he threw was a great curveball," Morris said, "one you can't take but one you can't hit."

Cash didn't take it and didn't hit it, swinging and missing to end the game. Miami's players rushed Neu, who had delivered Morris his first national championship in six trips to Omaha.

The last time a Hurricanes closer had stood on the mound at the end of a championship game, Robbie Morrison had served up a game-winning home run to Louisiana State's Warren Morris. That loss haunted Jim Morris for three years. Neu wouldn't allow a repeat.

"I had '96 on my mind, and I'm sure our coaches did too," Hill said. "But Mike Neu did the job for us. We scratched and clawed for runs, and Mike closed it out for us like he had all year."

All according to plan. ∎

# Jennings claims POY with old-fashioned play

By **JOHN MANUEL**

**J**ason Jennings is old fashioned. Nobody's got a problem with that, least of all Jennings himself.

At 6-foot-2, 235 pounds, with a closely shaved head and thick build, he has the Texas country-boy look down pat. A junior righthander/DH at Baylor, Jennings is an academic All-American for whom studying is as serious as cancer. He talks in a measured, almost deliberate tone, probably inherited from his grandfather James, a longtime public address announcer for the Dallas Cowboys.

In the span of a little more than a month, Jennings was pretty busy. He got engaged; led Baylor to a school-record win total; got drafted; was named the Big 12 Conference player of the year; led the Bears to within two innings of the College World Series; and won the College Player of the Year award.

The draft and all the awards capped an amazing month for Jennings, but he should

Jason Jennings earned his keep at Baylor as a formidable two-way player. He won National League Rookie of the Year for the Rockies in 2002 and posted a 4.95 ERA in nine big league seasons.

be used to it—he's had an amazing career. The only disappointment in the entire season came in the super regionals, where Jennings allowed six runs in four innings as Oklahoma State ousted the host Bears. Jennings got the loss in relief in the final game, unable to retire a batter on one day of rest.

Jennings was Baylor's closer as a freshman, going 3-5, 2.90 with 10 saves, and he holds all the school's saves records. He moved into the rotation last year, going 11-4, 5.08 with two saves while batting .327-18-58 and earning third-team All-America honors. He spent the last two summers pitching and hitting for Team USA.

Jennings' talents to hit and pitch with equal aplomb make him especially valuable in today's game. With just 11.7 scholarships available, effective two-way players are crucial. "I'm two players, in that sense," Jennings said.

Jennings' special pitching talent and his lack of quickness have persuaded Bears coach Steve Smith to keep him as a DH when he wasn't pitching.

"I saw him catching in high school," Smith said, "and I have never seen a guy get the ball to second base like that. He did it without even moving his feet.

"I wanted to work him at first base to give us more options, and he played some first for Team USA last summer. But my assistants reminded me he can't run out of sight by tomorrow, so we just kept him at DH."

Jennings has heard the knocks about his size before, and he admits he's not fleet of foot. But this year, with his dominance on the mound (13-2, 2.58) and in the batter's box (.386-17-68), he has turned the weight question into an answer.

"He's durable as hell," Rockies scouting director Pat Daugherty said after drafting Jennings 16th overall. "He's never missed a start and he's never been hurt."

That durability has its roots in Jennings' generous hips and thighs.

Jennings knows he's also going to have to turn away from hitting when his pro career begins. That lack of quickness, and his low-90s, hard-sinking fastball and plus slider, make for a combination better suited for pitching. Jennings was excited to go to a National League team, so he'll still get to hit.

Smith also thinks it's a combination made for Coors Field—particularly at the plate.

"I'd pay to see his first at-bat," Smith said with a laugh. "When I saw that he went to Colorado, I called him and said, 'This is awesome. You're going to hit some bombs there.' He was so excited.

"Jason's going to step in with his back foot dug in. He's going to open up in his big stance, and I'm going to laugh when the pitcher steps off, wipes his brow and just kind of says 'whew.' He ain't gonna look like no pitcher."

What an old-fashioned notion: a pitcher who can hit. ∎

# TOP PLAYERS OF 1999

## ALL-AMERICA TEAM

| Pos | Player | School | Yr | AVG | AB | R | H | HR | RBI | SB |
|-----|--------|--------|-----|-----|-----|-----|-----|-----|-----|-----|
| C | Josh Bard | Texas Tech | Jr | .353 | 238 | 49 | 84 | 13 | 92 | 1 |
| 1B | Jon Palmieri | Wake Forest | Sr | .412 | 272 | 81 | 112 | 18 | 94 | 19 |
| 2B | Marshall McDougall | Florida State | Jr | .419 | 301 | 104 | 126 | 28 | 106 | 22 |
| 3B | Xavier Nady | California | So | .374 | 227 | 56 | 85 | 23 | 62 | 5 |
| SS | Willie Bloomquist | Arizona State | Jr | .394 | 254 | 95 | 100 | 10 | 84 | 32 |
| OF | Matt Cepicky | SW Missouri State | Jr | .414 | 222 | 90 | 92 | 30 | 100 | 7 |
| OF | Daylan Holt | Texas A&M | So | .341 | 287 | 78 | 98 | 34 | 105 | 9 |
| OF | Keith Reed | Providence | Jr | .398 | 274 | 73 | 109 | 17 | 79 | 15 |
| DH | Ken Harvey | Nebraska | Jr | .478 | 224 | 77 | 107 | 23 | 86 | 13 |
| UT | Jason Jennings | Baylor | Jr | .386 | 233 | 52 | 90 | 17 | 68 | 1 |

| Pos | Pitcher | School | Yr | W | L | ERA | G | SV | IP | H | BB | SO |
|-----|---------|--------|-----|-----|-----|-----|-----|-----|-----|-----|-----|-----|
| SP | Kurt Ainsworth | Louisiana State | So | 13 | 6 | 3.45 | 22 | 1 | 130 | 114 | 48 | 157 |
| SP | Mike MacDougal | Wake Forest | Jr | 13 | 3 | 2.62 | 17 | 0 | 120 | 88 | 65 | 117 |
| SP | Ben Sheets | NE Louisiana | Jr | 14 | 1 | 3.11 | 18 | 2 | 116 | 100 | 31 | 156 |
| SP | Barry Zito | Southern California | Jr | 12 | 3 | 3.28 | 17 | 0 | 113 | 93 | 58 | 154 |
| RP | Jay Gehrke | Pepperdine | Jr | 1 | 1 | 0.86 | 31 | 18 | 31 | 19 | 12 | 40 |
| UT | Jason Jennings | Baylor | Jr | 13 | 2 | 2.58 | 22 | 1 | 147 | 102 | 50 | 172 |

## SECOND TEAM

C—Casey Dunn, Auburn. **1B**—Ben Broussard, McNeese State. **2B**—James Jurries, Tulane. **3B**—Ryan Gripp, Creighton. **SS**—Brian Roberts, South Carolina. **OF**—Larry Bigbie, Ball State; Patrick Boyd, Clemson; and Bill Scott, UCLA. **DH**—Tag Bozied, San Francisco. **UT**—Mike Dwyer, Richmond. **SP**—Mario Ramos, Rice; Brent Schoening, Auburn; Nick Stocks, Tampa; and Jason Young, Stanford. **RP**—Jim Journell, Illinois.

## THIRD TEAM

C—Dane Sardinha, Pepperdine. **1B**—Sean McGowan, Boston College. **2B**—Eric Nelson, Baylor. **3B**—Andrew Beinbrink, Arizona State. **SS**—Bobby Hill, Miami. **OF**—Lamont Matthews, Oklahoma State; Spencer Oborn, Cal State Fullerton; and Steve Salargo, East Carolina. **DH**—Andy Phillips, Alabama. **UT**—Peyton Lewis, Creighton. **SP**—Casey Burns, Richmond; Phil Devey, Southwestern Louisiana; Todd Moser, Florida Atlantic; and David Walling, Arkansas. **RP**—Chris Russ, Texas A&M.

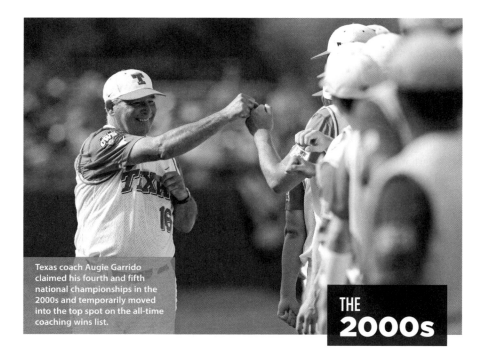

Texas coach Augie Garrido claimed his fourth and fifth national championships in the 2000s and temporarily moved into the top spot on the all-time coaching wins list.

THE
**2000s**

# TOP 25 PROGRAMS OF THE 2000s

Fresno State won the 2008 College World Series, yet fell just outside the top 25 with 92 points.
See Introduction (Page 4) for a key to abbreviations and scoring. Category leaders in **bold**.

| No. | School | Regional | Super | CWS | Title | AA1 | AA2 | AA3 | Top 10 | MLB | Points |
|-----|--------|----------|-------|-----|-------|-----|-----|-----|--------|-----|--------|
| 1. | Rice | **10** | **8** | 5 | 1 | **7** | 6 | 3 | 33 | 15 | 283 |
| 2. | Texas | **10** | 6 | **6** | 2 | 4 | 7 | 2 | 28 | 12 | 277 |
| 3. | Cal State Fullerton | **10** | **8** | **6** | 1 | 2 | 5 | 5 | 27 | 17 | 265 |
| 4. | Miami | **10** | **8** | 5 | 1 | 3 | 6 | 2 | 33 | 14 | 260 |
| 5. | Louisiana State | 8 | 7 | 5 | 2 | 4 | 2 | 3 | 23 | 21 | 255 |
| 6. | Stanford | 8 | 6 | 5 | 0 | 6 | 3 | 3 | **34** | 23 | 234 |
| 7. | Arizona State | **10** | 5 | 3 | 0 | **7** | 6 | 2 | 32 | 21 | 225 |
| 8. | Florida State | **10** | **8** | 2 | 0 | **7** | 8 | 2 | 19 | 8 | 216 |
| 9. | South Carolina | **10** | 7 | 3 | 0 | 4 | 5 | 6 | 22 | 11 | 209 |
| 10. | North Carolina | 9 | 5 | 4 | 0 | 3 | 4 | 9 | 25 | 14 | 204 |
| 11. | Clemson | 9 | 7 | 3 | 0 | 4 | 1 | 2 | 30 | 10 | 191 |
| 12. | Georgia Tech | 9 | 5 | 2 | 0 | 4 | 4 | 4 | 28 | 12 | 180 |
| 13. | Nebraska | 8 | 4 | 3 | 0 | 3 | 4 | 2 | 21 | 14 | 164 |
| 14. | Oregon State | 4 | 3 | 3 | 2 | 3 | 1 | 0 | 17 | 10 | 156 |
| 15. | Georgia | 6 | 4 | 4 | 0 | 2 | 0 | 3 | 17 | 6 | 137 |
| 16. | Tulane | 8 | 3 | 2 | 0 | 3 | 1 | 4 | 18 | 12 | 137 |
| 17. | Southern California | 4 | 4 | 2 | 0 | 3 | 2 | 2 | 21 | 14 | 128 |
| 18. | Long Beach State | 7 | 2 | 0 | 0 | 2 | 2 | 2 | 27 | 24 | 120 |
| 19. | Arizona | 5 | 2 | 1 | 0 | 4 | 2 | 1 | 23 | 15 | 115 |
| 20. | Mississippi | 8 | 4 | 0 | 0 | 2 | 1 | 1 | 21 | 10 | 114 |
| 21. | Florida | 8 | 3 | 1 | 0 | 2 | 1 | 3 | 16 | 6 | 112 |
| 22. | Arkansas | 8 | 3 | 2 | 0 | 0 | 2 | 0 | 13 | 7 | 107 |
| 23. | Houston | 6 | 3 | 0 | 0 | 5 | 1 | 0 | 17 | 9 | 105 |
| 24. | Baylor | 8 | 2 | 1 | 0 | 2 | 0 | 2 | 21 | 6 | 105 |
| 25. | Wichita State | 9 | 2 | 0 | 0 | 1 | 4 | 1 | 20 | 0 | 98 |

# New decade brings new balance and parity

By **MATT EDDY**

**A** confluence of events that transpired as college baseball entered the 2000s helped usher the game away from the high-scoring "gorilla ball" style of play that characterized the mid-to-late 1990s and into a period of unrivaled parity and balance.

In the 2000s, both traditional powers and newcomers had their moments in the spotlight. Cal State Fullerton, Louisiana State, Miami and Texas all added a national championship or two to their rich histories, and Stanford played for a title three times in four years to open the decade.

But the 2000s also saw the rise of Rice, one of the more unlikely college powers based on the private research university having the smallest enrollment of any Division I football school. Adding to Rice's intrigue was the fact that coach Wayne Graham didn't land his first Division I coaching gig until he was 54. His lengthy history in the game included a brief major league career in which he played for Casey Stengel on the 1964 Mets and 11 seasons at San Jacinto JC, north of Houston, where he coached both Roger Clemens and Andy Pettitte.

While Rice had developed No. 1 overall draft pick Matt Anderson and long-time major league star Lance Berkman in the late 1990s, the program was about to reach new heights in the 2000s by making five trips to Omaha and recording a .753 winning percentage that led Division I. The Owls' timing was impeccable. The

## TOP 10 STORYLINES OF THE 2000s

**1** **POPULARITY CONTEST.** ESPN's coverage of the postseason helped broaden fan appeal. Beginning in 2003, the network carried super regionals and every CWS game, while introducing and a best-of-3 championship series.

**2** **TURNSTILES TURN.** Total attendance at the CWS topped 300,000 fans for the first time in 2006 and never dipped below that number through the end of the 2010s.

**3** **EAGER BEAVERS.** Oregon State returned to Omaha for the first time in more than 50 years in 2005, then won consecutive titles in 2006-07, helping to break the stranglehold of California, Texas and Southwest-based schools.

**4** **RAISING THE BAR.** Louisiana State cemented itself as *the* program of the BA era with CWS titles five and six book-ending the decade.

**5** **GIVING A HOOT.** Rice, a private university with the smallest enrollment of any D-I football school, rose to national prominence with coach Wayne Graham and a parade of pitchers.

**6** **COACHING PANTHEON.** Texas coach Augie Garrido captures his fourth and fifth CWS titles in 2002 and 2005, giving him five total. He moved into No. 1 on the all-time coaching wins list in 2003 and stayed there for 15 years.

**7** **NEW STANDARDS.** A uniform start date of March 1 (later moved to mid-February) and a limit on scholarships (27) and roster spots (35) per team were put into effect in 2008.

**8** **SHIFTING TIDE.** Offensive levels decreased in the early to middle portion of the decade, bottoming out at 6.1 runs per game in 2007.

**9** **DECADE OF THE PITCHER.** A record five pitchers win Player of the Year honors. Mark Prior, Jered Weaver, Andrew Miller, David Price and Stephen Strasburg all went on to MLB success.

**10** **CLOSE BUT NO CIGAR.** In an incredible five-year run, Stanford played for a national title in 2000, 2001 and 2003 but lost, while placing fourth at the CWS in both 1999 and 2002.

program developed a trio of Texas high school pitchers into aces at exactly the same time, then rode the right arms of Philip Humber, Jeff Niemann and Wade Townsend to the 2003 national championship and then a preseason No. 1 ranking in 2004.

While Rice failed to repeat as champions, the junior trio of Humber, Niemann and Townsend were all selected in the first eight picks of the 2004 draft. Other schools have equaled the Owls' record of three first-round picks in one draft class, but none has seen all three drafted among the top 10 picks.

Led by historic coach Augie Garrido, Texas challenged its in-state rival Rice for team of the decade honors by making regionals (10), reaching Omaha (six) and winning as many national titles (two—and they played for two others) as any other program in the 2000s. The separator was that Rice made a bigger impact on All-America teams and in the draft.

The decade of the 2000s also featured perhaps the most unlikely champion in history when Fresno State claimed the 2008 crown. The Bulldogs hold records for a College World Series champion for most losses (31) and lowest regional seed (No. 4).

North Carolina also emerged as a national power in the 2000s and reached the CWS four times in the decade, equalling their career Omaha appearances prior to 2000. The Tar Heels played for a national championship in both 2006 and 2007 but lost both times to an emerging power from a part of the country not previously associated with CWS glory.

While the programs referenced thus far—Fullerton, LSU, Miami, Texas, Rice, Fresno State, UNC—had varied levels of baseball tradition, they all fit the general CWS finalist archetype in that those schools were based in either California, Texas or the Southeast.

Enter Oregon State, the nontraditional power that twice defeated North Carolina and broke molds along the way. Feeding into a burgeoning hotbed of baseball talent in the Pacific Northwest, the Beavers reached Omaha for the first time in 53 years in 2005, led by Oregon-born junior outfielder Jacoby Ellsbury. While that team went two-and-out at the CWS, two OSU freshmen—catcher Mitch Canham and shortstop Darwin Barney—would help lead the Beavers to consecutive national titles in 2006 and 2007 after Ellsbury was drafted in the first round in 2005.

# ALL-AMERICA TEAM OF THE DECADE

| POS, PLAYER, SCHOOL | SUMMARY |
| --- | --- |
| C Buster Posey, Florida State | Shifted to C as SO, then hit .463-26-93 as JR, missing national triple crown by 2 HR |
| 1B Dustin Ackley, North Carolina | Led nation in hitting as FR and JR; hit .412 in Tar Heels career, set CWS hits record |
| 2B Rickie Weeks, Southern | Three-time All-American is all-time Division I leader with .465 AVG, .927 SLG |
| 3B Alex Gordon, Nebraska | Two-time first-team All-American led Huskers to Omaha as POY in 2005 |
| SS Stephen Drew, Florida State | Won 2002 Freshman of the Year; hit .354/.449/.667 as three-year All-American |
| OF Jacoby Ellsbury, Oregon State | Keyed OSU turnaround; hit .406, 6 HR, 26 SB in 2005 as first-team All-American |
| OF Kellen Kulbacki, J. Madison | Hit .464-24-75 in epic SO year in 2006 in first of two first-team All-America years |
| OF Carlos Quentin, Stanford | Three-year starter helped lead Cardinal to Omaha each year from 2001-03 |
| DH Khalil Greene, Clemson | All-time D-I leader with 95 2B; hit .470-27-91 as a SR in 2002 POY season |
| UT Joe Savery, Rice | LHP/1B made impact on mound (24-7, 2.69) and at plate (.447 OBP) for 3 years |
| SP David Price, Vanderbilt | Huge JR year (11-1, 2.63, 194 SO, 133 IP) makes him POY, No. 1 overall draft pick |
| SP Mark Prior, Southern Cal | Led nation with 201 SO in 2001 POY season, went 15-1, 1.69 in celebrated season |
| SP Stephen Strasburg, San Diego St. | Led nation with 1.32 ERA, 195 SO in 2009; his 16.1 SO/9 best ever for P with 100 IP |
| SP Jered Weaver, Long Beach St. | In a 2004 season for the ages, led nation with 15 W, 213 SO to go with 1.63 ERA |
| RP Huston Street, Texas | Key component to Omaha trips in 2002-04; tied for career CWS record with 5 SV |

Oregon State's success inspired other cold-weather programs, particularly in the Pacific Northwest. Oregon restored its long-dormant program in 2009, while Washington would build to its first ever CWS appearance in 2018. The circle was completed when California programs began recruiting players from Oregon and Washington, rather than vice versa.

The emergence of Oregon State as a national power and class of the Pacific-10 Conference further spotlighted how far the traditional West powers had receded in this era of balance. Southern California won the wild 1998 CWS and made return trips to Omaha in 2000 and 2001—but none after that. Arizona State, the team that finished runner-up to USC in 1998, won more games than any Pac-10 school in the 2000s and made the NCAA Tournament every year. Yet the Sun Devils failed to break through in Omaha, even with teams loaded with future big leaguers such as Dustin Pedroia, Andre Ethier, Jason Kipnis, Mike Leake and first-round talents Ike Davis and Brett Wallace.

Now let's examine the reasons why parity and balance were hallmarks of the 2000s.

(1) The reduction in scholarships to 11.7 in 1991 combined with the limitations placed on total scholarships (27) and roster size (35) in 2008 effectively prevented schools from hoarding talent and encouraged the spread of players to a larger number of programs.

(2) New bat standards introduced in 2000 resulted in a lower level of run scoring, particularly from 2000 to 2007, and fostered an environment where pitching, defense and small ball were viable strategies. Thus teams with shallow lineups but two or three dominant pitchers could thrive—even in Omaha, where the margins of victory were shrinking.

(3) The depressed scoring contributed to the greatest decade for pitcher achievement in college baseball since the introduction of the aluminum bat in 1974. A record five pitchers won the Player of the Year award in the 2000s, and three of the POYs still occupy places in the Division I record book. Stephen Strasburg in 2009 recorded the highest single-season strikeout rate (16.1 per nine innings) for any pitcher with at least 100 innings, while Jered Weaver (2004) and Mark Prior (2001) rank sixth and 14th for strikeouts in a single season.

(4) When the NCAA expanded the tournament to 64 teams in 1999, it not only introduced a greater number of potential champions, it also randomized the winner to a degree by creating super regionals. The greater the number of rounds to navigate, the more teams are rewarded for their survival skills—and fortune—rather than greatness.

(5) With the NCAA Tournament expansion came a doubling of regional sites from eight to 16. This created a dynamic where more schools per year could host a regional and make money, often significant money. In turn, a greater number of schools strived to compete—even northern programs and even those in the Big Ten Conference, which had been a CWS non-factor for years until Indiana and Michigan reached Omaha in the 2010s.

(6) ESPN expanded television coverage of the College World Series in 2003, while also introducing the best-of-three championship series. For the first time, the network broadcasted every super regional and CWS game, enhancing visibility of the sport. ∎

## TEAM OF THE DECADE

### 2004 Cal State Fullerton

With a team boasting eight future big leaguers, including tenured veterans Justin Turner and Kurt Suzuki, the Titans won the Big West Conference even with stout competition from Long Beach State and Player of the Year Jered Weaver. At the College World Series, Fullerton went 5-1 and swept a Texas team at the peak of its powers in the finals. With his victory, Titans coach George Horton bettered his mentor, Longhorns coach Augie Garrido.

Brad Hawpe celebrates with the Louisiana State band following the Tigers' 6-5 victory against Stanford in the College World Series championship game.

2000

# LSU adds to legacy with fifth national title

By **JOHN MANUEL**

**T**he tag of "Program of the '90s" no longer suffices for coach Skip Bertman and Louisiana State.

The Tigers (52-17) added to their illustrious legacy on June 17 at Rosenblatt Stadium. After a pair of home runs by seniors Blair Barbier and Jeremy Witten tied the game in the bottom of the eighth inning, senior catcher Brad Cresse added to his national RBI lead in dramatic fashion in the ninth. Cresse lined an 0-1 slider from Stanford righthander Justin Wayne for a single into left field, scoring Ryan Theriot from second base and giving the Tigers a 6-5 victory for their fifth College World Series championship.

**FROM THE ISSUE:**
JULY 10-23, 2000

All of the titles have come since 1991—the others came in '93, '96 and '97—leaving just five for the rest of the nation to fight over. Only Southern California, with 12, has won more national titles than LSU. Arizona State is the only other school with five.

"This team is as close and courageous as any I have had in 42 years," said Bertman, just finishing his 17th—but, he stressed, not final—year in Baton Rouge. "I can honestly say this is the best one (of the national championships)."

Bertman and LSU certainly have the most flair for the dramatic. This was the third time in CWS history that the national championship had been won in the bottom of the ninth inning, and it has happened twice with the Tigers.

The last time it happened—Warren Morris' two-run, walk-off homer to beat Miami 10-9 in 1996—was probably the greatest moment in college baseball history. Morris had not homered all season leading up to that swing. Previously, USC beat Southern Illinois in its final at-bat in 1968.

Cresse, on the other hand, led the nation in home runs in 2000 with 30, so perhaps a single was evidence of some Cajun karma at work. "I dreamed of winning the College World Series with a home run," said Cresse, who was a freshman for LSU's last championship in 1997. "But I'll take a single."

Cresse was in the midst of what he called a "miserable Series for me personally."

## TOP TEAMS
### 2000 COLLEGE WORLD SERIES STANDINGS

| School | Conference | Record | CWS | Coach |
| --- | --- | --- | --- | --- |
| Louisiana State | Southeastern | 52–17 | 4–0 | Skip Bertman |
| Stanford | Pacific-10 | 50–16 | 3–1 | Mark Marquess |
| Florida State | Atlantic Coast | 53–19 | 2–2 | Mike Martin |
| Louisiana–Lafayette | Sun Belt | 49–20 | 2–2 | Tony Robichaux |
| Clemson | Atlantic Coast | 51–18 | 1–2 | Jack Leggett |
| Southern California | Pacific-10 | 44–20 | 1–2 | Mike Gillespie |
| San Jose State | Western Athletic | 41–24 | 0–2 | Sam Piraro |
| Texas | Big 12 | 46–21 | 0–2 | Augie Garrido |

## NATIONAL CHAMPION
## LOUISIANA STATE

Led by coach Skip Bertman, LSU won its fifth national title in 10 years. The Tigers cruised through the postseason, going 13-0, capped by a 6-5 victory against Stanford in the championship game. Brad Cresse drove home the game-winner in the ninth.

Entering the bottom of the ninth, Cresse was 1-for-12 with eight strikeouts. The last two strikeouts came against Wayne—Stanford's single-season wins leader and the No. 5 overall pick in the draft earlier this month.

Cresse came to the plate after Theriot had led off with a single to left. Freshman second baseman Mike Fontenot drew a walk to follow, setting the stage for Cresse.

"We'd thrown him six sliders in a row," said Wayne, who courageously faced the media after taking the loss. "It didn't seem like he had a good idea of what to do with it, and all of a sudden he does. I left it up, and I needed a double play there. He did a great job of extending his bat to get to it."

Louisiana State's players seemed to have no idea what to do with Wayne for his first three innings. Cardinal coach Mark Marquess went with junior righthander Jason Young for the first four innings, and Young pitched well, giving up LSU's first two runs in the second but settling down in the third and fourth. Marquess turned to Wayne, who last pitched on June 11, in the fifth, and the Hawaii native proceeded to dominate the Tigers for three innings. He struck out seven, three of them looking, and silenced the partisan crowd of 24,282.

LSU was getting its own lift on the mound, though, from senior righthander Trey Hodges, who earned the CWS Most Outstanding Player award. In getting his second victory of the CWS, Hodges gave up just two hits and one walk in four innings while striking out four. The Cardinal (50-16) had roughed up LSU starter Brian Tallet for 11 hits in the first five-plus innings, but Hodges kept the Tigers within striking distance.

With a team batting average of .341 coming into the game, LSU wasn't likely going to finish with just two runs. The Tigers won their final 13 games this postseason, with five of the last six wins coming against some of the most talented pitchers in the nation. Against

---

# 2000 NEWSMAKERS

**Ray Tanner** of **South Carolina** becomes the first to be recognized as Coach of the Year despite not taking his team to Omaha. The Gamecocks went 25-5 in Southeastern Conference play—which included a single-season record 17 straight wins against SEC opponents—on their way to a 56-10 record. South Carolina was ranked No. 1 in the country for five weeks—more than any other team—and held the No. 1 seed in the country heading into the NCAA Tournament, where they were upset by Louisiana-Lafayette in super regionals.

The **NCAA** required bats to be slightly heavier and narrower. As a result, offense continued to wane from the "gorilla ball" heyday. Compared with the offensive apex year of 1998, home runs (0.80 per game) declined by 20 percent and runs scored (6.53 per game) dropped 8 percent from the record 7.12. Many coaches pointed to a new, less-lively baseball produced by Rawlings—rather than the old ball from Wilson—as the reason.

**Georgia Tech** third baseman **Mark Teixeira** nearly won the **Atlantic Coast Conference** triple crown by hitting .427 (first) with 18 home runs (first) and 80 RBIs (second).

**FINAL TOP 25 FOR 2000**

1. Louisiana State*
2. #Stanford*
3. Florida State*
4. South Carolina
5. Southern California*
6. Georgia Tech
7. Clemson*
8. Nebraska
9. Louisiana-Lafayette*
10. Texas*
11. Houston
12. Arizona State
13. Miami
14. Baylor
15. Mississippi State
16. Loyola Marymount
17. UCLA
18. San Jose State*
19. Penn State
20. Florida
21. Wake Forest
22. Cal State Fullerton
23. Rutgers
24. Alabama
25. Auburn

* Reached College World Series
# Preseason No. 1

# IN RETROSPECT: 2000 DRAFT

### Top 10 Draft Picks From College
With overall selection number (Ov), drafting team (Team) and rank on Baseball America draft board (BA).

| Player | Pos | School | Ov | Team | BA |
|---|---|---|---|---|---|
| Adam Johnson | RHP | Cal State Fullerton | 2 | Twins | 13 |
| Justin Wayne | RHP | Stanford | 5 | Expos | 20 |
| Joe Borchard | OF | Stanford | 12 | White Sox | 12 |
| Beau Hale | RHP | Texas | 14 | Orioles | 6 |
| Chase Utley | 2B | UCLA | 15 | Phillies | 25 |
| Billy Traber | LHP | Loyola Marymount | 16 | Mets | 26 |
| Ben Diggins | RHP | Arizona | 17 | Dodgers | 16 |
| Chris Bootcheck | RHP | Auburn | 20 | Angels | 8 |
| Blake Williams | RHP | SW Texas State | 24 | Cardinals | – |
| David Parrish | C | Michigan | 28 | Yankees | – |

### Top 10 Major League Players From College Draft Class
With draft round and Baseball-Reference.com total for wins above replacement (WAR) through 2019.

| Player | Pos | School | Rd | Ov | Team | WAR |
|---|---|---|---|---|---|---|
| Chase Utley | 2B | UCLA | 1 | 15 | Phillies | 65.4 |
| Cliff Lee | LHP | Arkansas | 4 | 105 | Expos | 43.5 |
| Brandon Webb | RHP | Kentucky | 8 | 249 | D-backs | 31.0 |
| Jason Bay | OF | Gonzaga | 22 | 645 | Expos | 24.6 |
| David DeJesus | OF | Rutgers | 4 | 104 | Royals | 23.2 |
| Josh Willingham | OF | North Alabama | 17 | 491 | Marlins | 18.8 |
| Chris Young | RHP | Princeton | 3 | 89 | Pirates | 17.3 |
| Freddy Sanchez | 2B | Oklahoma City | 11 | 332 | Red Sox | 15.9 |
| Clint Barmes | SS | Indiana State | 10 | 287 | Rockies | 15.6 |
| Ryan Church | OF | Nevada | 14 | 426 | Indians | 9.1 |

UCLA in the super regional, LSU beat Rob Henkel, a projected first-round pick who fell to the third round; and Josh Karp, a projected first-rounder for 2001. In the CWS, LSU beat Texas starter Beau Hale, a first-round pick in this year's draft; Southern California righthander Mark Prior, a projected first-rounder fir 2001; and then Stanford's Young—a second-rounder to the Rockies this year—and Wayne.

"I don't know of any team that has beaten those kinds of pitchers," said Witten, a fifth-year senior outfielder. "Young and Wayne were the best pitchers we've seen all year. It was pretty dull in the dugout, but then Blair's hit sparked us."

Barbier, a senior third baseman who was not drafted this year, homered twice in the CWS opener against Hale. He faced Wayne in the bottom of the eighth with LSU trailing 5-2 after Brad Hawpe had fouled out to the catcher to end a nine-pitch at-bat.

Barbier was up to the task, hitting Wayne's eighth pitch of the at-bat, a changeup, just over the left field wall for a homer. The crowd immediately came to life, and a rattled Wayne walked Wally Pontiff to follow. After Cedrick Harris lined out to right field, Witten came to the plate as the tying run. Again, Wayne got ahead in the count 1-2, but Witten fouled off a pitch. Then he drilled a two-run homer to left to tie the game and circled the bases waving a fist, exhorting the already delirious crowd and his jubilant teammates.

"They hit two home runs in big spots," Marquess said. "They won those big spots.

"That's what I told our team, that they had nothing to be ashamed of. Sometimes you lose it, you give it away, and sometimes you get beat. We got beat. We didn't give it to them. Justin had good stuff and pitched very well. He's disappointed now, but shoot, he won 15 games, he pitched well all year. He got his pitches up, and they hit them out." ■

# Teixeira shoulders every challenge

By **JOHN MANUEL**

**M**ark Teixeira makes his own decisions.

He's the one who turned down the Red Sox in the 1998 draft, not some agent acting as his "adviser." He's the one who picked Georgia Tech over Stanford, Miami, Clemson and Arizona State.

He's the 20-year-old sophomore third baseman so mature, so together and so good, his Georgia Tech teammates voted him one of their three team captains.

"He's so good, he really benefits everyone around him," Yellow Jackets coach Danny Hall said. "He wears the target on his back. He takes all the bullets for us. He really shoulders a lot of responsibility."

At 6-foot-2, 218 pounds—with broad, muscular shoulders for all that responsibility—Teixeira wears the target well. As mature as he is off the field, Teixeira oozes maturity on it, from his plate approach to his reaction to wearing that target on his

Georgia Tech's Mark Teixeira was the rare sophomore to win College Player of the Year. His 14-year major league career included 409 homers, three all-star bids and five Gold Gloves at first base.

back. Teixeira drew 67 walks, just nine shy of former Yellow Jackets star Jason Varitek's Atlantic Coast Conference record, set in 1994.

"I think, definitely in conference play, everybody was scared to death of him," Hall said. "I think the game plan was that he was the guy you wouldn't let beat you. After what he did as a freshman and in the Cape Cod League, everybody lives in fear of him."

And he's the College Player of the Year, earning the award as much with his presence as with his stats. But still, the numbers speak for themselves.

Teixeira led the ACC in average (.427) and home runs (18) but trailed teammate Bryan Prince in RBIs (80). Throw in the doubles (21) and walks, and Teixeira ended up with Ruthian slugging (.772) and on-base (.549) percentages. And he led the Yellow Jackets in stolen bases with 13.

The average and power are expected from a player unanimously voted the Cape Cod League's top prospect. His 13 stolen bases, though, hint at Teixeira's motivation.

In Baseball America's 1998 Draft Preview, Teixeira read that scouts thought he had a "dead lower half." It rankled him—still does, he said. It probably didn't help that Red Sox scouting director Wayne Britton, talking to Teixeira after a high school game that spring, asked him to lift his uniform pants and then squeezed his legs.

"(Britton) said he wanted to make sure his legs were muscular," Mark's mother Margie said. "That kind of thing just motivates him."

Teixeira has a field day rising to challenges, which endears him to baseball officials. He started swinging a bat as soon as he could walk, always from the right side. He was an accomplished hitter by age 10, but his dad thought it came too easily. That's when he encouraged Mark to try switch-hitting.

"He was already playing up in age level, so I told him switch-hitting was the next step up for him to take," father John said. "When he first started, he wasn't comfortable, and he was just trying to put the bat on the ball. But I told him, 'You need to be able to drive the ball from both sides of the plate, or it's not worth it.' "

Now nobody can say which is Teixeira's better side. He's the second sophomore to earn the POY nod, and he looks forward to the chance to repeat in 2001, when he figures to be one of the first players picked in the draft.

Teixeira said he's ready for the draft, and if he didn't have to wait a year, he wouldn't.

"I'd be lying if I told you I was pleased with my defense the last two years, but I think I'm ready for pro ball," Teixeria said.

"I like to set challenges up for myself and fulfill them. One of my goals this year was to be ACC player of the year, and I did that. I wanted our team to win the ACC and get back to regionals, and we did that. Now, I'm ready for the next challenge." ■

# TOP PLAYERS OF 2000

## ALL-AMERICA TEAM

| Pos | Player | School | Yr | AVG | AB | R | H | HR | RBI | SB |
|-----|--------|--------|----|-----|----|----|----|----|-----|-----|
| C | Dane Sardinha | Pepperdine | Jr | .353 | 232 | 52 | 82 | 17 | 72 | 6 |
| 1B | Todd Faulkner | Auburn | Jr | .423 | 248 | 71 | 105 | 22 | 103 | 3 |
| 2B | Chase Utley | UCLA | Jr | .382 | 283 | 81 | 108 | 22 | 69 | 15 |
| 3B | Mark Teixeira | Georgia Tech | So | .427 | 241 | 104 | 103 | 18 | 80 | 13 |
| SS | Tim Hummel | Old Dominion | Jr | .408 | 223 | 66 | 91 | 8 | 68 | 22 |
| OF | Gabe Gross | Auburn | So | .430 | 237 | 83 | 102 | 13 | 86 | 16 |
| OF | Mitch Jones | Arizona State | Sr | .357 | 249 | 79 | 89 | 27 | 92 | 9 |
| OF | Bill Scott | UCLA | Jr | .421 | 266 | 75 | 112 | 21 | 76 | 1 |
| DH | Brad Cresse | Louisiana State | Sr | .388 | 273 | 73 | 106 | 30 | 106 | 1 |
| UT | Ben Diggins | Arizona | So | .336 | 122 | 33 | 41 | 9 | 34 | 2 |

| Pos | Pitcher | School | Yr | W | L | ERA | G | SV | IP | H | BB | SO |
|-----|---------|--------|----|----|----|-----|----|----|----|----|----|----|
| SP | Kip Bouknight | South Carolina | Jr | 17 | 1 | 2.81 | 19 | 0 | 144 | 121 | 34 | 143 |
| SP | Kyle Crowell | Houston | Jr | 13 | 3 | 2.86 | 23 | 0 | 138 | 117 | 27 | 117 |
| SP | Lenny DiNardo | Stetson | So | 16 | 1 | 1.90 | 20 | 0 | 133 | 112 | 27 | 132 |
| SP | Justin Wayne | Stanford | Jr | 15 | 4 | 3.21 | 20 | 0 | 143 | 121 | 44 | 153 |
| RP | Charlie Thames | Texas | Jr | 4 | 2 | 2.22 | 42 | 19 | 77 | 60 | 19 | 82 |
| UT | Ben Diggins | Arizona | So | 10 | 4 | 3.83 | 17 | 0 | 113 | 111 | 63 | 127 |

## SECOND TEAM
**C**—Casey Myers, Arizona State. **1B**—Brad Hawpe, Louisiana State. **2B**—Sam Bozanich, Alabama. **3B**—Justin Gemoll, Southern California. **SS**—Darren Fenster, Rutgers. **OF**—Joe Borchard, Stanford; Michael Campo, Penn State; and Chris Smith, Florida State. **DH**—Frank Corr, Stetson. **UT**—Jason Dubois, Virginia Commonwealth. **SP**—Rik Currier, Southern California; Beau Hale, Texas; Shane Komine, Nebraska; and Brian Tallet, Louisiana State. **RP**—Scott Barber, South Carolina.

## THIRD TEAM
**C**—Scott Walter, Loyola Marymount. **1B**—Garrett Atkins, UCLA. **2B**—Chris Burke, Tennessee. **3B**—Xavier Nady, California. **SS**—Keoni DeRenne, Arizona. **OF**—Tyrell Godwin, North Carolina; Joe Inglett, Nevada; and Tim Olson, Florida. **DH**—Matt Easterday, Georgia Southern. **UT**—Jeff Bajenaru, Oklahoma. **SP**—Kenny Baugh, Rice; Chad Hawkins, Baylor; Billy Traber, Loyola Marymount; and Cory Vance, Georgia Tech. **RP**—Cory Scott, East Carolina.

Miami players celebrate their 12-1 rout of Stanford in the College World Series championship game. The Hurricanes won their second title in three years.

2001

# Hurricanes spoil West Coast party

By **JOHN MANUEL**

**W**hen the College World Series began, Miami received as little attention as the nation's top-ranked team could. After all, President George W. Bush was in town, and so was Nebraska, the first time the home-state Huskers had appeared in the CWS in school history.

On the field, the three West Coast teams—Cal State Fullerton, Southern California and Stanford—were getting all the ink. All three had played each other during the season and employed a similar style. They relied heavily on defense and pitching—with aces Mark Prior (USC), Kirk Saarloos (Fullerton) and Jeremy Guthrie (Stanford)—while using opportunistic offenses.

**FROM THE ISSUE:**
JULY 9-22, 2001

Considering the Titans had rolled into Miami in late March and handed the Hurricanes their first-ever three-game sweep at Mark Light Stadium, it was easy to see why the West Coast teams were seen as the favorites.

"We know what kind of teams Southern California had and Stanford had," Cal State Fullerton coach George Horton said midway through the CWS. "They have a lot of talent on the mound and they come out and compete. You look at those teams, Long Beach State, Pepperdine—we think West Coast ball is represented well every year, and especially this year.

"My assistant coach Dave Serrano said to me early in the year that the national champion would come out of the West. This is no disrespect to Miami, but we think that the West Coast teams are very fine baseball teams."

Miami agrees, but the Hurricanes have always had a West Coast flavor under coach Jim Morris. Making his seventh trip to the CWS in eight years, Morris said Miami's recruiting territory includes South Florida and California.

"If we can recruit those two places," he said, "we'll have a pretty good team."

Pretty good indeed. The Hurricanes in 2001 learned from their West Coast brethren after getting swept by the Titans. They bunted. They defended. They stole bases and played with intensity any team from any part of the country would envy.

## TOP TEAMS
### 2001 COLLEGE WORLD SERIES STANDINGS

| School | Conference | Record | CWS | Coach |
|---|---|---|---|---|
| Miami | Independent | 53–12 | 4–0 | Jim Morris |
| Stanford | Pacific-10 | 51–17 | 3–1 | Mark Marquess |
| Cal State Fullerton | Big West | 48–18 | 2–2 | George Horton |
| Tennessee | Southeastern | 48–20 | 2–2 | Rod Delmonico |
| Southern California | Pacific-10 | 45–19 | 1–2 | Mike Gillespie |
| Tulane | Conference USA | 56–13 | 1–2 | Rick Jones |
| Georgia | Southeastern | 47–22 | 0–2 | Ron Polk |
| Nebraska | Big 12 | 50–16 | 0–2 | Dave van Horn |

## NATIONAL CHAMPION
### MIAMI

Miami co-opts a West Coast-style attack and beats USC and Stanford at their own game, routing the Cardinal 12-1 in the championship game. The Hurricanes claim their fourth title and their second under coach Jim Morris in the last three years.

They refocused, and with significant help from a pair of Californians, the Canes went on a late-season tear straight through the CWS. Miami won its last 17 games—the final four coming in Omaha, with wins against USC and Stanford.

The last was a 12-1 drubbing of the Cardinal in the national championship game, tying for the most lopsided victory in championship game history and earning the Hurricanes their fourth national title and second in three years.

"The style of play is a lot different from one part of the country to another," said third baseman Kevin Howard, out of Thousand Oaks, Calif. "A lot of teams in the South or East try to sit back and wait for a home run. But I knew it would be easy to adapt to the way Miami plays. We play a West Coast style of baseball."

Morris' first championship club had a similar wake-up call against Fullerton's Big West Conference rival, Long Beach State, in 1999. Those Canes lost the first game at Long Beach before a team meeting got them back on track, and they finished that season on an 11-game winning streak. The 2001 team had a meeting after the sweep against Fullerton, called by outfielder Charlton Jimerson.

The square-jawed, muscular Jimerson looks like anything but a laid-back Californian. A little-used senior, Jimerson was attending Miami on an academic scholarship but was starting to harness the talent that prompted the Astros to draft him in the fifth round.

He got the Hurricanes together and initiated a clear-the-air meeting after the Fullerton series. Miami never looked back, going 28-3 to close the season.

At Rosenblatt Stadium, Jimerson set the tone. He led off the bottom of the first inning of Miami's opener, a 21-13 win against Tennessee, with a solo homer. He did the same against Southern California senior righthander Rik Currier to kick off the Hurricanes' second-round showdown against the Trojans.

# 2001 NEWSMAKERS

**Nebraska** made its first ever trip to the CWS, led by 5-foot-9 All-American starter **Shane Komine**. The "Hawaiian Punchout" ranked fourth in the nation with 157 strikeouts. The Huskers hosted a regional for the first time in program history and swept a powerful Rice team in super regionals.

Preseason No. 1 **Georgia Tech** got off to a hot start before fading and finished the season outside the top 25. Third baseman **Mark Teixeira**, the reigning Player of the Year, started 12-for-24 with four home runs and 11 RBIs but broke his right ankle in early February. The injury cost him all but 16 games.

**Kent State** two-way player **John Van Benschoten** led the nation with 31 home runs and a .982 slugging percentage. The right-right first baseman/closer entered his junior year a relative unknown but spent the previous summer adding muscle to his 6-foot-4 frame at the IMG Academy in Bradenton, Fla. .

A **Virginia** athletic department task force recommended making the baseball program a "fourth-tier" sport, with no scholarships and a limited budget. In the end, an anonymous donor contributed $2 million to save the program.

## FINAL TOP 25 FOR 2001

1. Miami*
2. Stanford*
3. Cal State Fullerton*
4. Southern California*
5. Tulane*
6. Nebraska*
7. Georgia*
8. Tennessee*
9. Louisiana State
10. Florida State
11. East Carolina
12. South Carolina
13. Rice
14. Central Florida
15. Notre Dame
16. Pepperdine
17. Clemson
18. Wake Forest
19. Mississippi State
20. Florida International
21. Texas Tech
22. Arizona State
23. South Alabama
24. Winthrop
25. Rutgers

* Reached College World Series
# Georgia Tech ranked as the preseason No. 1

# IN RETROSPECT: 2001 DRAFT

## Top 10 Draft Picks From College
With overall selection number (Ov), drafting team (Team) and rank on Baseball America draft board (BA).

| Player | Pos | School | Ov | Team | BA |
|---|---|---|---|---|---|
| Mark Prior | RHP | Southern California | 2 | Cubs | 1 |
| Dewon Brazelton | RHP | Middle Tenn. State | 3 | Rays | 5 |
| Mark Teixeira | 3B | Georgia Tech | 5 | Rangers | 2 |
| Josh Karp | RHP | UCLA | 6 | Expos | 13 |
| Chris Smith | LHP | Cumberland | 7 | Orioles | 17 |
| John Van Benschoten | 1B | Kent State | 8 | Pirates | 7 |
| Chris Burke | SS | Tennessee | 10 | Astros | 25 |
| Kenny Baugh | RHP | Rice | 11 | Tigers | 23 |
| Jake Gautreau | 3B | Tulane | 14 | Padres | 12 |
| Gabe Gross | OF | Auburn | 15 | Blue Jays | 16 |

## Top 10 Major League Players From College Draft Class
With draft round and Baseball-Reference.com total for wins above replacement (WAR) through 2019.

| Player | Pos | School | Rd | Ov | Team | WAR |
|---|---|---|---|---|---|---|
| Mark Teixeira | 1B | Georgia Tech | 1 | 5 | Rangers | 51.8 |
| Dan Haren | RHP | Pepperdine | 2 | 72 | Cardinals | 35.0 |
| Kevin Youkilis | 3B | Cincinnati | 8 | 243 | Red Sox | 32.6 |
| Jason Bartlett | SS | Oklahoma | 13 | 390 | Padres | 18.3 |
| Dan Uggla | 2B | Memphis | 11 | 338 | D-backs | 17.5 |
| C.J. Wilson | LHP | Loyola Marymount | 5 | 141 | Rangers | 17.4 |
| Mark Prior | RHP | Southern Calif. | 1 | 2 | Cubs | 16.6 |
| Ryan Howard | 1B | Missouri State | 5 | 140 | Phillies | 15.0 |
| Luke Scott | OF | Oklahoma State | 9 | 277 | Indians | 11.9 |
| Noah Lowry | LHP | Pepperdine | 1 | 30 | Giants | 10.0 |

In the end, that kind of offense and overall pitching depth were the most important differences between Miami and the West Coast teams whose style it appropriated.

With previous closers like Danny Graves, Jay Tessmer, Robbie Morrison and Michael Neu, Morris has cultivated great college closers, and he found another in freshman righthander George Huguet. The Miami native picked up his 14th save in the 4-3 victory against USC after Morris used three middle relievers to get his closer the ball.

For the tournament, Morris used 10 different pitchers, such as lefty specialist Andrew Cohn and submarining righty Luke DeBold, who worked in every game of the CWS and gave up one run in 6.1 innings.

Huguet wasn't needed in the championship game because, for all its pitching and defense, Miami also hit a little. Miami's offense was built around speed, shown by a national-best 228 steals in 273 attempts.

Realizing he had no true cleanup hitter, Morris pooled his speed at the top of the lineup, batting Jimerson (31 steals) leadoff ahead of outfielder Mike Rodriguez (53) and shortstop Javy Rodriguez, who had a Division I-best 66. Line-drive hitters such as DH Danny Matienzo and Howard made up the middle of the order.

Miami showed all its weapons in the championship game: speed and power, pitching and defense. It looked easy, the way it should for a No. 1 team. And to its West Coast foes, it had to look familiar. But the Hurricanes made sure the CWS was no West Coast party.

"This frankly wasn't much of a game," Stanford coach Mark Marquess said when it was over. "We made a couple mistakes, and they just jumped all over us.

"That's why they're national champions." ∎

# Award-winner Prior sets mound tone

By **JOHN MANUEL**

**G**orilla ball may not be dead, as the 2001 College World Series showed. The bats are still metal, still making good hitters out of mediocre ones.

But the CWS also showed good pitching can still beat good hitting, no matter how many advantages those hitters have. The evidence was all over college baseball this year, no matter where you looked. It's most obvious on the All-America teams that this was the Year of the Pitcher.

If you didn't have an ERA under 2.00, you didn't make the first team in 2001. Too many pitchers were dominant to allow for someone who was merely very good.

The bar was higher in 2001, and Southern California's Mark Prior was the one who kept erasing the old mark. The statistics tell part of the story about why Prior is the College Player of the Year, becoming just the fourth pitcher (excluding two-way players) to win the award.

Mark Prior lived up to expectations as a USC junior and went No. 2 overall in the draft to the Cubs. He rocketed to the majors and nearly won the Cy Young Award in 2003 before injuries felled him.

Prior became just the 14th pitcher in Division I history to post 200 strikeouts in a season—trying for 12th-best all-time—and he did it in the most efficient manner possible. While going 15-1, 1.69, Prior struck out 202 while walking just 18 in 139 innings. He gave up 100 hits, just five of them home runs. In Prior's lone CWS start, Georgia patted itself on the back for scratching out four runs in seven innings during an 11-5 loss.

Apparently, other teams realized attacking Prior was their best way to answer his unique combination of power, command and poise. In the month entering the CWS, Prior appeared mortal. He followed a 13-day layoff with his worst start of the year, a seven-inning, six-run (four earned) effort against Washington State. Prior again appeared mortal at Oregon State, striking out a season-low five in seven innings. Of course, he gave up three runs and got the win, which mattered most to the 6-foot-5 junior righthander.

Prior also wanted to make sure he was healthy. It is this devotion to functional fitness that might help Prior avoid the poor professional fates of his "best college pitcher ever" predecessors. So he turned again to personal pitching guru Tom House for advice.

"I was a little tired and lost a little rhythm after the layoff," Prior said. "Tom told me the reason I wasn't pitching the way I did before the layoff was my body had gotten used to that time, to not working so hard. So I had to really step up my workouts and work hard to get my rhythm back.

"I was a little tired, but I felt I pitched well in the regional and super regional."

By any standard, except maybe his own of earlier in the season, he did. Against Pepperdine, Prior gave up 11 hits but just two runs while striking out 14 in eight innings. The Trojans rallied for a 4-3 win with three runs in the bottom of the ninth against fellow All-American Noah Lowry. In the super regional, Prior gave up only one first-inning run to Florida International before finishing with eight straight zeroes in a 5-1 victory.

Certainly, Prior had competition for the award, coming first from the pitchers on the All-America first team.

Lowry and Pepperdine almost ended Prior's season in the regional, dominating Southern California until running out of gas in the ninth. Central Florida righthander Justin Pope broke Roger Clemens' Division I record for consecutive scoreless innings, while Notre Dame's Aaron Heilman won all 15 of his starts. And perhaps no pitcher did more for his team by himself than Middle Tennessee State's Dewon Brazelton, who won 47 percent of his team's Sun Belt Conference games.

None of them faced the consistent level of competition as Prior. None of them were quite as dominant, and none faced the spotlight and the pressure quite like Prior.

In the Year of the Pitcher, it took better pitching to beat good pitching. And no one pitched better than Mark Prior. ■

# TOP PLAYERS OF 2001

## ALL-AMERICA TEAM

| Pos | Player | School | Yr | AVG | AB | R | H | HR | RBI | SB |
|-----|--------|--------|----|-----|-----|-----|-----|-----|-----|-----|
| C | Kelly Shoppach | Baylor | Jr | .397 | 234 | 51 | 93 | 12 | 69 | 4 |
| 1B | John Van Benschoten | Kent State | Jr | .440 | 225 | 74 | 99 | 31 | 84 | 23 |
| 2B | Michael Woods | Southern | Jr | .453 | 170 | 68 | 77 | 14 | 54 | 32 |
| 3B | Jeff Baker | Clemson | So | .369 | 233 | 66 | 86 | 23 | 75 | 5 |
| SS | Chris Burke | Tennessee | Jr | .435 | 271 | 105 | 118 | 20 | 60 | 49 |
| OF | John Cole | Nebraska | Jr | .418 | 239 | 71 | 100 | 11 | 61 | 28 |
| OF | Shelley Duncan | Arizona | Jr | .338 | 228 | 64 | 77 | 24 | 78 | 3 |
| OF | John-Ford Griffin | Florida State | Jr | .450 | 251 | 79 | 113 | 19 | 75 | 11 |
| DH | Jake Gautreau | Tulane | Jr | .355 | 290 | 82 | 103 | 21 | 96 | 8 |
| UT | Cory Sullivan | Wake Forest | Sr | .390 | 264 | 85 | 103 | 13 | 67 | 27 |

| Pos | Pitcher | School | Yr | W | L | ERA | G | SV | IP | H | BB | SO |
|-----|---------|--------|----|-----|-----|------|-----|-----|-----|-----|-----|-----|
| P | Dewon Brazelton | Middle Tenn. State | Jr | 13 | 2 | 1.42 | 15 | 0 | 127 | 82 | 24 | 154 |
| P | Aaron Heilman | Notre Dame | Sr | 15 | 0 | 1.74 | 15 | 0 | 114 | 70 | 31 | 111 |
| P | Noah Lowry | Pepperdine | Jr | 14 | 2 | 1.71 | 18 | 1 | 121 | 88 | 41 | 142 |
| P | Justin Pope | Central Florida | Jr | 15 | 1 | 1.68 | 17 | 0 | 123 | 97 | 27 | 158 |
| P | Mark Prior | Southern California | Jr | 15 | 1 | 1.69 | 20 | 0 | 139 | 100 | 18 | 202 |
| UT | Cory Sullivan | Wake Forest | Sr | 7 | 0 | 3.52 | 13 | 0 | 77 | 72 | 36 | 54 |

## SECOND TEAM

C—Casey Myers, Arizona State. 1B—Dan Johnson, Nebraska. 2B—Chris O'Riordan, Stanford. 3B—Kevin Youkilis, Cincinnati. SS—Jeff Keppinger, Georgia Tech. OF—Matt Davis, Virginia Commonwealth; Greg Dobbs, Oklahoma; and Jason Knoedler, Miami (Ohio). DH—Ryan Brunner, Northern Iowa. UT—Dan Haren, Pepperdine. SP—Jason Arnold, Central Florida; Kenny Baugh, Rice; Nate Fernley, Brigham Young; and Shane Komine, Nebraska. RP—Kirk Saarloos, Cal State Fullerton.

## THIRD TEAM

C—Tim Whittaker, South Carolina. 1B—Aaron Clark, Alabama. 2B—Dan Uggla, Memphis. 3B—Jack Hannahan, Minnesota. SS—Brendan Harris, William & Mary. OF—Todd Linden, Louisiana State; Steve Stanley, Notre Dame; Rickie Weeks, Southern. DH—Brian Baron, UCLA. UT—Barry Matthews, Gonzaga. SP—Willie Collazo, Florida International; Rik Currier, Southern California; Lee Gronkiewicz, South Carolina; and Jeremy Guthrie, Stanford. RP—Ben Thurmond, Winthrop.

# 2002

College World Series
Most Outstanding Player
Huston Street (25) greets
teammates during Texas'
12-6 championship
game victory against
South Carolina.

# Texas' powerful mix leads to fifth CWS crown

By **JOHN MANUEL**

FROM THE ISSUE:
JULY 22–AUG. 4, 2002

As South Carolina came through the loser's bracket at the 2002 College World Series, coach Ray Tanner reminded everyone that nothing came easy for the Gamecocks.

South Carolina, blown out 11-0 by Georgia Tech in its CWS opener, came back to beat Nebraska, Georgia Tech and Clemson—twice—to make it to the championship game. The Gamecocks were one win away from becoming the second team under the two-bracket CWS format to incur an opening loss and win the national championship.

Then Tanner's club ran into a team that made the game look easy, even though it had its own tough road. Texas may have been undefeated in Omaha, but it had to sweat out a trio of one-run games.

The Longhorns may have done so with the tournament's best closer, freshman right-hander Huston Street, but only after suffering several early season setbacks while trying to find the right man for the job. Texas may have shown a more balanced offense, but only after adjusting to the preseason loss of outfielder Ben King, its RBI leader in 2001.

And the Horns may have had the coach with the most CWS experience in Augie Garrido, who had won the championship three previous times with Cal State Fullerton, but not with the pressure that goes with coaching at Texas.

With all that, Garrido's Longhorns still made the school's fifth CWS championship look easy. They added power to their pitching-and-defense mix to beat the Gamecocks 12-6 in the championship game.

"This team was very similar to those Fullerton teams," Garrido said. "It has a lot of speed, which you have to have to defend, particularly at Disch-Falk Field. It has good pitching. And we have added power, which was a factor in today's game."

Garrido was famous at Fullerton for a West Coach approach heavy on bunting and running, with an accent on pitching and a scarcity of power hitters. That approach fits Disch-Falk but not Rosenblatt Stadium, expanded for the 2002 CWS but still a hitter's park.

The 2002 Longhorns went through plenty, because nothing went according to plan.

## TOP TEAMS
### 2002 COLLEGE WORLD SERIES STANDINGS

| School | Conference | Record | CWS | Coach |
|---|---|---|---|---|
| Texas | Big 12 | 57–15 | 4–0 | Augie Garrido |
| South Carolina | Southeastern | 57–18 | 4–2 | Ray Tanner |
| Clemson | Atlantic Coast | 54–17 | 2–2 | Jack Leggett |
| Stanford | Pacific-10 | 47–18 | 2–2 | Mark Marquess |
| Georgia Tech | Atlantic Coast | 52–16 | 1–2 | Danny Hall |
| Notre Dame | Big East | 50–18 | 1–2 | Paul Mainieri |
| Nebraska | Big 12 | 47–21 | 0–2 | Dave Van Horn |
| Rice | Western Athletic | 52–14 | 0–2 | Wayne Graham |

### NATIONAL CHAMPION
### TEXAS

Coach Augie Garrido guided Texas to the program's fifth title by defeating South Carolina 12-6 in the championship game. He succeeded all-time Division I wins leader Cliff Gustafson in Austin, so he had huge shoes to fill. Garrido would add another title in 2005.

First, there were newcomers to indoctrinate, like righthander Alan Bomer, the erstwhile Iowa State ace who transferred to Austin after the Cyclones dropped baseball.

Then came King's injury, which required Tommy John surgery, and deprived Texas of perhaps its most talented player. Shortstop Omar Quintanilla, the team's leading hitter as a freshman, missed the first third of the season serving an NCAA suspension. And in May, leadoff hitter Tim Moss was arrested on misdemeanor charges following an altercation with another student, though he never missed a game.

The Longhorns had more than enough depth to compensate for their adversity. While Quintanilla sat, junior college transfer Brendan Fahey asserted himself as a steady defender with a solid bat who could play virtually anywhere. Fahey settled in at shortstop for the stretch run, with Quintanilla at third base.

King's injury opened space for outfielders like Dustin Majewski, who didn't become an everyday player until March. He finished as the team's top hitter and was the outstanding player of both the Big 12 Conference tournament and Texas' regional.

Outfielder Chris Carmichael, a senior who missed 2001 with a broken right wrist, still got squeezed out, starting one game since March. Garrido played a hunch by starting tin the championship game, and he proved just how deep the Longhorns' bench was.

Carmichael struck the game's decisive blow in the fifth. His three-run homer, making the score 7-2, was just his second of the year but showed the team's newfound commitment to power. Carmichael's blast—Texas' 68th of the season—set a program record.

Carmichael was met by a mob of teammates at the plate, another indication that Garrido's proclamations during the CWS about his team's closeness were accurate.

"Every team reacts to adversity differently," Fahey said. "Championship teams stay together and find ways to keep winning."

# 2002 NEWSMAKERS

Freshman of the Year **Stephen Drew** stepped into a starting role at **Florida State** and hit .402 with 16 home runs despite missing eight weeks with a broken left foot. Fueled by Drew's return, the Seminoles ranked No. 1 at the close of the regular season after winning their final 15 **Atlantic Coast Conference** games, sweeping through the ACC tournament and taking a 25-game winning streak into super regionals. The ride ended there at the hands of Notre Dame in an upset defeat.

Coach of the Year **Augie Garrido** guided **Texas** to a CWS championship in his sixth season in Austin, becoming the first coach to claim titles at two different schools (he won three at Cal State Fullerton) and the first to win the CWS in four different decades (1979, 1984, 1995, 2002 and later 2005).

The **NCAA** mandated reduced air travel for regionals in the wake of the Sept. 11, 2001, terrorist attacks. This forced regional teams into tight geographical constraints. The resulting unbalanced fields yielded the most difficult regional in history, when **Stanford** hosted **Long Beach State**, **Cal State Fullerton** and **San Jose State**. All four clubs ranked in the top 25 at the time.

## FINAL TOP 25 FOR 2002

1. Texas*
2. South Carolina*
3. Clemson*
4. #Stanford*
5. Rice*
6. Notre Dame*
7. Florida State
8. Georgia Tech*
9. Nebraska*
10. Houston
11. Louisiana State
12. Wake Forest
13. Alabama
14. Southern California
15. Florida
16. Richmond
17. North Carolina
18. Cal State Northridge
19. Florida Atlantic
20. Miami
21. Long Beach State
22. Arizona State
23. Wichita State
24. San Jose State
25. Arkansas

* Reached College World Series
# Preseason No. 1

# IN RETROSPECT: 2002 DRAFT

## Top 10 Draft Picks From College
With overall selection number (Ov), drafting team (Team) and rank on Baseball America draft board (BA).

| Player | Pos | School | Ov | Team | BA |
|--------|-----|--------|----|------|-----|
| Bryan Bullington | RHP | Ball State | 1 | Pirates | 3 |
| Jeff Francis | LHP | British Columbia | 9 | Rockies | 15 |
| Drew Meyer | SS | South Carolina | 10 | Rangers | 27 |
| Joe Saunders | LHP | Virginia Tech | 12 | Angels | 17 |
| Khalil Greene | SS | Clemson | 13 | Padres | 35 |
| Russ Adams | SS | North Carolina | 14 | Blue Jays | 19 |
| Nick Swisher | 1B | Ohio State | 16 | Athletics | 34 |
| Royce Ring | LHP | San Diego State | 18 | White Sox | 26 |
| Bobby Brownlie | RHP | Rutgers | 21 | Cubs | 6 |
| Jeremy Guthrie | RHP | Stanford | 22 | Indians | 11 |

## Top 10 Major League Players From College Draft Class
With draft round and Baseball-Reference.com total for wins above replacement (WAR) through 2019.

| Player | Pos | School | Rd | Ov | Team | WAR |
|--------|-----|--------|----|----|------|-----|
| Curtis Granderson | OF | Illinois-Chicago | 3 | 80 | Tigers | 47.3 |
| Nick Swisher | OF | Ohio State | 1 | 16 | Athletics | 22.0 |
| Jeremy Guthrie | RHP | Stanford | 1 | 22 | Indians | 17.8 |
| Rich Hill | LHP | Michigan | 4 | 112 | Cubs | 13.6 |
| Joe Blanton | RHP | Kentucky | 1 | 24 | Athletics | 11.8 |
| Jesse Crain | RHP | Houston | 2 | 61 | Twins | 11.4 |
| Pat Neshek | RHP | Butler | 6 | 182 | Twins | 10.8 |
| Chris Denorfia | OF | Wheaton (Mass.) | 19 | 555 | Reds | 10.5 |
| Jeff Francis | LHP | British Columbia | 1 | 9 | Rockies | 9.6 |
| Joe Saunders | LHP | Virginia Tech | 1 | 12 | Angels | 8.6 |

But clearing up Bomer's closer role ended up helping the Longhorns the most. While Bomer won two of his first three starts, Garrido and pitching coach Frank Anderson decided to try the righthander as the closer. After he blew a 6-1 lead at Stanford in late March, Anderson gave Street a try at the role.

Street became the first player to save four games in one CWS and got the last five outs of the title game, including striking out Gamecocks slugger Yaron Peters, who led the Southeastern Conference in home runs, when he was the tying run in the eighth inning.

As for Bomer, he rebounded from his closer experiment to win games that clinched regional and super regional titles, then started the first of two CWS victories against Stanford to finish second on the team with 11 wins.

Sophomore lefthander Justin Simmons also rebounded in Omaha. After winning his first 14 decisions, he stumbled in his last four appearances prior to the CWS, giving up 11 runs in 11.1 innings. Simmons' offspeed repertoire was sharp in Omaha. He beat Rice in the opener, and with relief help held the Gamecocks at bay in the championship game.

It was Simmons' 16th victory, most in the nation, while Street got his 14th save. Carmichael's homer provided the unexpected element that every CWS championship seems to have. And Garrido, in becoming just the third head coach to win four national titles and the first to do so at two schools and over four decades, provided the perspective.

"I have talked about expecting the unexpected, and (Carmichael) provided that," Garrido said. "He overcame injuries and played out the year as a reserve, and still was able to come through."

"He's an example of how our whole bench played. He earned it. It's good stuff." ∎

# Clemson's Greene can't hide talent anymore

By **JOHN MANUEL**

**W**hen Brooks Carey played for the Rookie-level Bluefield Orioles in 1978, he was struck by the athleticism and skills of a 17-year-old shortstop.

Cal Ripken Jr. stood out on a team that won 19 games. Future Hall of Famers tend to do that.

Carey didn't have quite the same skill level and went into coaching, eventually becoming head coach at Key West (Fla.) High. Around 1990, he noticed a Little Leaguer in town who stood out almost as much as Ripken had.

"You could see he was different, this little kid who looks about the same as he does now, but who could really, really play," Carey said. "You could see the talent."

Seven years later, Carey was coaching Khalil Greene for Key West High, the little kid having grown up a bit but still standing out from the crowd. Carey had coaxed Ripken to come to the Keys for a fundraiser

Clemson shortstop Khalil Greene stands as the all-time D-I leader with 95 doubles, and he ranks top 10 in hits, totals bases and assists. He spent seven uneven years in the majors, mostly with the Padres.

and had his old friend throw out the first pitch before a Key West game.

"You got any good players?" Ripken asked as he came to the dugout.

"Yeah, the shortstop, Greene," Carey replied. "You should watch him."

About then, Greene slammed a 400-foot homer to left field to open the game. By the time Ripken left, Greene had a couple more hits and a recommendation from the Orioles star, one that wasn't heeded in the 1998 draft.

In fact, no one drafted Khalil Greene out of high school, a fact that seems impossible after his enormous senior season for Clemson. All he did in 2002 was redefine everyone's expectations for him, the way Ripken redefined the shortstop position.

"Nothing Khalil does surprises me anymore," Clemson coach Jack Leggett said. "Whenever we need a hit, he gets a hit. When we need a play, he makes a play."

Greene went from a 14th-round pick of the Cubs in 2001 to the 13th overall selection by the Padres in 2002. His offensive feats, defensive gems and overall dominance made him an easy selection as the College Player of the Year.

Greene thought he would be playing pro ball after leading Carey's Conchs to a Florida 3-A title and ending his career as the school's all-time hits and runs leader. Carey said the Cardinals approached Greene with a six-figure bonus offer if he would move to catcher out of high school, but Greene refused. He wasn't drafted at all.

"That's one of the things I respect the most about him—he believed so much in himself as an infielder, he wouldn't accept a move even though he wanted to play pro ball," Carey said. "He was extremely insulted that he wasn't drafted, though."

Scouts who saw Greene in his first two seasons at Clemson marveled at his savvy and instincts, which helped him step right into the lineup as a freshman.

He was emerging as one of the nation's top third basemen entering his junior year, but for the first time baseball didn't come easy. He pressed at the plate, slumping to the .260s before finishing with a flourish to end the season with a .303 average. The Cubs drafted him, but Greene said he didn't seriously consider signing.

Greene returned for his senior season and his assault on the record books started almost immediately. He got off to a monster start that included a 14-game hitting streak and eventually became just the second player in Division I history to pass 400 career hits.

Greene finished the year with a .470 average to go with 27 home runs and 91 RBIs.

Mike Rikard, the Padres area scout who will try to sign Greene, said of his late-season hit streak, "It's like he's playing PlayStation. He just gets a hit or hits a home run or makes a play whenever he wants."

The last thing Greene wants, those who know him agree, is the limelight.

Too bad, Khalil. You're too good to ignore anymore. ■

# TOP PLAYERS OF 2002

## ALL-AMERICA TEAM

| Pos | Player | School | Yr | AVG | AB | R | H | HR | RBI | SB |
|-----|--------|--------|----|----|----|----|----|----|----|----|
| C | Tony Richie | Florida State | So | .353 | 249 | 59 | 88 | 13 | 75 | 1 |
| 1B | Yaron Peters | South Carolina | Sr | .377 | 281 | 81 | 106 | 29 | 95 | 6 |
| 2B | Russ Adams | North Carolina | Jr | .370 | 254 | 75 | 94 | 7 | 55 | 45 |
| 3B | Jeff Baker | Clemson | Jr | .325 | 265 | 71 | 86 | 25 | 87 | 17 |
| SS | Khalil Greene | Clemson | Sr | .470 | 285 | 93 | 134 | 27 | 91 | 17 |
| OF | Sam Fuld | Stanford | So | .375 | 293 | 67 | 110 | 8 | 47 | 8 |
| OF | Bobby Malek | Michigan State | Jr | .402 | 219 | 66 | 88 | 16 | 66 | 16 |
| OF | Steve Stanley | Notre Dame | Sr | .439 | 271 | 77 | 119 | 1 | 36 | 32 |
| DH | Rickie Weeks | Southern | So | .495 | 198 | 82 | 98 | 20 | 96 | 10 |
| UT | Jesse Crain | Houston | Jr | .309 | 262 | 51 | 81 | 11 | 47 | 3 |

| Pos | Pitcher | School | Yr | W | L | ERA | G | SV | IP | H | BB | SO |
|-----|---------|--------|----|----|----|----|----|----|----|----|----|----|
| SP | Bryan Bullington | Ball State | Jr | 11 | 3 | 2.84 | 15 | 0 | 105 | 88 | 18 | 139 |
| SP | Jeremy Guthrie | Stanford | Jr | 13 | 2 | 2.51 | 20 | 0 | 158 | 138 | 36 | 136 |
| SP | Tim Stauffer | Richmond | So | 15 | 3 | 1.54 | 20 | 0 | 146 | 110 | 34 | 140 |
| SP | Brad Sullivan | Houston | So | 13 | 1 | 1.82 | 18 | 0 | 129 | 80 | 49 | 157 |
| RP | Royce Ring | San Diego State | Jr | 5 | 1 | 1.85 | 36 | 17 | 39 | 29 | 13 | 54 |
| UT | Jesse Crain | Houston | Jr | 4 | 0 | 0.23 | 27 | 10 | 38 | 22 | 10 | 46 |

## SECOND TEAM

**C**—Chris Snyder, Houston. **1B**—Vince Sinisi, Rice. **2B**—Brian Burgamy, Wichita State. **3B**—Pat Osborn, Florida. **SS**—Stephen Drew, Florida State. **OF**—Curtis Granderson, Illinois-Chicago; Darryl Lawhorn, East Carolina; and Chris Maples, North Carolina. **DH**—John McCurdy, Maryland. **UT**—Ben Fritz, Fresno State. **SP**—Kyle Bakker, Georgia Tech; Shane Komine, Nebraska; Justin Simmons, Texas; and Kyle Sleeth, Wake Forest. **RP**—Blake Taylor, South Carolina.

## THIRD TEAM

**C**—Chris Westervelt, Stetson. **1B**—James Jurries, Tulane. **2B**—Tim Moss, Texas. **3B**—Ryan Barthelemy, Florida State. **SS**—Drew Meyer, South Carolina. **OF**—Joey Gomes, Santa Clara; Adam Greenberg, North Carolina; and Brian Wright, North Carolina State. **DH**—Jed Morris, Nebraska. **UT**—Wes Whisler, UCLA. **SP**—Abe Alvarez, Long Beach State; Alex Hart, Florida; Philip Humber, Rice; and Wes Littleton, Cal State Fullerton. **RP**—David Bush, Wake Forest.

Jeff Niemann and Philip Humber (back to camera), two of Rice's three aces, embrace following the Owls' CWS victory in the first ever best-of-three championship series.

**2003**

# Owls soar to first national crown

By **JOHN MANUEL**

R ice University won the College World Series. Consider that for a moment. Rice, with the smallest enrollment (2,600) of any Division I football school. Rice, which was left out when the old Southwest Conference melted and the Big 12 Conference swallowed what it thought were the SWC's four best programs. Rice, a school with elite academic credentials and a 91 percent graduation rate for its athletes.

**FROM THE ISSUE:**
JULY 21–AUG. 3, 2003

But this was also an Owls program making its fourth trip to Omaha since 1997, a team that expected to get to the CWS. The Owls had a 30-game winning streak during the regular season with a pitching staff full of power arms, an airtight defense and a coach whose lineage and legacy are nearly unmatched at any level of baseball.

That coach is Wayne Graham. And he wasn't surprised that Rice won a national championship in baseball—the first for the school in any team sport—by beating Stanford 14-2 at Rosenblatt Stadium in the finale of the new best-of-three championship format.

Look right there in the Owls' media guide, where Graham throws down the gauntlet. Question: "What's left?" Answer: "A national championship for Rice; I know it's possible."

His team proved him right with a performance Graham called "a tribute to pitching and defense." Rice did it with a trio of sophomore righthanders—Phillip Humber, Jeff Niemann and Wade Townsend—who anchored the rotation, combining for 39 victories on the season and 458 of a school-record 653 strikeouts.

In Omaha, the Owls were without Jeff Jorgensen, who came to Rice on a track scholarship but had a broken foot. And they had to weather a slump from sophomore first baseman Vincent Sinisi, their top hitter who went 4-for-25 in the CWS.

To top it off, junior left fielder Chris Kolkhorst dislocated his left kneecap during the first game of the finals, when he tripped over a bullpen mound while chasing a fly ball. Kolkhorst resolutely played on, and in the clincher he went 3-for-4 with a pair of doubles, two RBIs and three runs scored.

Humber, however, was the story of the finale. He had won 17 consecutive decisions

## TOP TEAMS
### 2003 COLLEGE WORLD SERIES STANDINGS

| School | Conference | Record | CWS | Coach |
|---|---|---|---|---|
| Rice | Western Athletic | 58–12 | 5–1 | Wayne Graham |
| Stanford | Pacific-10 | 51–18 | 5–3 | Mark Marquess |
| Cal State Fullerton | Big West | 50–16 | 2–2 | George Horton |
| Texas | Big 12 | 50–20 | 2–2 | Augie Garrido |
| Miami | Independent | 45–17–1 | 1–2 | Jim Morris |
| South Carolina | Southeastern | 45–22 | 1–2 | Ray Tanner |
| Louisiana State | Southeastern | 45–22 | 0–2 | Smoke Laval |
| SW Missouri State | Missouri Valley | 40–26 | 0–2 | Keith Guttin |

## NATIONAL CHAMPION
### RICE

A 66-year-old Wayne Graham guided Rice to the program's first and only national title. The Owls rode a fearsome rotation featuring three future first-round picks to victory against Stanford in the first-ever best-of-three CWS championship series.

**161**

dating back to his Freshman All-America 2002 season, but lost his last two heading into the CWS. The team's No. 3 starter behind Niemann and Townsend, Humber struggled in his first Omaha start, striking out eight but walking five and hitting a CWS-record three consecutive batters against Texas. He lasted just 3.2 innings as the Owls rallied to victory, but the redemption was clearly on his mind.

Stanford had stunned Niemann, who was trying to become the NCAA's first pitcher to go 18-0, with three runs in the first inning of the championship opener, but Niemann recovered, as did the Owls. Rice chipped away and won 4-3 in 10 innings when Cardinal reliever Kodiak Quick threw away a routine two-out grounder.

Stanford's aggressive offense, led by senior catcher Ryan Garko and outfielders Danny Putnam and Carlos Quentin, then attacked Niemann's roommate Townsend, who had won 11 of 12 decisions but got the game loss in Stanford's 8-2 victory in Game 2. The Cardinal jumped to a 3-1 lead, then got five in the seventh as Townsend fell apart and Sinisi, who had made one error all season, made two in the frame.

So Humber got the ball with the season on the line. He had two games to take notes on how to attack the Cardinal and formulated an excellent game plan. While Humber runs his fastball into the low 90s, he relied on his curveball and split-finger fastball in the championship game, throwing offspeed stuff in fastball counts and keeping Stanford's hitters off balance. When he needed it, he had a 92 mph fastball at the ready.

The result was the first complete game in a series clincher since Louisiana State's Brett Laxton struck out 16 against Wichita State in 1993. Humber gave up just five hits.

After being overshadowed by Niemann and Townsend all season, Humber shined the brightest when it mattered most.

"(Stanford is) a first-pitch fastball team, and I wanted to stay away from that, get my

# 2003 NEWSMAKERS

■ **ESPN** purchased the rights to the **College World Series** and adopted a best-of-three championship series, expanding the event to 11 days with every game televised. Previously, CBS had carried two games from Omaha, including the one-game championship. The ratings for the 2003 finals were similar despite the event moving from network TV to cable.

■ **Rice** coach **Wayne Graham**, 66, won his first and only CWS, defeating rival Texas twice in Omaha. He reached the majors briefly as a player in the early 1960s and later coached five national champions at San Jacinto (Texas) JC, where he worked with **Roger Clemens** and **Andy Pettitte**. Graham got his first Division I coaching gig at age 54 and led Rice to its first-ever regional appearance in 1995, his fourth year at the school. The Owls didn't miss the NCAA Tournament again until his final season in 2018.

■ **Southern** second baseman and Player of the Year **Rickie Weeks** finished three years in the **Southwestern Athletic Conference** as the all-time Division I leader for batting average (.465) and slugging (.927) for players with at least 200 at-bats.

| FINAL TOP 25 FOR 2003 |
| --- |
| 1. Rice* |
| 2. Stanford* |
| 3. Cal State Fullerton* |
| 4. Texas* |
| 5. Louisiana State* |
| 6. Florida State |
| 7. Arizona State |
| 8. Miami* |
| 9. Long Beach State |
| 10. South Carolina* |
| 11. Baylor |
| 12. North Carolina State |
| 13. Nebraska |
| 14. Texas A&M |
| 15. Southern Mississippi |
| 16. SW Missouri State* |
| 17. #Georgia Tech |
| 18. Auburn |
| 19. North Carolina |
| 20. Nevada-Las Vegas |
| 21. Ohio State |
| 22. Houston |
| 23. Florida Atlantic |
| 24. Mississippi State |
| 25. Washington |
| * Reached College World Series |
| # Preseason No. 1 |

# IN RETROSPECT: 2003 DRAFT

### Top 10 Draft Picks From College
With overall selection number (Ov), drafting team (Team) and rank on Baseball America draft board (BA).

| Player | Pos | School | Ov | Team | BA |
|---|---|---|---|---|---|
| Rickie Weeks | 2B | Southern | 2 | Brewers | 3 |
| Kyle Sleeth | RHP | Wake Forest | 3 | Tigers | 6 |
| Tim Stauffer | RHP | Richmond | 4 | Padres | 10 |
| Paul Maholm | LHP | Mississippi State | 8 | Pirates | 17 |
| Michael Aubrey | 1B | Tulane | 11 | Indians | 8 |
| Aaron Hill | SS | Louisiana State | 13 | Blue Jays | 19 |
| Ryan Wagner | RHP | Houston | 14 | Reds | 18 |
| Brian Anderson | OF | Arizona | 15 | White Sox | 27 |
| David Murphy | OF | Baylor | 17 | Red Sox | 38 |
| Brad Snyder | OF | Ball State | 18 | Indians | 26 |

### Top 10 Major League Players From College Draft Class
With draft round and Baseball-Reference.com total for wins above replacement (WAR) through 2019.

| Player | Pos | School | Rd | Ov | Team | WAR |
|---|---|---|---|---|---|---|
| Ian Kinsler | 2B | Missouri | 17 | 496 | Rangers | 57.2 |
| Aaron Hill | 2B | Louisiana State | 1 | 13 | Blue Jays | 23.7 |
| Jonathan Papelbon | RHP | Mississippi State | 4 | 114 | Red Sox | 23.5 |
| Michael Bourn | OF | Houston | 4 | 115 | Phillies | 22.8 |
| Andre Ethier | OF | Arizona State | 2 | 62 | Athletics | 21.2 |
| Scott Baker | RHP | Oklahoma State | 2 | 58 | Twins | 15.6 |
| Brendan Ryan | SS | Lewis-Clark State | 7 | 215 | Cardinals | 15.1 |
| Shaun Marcum | RHP | Missouri State | 3 | 80 | Blue Jays | 13.5 |
| Brad Ziegler | RHP | Missouri State | 20 | 595 | Phillies | 12.9 |
| Paul Maholm | LHP | Mississippi State | 1 | 8 | Pirates | 11.9 |

curve over and then use my split to get outs," Humber said. "Last time, I was trying too hard to miss bats, but this time I trusted my stuff and let my defense work for me."

The Cardinal had no defense for the Owls, who jumped to a 4-0 lead as freshman Mark Romanczuck walked six of the 10 batters he faced. The lefthander, who was 12-0, 3.39 coming into Omaha, was dreadful at Rosenblatt, going 0-2, 11.42.

Rice romped to a 14-2 victory in Game 3, the largest margin ever in a CWS clincher.

That was despite the efforts of junior righthander John Hudgins, who claimed the CWS Most Outstanding Player trophy. He beat South Carolina with eight shutout innings in the Cardinal's CWS opener, then beat Cal State Fullerton in the bracket championship. He also won Game 2 of the championship series. Hudgins' three CWS wins tied a record, as did his four career wins, but he was unavailable in the finale.

Some would say that time is winding down for the 66-year-old Graham, but they would be sadly mistaken. He's only getting better and has no plans for retirement.

"I've said it before: I'll go on a baseball field," he joked after the title was won.

Graham didn't get his first Division I head coaching job until he was 54, but he has been a perfect fit for the Owls. Rice had never made a regional trip until year four under Graham, in 1995. Now they are the Western Athletic Conference's perennial champion, an Omaha regular and consistent stop on the road for pro scouts.

With the talent returning for 2004, the Owls will once again be expected to come back to the CWS. And now, they'll be expected to win it. At least Graham thinks so.

"It's redemption. It's validation. It's all those words," he said. "We had a lot to prove, and we still have a lot to prove. We want to do it again." ∎

# Weeks set to become Brewers' best bet

By **DREW OLSON**

There wasn't much else Rickie Weeks could have done for Southern.

He flirted with .500 all spring, stole 31 bases and hit 16 homers. He led the Jaguars to the postseason, then sparked Southern to a regional win with a two-run homer. And he finished his career with a .473 average, best in Division I history.

So now, Weeks will be expected to do a lot to help the Brewers.

Trying to dig out from the rubble of 10 straight losing seasons, the Brewers chose Southern's standout second baseman with the No. 2 overall pick. It was nearly as easy for Baseball America to make Weeks its College Player of the Year.

A pick that high brings an enormous amount of pressure, for both the player and the club. After watching Weeks work out, Brewers scouting director Jack Zduriencik had no second thoughts about the second selection.

Rickie Weeks played for Team USA in both 2001 and 2002, and he still holds D-I career marks for average (.465) and slugging (.927). He hit 161 homers and swiped 132 bats in 14 big leagues seasons.

"We've seen the kid play for three years," Zduriencik said. "His athleticism was always impressive. He can run. He can throw. He's strong. He has great instincts. He's played all three positions in the middle of the field—shortstop, center field and second base. He could realistically play any of those three spots. But he finally settled into one position, and I saw marked improvement as he got comfortable at second base.

"For us, when you think about this organization and where we're heading and what's coming, it's a good fit. He's 20 years old. He's going to get better. Like all young kids, he just needs some fine-tuning of his game. He's going to get that. I just can't wait to get him in a uniform."

While wearing the uniform of the Jaguars, Weeks transformed himself from a skinny, largely unnoticed and under-recruited high school player to a two-time NCAA batting champion. Weeks hit .493 as a senior as he helped his team to a 43-5 record. For his career, he went 65-for-66 on stolen base attempts.

Brewers general manager Doug Melvin watched Weeks play in Baton Rouge this spring and met him in the parking lot after the game. "He had a nice, firm handshake," Melvin said. "You like to see that."

Weeks' hands are continually noticed by scouts, who compare his wrist strength to that of Hank Aaron and his bat speed to major leaguers Gary Sheffield and Alfonso Soriano.

"That blew my mind right there," Weeks said of the comparisons. "I don't pay much attention to that. Hopefully, I'll come out, do my best and turn some heads."

Weeks said his bat speed is just a natural phenomenon. "I have a quick bat, but to tell the truth, I don't know where it comes from," he said. "It just comes naturally. You try to work on a few things, but it's pretty much natural."

Weeks' hands gain attention on defense, as well. Though some scouts worried about his defense at second base, he looked sharp during his workout in Milwaukee.

"We had heard that he was a little unrefined with the glove, but he looked very smooth—a very quick release," Brewers manager Ned Yost said. "He turned two very well—his transfer was very impressive."

Because he had not signed a contract, Weeks was under no obligation to put his skills on display for the Brewers. The fact that he did was surprising to some, which Weeks couldn't understand.

"I came here to prove myself and to try to build a relationship with the people who I am going to be with for the long run," he said. "Milwaukee is a great team, headed in the right direction with the coaching staff it has. I'm just going to work hard and see what happens."

What has already happened for Weeks has been plenty impressive. ■

# TOP PLAYERS OF 2003

## ALL-AMERICA TEAM

| Pos | Player | School | Yr | AVG | AB | R | H | HR | RBI | SB |
|-----|--------|--------|----|----|----|----|----|----|----|----|
| C | Ryan Garko | Stanford | Sr | .402 | 259 | 64 | 104 | 18 | 92 | 2 |
| 1B | Michael Aubrey | Tulane | Jr | .420 | 243 | 70 | 102 | 18 | 79 | 19 |
| 2B | Rickie Weeks | Southern | Jr | .479 | 163 | 82 | 78 | 16 | 66 | 28 |
| 3B | Brian Snyder | Stetson | Jr | .396 | 227 | 65 | 90 | 11 | 55 | 12 |
| SS | Aaron Hill | Louisiana State | Jr | .358 | 265 | 68 | 95 | 9 | 67 | 9 |
| OF | Dustin Majewski | Texas | Sr | .391 | 274 | 62 | 107 | 12 | 85 | 21 |
| OF | David Murphy | Baylor | Jr | .413 | 293 | 84 | 121 | 11 | 67 | 3 |
| OF | Brad Snyder | Ball State | Jr | .405 | 200 | 68 | 81 | 14 | 61 | 20 |
| DH | Mitch Maier | Toledo | Jr | .448 | 194 | 59 | 87 | 9 | 61 | 29 |
| UT | Scott Beerer | Texas A&M | Jr | .335 | 245 | 44 | 82 | 11 | 57 | 5 |

| Pos | Pitcher | School | Yr | W | L | ERA | G | SV | IP | H | BB | SO |
|-----|---------|--------|----|----|----|----|----|----|----|----|----|----|
| SP | David Marchbanks | South Carolina | Jr | 15 | 3 | 2.73 | 21 | 0 | 135 | 148 | 25 | 97 |
| SP | Jeff Niemann | Rice | So | 17 | 0 | 1.70 | 22 | 1 | 137 | 96 | 35 | 156 |
| SP | Wade Townsend | Rice | So | 11 | 2 | 2.20 | 29 | 5 | 119 | 80 | 46 | 164 |
| SP | Jered Weaver | Long Beach State | So | 14 | 4 | 1.96 | 19 | 0 | 133 | 87 | 20 | 144 |
| RP | Ryan Wagner | Houston | So | 6 | 5 | 1.93 | 38 | 15 | 79 | 39 | 21 | 148 |
| UT | Scott Beerer | Texas A&M | Jr | 6 | 1 | 1.82 | 27 | 13 | 49 | 32 | 12 | 58 |

### SECOND TEAM

C—Tony Richie, Florida State. 1B—Jeff Larish, Arizona State. 2B—Luke Appert, Minnesota. 3B—Jamie D'Antona, Wake Forest. SS—Dustin Pedroia, Arizona State. OF—Brian Anderson, Arizona; Josh Anderson, Eastern Kentucky; and Carlos Quentin, Stanford. DH—Jeremy Cleveland, North Carolina. UT—Micah Owings, Georgia Tech. SP—Abe Alvarez, Long Beach State; Scott Lewis, Ohio State; Justin Orenduff, Va. Commonwealth; and Tim Stauffer, Richmond. RP—Huston Street, Texas.

### THIRD TEAM

C—Jake Fox, Michigan. 1B—Matt Hooper, Nebraska. 2B—Lee Curtis, College of Charleston. 3B—Conor Jackson, California. SS—Stephen Drew, Florida State. OF—Jeff Cook, Southern Mississippi; Chris Durbin, Baylor; and Clint King, Southern Mississippi. DH—Billy Becher, New Mexico State. UT—Ryan Gordon, UNC Greensboro. SP—Randy Beam, Florida Atlantic; John Hodgins, Stanford; Paul Maholm, Mississippi State; and Tom Mastny, Furman. RP—Will Fenton, Washington.

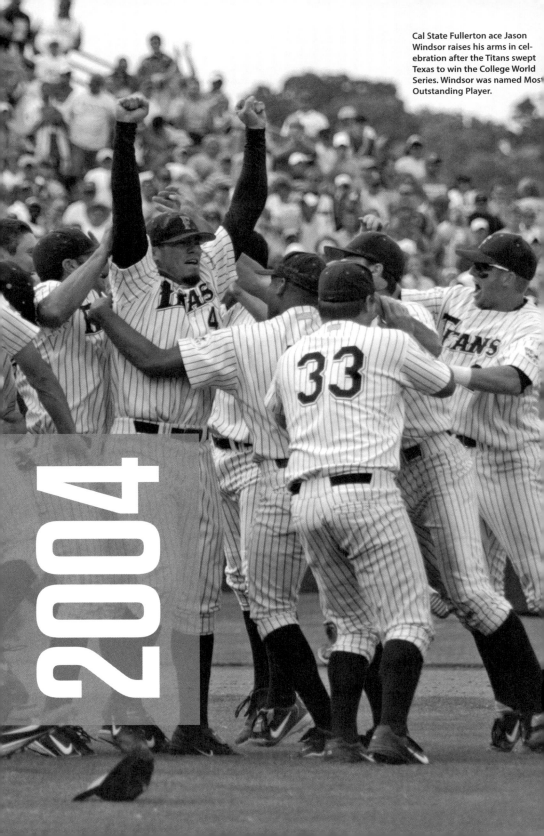

Cal State Fullerton ace Jason Windsor raises his arms in celebration after the Titans swept Texas to win the College World Series. Windsor was named Most Outstanding Player.

2004

# Fullerton completes Titanic turnaround

### By **WILL KIMMEY**

C al State Fullerton reached the College World Series despite a 15-16 start to the season because of Titanic contributions from catcher Kurt Suzuki and the one-two punch of Jason Windsor and Ricky Romero on the mound.

The trio also drove Fullerton's two-game championship series sweep of favored Texas, with Windsor throwing his second complete game of the CWS and Suzuki driving in the decisive run in a 3-2, title-clinching win.

"Not to take anything away from the other Titans battling in our dugout, but what a fitting conclusion to have Jason Windsor on the mound to win it and Kurt Suzuki getting the winning hit," Fullerton coach George Horton said. "That's the way to win it."

Suzuki, a first-team All-American, was mired in a 2-for-22 slump before living up to his Kurt Klutch nickname. He shot a single to left field to drive home the deciding run.

"There's no mystery that I had nothing to show for the series," Suzuki said. "I knew I just wanted to hit the ball somewhere. I had frustrations, but I couldn't let that bother me. I had 24 other teammates that I was trying to win a national championship for."

It marked the first national title as a head coach for Horton, who served as an assistant on the 1995 Titans championship team coached by Augie Garrido, who has since moved on to Texas. Fullerton became the sixth school to win at least four titles.

Windsor dominated the CWS and earned Most Outstanding Player honors, allowing just two runs in 21 innings while notching two wins and a save. He racked up 29 strikeouts against six walks while throwing 322 pitches in a nine-day span.

"It hasn't sunk in yet," he said. "It'll take a few days of relaxing before it does. I look at it on paper and I don't believe it's me. It just feels great."

Texas entered the championship series with a decided pitching edge. The Longhorns staff was the nation's deepest, and Texas had played one fewer game to reach the finals than Fullerton. Texas' greatest advantage looked to be in the bullpen.

Because of Huston Street, J. Brent Cox and Buck Cody, the Longhorns entered the CWS

**FROM THE ISSUE:**
JULY 19–AUG. 1, 2004

## TOP TEAMS
### 2004 COLLEGE WORLD SERIES STANDINGS

| School | Conference | Record | CWS | Coach |
|---|---|---|---|---|
| Cal State Fullerton | Big West | 47–22 | 5–1 | George Horton |
| Texas | Big 12 | 58–15 | 3–2 | Augie Garrido |
| South Carolina | Southeastern | 53–17 | 3–2 | Ray Tanner |
| Georgia | Southeastern | 45–23 | 2–2 | David Perno |
| Arizona | Pacific-10 | 36–27–1 | 1–2 | Andy Lopez |
| Miami | Independent | 50–13 | 1–2 | Jim Morris |
| Arkansas | Southeastern | 45–24 | 0–2 | Dave van Horn |
| Louisiana State | Southeastern | 46–19 | 0–2 | Smoke Laval |

## NATIONAL CHAMPION
### CAL STATE FULLERTON

The student defeated the teacher as the Titans swept Texas in the championship series. Fullerton coach George Horton served as Augie Garrido's assistant for seven years before succeeding him in the dugout when Garrido left for Texas in 1997.

finals having won 41 of 42 games when they held a lead after five innings. But both of the Titans' victories in the championship series against Texas featured such comebacks.

"Pitching-wise they go eight or nine deep," Horton said. "But I told our guys not to worry because you only have to face one of them at a time."

Fullerton's bullpen had not won a game since April 18 and had recorded just five saves entering the Texas series. The question mark turned into an exclamation point during the CWS, when Titans relievers pitched eight shutout innings at Rosenblatt Stadium.

The Titans also received an unexpected pitching boost from junior lefthander Scott Sarver. Making his second appearance since May 11, Sarver held South Carolina without a run for six-plus innings of a 4-0 win that sent Fullerton into the championship series.

Windsor worked the final three innings to finish the second Titans shutout of the Gamecocks—the first came in the CWS opener. They hadn't been held scoreless this year before Omaha.

"Scott Sarver, what a great story that kid is," Horton said. "Not in our wildest dreams did we think he would shut out South Carolina, a team that swings the bat real well. He looked like he was an All-American."

After Cal State Fullerton right fielder Bobby Andrews squeezed a fly ball for the final out of the 2004 CWS, Titans players immediately piled into a throbbing mass of humanity on the pitcher's mound as they celebrated the national championship they earned with a 3-2 win.

Horton exchanged hugs with his staff, thanking them for their advice and teamwork throughout a sometimes trying season. He found his family in the stands and made eye contact to thank them for their sacrifices and contributions that allowed him to reach the pinnacle of his coaching career.

# 2004 NEWSMAKERS

Preseason No. 1 **Rice** looked like a strong bet to repeat as national champions after returning righthanders **Philip Humber**, **Jeff Niemann** and **Wade Townsend**. But Texas Southern, a team that had gone 18-31 during the season, stunned the Owls in regional play in one of the biggest upsets in college baseball history. Rice fell to the Tigers 4-3 when Humber surrendered a three-run, eighth inning home run.

The 10-member **NCAA** Division I baseball issues committee approved changes to the college calendar, effective for the 2006-07 school year. Changes included a uniform start date of March 1, a Feb. 1 start date for spring practices and the instal-lation of a 45-day window from September through November for teams to use for fall practice.

The **Southeastern Conference** set or tied records by getting nine NCAA Tournament bids, six No. 1 seeds, five regional host sites and four College World Series entrants. **Mississippi State**, the ninth SEC team in the 64-team tournament, made it with-out participating in the SEC Tournament and despite having a losing record (13-17) in conference play.

## FINAL TOP 25 FOR 2004

1. Cal State Fullerton*
2. Texas*
3. South Carolina*
4. Miami*
5. Georgia*
6. Arkansas*
7. Louisiana State*
8. East Carolina
9. Stanford
10. Georgia Tech
11. #Rice
12. Arizona*
13. Long Beach State
14. Florida State
15. Notre Dame
16. Florida
17. Vanderbilt
18. Oral Roberts
19. Tulane
20. Texas A&M
21. Washington
22. Arizona State
23. Mississippi
24. Virginia
25. Oklahoma

* Reached College World Series
# Preseason No. 1

# IN RETROSPECT: 2004 DRAFT

## Top 10 Draft Picks From College
With overall selection number (Ov), drafting team (Team) and rank on Baseball America draft board (BA).

| Player | Pos | School | Ov | Team | BA |
|---|---|---|---|---|---|
| Justin Verlander | RHP | Old Dominion | 2 | Tigers | 7 |
| Philip Humber | RHP | Rice | 3 | Mets | 5 |
| Jeff Niemann | RHP | Rice | 4 | Rays | 2 |
| Jeremy Sowers | LHP | Vanderbilt | 6 | Indians | 10 |
| Wade Townsend* | RHP | Rice | 8 | Orioles | 9 |
| Thomas Diamond | RHP | New Orleans | 10 | Rangers | 11 |
| Jered Weaver | RHP | Long Beach State | 12 | Angels | 1 |
| Bill Bray | LHP | William & Mary | 13 | Expos | 36 |
| Stephen Drew | SS | Florida State | 15 | D-backs | 3 |
| David Purcey | LHP | Oklahoma | 16 | Blue Jays | 18 |

\* Did not sign

## Top 10 Major League Players From College Draft Class
With draft round and Baseball-Reference.com total for wins above replacement (WAR) through 2019.

| Player | Pos | School | Rd | Ov | Team | WAR |
|---|---|---|---|---|---|---|
| Justin Verlander | RHP | Old Dominion | 1 | 2 | Tigers | 70.9 |
| Dustin Pedroia | 2B | Arizona State | 2 | 6y5 | Red Sox | 51.7 |
| Ben Zobrist | 2B | Dallas Baptist | 6 | 184 | Astros | 45.2 |
| Jered Weaver | RHP | Long Beach State | 1 | 12 | Angels | 34.4 |
| Hunter Pence | OF | Texas-Arlington | 2 | 64 | Astros | 31.3 |
| J.A. Happ | LHP | Northwestern | 3 | 92 | Phillies | 21.8 |
| Kurt Suzuki | C | Cal State Fullerton | 2 | 67 | Athletics | 20.3 |
| Stephen Drew | SS | Florida State | 1 | 15 | D-backs | 17.0 |
| Jason Vargas | LHP | Long Beach State | 2 | 68 | Marlins | 16.9 |
| Chris Iannetta | C | North Carolina | 4 | 110 | Rockies | 15.5 |

Then he went in search of the man who made it all possible. A crestfallen Garrido was in the Texas dugout.

"I tip-toed over there and said, 'Thanks for the opportunity,' " Horton said. "Who knows where I'd be without him?"

Maybe Horton would still be coaching at Cerritos (Calif.) Junior College. Maybe he never would have had the urge to enter the profession had he not played under Garrido at Fullerton in 1975 and '76. Had Horton not joined Garrido's staff at Fullerton in 1991, he wouldn't be the coach he is today.

Garrido and Horton shared much during their six years together, when Garrido was Fullerton's head coach and Horton his associate head coach. They have their own styles—with Garrido the type to live in the moment and Horton one who likes to meticulously plan—but incorporated their ideas together for the greater good: developing players and young men, and ultimately success on the field.

Horton has made four trips to Omaha since replacing Garrido, who left for Texas prior to the 1997 season. He had never reach the title game before this year. Garrido owns four national championships, including one won with the Longhorns in 2002.

Winning the championship against the benchmark of success at Fullerton should have been the best validation Horton could find. But it was bittersweet.

"On one hand, this is equally special to accomplish this against your mentor who taught you so much, who built Fullerton into a great program," he said. "But my heart goes out to them because they are 180 degrees from what we are feeling right now."

"I think about Augie and hopefully his heart mends quickly." ∎

# Weaver settles for personal honor

By **WILL KIMMEY**

**D**espite all he accomplished, Jered Weaver likely will remember the 2004 season as a disappointment. How could he? After all, he blossomed from Jeff Weaver's little brother to the best pitcher in college baseball. He enjoyed a junior season at Long Beach State that statistically rivaled Mark Prior's 2001 campaign at Southern California. Weaver set school records for strikeouts in a game (17), season (213) and career (431), while also notching first place in career wins and innings. He easily earned College Player of the Year honors.

Weaver's strikeouts tied him for sixth-best season all time with Arizona State lefthanded greats Floyd Bannister (1976) and Eddie Bane (1972). He walked just 21, or one-tenth as many batters as he struck out.

The Angels selected him in the first round of the draft, putting him closer to fulfilling his dream of becoming a major leaguer.

Long Beach State's Jered Weaver turned in a season for the ages, going 15-1, 1.63 with a 213-21 SO-BB ratio. In 12 big league seasons he won 150 games, recorded a 3.63 ERA and made three all-star teams.

Heck, he even helped topple a nemesis in Stanford, ending its streak of consecutive College World Series appearances at five. The Cardinal had bounced the Dirtbags from the NCAA Tournament the last four years, and knocked brother Jeff's Fresno State team out of the postseason five years ago.

Yet in Weaver's mind, he fell short.

"I'm here for one reason: to get to Omaha," he said midway through the season. "It's been my dream to get drafted and be a big leaguer. But first I want to get to Omaha."

Weaver did his part to reach that goal. He was as good in his final start as he was all year in compiling a 15-1, 1.62 record. The 6-foot-7 righthander struck out 12 batters and allowed two runs—one earned—on five hits in 7.2 innings in the super regional opener against Arizona. But the feisty Wildcats scored four ninth-inning runs that night, then won an 11-inning, 4-3 battle in the final game of the series to end Long Beach State's season—and likely Weaver's college career—one game shy of the CWS.

Weaver's unwavering desire to get to Omaha underlines his team-first attitude. He settled on Long Beach State as his college choice because he loved the program's scrappy, hard-working mindset that begat the Dirtbags nickname. He views his success simply as a means for his team to succeed, not a vehicle for personal stardom.

"He doesn't want special treatment," Long Beach State coach Mike Weathers said.

"The guy is a good teammate. In our program, no one player is bigger than anyone else, and he fits that. They don't call him big leaguer or prima donna or whatever."

When he was not pitching, Weaver was often the first guy out of the dugout to congratulate teammates. He spent his time between starts sticking close by Weathers' side, discussing in-game strategy with the coach. "He's real interested, involved," Weathers said.

Sometimes, he gets too involved. One Tuesday in late April, Weaver asked Weathers to put him on the mound during a 2-1 win at UCLA. He had thrown 122 pitches and registered 14 strikeouts in seven innings the previous Friday, but he told the coach he felt fine.

"He was dead serious," Weathers recalled. "So I told him, 'We don't do that.' "

Weaver might have been thinking the same thing as the final Arizona game headed to extra innings. All he could do was watch.

"He hates to lose almost more than he enjoys winning," pitching coach Troy Buckley said. "Winning is fleeting because you have to start preparing for the next time. Losing can linger because of the feeling of failure.

"It's pain. It leads to more concentration and discipline."

It's too soon for that pain to have subsided quite yet. But at some point in a month, or a year, Weaver can look back and remember authoring one of the greatest seasons ever by a college pitcher. ∎

# TOP PLAYERS OF 2004

## ALL-AMERICA TEAM

| Pos | Player | School | Yr | AVG | AB | R | H | HR | RBI | SB |
|-----|--------|--------|-----|-----|-----|-----|-----|-----|-----|-----|
| C | Kurt Suzuki | Cal State Fullerton | Jr | .413 | 252 | 77 | 104 | 16 | 87 | 9 |
| 1B | Mike Ferris | Miami (Ohio) | Jr | .361 | 208 | 61 | 75 | 21 | 62 | 3 |
| 2B | Jed Lowrie | Stanford | So | .399 | 233 | 72 | 93 | 17 | 68 | 6 |
| 3B | Alex Gordon | Nebraska | So | .365 | 211 | 64 | 77 | 18 | 75 | 12 |
| SS | Dustin Pedroia | Arizona State | Jr | .395 | 233 | 76 | 92 | 9 | 48 | 8 |
| OF | Brad Corley | Mississippi State | So | .395 | 266 | 62 | 105 | 12 | 83 | 21 |
| OF | Eddy Martinez-Esteve | Florida State | So | .385 | 270 | 57 | 104 | 19 | 81 | 8 |
| OF | Danny Putnam | Stanford | Jr | .378 | 249 | 61 | 94 | 16 | 62 | 6 |
| DH | Warner Jones | Vanderbilt | So | .414 | 268 | 55 | 111 | 11 | 74 | 12 |
| UT | Stephen Head | Mississippi | So | .357 | 213 | 39 | 76 | 11 | 49 | 0 |

| Pos | Pitcher | School | Yr | W | L | ERA | G | SV | IP | H | BB | SO |
|-----|---------|--------|-----|-----|-----|-----|-----|-----|-----|-----|-----|-----|
| SP | Matt Fox | Central Florida | Jr | 14 | 2 | 1.85 | 17 | 0 | 112 | 78 | 32 | 125 |
| SP | J.P. Howell | Texas | Jr | 15 | 2 | 2.13 | 24 | 1 | 135 | 90 | 53 | 166 |
| SP | Wade Townsend | Rice | Jr | 12 | 0 | 1.80 | 18 | 2 | 120 | 74 | 45 | 148 |
| SP | Jered Weaver | Long Beach State | Jr | 15 | 1 | 1.62 | 19 | 0 | 144 | 81 | 21 | 213 |
| RP | Nate Moore | Troy | Jr | 9 | 4 | 1.25 | 32 | 8 | 65 | 42 | 16 | 84 |
| UT | Stephen Head | Mississippi | So | 6 | 3 | 2.82 | 17 | 5 | 70 | 68 | 19 | 56 |

## SECOND TEAM

**C**—Landon Powell, South Carolina. **1B**—Josh Brady, Texas Tech. **2B**—Jarrett Hoffpauir, Southern Mississippi. **3B**—Matt Macri, Notre Dame. **SS**—Stephen Drew, Florida State. **OF**—Jeff Frazier, Rutgers; Chris Rahl, William & Mary; and Richie Robnett, Fresno State. **DH**—Ryan Jones, East Carolina. **UT**—Brian Bogusevic, Tulane. **SP**—Philip Humber, Rice; Justin Hoyman, Rice; Mike Pelfrey, Wichita State; and Jason Windsor, Cal State Fullerton. **RP**—Huston Street, Texas.

## THIRD TEAM

**C**—Chris Iannetta, North Carolina. **1B**—Jim Burt, Miami. **2B**—Eric Patterson, Georgia Tech. **3B**—Brad McCann, Clemson. **SS**—Brian Bixler, Eastern Michigan. **OF**—J.C. Holt, Louisiana State; Marshall Hubbard, North Carolina; and Eric Nielsen, Nevada-Las Vegas. **DH**—Jeff Fiorentino, Florida Atlantic. **UT**—Joe Koshansky, Virginia. **SP**—Matt Campbell, South Carolina; Cesar Carrillo, Miami; Wade LeBlanc, Alabama; and Glen Perkins, Minnesota. **RP**—Chad Blackwell, South Carolina.

**2005**

Texas coach Augie Garrido flashes the "Hook 'em Horns" sign after the Longhorns completed a championship series sweep of Florida. It was Garrido's fifth CWS title.

# Ups and downs fortified Texas for title run

By **WILL KIMMEY**

I n its record 32nd trip to the College World Series, Texas made winning look easy. The Longhorns never trailed on their way to winning five straight games and the school's sixth national championship.

J. Brent Cox, though, knows it wasn't easy. He remembers standing on the mound in the ninth inning of Texas' decisive super regional game at Mississippi with a 6-4 lead, two outs and runners at first and second base. Lefthanded-hitting Stephen Head stepped to the plate, where his 19th home run of the season could send the Rebels to the CWS.

Cox had allowed four runs to take the loss in the first game of the series, and he escaped a bases-loaded, one-out jam to preserve a 3-1 win in the second. He worked the count to 2-2 before deciding on his trademark slider. The pitch slipped out of his hand, breaking knee-high, but too far inside. Head swung and missed at ball three, and Texas advanced to Omaha for the fourth consecutive season.

That's how close things came for the Longhorns in 2005, when they didn't always look dominant but usually produced at important times. If one ground ball, or one pitch, had been an inch or two off, they might not have even had the chance to win their second national title in four years. But close calls and tough losses—in personnel and on the field—weren't enough to stop Texas from steamrolling through Omaha and sweeping Florida in the championship round.

"We all knew coming in that this was a team with experience," said coach Augie Garrdio, whose second title at Texas and fifth overall tied him with LSU's Skip Bertman for the second most by any coach. "It's one thing to have it, it's another thing to be able to use it to enrich your performances. And that's what the players did."

Texas became just the second team to win the CWS without being a top eight national seed since the 64-team format began in 1999. The Longhorns did it by playing their pitching-and-defense style to near perfection, allowing seven runs in five CWS games with just two errors.

**FROM THE ISSUE:**
JULY 18-31, 2005

## TOP TEAMS

### 2005 COLLEGE WORLD SERIES STANDINGS

| School | Conference | Record | CWS | Coach |
|---|---|---|---|---|
| Texas | Big 12 | 56–16 | 5–0 | Augie Garrido |
| Florida | Southeastern | 48–23 | 3–3 | Pat McMahon |
| Arizona State | Pacific-10 | 42–25 | 3–2 | Pat Murphy |
| Baylor | Big 12 | 46–24 | 2–2 | Steve Smith |
| Nebraska | Big 12 | 57–15 | 1–2 | Mike Anderson |
| Tulane | Conference USA | 56–12 | 1–2 | Rick Jones |
| Oregon State | Pacific-10 | 46–12 | 0–2 | Pat Casey |
| Tennessee | Southeastern | 43–21 | 0–2 | Rod Delmonico |

## NATIONAL CHAMPION
### TEXAS

Coach Augie Garrido captured his fifth national championship and second in four years at Texas. It was the Longhorns' second CWS title of the 2000s and sixth in program history. They swept the field in Omaha, never trailing in any game.

They stayed with small ball on offense, executing 10 successful sac bunts, but showed power in cracking seven home runs after totaling 49 in the 67 games before Omaha.

"We had a little of an underdog role coming into the postseason," said catcher Taylor Teagarden, who batted .350 in the CWS. "We knew that in the back of our minds that if we played Texas baseball—play great defense and pitch well—we were going to win some games. And that's what happened. Things worked out for us."

Texas started the year 16-0 and cruised along until meeting Baylor in the first conference series of the year. The Bears handed the Longhorns their first Big 12 Conference series sweep since 1999. Texas survived that pratfall, and several more, always finding a way to battle back: a 16-inning game at Nebraska, its first-ever conference series loss to Kansas and finishing in third place in the conference for the first time since 2000.

The Longhorns also weathered injuries to infielders Seth Johnston (arm), David Maroul (leg) and Chance Wheeless (shoulder), as well as Teagarden.

Garrido told his players that great teams grow stronger by recovering from these setbacks, developing a survivor's instinct.

"This is the toughest year we've ever been through," Johnston said. "I think this team has learned so much because of the struggles we went through. It made us a lot tighter and a lot stronger."

Texas also took a rugged path to Omaha, battling back after early losses to Arkansas in regionals and Mississippi in super regionals. The Longhorns faced five elimination games, a strong contrast to their perfect run into Omaha a year ago, when they breezed through the tournament and the first week of the CWS without a loss before getting swept by Cal State Fullerton in the final. That loss hadn't left their thoughts.

"Last year we were just unbelievable," Teagarden said. "We were by far the best team

# 2005 NEWSMAKERS

Coach of the Year **Rick Jones** guided **Tulane** to a program-record 56 wins and its second CWS appearances in five years. Led by **Brian Bogusevic** and **Micah Owings**, the Green Wave ranked as the preseason No. 1 team and carried that ranking into Omaha. Tulane suffered a crushing loss to Baylor in a CWS elimination game in which it squandered a 7-0 lead. Tragedy struck in September, when Hurricane Katrina ravaged New Orleans and forced the baseball team's relocation to nearby Zephyr Field, home of the Triple-A franchise, for 2006 and 2007.

A record 263,475 fans filled Rosenblatt Stadium at the **College World Series**, and the average session attendance of 23,952 also set a record. Nebraska fans flocked to see the home-state Huskers. They camped overnight to secure tickets, flooded parking lots and turned the stands into a sea of red, providing a home-field feel in what was supposed to be a neutral site.

**Florida State** outfielder **Shane Robinson** authored a 40-game hitting streak to become the seventh player in Division I history to reach 40. He batted .427 and led the nation with 122 hits and 96 runs.

## FINAL TOP 25 FOR 2005

1. Texas*
2. Florida*
3. #Tulane*
4. Baylor*
5. Nebraska*
6. Arizona State*
7. Oregon State*
8. Tennessee*
9. Cal State Fullerton
10. Mississippi
11. Georgia Tech
12. Arizona
13. Rice
14. Clemson
15. Miami
16. Florida State
17. Southern California
18. Louisiana State
19. Long Beach State
20. Alabama
21. Missouri
22. Mississippi State
23. Coastal Carolina
24. Pepperdine
25. South Carolina

\* Reached College World Series
\# Preseason No. 1

# IN RETROSPECT: 2005 DRAFT

### Top 10 Draft Picks From College
With overall selection number (Ov), drafting team (Team) and rank on Baseball America draft board (BA).

| Player | Pos | School | Ov | Team | BA |
|---|---|---|---|---|---|
| Alex Gordon | 3B | Nebraska | 2 | Royals | 2 |
| Jeff Clement | C | Southern California | 3 | Mariners | 15 |
| Ryan Zimmerman | 3B | Virginia | 4 | Nationals | 9 |
| Ryan Braun | 3B | Miami | 5 | Brewers | 14 |
| Ricky Romero | LHP | Cal State Fullerton | 6 | Blue Jays | 13 |
| Troy Tulowitzki | SS | Long Beach State | 7 | Rockies | 4 |
| Wade Townsend | RHP | Rice | 8 | Rays | 18 |
| Mike Pelfrey | RHP | Wichita State | 9 | Mets | 5 |
| Trevor Crowe | OF | Arizona | 14 | Indians | 29 |
| Lance Broadway | RHP | Texas Christian | 15 | White Sox | 48 |

### Top 10 Major League Players From College Draft Class
With draft round and Baseball-Reference.com total for wins above replacement (WAR) through 2019.

| Player | Pos | School | Rd | Ov | Team | WAR |
|---|---|---|---|---|---|---|
| Ryan Braun | OF | Miami | 1 | 5 | Brewers | 48.2 |
| Troy Tulowitzki | SS | Long Beach State | 1 | 7 | Rockies | 44.2 |
| Brett Gardner | OF | Coll. of Charleston | 3 | 109 | Yankees | 41.6 |
| Ryan Zimmerman | 3B | Virginia | 1 | 4 | Nationals | 37.8 |
| Alex Gordon | OF | Nebraska | 1 | 2 | Royals | 36.4 |
| Jacoby Ellsbury | OF | Oregon State | 1 | 23 | Red Sox | 31.1 |
| Chase Headley | 3B | Tennessee | 2 | 66 | Padres | 26.1 |
| Jed Lowrie | 2B | Stanford | 1s | 45 | Red Sox | 17.5 |
| Matt Joyce | OF | Florida Southern | 12 | 360 | Tigers | 14.9 |
| Marco Estrada | RHP | Long Beach State | 6 | 174 | Nationals | 12.5 |

in college baseball. (Fullerton) just came out and played a little bit better than us. We might have given in a little bit to the hype of the championship series, thinking we were going to roll through Fullerton. We knew coming out here (this year) losing a game in the regional and super regional that nothing comes free.

"It's not overrated to say that experience helps. So many of these guys have been to Omaha. We're going to get the job done and perform in clutch situations. Losing a game to Arkansas might have been a little bit of a letdown on our part. But losing a game to Mississippi, that definitely wasn't a letdown. That was the best team we played all year. The biggest advantage for us was going to Mississippi and playing at their place.

"Coming in here, we're almost the home team at some point. Once we got through that, we felt like we could handle anyone."

Johnston's career resembled Texas' 2005 season, with ups and downs leading to development and the ultimate payoff. He didn't make the travel roster as a freshman, moved into a part-time role as a sophomore, earned regular duty as a junior and became the team leader and best hitter as a senior. He turned down signing with the Orioles as a seventh-rounder last year to return for his senior season, and he hit .378, earned second-team All-America honors and was a fifth-round pick of the Padres.

As the Texas players gathered themselves after the dogpile, Johnston held two shirts. One was the standard-issue national champions shirt, while the other showed Johnston's head superimposed on Darth Vader's body, with the text: "Return of the Seth."

"I came in my freshman year and won the national championship and finish my senior year winning the national championship," he said. "You can't ask for anything more." ■

# Gordon wins Player of the Year honors

By **JOHN MANUEL**

**W**hen historians—all right, Baseball Americans—look back at the 2005 season in college baseball, they may consider this the Year of the Third Baseman.

Never before have three college hitters who play the same position gone in the first five picks of the draft, dating back to 1965. But teams liked college third basemen so much in 2005, they couldn't help themselves.

Ryan Braun was the Freshman of the Year in 2003 and rebounded from an injury-plagued sophomore season to pace Miami's offense as a junior. His all-around tools prompted the Brewers to draft him fifth overall, envisioning him as the final piece in a future infield with Prince Fielder, Rickie Weeks and J.J. Hardy.

One pick earlier, the Nationals drafted Virginia's Ryan Zimmerman, the best defensive player in the country. Several

Nebraska's Alex Gordon edged a deep field of third basemen to claim Player of the Year. He developed into a star for the Royals, making three all-star teams and winning six Gold Gloves in left field.

scouts agreed Zimmerman has the hands, arm strength and footwork to give shortstop a try in professional baseball. But they also agreed, why move a Gold Glove-caliber player from a position he has clearly mastered?

And while Zimmerman hit a team-best .468 last summer, Gordon adjusted to wood bats over the course of the summer and reversed a slow start. He batted .388 and was Team USA's top hitter in the World University Championship in Taiwan, helping lead Team USA to a gold medal.

Gordon's response? The day he was back home in Lincoln, Neb., after his Team USA tour he grabbed his bats and went back into the batting cage.

Gordon's work ethic extended to the field, where he rededicated himself to being the best defender he can be. The combination allowed him to hit .382 with 18 home runs and 23 stolen bases in 26 attempts, leading the Cornhuskers back to regional play after a one-year absence and ultimately back to Omaha.

It also helped cement his status as the top college prospect for the 2005 draft, and the Royals—whom he grew up rooting for—selected him with the second overall pick.

For his performance—standing out in a crowded field, not just of third basemen but of star players—Gordon is the College Player of the Year.

If getting beat out by Zimmerman for the third base job was a wake-up call, Gordon wanted to prove to scouts that he was wide awake. That's even as he was being lulled to sleep by teams that wouldn't give him a good pitch to hit.

"We tried everything with Gordon," one coach said when sizing up the Cornhuskers. "We hit him, we tried to go in and tried to go away. You have to go hard in and then soft away. Just don't let him beat you."

Easier said than done. Stay away from Gordon, and he has the power to drive balls to the other field, a part of his game that has evolved from weakness to strength over his college career. Come inside, and he has the bat speed to get around on even the best fastballs. Miss over the middle . . . well, even being pitched around, he slammed 18 home runs this spring, seven of them in Big 12 Conference play.

Gordon had to perform the way he did to stand out from the crowd of third basemen in the country this season. Beyond the big three, the position featured Tennessee's Chase Headley, who hit .387 with a sterling 60-22 walk-strikeout ratio; Georgia Tech sophomore Wes Hodges as well as a pair of hard-hitting freshmen, Tulane's Brad Emaus (.346, 13 home runs) and Fresno State's Beau Mills (.319, 22 home runs).

When it came to quality third basemen, college baseball had plenty of competition. As Gordon found last summer, competition can push a player to be his best.

In 2005, the Year of the Third Basemen, Gordon was at his best. ■

# TOP PLAYERS OF 2005

## ALL-AMERICA TEAM

| Pos | Player | School | Yr | AVG | AB | R | H | HR | RBI | SB |
|-----|--------|--------|----|-----|----|----|----|----|-----|-----|
| C | Jeff Clement | Southern California | Jr | .348 | 230 | 52 | 80 | 15 | 54 | 5 |
| 1B | Matt LaPorta | Florida | So | .328 | 265 | 75 | 87 | 26 | 79 | 3 |
| 2B | Jim Negrych | Pittsburgh | So | .349 | 186 | 52 | 65 | 16 | 59 | 11 |
| 3B | Alex Gordon | Nebraska | Jr | .372 | 253 | 79 | 94 | 19 | 66 | 23 |
| SS | Tyler Greene | Georgia Tech | Jr | .372 | 269 | 76 | 100 | 12 | 72 | 31 |
| OF | Trevor Crowe | Arizona | Jr | .403 | 263 | 83 | 106 | 9 | 54 | 27 |
| OF | Jacoby Ellsbury | Oregon State | Jr | .406 | 244 | 56 | 99 | 6 | 48 | 26 |
| OF | Shane Robinson | Florida State | So | .427 | 286 | 96 | 122 | 6 | 43 | 49 |
| DH | Ryan Braun | Miami | Jr | .388 | 219 | 70 | 85 | 18 | 76 | 23 |
| UT | Mike Costanzo | Coastal Carolina | Jr | .379 | 240 | 74 | 91 | 16 | 67 | 8 |

| Pos | Pitcher | School | Yr | W | L | ERA | G | SV | IP | H | BB | SO |
|-----|---------|--------|----|----|----|-----|----|-----|-----|-----|-----|-----|
| SP | Lance Broadway | Texas Christian | Jr | 15 | 1 | 1.62 | 19 | 0 | 117 | 83 | 35 | 151 |
| SP | Dallas Buck | Oregon State | So | 12 | 1 | 2.09 | 19 | 1 | 129 | 90 | 51 | 118 |
| SP | Luke Hochevar | Tennessee | Jr | 15 | 3 | 2.26 | 19 | 0 | 140 | 104 | 54 | 154 |
| SP | Ian Kennedy | Southern California | So | 12 | 3 | 2.54 | 18 | 0 | 117 | 85 | 38 | 158 |
| RP | Craig Hansen | St. John's | Jr | 3 | 2 | 1.68 | 31 | 14 | 64 | 38 | 20 | 85 |
| UT | Mike Costanzo | Coastal Carolina | Jr | 8 | 1 | 2.13 | 37 | 14 | 55 | 44 | 24 | 69 |

## SECOND TEAM
C—Nick Hundley, Arizona. 1B—Steve Pearce, South Carolina. 2B—Chris Campbell, College of Charleston. 3B—Ryan Zimmerman, Virginia. SS—Seth Johnston, Texas. OF—Daniel Carte, Winthrop; Eli Iorg, Tennessee; and Brian Pettway, Mississippi. DH—Kris Harvey, Clemson. UT—Joe Savery, Rice. SP—Cesar Carrillo, Miami; Mike Pelfrey, Wichita State; Ricky Romero, Cal State Fullerton; and Max Scherzer, Missouri. RP—J. Brent Cox, Texas.

## THIRD TEAM
C—Mike Ambort, Lamar. 1B—Aaron Bates, North Carolina State. 2B—Adam Davis, Florida. 3B—Chase Headley, Tennessee. SS—Cliff Pennington, Texas A&M. OF—Brett Gardner, College of Charleston; Ryan Patterson, Louisiana State; and Sergio Pedroza, Cal State Fullerton. DH—Nolan Reimold, Bowling Green. UT—Micah Owings, Tulane. SP—Brian Bogusevic, Tulane; Matt Green, Louisiana-Monroe; Kevin Slowey, Winthrop; and Matt Torra, Massachusetts. RP—Neil Jamison, Long Beach State.

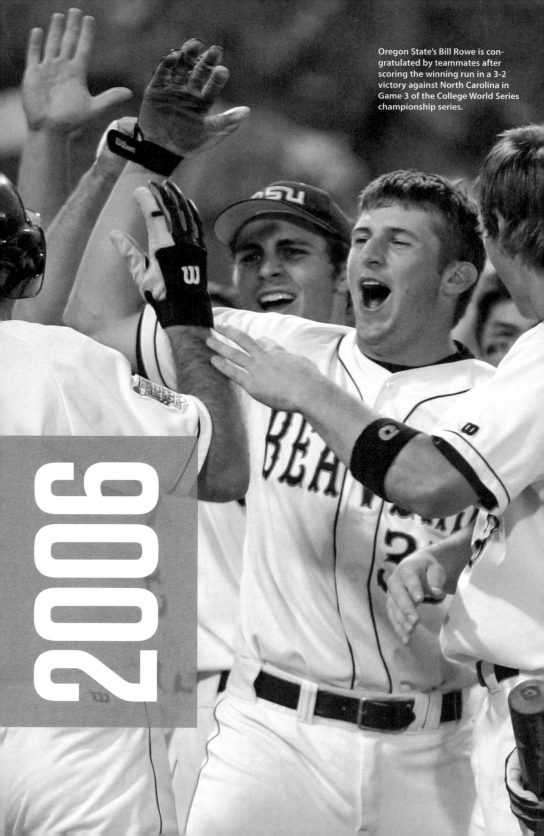

Oregon State's Bill Rowe is congratulated by teammates after scoring the winning run in a 3-2 victory against North Carolina in Game 3 of the College World Series championship series.

**2006**

# Beavers bounce back from losses to win CWS

By **WILL KIMMEY**

**B**ill Rowe's father Douglas is an actor who has made appearances in M*A*S*H, Star Trek and ER. So naturally, Oregon State's senior first baseman was asked what kind of script he'd write for the Beavers before the finals of the College World Series.

"I told him Jonah would come back on short days' rest and Gundy would come in with two on and two out," Rowe said. "I was standing there at first base watching it happen."

If Rowe hadn't been, he might not have believed the ending. Starter Jonah Nickerson worked into the seventh inning for the third time in eight days, and closer Kevin Gunderson came out of the bullpen with two on in the ninth, but there was only one out.

**FROM THE ISSUE:**
JULY 17-30, 2006

The one thing Rowe left out was the excitement he would feel rounding third base with the go-ahead run in the bottom of the eighth inning. He scored when North Carolina second baseman Bryan Steed fielded a routine grounder with two outs but threw wide of first base, allowing Rowe to race home from second base.

Oregon State held on for a 3-2 win, coming out on the positive end of its sixth straight elimination game in front of 18,565 spectators at Rosenblatt Stadium. Just as they had in bracket play, the Beavers lost the first game of the championship series to North Carolina but didn't lose again.

"The will of this team, we tried to compete hard and never give up," center fielder Tyler Graham said. "We can play with anyone in the country. We never doubted ourselves and from there we just took the national championship."

Oregon State's path to becoming the Northern-most national champion since Minnesota won it all in 1964 was nearly as unlikely as a team from that latitude winning a title in a sport dominated by teams from California, Florida, Texas and the rest of the Sun Belt. The Beavers (50-16) set a record by winning six elimination games and became the first team to lose two games in Omaha and still leave as champions. They also tied Stanford's 2003 mark by playing eight times at Rosenblatt Stadium.

## TOP TEAMS
### 2006 COLLEGE WORLD SERIES STANDINGS

| School | Conference | Record | CWS | Coach |
|---|---|---|---|---|
| Oregon State | Pacific-10 | 50–16 | 6–2 | Pat Casey |
| North Carolina | Atlantic Coast | 54–15 | 4–2 | Mike Fox |
| Cal State Fullerton | Big West | 50–15 | 2–2 | George Horton |
| Rice | Conference USA | 57–13 | 2–2 | Wayne Graham |
| Clemson | Atlantic Coast | 53–16 | 1–2 | Jack Leggett |
| Miami | Atlantic Coast | 42–24 | 1–2 | Jim Morris |
| Georgia | Southeastern | 47–23 | 0–2 | David Perno |
| Georgia Tech | Atlantic Coast | 50–18 | 0–2 | Danny Hall |

## NATIONAL CHAMPION
### OREGON STATE

The Beavers lost their CWS opener then staved off elimination by winning four straight games. They dropped the first game of the championship series to UNC, too, before winning two straight. OSU set a CWS record by winning six elimination games.

Oregon State became the second team in the last 26 years to win the CWS after losing its first game, following Southern California, which turned the trick in 1998. The Beavers followed their opening-game loss by winning four elimination games in four days, toppling Georgia, Miami and top-ranked Rice twice.

Nickerson earned wins in the first and last of those wins—with just two days' rest in between—to get his team into the championship series against a North Carolina team that was undefeated in the NCAA tournament and fully rested on the mound.

After North Carolina earned a 4-3 win in the opener, it didn't look like Nickerson would even get the chance to make his CWS record-tying third start. But he did, and he worked 6.2 innings, allowing just two unearned runs to leave with both a national championship and the Most Outstanding Player award. Those are the spoils for someone who throws 323 pitches in eight days and doesn't allow an earned run for his final 16.1 innings.

Nickerson didn't earn the win in the finale, but he kept his team in position. UNC got to him in the top of the fifth, a frame that saw two impressive Oregon State streaks end. Jay Cox reached on the first OSU error in 51.1 innings in Omaha and scored two batters later on an RBI double by Seth Williams. That run, and the one that followed, was unearned, the first such runs the Beavers had allowed in the NCAA Tournament.

Nickerson threw his 300th pitch in eight days in the sixth inning, and North Carolina had a chance to take the lead and knock him out of the game with runners at the corners and one out. But UNC ran itself out of the inning when Tim Federowicz grounded to third base. Shea McFeely threw out Josh Horton at home, then Cox, who was on first base, got caught in a rundown between second and third base to end the inning.

"I knew if I pitched my best, we would keep playing," said Nickerson, who paid $85 for a massage at the team hotel Friday.

# 2006 NEWSMAKERS

A record 11 **College World Series** games were decided by one or two runs. Teams combined to average 8.9 runs per game, the second lowest average at the CWS (only 2005 was lower) since 1974, the first year of the aluminum bat. All the close games helped drive viewership on ESPN, especially during the championship series that pitted first-time finalists **North Carolina** and **Oregon State**.

**Louisiana State** coach **Smoke Laval** was pressured to resign in the face of declining attendance and after the Tigers failed to qualify for the NCAA Tournament for the first time since 1988. Athletic director **Skip Bertman**, the decorated former coach, chose Notre Dame's **Paul Mainieri** as Laval's replacement.

The **Academic Progress Report** released by the NCAA impacted 10 baseball programs, including CWS participants **Texas** and **Tennessee**. The affected schools lost the maximum of 1.17 scholarships, a figure based on 10 percent of the sport's limit of 11.7 scholarships. The APR reflected data for the 2003-04 and 2004-05 academic years and measured a school's retention of student-athletes and their progress toward graduation.

**FINAL TOP 25 FOR 2006**

1. Oregon State*
2. North Carolina*
3. Cal State Fullerton*
4. Rice*
5. Clemson*
6. Georgia*
7. Georgia Tech*
8. Miami*
9. Oklahoma
10. Alabama
11. Mississippi
12. #Texas
13. South Carolina
14. College of Charleston
15. Nebraska
16. Virginia
17. Oral Roberts
18. Missouri
19. Stanford
20. Kentucky
21. Pepperdine
22. Fresno State
23. Oklahoma State
24. Houston
25. Wichita State

* Reached College World Series
# Preseason No. 1

# IN RETROSPECT: 2006 DRAFT

**Top 10 Draft Picks From College**
With overall selection number (Ov), drafting team (Team) and rank on Baseball America draft board (BA).

| Player | Pos | School | Ov | Team | BA |
|---|---|---|---|---|---|
| Greg Reynolds | RHP | Stanford | 2 | Rockies | 5 |
| Evan Longoria | 3B | Long Beach State | 3 | Rays | 4 |
| Brad Lincoln | RHP | Houston | 4 | Pirates | 3 |
| Brandon Morrow | RHP | California | 5 | Mariners | 10 |
| Andrew Miller | LHP | North Carolina | 6 | Tigers | 1 |
| Drew Stubbs | OF | Texas | 8 | Reds | 11 |
| Tim Lincecum | RHP | Washington | 10 | Giants | 2 |
| Max Scherzer | RHP | Missouri | 11 | D-backs | 8 |
| Tyler Colvin | OF | Clemson | 13 | Cubs | – |
| Matt Antonelli | 3B | Wake Forest | 17 | Padres | 27 |

**Top 10 Major League Players From College Draft Class**
With draft round and Baseball-Reference.com total for wins above replacement (WAR) through 2019.

| Player | Pos | School | Rd | Ov | Team | WAR |
|---|---|---|---|---|---|---|
| Max Scherzer | RHP | Missouri | 1 | 11 | D-backs | 60.3 |
| Evan Longoria | 3B | Long Beach State | 1 | 3 | Rays | 54.2 |
| Justin Turner | 3B | Cal State Fullerton | 7 | 204 | Reds | 27.9 |
| Tim Lincecum | RHP | Washington | 1 | 10 | Giants | 19.7 |
| Doug Fister | RHP | Fresno State | 7 | 201 | Mariners | 19.6 |
| Daniel Murphy | 2B | Jacksonville | 13 | 394 | Mets | 18.9 |
| David Freese | 3B | South Alabama | 9 | 273 | Padres | 17.2 |
| Ian Kennedy | RHP | Southern Calif. | 1 | 21 | Yankees | 16.8 |
| David Robertson | RHP | Alabama | 17 | 524 | Yankees | 15.9 |
| Jeff Samardzija | RHP | Notre Dame | 5 | 149 | Cubs | 15.0 |

Nickerson's relief was only slightly more rested than he was. Righthander Dallas Buck, who went 6.1 innings in the first game of the championship series, started lobbying to enter the game in the sixth inning. He got his wish in the eighth, entering with two runners on and no outs.

Buck induced a ground out from Cox before walking the bases loaded. Then he struck out Williams and Benji Johnson back to back, the second strikeout ending the inning as Horton raced down the third base line on a 1-2 pitch in what would have been a straight steal attempt of home.

North Carolina earned one more chance in the ninth inning. It got a one-out single followed by a walk to bring up Horton, its top hitter and the ACC batting champion. Gunderson, who pitched a season-long 5.1 innings the day before, came out of the bullpen to get Horton to hit into a force play. North Carolina's last chance was Chad Flack, who hit two homers, including the game-winner, against Alabama in the super regional. Flack made solid contact, but his fly ball ended up in Graham's glove.

"If I could take all their arm pain and put it in mine, I would," Rowe said. "They deserve it."

North Carolina scored 11 of its 13 runs in the championship series with two outs, but left the tying run on third base in the top of the ninth. It marked Gunderson's 20th save of the season, giving him sole possession of the Division I lead. But the 5-foot-10, 165-pound lefthander was more concerned with sole possession of something else that belonged to the NCAA: the national championship trophy.

Just as Rowe had envisioned. ■

# Dominant Miller leads UNC back to Omaha

By **WILL KIMMEY**

Andrew Miller's 13-2, 2.48 season stands as a key reason for North Carolina's first College World Series berth since 1989. But the junior lefthander would rather be known as one of many Tar Heels piled atop one another after Chad Flack's game-ending home run to clinch a super regional series win at Alabama.

"I think he kind of feels uncomfortable talking about himself," North Carolina coach Mike Fox said of his junior lefthander. "You know how kids can be, they don't want people to think they think they're better than anybody. His parents said he's always been like that. Even in high school he didn't really want the attention. He's a big kid at heart and a great teammate."

But Miller, all 6 feet and 6 inches of him, can't hide from the attention now. His dominant junior season, in which he posted a 119-36 strikeout-walk ratio and allowed seven extra-base hits (and only one home run) in 111 innings, not only helped him meet a personal goal of reaching Omaha, but also earned him the College Player of the Year award.

Six-foot-6 Andrew Miller towered over a deep pitching class to become the first lefty to win College Player of the Year. After flaming out as a starter in the majors, he developed into a relief ace.

"I appreciate all the awards and the accolades, but the biggest memory for me is going to be we went to Omaha and what we accomplished there," Miller said. "I certainly wouldn't want to have a good year on a team that's not as good. I've never really been a part of a team like this."

Miller becomes the sixth pitcher to win the award in the last 25 years and the first lefthander to ever claim the award. The honor—and humility—came in the middle of perhaps the best week in Miller's life. The Tigers drafted him sixth overall on a Tuesday, and three days later he struck out 11 Alabama batters over seven innings without allowing an earned run to put his team only one game from Omaha. He used his mid-90s four-seam fastball, 88-90 mph two-seamer and power slider to dominate the Crimson Tide.

"There's a reason he's the sixth pick in the draft. He's a great pitcher, and it's really hard to solve a guy like that," said Alabama leadoff man Emeel Salem, who struck out three times against Miller after hitting .356 during the season as the only consensus selection on the all-Southeastern Conference first team.

"He has three pitches and even movement on a 97 (mph) fastball. We didn't capitalize when we had chances, but he didn't make enough mistakes for us to get anything going."

Good luck blending in after a game like that.

Even Alabama fans were asking for Miller's autograph the next day. After honoring those requests, Miller settled into the North Carolina bullpen. Mr. All-American (the only player on both BA's preseason and postseason first teams) was down there holding a walkie-talkie, serving as the team's communicator by relaying the coaches' wishes from the dugout as to which relievers should warm up.

That perch gave Miller a great viewpoint to watch Flack's heroics. "The greatest performance in the most exciting baseball game I've ever seen," Miller said of the sophomore first baseman giving UNC a 5-4 lead with a three-run homer in the eighth inning and then turning a 7-6 deficit into an 8-7 win with a two-out, two-run, walk-off homer in the bottom of the ninth to clinch the super regional.

"I just ran in from the bullpen as fast as I could," Miller said. "I basically was right with Chad rounding third base. It was a unique feeling. I don't think I've ever had."

Fox, who was coaching third base, said he will never forget the look on Miller's face as he sprinted past, walkie-talkie still in hand, to join Flack and the rest of the team in a giant celebratory mass. It was all arms, legs, hats and cleats.

Nearly impossible to discern any particular player.

Just all Tar Heels. Just the way Miller likes it. ■

# TOP PLAYERS OF 2006

## ALL-AMERICA TEAM

| Pos | Player | School | Yr | AVG | AB | R | H | HR | RBI | SB | BB | SO |
|-----|--------|--------|----|----|----|----|----|----|----|----|----|----|
| C | Matt Wieters | Georgia Tech | So | .355 | 251 | 72 | 92 | 15 | 71 | 3 | 56 | 39 |
| 1B | Mark Hamilton | Tulane | Jr | .336 | 235 | 61 | 79 | 29 | 69 | 2 | 51 | 42 |
| 2B | Jim Negyrch | Pittsburgh | Jr | .396 | 182 | 41 | 72 | 11 | 60 | 6 | 40 | 42 |
| 3B | Pedro Alvarez | Vanderbilt | Fr | .329 | 240 | 70 | 79 | 22 | 64 | 7 | 57 | 64 |
| SS | Brian Friday | Rice | So | .353 | 269 | 66 | 95 | 9 | 57 | 17 | 30 | 51 |
| OF | Kellen Kulbacki | James Madison | So | .464 | 194 | 68 | 90 | 24 | 75 | 13 | 30 | 32 |
| OF | Cole Gillespie | Oregon State | Jr | .374 | 238 | 83 | 89 | 13 | 57 | 15 | 46 | 37 |
| OF | Tyler Colvin | Clemson | Jr | .356 | 281 | 64 | 100 | 13 | 70 | 23 | 28 | 42 |
| DH | Ryan Strieby | Kentucky | Jr | .343 | 233 | 60 | 80 | 20 | 77 | 2 | 46 | 39 |
| UT | Brad Lincoln | Houston | Jr | .295 | 224 | 35 | 66 | 14 | 53 | 5 | 24 | 41 |

| Pos | Pitcher | School | Yr | W | L | ERA | G | SV | IP | H | BB | SO |
|-----|---------|--------|----|----|----|----|----|----|----|----|----|----|
| SP | Andrew Miller | North Carolina | Jr | 13 | 2 | 2.48 | 20 | 1 | 123 | 100 | 40 | 133 |
| SP | Tim Lincecum | Washington | Jr | 12 | 4 | 1.94 | 22 | 3 | 125 | 75 | 63 | 199 |
| SP | Eddie Degerman | Rice | Sr | 13 | 2 | 2.00 | 20 | 0 | 131 | 78 | 56 | 172 |
| SP | Wes Roemer | Cal State Fullerton | So | 13 | 2 | 2.38 | 21 | 1 | 155 | 126 | 7 | 145 |
| RP | Cole St. Clair | Rice | So | 7 | 2 | 1.82 | 37 | 11 | 74 | 39 | 26 | 100 |
| UT | Brad Lincoln | Houston | Jr | 12 | 2 | 1.69 | 17 | 0 | 128 | 91 | 32 | 152 |

## SECOND TEAM

C—Kody Valverde, Alabama. 1B—Craig Cooper, Notre Dame. 2B—Justin Turner, Cal State Fullerton. 3B—Evan Longoria, Long Beach State. SS—Emmanuel Burris, Kent State. OF—Jacob Dempsey, Winthop; Jon Jay, Miami; and Drew Stubbs, Texas. DH—Josh Horton, North Carolina. UT—Sean Doolittle, Virginia. SP—Jake arrieta, Texas Christian; Jonah Nickerson, Oregon State; Nick Schmidt, Arkansas; and Steven Wright, Hawaii. RP—Don Czyz, Kansas.

## THIRD TEAM

C—Jordan Newton, Western Kentucky. 1B—Andy D'Alessio, Clemson. 2B—Damon Sublett, Wichita State. 3B—Josh Rodrigues, Rice. SS—Zach Cozart, Mississippi. OF—Corey Brown, Oklahoma State; John Raynor, UNC Wilmington; and Joey Side, Georgia. DH—Chad Huffman, Texas Christian. UT—Mike Felix, Troy. SP—Lauren Gagnier, Cal State Fullerton; Danny Ray Herrera, New Mexico; Wade LeBlanc, Alabama; and P.J. Walters, Alabama. RP—Josh Fields, Georgia.

Oregon State celebrates after winning the 2007 College World Series, giving them back-to-back national championships.

**2007**

# Beavers prove their mettle in Omaha again

By **AARON FITT**

**FROM THE ISSUE:**
JULY 16-29, 2007

**D**arwin Barney emerged from the gaggle of Oregon State players draped in white "National Championship" T-shirts, took a few steps toward home plate, then wheeled around and yelled, "Mitch! Mitch! Let's go!"

A moment later, Mitch Canham forced his way through the throng. Barney put his left arm around Canham's shoulders, and the duo approached the makeshift platform set up near the plate. Together, the two juniors hoisted the national championship trophy over their heads and posed for pictures. Then they turned to teammates, calling, "Hey everybody, get in here!"

It wasn't the first time Barney and Canham have led their teammates during the past three years, but it might be the last. The pair put the finishing touches on one of the great three-year runs in college baseball history, leading the Beavers in a 9-3 win against North Carolina and their second consecutive national title, capping off their third straight trip to the College World Series. Appropriately, Barney's two-run homer in the second inning—with Canham on first base—gave Oregon State the lead for good.

But Barney and Canham weren't thinking about the last three years. They were thinking about the 2007 Beavers, whose improbable run through the postseason made them the first team ever to finish with a sub-.500 record in its conference and win the title.

"All I can think about right now is what just happened between those lines," Barney said. "The men who we brought together and that I've been with since September, that's what's most special to me right now. The past three years of my career, it's been fun, but right now it's all about the team, and it's about every single one of these guys contributing today."

That team-first attitude has defined the Beavers during their remarkable run, and they proved to be the best, most complete team in the nation by simply dominating the 2007 CWS. Oregon State won its final 10 games in the postseason and became the first team

## TOP TEAMS

### 2007 COLLEGE WORLD SERIES STANDINGS

| School | Conference | Record | CWS | Coach |
|---|---|---|---|---|
| Oregon State | Pacific-10 | 49–18 | 5–0 | Pat Casey |
| North Carolina | Atlantic Coast | 57–16 | 4–3 | Mike Fox |
| Rice | Conference USA | 56–14 | 2–2 | Wayne Graham |
| UC Irvine | Big West | 47–17–1 | 2–2 | Dave Serrano |
| Arizona State | Pacific-10 | 49–15 | 1–2 | Pat Murphy |
| Louisville | Big East | 47–24 | 1–2 | Dan McDonnell |
| Cal State Fullerton | Big West | 38–25 | 0–2 | George Horton |
| Mississippi State | Southeastern | 38–22 | 0–2 | Ron Polk |

## NATIONAL CHAMPION
### OREGON STATE

The Beavers went a perfect 5-0 in Omaha to repeat as CWS champions. They defeated North Carolina 11-4 and 9-3 in the best-of-three championship series. OSU became the fifth team to win the CWS in back-to-back years.

ever to win four consecutive CWS games by six or more runs.

For a while, it was uncertain Oregon State would make it into the NCAA Tournament to have a chance to defend its title. The Beavers started the season with a bang, when four pitchers combined to throw a no-hitter against Hawaii-Hilo. OSU kept rolling from there, despite playing its first 17 games away from home, and the Beavers were sitting pretty at 23-3, ranked No. 4 in the nation heading into Pac-10 Conference play.

But the Beavers finished just 10-14 in conference, good enough for sixth place, and they were shipped to the Charlottesville regional as a No. 3 seed. After winning their opener against Rutgers, the Beavers dropped a 13-inning classic to host Virginia, putting them in position to have to win three consecutive elimination games.

Rain forced OSU to play two games on Monday during regionals, and after winning the first game against Rutgers, Oregon State trailed the Cavaliers 3-1 heading into the eighth inning of the nightcap. That's when everything clicked into place—and the Beavers wouldn't lose again in 2007.

They came back to beat Virginia with three runs in the eighth inning, then took the decisive game of the regional the next day. They swept Michigan in two games at the Corvallis Super Regional before vanquishing Cal State Fullerton, Arizona State and UC Irvine to earn a rematch with the Tar Heels in the CWS finals. Oregon State cruised to an 11-4 win in the first game against UNC, then sent Mike Stutes to the mound in Game 2.

North Carolina actually grabbed a 1-0 lead in the first inning, the first time OSU had trailed in its last 61 innings. But Stutes minimized the damage by getting Seth Williams to fly out to center with runners on the corners. Stutes settled down after that, holding the Tar Heels to three runs on seven hits over 5.1 innings.

Oregon State seemed energized after escaping the rocky UNC first inning with only

# 2007 NEWSMAKERS

**Vanderbilt** boasted three first-team All-Americans: third baseman **Pedro Alvarez**, starter **David Price** and reliever **Casey Weathers**. The Commodores won the Southeastern Conference Tournament and hosted a regional, where they bowed out to Michigan.

Coach of the Year **Dave Serrano** led **UC Irvine** to its first-ever College World Series appearance. The Anteaters had not previously won a regional game. The UCI baseball program was in its sixth season since being reinstated after a 10-year hiatus.

The **NCAA** approved a legislative reform package aimed at improving baseball's standing on the **Academic Progress Report**, which holds institutions accountable for the eligibility and retention of student-athletes. Beginning in 2008, players must sit out a season after transferring. Also, all players must be academically certified in the fall to prevent course loading in the fall and taking too few classes in the spring. The reform also introduced limits on scholarships (27 players) and roster size (35). Additionally, all scholarship players will have to receive at least a 25 percent aid package.

## FINAL TOP 25

1. Oregon State*
2. North Carolina*
3. #Rice*
4. UC Irvine*
5. Arizona State*
6. Vanderbilt
7. Louisville*
8. Mississippi State*
9. Cal State Fullerton*
10. South Carolina
11. Texas
12. Texas A&M
13. Wichita State
14. Florida State
15. Clemson
16. Virginia
17. Mississippi
18. San Diego
19. Michigan
20. Coastal Carolina
21. Arkansas
22. UCLA
23. Oklahoma State
24. Missouri
25. Texas Christian

* Reached College World Series
# Preseason No. 1

# IN RETROSPECT: 2007 DRAFT

**Top 10 Draft Picks From College**
With overall selection number (Ov), drafting team (Team) and rank on Baseball America draft board (BA).

| Player | Pos | School | Ov | Team | BA |
|---|---|---|---|---|---|
| David Price | LHP | Vanderbilt | 1 | Devil Rays | 1 |
| Daniel Moskos | LHP | Clemson | 4 | Pirates | 8 |
| Matt Wieters | C | Georgia Tech | 5 | Orioles | 2 |
| Ross Detwiler | LHP | Missouri State | 6 | Nationals | 6 |
| Matt LaPorta | 1B | Florida | 7 | Brewers | 20 |
| Casey Weathers | RHP | Vanderbilt | 8 | Rockies | 22 |
| Beau Mills | 3B | Lewis-Clark State | 13 | Indians | 12 |
| Joe Savery | LHP | Rice | 19 | Phillies | 21 |
| J.P. Arencibia | C | Tennessee | 21 | Blue Jays | 57 |
| Nick Schmidt | LHP | Arkansas | 23 | Padres | 26 |

**Top 10 Major League Players From College Draft Class**
With draft round and Baseball-Reference.com total for wins above replacement (WAR) through 2019.

| Player | Pos | School | Rd | Ov | Team | WAR |
|---|---|---|---|---|---|---|
| Josh Donaldson | 3B | Auburn | 1s | 48 | Cubs | 44.8 |
| David Price | LHP | Vanderbilt | 1 | 1 | Rays | 39.7 |
| Corey Kluber | RHP | Stetson | 4 | 134 | Padres | 33.1 |
| Todd Frazier | 3B | Rutgers | 1s | 34 | Reds | 26.0 |
| Jake Arrieta | RHP | Texas Christian | 5 | 159 | Orioles | 25.5 |
| Jordan Zimmermann | RHP | Wis.-Stevens Point | 2 | 67 | Nationals | 21.3 |
| Matt Wieters | C | Georgia Tech | 1 | 5 | Orioles | 18.4 |
| Jonathan Lucroy | C | Louisiana-Lafayette | 3 | 101 | Brewers | 18.0 |
| Zack Cozart | SS | Mississippi | 2 | 79 | Reds | 15.8 |
| Steve Cishek | RHP | Carson-Newman | 5 | 166 | Marlins | 12.4 |

one run on the board, and Barney's two-run homer to left keyed a three-run inning that chased North Carolina starter Luke Putkonen.

Closer Andrew Carignan replaced Putkonen and kept the Tar Heels in the game by allowing two runs over 3.2 innings. But UNC had no answer for Oregon State's two-run seventh and ninth innings. The Beavers got much of their production from the No. 6 and No. 7 spots in the lineup, where outfielders John Wallace and Scott Santschi combined to go 6-for-7 with three runs and three RBIs.

Freshman righthander Jorge Reyes was named the CWS Most Outstanding Player after starting and winning Oregon State's opener against Cal State Fullerton and its CWS final opener against North Carolina. Reyes has already etched his name alongside former Beaver greats—and he has at least two more years remaining in Corvallis.

"Jorge is lights out. You can see it in his eyes. You can see it in his mannerisms," Barney said.

For Barney, Canham, Stutes and the other OSU players who are likely now headed to the professional ranks, their legacy is already secure, and they leave their program in capable hands. There can be no doubting that Oregon State—which didn't even make the NCAA Tournament field from 1987 through 2004—is now a college baseball super-power, and not just because the Beavers joined elite programs Louisiana State, Stanford, Southern California and Texas as the only schools to repeat as national champions.

"I don't have to convince these guys that they're Texas or USC, because they're Oregon State," Beavers coach Pat Casey said. "We don't need to be anybody but who we are, and tonight in Omaha, Nebraska, we're the best club in the country." ∎

# David Price: Straight from the source(s)

By **AARON FITT**

What more can we say about David Price? We ranked the Vanderbilt lefthander No. 1 on our preseason draft prospects list and kept him there all year long; we chronicled his amazing weekly exploits for the Commodores this spring, when he went 11-1, 2.63 with 194 strikeouts and 31 walks in 133 innings; and we detailed his inevitable selection as the No. 1 pick in the 2007 draft by the Devil Rays.

Now that Price can add the label of College Player of the Year to his impressive résumé, we'll let other people do the talking. We asked those who have coached Price, those who have coached against him, and even Price himself to try to put his season and his talent into historical context.

Vanderbilt's David Price went wire-to-wire as the top draft prospect in 2007. He quickly embarked on a big league career that includes a Cy Young Award, a World Series ring and five All-Star nods.

### Vanderbilt coach Tim Corbin:

"As good as he is for your team when he's pitching, he drives the level of energy for your team up three or four notches when he's not playing because he's an active participant. He leans over the railing with a fungo bat in his hand—and he doesn't miss a pitch. He's like an extension of a coach, he's into every single pitch. He's the first one off the bench every single time—not second or third, he's first. He's so competitive, he doesn't want to finish second in anything. It's not a put-on, it's just what he does. He likes the fact that he is a good teammate, and when you tell him that, it makes him smile and it makes him feel proud. Even at the major league level, you can't minimize it. He's going to be a tremendous clubhouse person.

"He's a very jovial locker-room guy. He's got something going with everyone on the team. His continual text messages, his leaving of notes to coaches. Even before we played Michigan on the last day, he left a note on my desk. It said, 'If you're too scared to coach this game, let me know. I'll coach this team. I can do anything I want to.' Even though it was a joke, that's how he feels, and it wasn't disrespectful in any way. For a kid who came in here from Murfreesboro, Tenn., he was kind of quiet and shy, but he's leaving here confident and verbal. He backed up everything he said."

### Texas Christian coach (and Team USA pitching coach) Jim Schlossnagle:

"You think of a lefty, he's got deception like Dontrelle Willis, but he's got more stuff. I've only seen Sandy Koufax pitch on video. But I'm trying to think of a loose-armed, loose-bodied lefty who has that great fastball, and Koufax is the only guy I come up with.

"It seems like every third year there's a guy that is supposed to be 'can't-miss,' but the thing about David Price that is can't miss is his absolutely off-the-charts makeup, from work ethic to team orientation to selflessness. On days he's not pitching, he's literally the bat boy. He was that all summer long for Team USA. That kid is team before self, more so than any other player I've ever been around. He's amazing. Mark Teixeira said one time to my team, 'There's big league ability all over the minor leagues, but there's very little big league makeup.' If I was ever going to put money on somebody, it would be David Price."

**Arkansas coach Dave Van Horn:**

"What made him so tough is that every Friday night, Vanderbilt knew they were going to win. That's such a positive when you're practicing during the week, going on the road to someone else's ballpark, you know you have David Price on the mound, he's going to give you eight quality innings, and you're going to be 1-0 going into Saturday.

"He reminds me more of a big leaguer than a college player. He just carried himself with the confidence, the athletic ability, the talent. He's going to be an All-Star one day."

**David Price:**

"This has been hands down the greatest year of my life. I give all the credit to my teammates. They helped me out a lot this year. This could have been a very, very stressful year, but there was no stress at all thanks to them." ∎

# TOP PLAYERS OF 2007

## ALL-AMERICA TEAM

| Pos | Player | School | Yr | AVG | OBP | SLG | AB | R | H | HR | RBI | SB |
|-----|--------|--------|----|-----|-----|-----|-----|-----|-----|-----|-----|-----|
| C | Matt Wieters | Georgia Tech | Jr | .358 | .480 | .592 | 218 | 42 | 78 | 10 | 59 | 2 |
| 1B | Brett Wallace | Arizona State | So | .415 | .495 | .702 | 248 | 73 | 103 | 15 | 75 | 11 |
| 2B | Tony Thomas | Florida State | Jr | .430 | .522 | .733 | 258 | 91 | 111 | 11 | 43 | 31 |
| 3B | Pedro Alvarez | Vanderbilt | So | .386 | .463 | .684 | 272 | 76 | 105 | 18 | 68 | 6 |
| SS | Todd Frazier | Rutgers | Jr | .377 | .502 | .757 | 247 | 87 | 93 | 22 | 65 | 25 |
| OF | Grant Desme | Cal Poly | Jr | .405 | .494 | .733 | 195 | 54 | 79 | 15 | 53 | 12 |
| OF | Kellen Kulbacki | James Madison | Jr | .398 | .538 | .785 | 191 | 56 | 76 | 19 | 49 | 9 |
| OF | Kyle Russell | Texas | So | .336 | .456 | .807 | 223 | 68 | 75 | 28 | 71 | 10 |
| DH | Matt LaPorta | Florida | Sr | .402 | .582 | .817 | 169 | 60 | 68 | 20 | 52 | 2 |
| UT | Joe Savery | Rice | Jr | .360 | .441 | .504 | 258 | 55 | 93 | 5 | 57 | 4 |

| Pos | Pitcher | School | Yr | W | L | ERA | SV | IP | H | BB | SO | AVG |
|-----|---------|--------|----|-----|-----|-----|-----|-----|-----|-----|-----|-----|
| SP | Preston Guilmet | Arizona | So | 12 | 2 | 1.87 | 0 | 135 | 100 | 34 | 146 | .205 |
| SP | Adam Mills | Charlotte | Sr | 14 | 2 | 1.01 | 0 | 143 | 93 | 27 | 141 | .188 |
| SP | David Price | Vanderbilt | Jr | 11 | 1 | 2.63 | 0 | 133 | 95 | 31 | 194 | .199 |
| SP | Jacob Thompson | Virginia | So | 11 | 0 | 1.50 | 0 | 114 | 79 | 32 | 101 | .198 |
| RP | Casey Weathers | Vanderbilt | Sr | 12 | 2 | 2.37 | 7 | 49 | 25 | 21 | 75 | .154 |
| UT | Joe Savery | Rice | Jr | 10 | 1 | 2.78 | 0 | 87 | 75 | 38 | 57 | .239 |

## SECOND TEAM

**C**—Buster Posey, Florida State. **1B**—Yonder Alonso, Miami. **2B**—Eric Sogard, Arizona State. **3B**—Brandon Waring, Wofford. **SS**—Jaime Pedroza, UC Riverside. **OF**—Corey Brown, Oklahoma State; Dominic de la Osa, Vanderbilt; and Brian Rike, Louisiana Tech. **DH**—Blake Stouffer, Texas A&M. **UT**—Zach Putnam, Michigan. **SP**—Bryan Henry, Florida State; Brian Matusz, San Diego; Nick Schmidt, Arkansas; and James Simmons, UC Riverside. **RP**—Pat Venditte, Creighton

## THIRD TEAM

**C**—Jonathan Lucroy, Louisiana-Lafayette. **1B**—Justin Smoak, South Carolina. **2B**—Tyler Mach, Oklahoma State. **3B**—Greg Sexton, William & Mary. **SS**—Brandon Hicks, Texas A&M. **OF**—Ryan Lavarnway, Yale; Danny Payne, Georgia Tech; and Boomer Whiting, Louisville. **DH**—Dustin Ackley, North Carolina. **UT**—Mitch Harris, Navy. **SP**—Josh Collmenter, Central Michigan; Barry Enright, Pepperdine; Scott Gorgen, UC Irvine; and Anthony Shawler, Old Dominion. **RP**—Andrew Carignan, North Carolina.

Fresno State closer Brandon Burke celebrates after recording the final out in a 6-1 victory against Georgia in the College World Series championship series.

2008

# Fresno State becomes unlikely champion

By **AARON FITT**

**FROM THE ISSUE:**
JULY 14-27, 2008

Robert Detwiler, a construction worker from Forest Knolls, Calif., raised his son to be tough.

When Fresno State sophomore outfielder Steve Detwiler tore a ligament in his thumb on a head-first slide April 1 against Long Beach State, doctors told him he had a choice. If Detwiler had sustained just a partial tear, he would have required season-ending surgery, but since he suffered a complete tear, he could opt to play through it and have surgery after the season. He couldn't do any more damage than had already been done.

"As soon as the doctor told me I had an option, there was no doubt in my mind what I was going to do," Detwiler said. "I know if Coach (Mike) Batesole thinks I was good enough to go, I was good enough to go."

He was much more than good enough on June 25, making Fresno awfully glad he waited to go under the knife. Detwiler went 4-for-4 with two home runs and a double and drove in all six of Fresno State's runs, powering the Bulldogs to a 6-1 win against Georgia and their first national championship.

Early in the College World Series, Detwiler struck out swinging three times, causing his thumb to pop out of place and giving him the worst pain he's gone through since sustaining the injury.

Robert Detwiler had no sympathy. Instead, in their nightly conversations, he made fun of his son for wincing every time he swung and missed.

"One swing of the bat makes a hero. That's what my pops told me every time I talk to him every night—just keep with it, stick with it, suck it up," Steve Detwiler said.

He entered the CWS finals batting just 4-for-39 in the NCAA Tournament, but he stuck with it and sucked it up. He didn't swing and miss much in the championship series, which spared him some extra pain. He finished with championship series records for hits (eight) homers (three) and RBIs (nine).

Detwiler got the scoring started in the decisive third game with a two-run home run to right field in the second. He followed with an RBI double to left-center field in the fourth,

## TOP TEAMS
### 2008 COLLEGE WORLD SERIES STANDINGS

| School | Conference | Record | CWS | Coach |
|--------|-----------|--------|-----|-------|
| Fresno State | Western Athletic | 47–31 | 5–2 | Mike Batesole |
| Georgia | Southeastern | 45–25–1 | 4–2 | David Perno |
| North Carolina | Atlantic Coast | 54–14 | 3–2 | Mike Fox |
| Stanford | Pacific-10 | 41–24–2 | 2–2 | Mark Marquess |
| Louisiana State | Southeastern | 49–19–1 | 1–2 | Paul Mainieri |
| Miami | Atlantic Coast | 53–11 | 1–2 | Jim Morris |
| Florida State | Atlantic Coast | 54–14 | 0–2 | Mike Martin |
| Rice | Conference USA | 47–15 | 0–2 | Wayne Graham |

## NATIONAL CHAMPION
### FRESNO STATE

Fresno State won two elimination games against Georgia to win the champion-ship series. The ultimate Cinderella team, the Bulldogs were the first team to reach the CWS as a No. 4 regional seed and had more losses (31) than any CWS champion ever.

**191**

then tacked on a mammoth three-run homer to left in the sixth, giving Fresno a 6-0 lead.

Georgia got on the board on Gordon Beckham's 28th homer of the year in the eighth, but never got within sniffing distance of Fresno State.

When a reporter asked Detwiler later about being a one-man wrecking crew in the decisive Game 3, he started to argue the point and spread the credit to his teammates, as is the Fresno way.

"He's giving too much credit away," lefthander Justin Wilson interjected.

Wilson should talk. He only wanted to discuss the defense, the hitting, the coaching and the bullpen—forget about his own splendid evening. The junior was masterful on three days' rest, allowing one run on five hits while striking out nine over eight innings. He finished with 129 pitches after throwing 112 against North Carolina last time out.

"It was over when I saw the look in his eye in the first inning," Batesole said. "There was no doubt in my mind it was over. I knew when I saw that look in his eye that he was going to give everything he had to bring it home. And that's exactly what happened."

Wilson went 2-0, 2.21 in three CWS starts, leading all pitchers in strikeouts (20) and innings (20). But Most Outstanding Player honors went to sophomore Tommy Mendonca, who tied the single-CWS record with four home runs in Omaha and played spectacular defense at third base.

Mendonca led a Fresno State power surge that was unprecedented in the post-gorilla ball era. Fresno scored 62 runs in Omaha to tie a CWS record set by Southern California in 1998—year of the infamous 21-14 national championship game. Fresno's 14 homers is the third-most by one team in Omaha, and the most since both USC and Louisiana State smacked 18 homers in that same 1998 CWS. Seven different players homered for Fresno in Omaha; no other team at the CWS even hit seven homers collectively.

# 2008 NEWSMAKERS

A pair of notable pitching achievements transpired on April 11. **San Diego State** sophomore **Stephen Strasburg** struck out 23 Utah batters in a game to set a Mountain West Conference record. Meanwhile, **Missouri** junior **Aaron Crow** authored 43 straight scoreless innings, believed to be the fourth-longest streak in modern Division I history.

The uniform **March 1 start date** went into effect, forcing all teams to play their entire 56-game schedule in 13 weeks. Many warm-weather programs struggled to adapt. They felt the drain on their pitching staffs and their study time because they were unaccustomed to playing four or five games per week.

Potent offenses and a lack of power arms in **Omaha** made the 2008 **CWS** the highest-scoring affair since the "gorilla ball" heyday of 1998. A total of 206 runs were scored, compared with 225 twenty years earlier. The .303 collective batting average was just the fourth time the eight teams combined to hit .300.

**Florida State** went 0-2 at the CWS for the sixth time in its 19 trips to Omaha. Only **Northern Colorado**, with seven, went two-and-out more often than the Seminoles.

**FINAL TOP 25 FOR 2008**

1. Fresno State*
2. Georgia*
3. North Carolina*
4. Miami*
5. Stanford*
6. Louisiana State*
7. Florida State*
8. Rice*
9. Arizona State
10. Cal State Fullerton
11. UC Irvine
12. Texas A&M
13. Wichita State
14. Arizona
15. North Carolina State
16. Coastal Carolina
17. Oklahoma State
18. San Diego
19. Missouri
20. Nebraska
21. Texas
22. Michigan
23. Texas Christian
24. Kentucky
25. Long Beach State

* Reached College World Series
# UCLA was preseason No. 1

# IN RETROSPECT: 2008 DRAFT

## Top 10 Draft Picks From College
With overall selection number (Ov), drafting team (Team) and rank on Baseball America draft board (BA).

| Player | Pos | School | Ov | Team | BA |
|---|---|---|---|---|---|
| Pedro Alvarez | 3B | Vanderbilt | 2 | Pirates | 1 |
| Brian Matusz | LHP | San Diego | 4 | Orioles | 2 |
| Buster Posey | C | Florida State | 5 | Giants | 4 |
| Yonder Alonso | 1B | Miami | 7 | Reds | 12 |
| Gordon Beckham | SS | Georgia | 8 | White Sox | 6 |
| Aaron Crow* | RHP | Missouri | 9 | Nationals | 5 |
| Jason Castro | C | Stanford | 10 | Astros | 21 |
| Justin Smoak | 1B | South Carolina | 11 | Rangers | 8 |
| Jemile Weeks | 2B | Miami | 12 | Athletics | 27 |
| Brett Wallace | 3B | Arizona State | 13 | Cardinals | 20 |

\* Did not sign

## Top 10 Major League Players From College Draft Class
With draft round and Baseball-Reference.com total for wins above replacement (WAR) through 2019.

| Player | Pos | School | Rd | Ov | Team | WAR |
|---|---|---|---|---|---|---|
| Buster Posey | C | Florida State | 1 | 5 | Giants | 42.1 |
| Brandon Crawford | SS | UCLA | 4 | 117 | Giants | 23.6 |
| Lance Lynn | RHP | Mississippi | 1s | 39 | Cardinals | 22.2 |
| Charlie Blackmon | OF | Georgia Tech | 2 | 72 | Rockies | 18.2 |
| Alex Avila | C | Alabama | 5 | 163 | Tigers | 15.9 |
| Josh Harrison | 2B | Cincinnati | 6 | 191 | Cubs | 13.1 |
| Logan Forsythe | 2B | Arkansas | 1s | 46 | Padres | 12.5 |
| Jason Castro | C | Stanford | 1 | 10 | Astros | 12.0 |
| Andrew Cashner | RHP | Texas Christian | 1 | 19 | Cubs | 11.5 |
| Wade Miley | LHP | SE Louisiana | 1s | 43 | D-backs | 11.1 |

The Bulldogs, meanwhile, swung out of their shoes facing that early deficit against a dominant Wilson, and they were never able to sustain any rallies.

Georgia managed to put its first two runners on base against Clayton Allison in a last-ditch rally in the ninth, causing Fresno State to summon Brandon Burke from the bullpen. He quickly got David Thoms to ground into a 4-6-3 double play, then issued a walk to Ryan Peisel to bring up Matt Olson. Olson lined Burke's first pitch to right field, where it was snared by—who else?—Detwiler for the final out.

Second baseman Erik Wetzel and first baseman Alan Ahmady mobbed Detwiler in right field, while the rest of the team buried Burke in a raucous dogpile behind the mound.

"I was directly next to Burke at the bottom of the pile, and we both after four seconds decided it's time to get up now, or we both might never pitch again," Wilson said.

Detwiler was late to arrive at the main dogpile after his mini-celebration in right field, but he finally joined his teammates, jumping on the top of the heap.

"He's the reason me and Wilson are hurt," Burke said.

Robert Detwiler would tell Burke to suck it up. That's what Steve did; now he gets to have surgery to remove a piece of ligament from his wrist and insert it into his thumb, followed by 12 weeks of rehab.

That's nothing for Detwiler—he's a tough kid. And besides, his thumb was the farthest thing from his mind after Fresno State won the national championship, his face glistening with sweat from the celebration, his eyes aglow with amazement and incredulity.

"It's the best feeling in the world, there's no words to describe it," Detwiler said. "This is what everybody wishes for, and I've got it." ∎

# All-around catcher Posey is top player

By **AARON FITT**

Three years ago, most scouts thought Buster Posey's future was on the mound. Two years ago, he was a standout freshman shortstop at Florida State. Last year, he moved behind the plate and was second-team All-America.

In 2008, Posey turned in one of the finest seasons ever by a college catcher, earning him the College Player of the Year award. Posey won the Atlantic Coast Conference triple crown by hitting .460 with 26 home runs and 92 RBIs. He led the nation in hitting and also on-base percentage (.564), slugging (.887), hits (119) and total bases (226). Posey also saved six games in nine appearances as FSU's closer.

Posey's stellar defense and leadership behind the plate helped carry the Seminoles to the brink of the College World Series for the first time since 2001. That entire package also made Posey the No. 5 overall pick in the draft by the Giants.

Florida State's Buster Posey turned in one of the best seasons ever by a college catcher. His first decade in the majors included an MVP, six all-star nods and three World Series rings with the Giants.

**Florida State coach Mike Martin:**

"I honestly think it was Posey's leadership more than anything else that got us through the regional (after losing the opener to Bucknell). He just has a calmness but yet a firmness about him that filters over to the freshmen. We really have a young club. So it's Posey's leadership more than anything. And of course when the leader produces like he did, it's almost unreal. I wanted to give him the second Bucknell game off from catching—I was going to DH him. He looked me in the eye and said one word: 'What?' Immediately the magic marker wrote '2' beside Posey.

"Posey will look you in the eye and say, 'I'm ready.' He is one of a kind. They just don't come along every five years like this guy. I've been here 34 years. I've never had a catcher used as a closer, never had a closer go out there and not give up a run in seven or eight appearances—and each time the game is on the line. He is one special player, and I'm proud to say student-athlete. Because that's what he is, he's a student-athlete."

**Miami coach Jim Morris:**

"Well, he destroyed us; he was outstanding. I've heard Mike Martin say he thinks (Posey) might be the best player ever to play at Florida State, and I would have to agree with him, and I've been competing against Florida State for 25 years. Every phase of the game—he can hit, throw, receive, hit home runs—he's just outstanding in every phase."

**Florida coach Kevin O'Sullivan:**

"As far as going from a shortstop/righthander and in only two years learning the catching position as well as he has is quite an accomplishment—and not only learning the post but excelling at it is quite amazing. He receives the ball well—it's clean, he's got a strong arm—and on top of that he's added some power to his bat as he's gone along. He's improved in all parts of his game. With his body, there's certainly more room for growth. He's an athletic kid, and who knows how much stronger he can get?"

**Tulane coach Rick Jones:**

"He's an outstanding receiver. He's got a great throwing arm, an accurate throwing arm, and that's why they close with him. When you watch him between innings, you can see he plays the game the right way. His numbers are throwback numbers, to 10 or 15 years ago—you just don't see those kind of numbers anymore."

**Buster Posey:**

"I'd say probably the biggest change for me since I got to Florida State is just my maturity as a player and understanding the game better.

"Being able to play under Coach Martin for three years and having two years of experience in the Cape Cod League, you learn the game a lot better. And I feel like I have a better understanding of the game and how it's played, how it should be played." ∎

# TOP PLAYERS OF 2008

## ALL-AMERICA TEAM

| Pos | Player | School | Yr | AVG | AB | R | H | HR | RBI | SB | BB | SO | OBP | SLG |
|-----|--------|--------|----|-----|-----|----|-----|----|-----|----|----|----|-----|-----|
| C | Buster Posey | Florida State | Jr | .460 | 248 | 88 | 114 | 26 | 92 | 5 | 55 | 27 | .564 | .887 |
| 1B | Justin Smoak | South Carolina | Jr | .383 | 235 | 63 | 90 | 23 | 72 | 1 | 57 | 28 | .505 | .757 |
| 2B | Josh Satin | California | Sr | .379 | 195 | 56 | 74 | 18 | 52 | 6 | 47 | 45 | .500 | .723 |
| 3B | Brett Wallace | Arizona State | Jr | .410 | 239 | 87 | 98 | 22 | 83 | 16 | 48 | 33 | .526 | .753 |
| SS | Gordon Beckham | Georgia | Jr | .401 | 252 | 90 | 101 | 26 | 72 | 17 | 50 | 30 | .513 | .802 |
| OF | Sawyer Carroll | Kentucky | Sr | .419 | 234 | 69 | 98 | 19 | 83 | 12 | 44 | 33 | .514 | .782 |
| OF | Blake Dean | Louisiana State | So | .359 | 256 | 62 | 92 | 20 | 70 | 4 | 34 | 42 | .439 | .680 |
| OF | Chris Shehan | Georgia Southern | Jr | .438 | 224 | 84 | 98 | 22 | 77 | 22 | 53 | 56 | .557 | .835 |
| DH | Yonder Alonso | Miami | Jr | .367 | 199 | 73 | 73 | 23 | 71 | 9 | 74 | 23 | .535 | .774 |
| UT | Ike Davis | Arizona State | Jr | .385 | 213 | 64 | 82 | 16 | 76 | 6 | 31 | 34 | .457 | .742 |

| Pos | Pitcher | School | Yr | W | L | ERA | G | SV | IP | H | BB | SO |
|-----|---------|--------|----|----|----|-----|----|----|-----|----|----|----|
| SP | Aaron Crow | Missouri | Jr | 13 | 0 | 2.35 | 15 | 0 | 107 | 85 | 38 | 127 |
| SP | Brian Matusz | San Diego | Jr | 12 | 2 | 1.71 | 15 | 0 | 105 | 83 | 22 | 141 |
| SP | Rob Musgrave | Wichita State | Sr | 12 | 1 | 2.51 | 16 | 0 | 111 | 99 | 22 | 101 |
| SP | Stephen Strasburg | San Diego State | So | 8 | 3 | 1.57 | 13 | 0 | 97 | 61 | 16 | 133 |
| RP | Scott Bittle | Mississippi | Jr | 7 | 1 | 1.78 | 27 | 8 | 71 | 35 | 30 | 130 |
| UT | Ike Davis | Arizona State | Jr | 4 | 1 | 2.25 | 16 | 4 | 24 | 17 | 4 | 30 |

## SECOND TEAM

**C**—Corey Kemp, East Carolina. **1B**—David Cooper, California. **2B**—Jemile Weeks, Miami. **3B**—Conor Gillaspie, Wichita State. **SS**—Reese Havens, South Carolina. **OF**—Tim Fedroff, North Carolina; Blake Tekotte, Miami; and Eric Thames, Pepperdine. **DH**—Nate Recknagel, Michigan. **UT**—Zach Putnam, Michigan. **SP**—Christian Friedrich, Eastern Kentucky; Scott Gorgen, UC Irvine; Chris Hernandez, Miami; and Mike Leake, Arizona State. **RP**—Andrew Cashner, Texas Christian.

## THIRD TEAM

**C**—Jason Castro, Stanford. **1B**—Dustin Ackley, North Carolina. **2B**—Johnny Giavotella, New Orleans. **3B**—Chris Dominguez, Louisville. **SS**—Grant Green, Southern California. **OF**—Collin Cowgill, Kentucky; Jason Kipnis, Arizona State; and Brian Van Kirk, Oral Roberts. **DH**—Erik Komatsu, Cal State Fullerton. **UT**—Josh Romanski, San Diego. **SP**—Barry Bowden, Southern Mississippi; Shooter Hunt, Tulane; Chance Ruffin, Texas; and Alex White, North Carolina. **RP**—Josh Fields, Georgia.

Louisiana State players celebrate their College World Series championship series victory against Texas. The Tigers ended the decade the same way they began it: with a national title.

2009

# Sixth title propels LSU back to the top

By **AARON FITT**

Louisiana State athletic director Joe Alleva waded through the throng around the Rosenblatt Stadium pitcher's mound and spotted Louis Coleman. With a hug and a handshake, Alleva said into Coleman's ear, "Thanks for coming back."

Moments earlier, Coleman had set off a wild celebration on that mound by striking out three straight Texas Longhorns to secure an 11-4 victory and the sixth national championship for LSU—the first since 2000. After getting Connor Rowe to swing through an 0-2 pitch, Coleman chucked his glove into the air and was speared to the ground by catcher Micah Gibbs. Within seconds, Coleman was enveloped by a writhing sea of yellow.

**FROM THE ISSUE:**
JULY 13-26, 2009

"There's no one better to close out that game than Louis," said LSU sophomore right-hander Anthony Ranaudo, who started Game 3 of the College World Series finals and picked up his 12th victory of the season with 5.1 innings of work. "What he did to sacrifice a year of professional ball to come back—he said he wanted to come back to win a national championship. I know everyone is happy he got to close it out for us and be the one at the bottom of the dogpile."

Ranaudo played his own key part in the clinching victory, though he didn't have his sharpest control, as evidenced by his five walks. The Tigers staked him to an early 4-0 lead, and though Texas battled back to tie the score in the fifth inning, Ranaudo kept the Tigers in the game until LSU's explosive offense could break it open with a five-run sixth.

"It's just the story of our year: When the pitcher might not have his best stuff, the hitters pick him up, and vice versa," Ranaudo said.

"I knew he was going to give us a chance," said LSU junior first baseman Sean Ochinko, who stepped into the cleanup spot and delivered four hits and three RBIs. "I put my head on the pillow last night knowing Anthony Ranaudo would give us a chance to win."

Knowing their ace was on the mound, the Tigers came out loose and confident, and CWS Most Outstanding Player Jared Mitchell put them on top with a three-run homer down the right field line in the first inning. After Texas tied the game at 4-4 with two

## TOP TEAMS
### 2009 COLLEGE WORLD SERIES STANDINGS

| School | Conference | Record | CWS | Coach |
|---|---|---|---|---|
| Louisiana State | Southeastern | 56–17 | 5–1 | Paul Mainieri |
| Texas | Big 12 | 50–16–1 | 4–2 | Augie Garrido |
| Arizona State | Pacific-10 | 51–14 | 2–2 | Pat Murphy |
| Arkansas | Southeastern | 41–24 | 2–2 | Dave van Horn |
| North Carolina | Atlantic Coast | 48–18 | 1–2 | Mike Fox |
| Virginia | Atlantic Coast | 49–15–1 | 1–2 | Brian O'Connor |
| Cal State Fullerton | Big West | 47–16 | 0–2 | Dave Serrano |
| Southern Mississippi | Conference USA | 40–26 | 0–2 | Corky Palmer |

## NATIONAL CHAMPION
### LOUISIANA STATE

The Tigers claim their second title of the 2000s and the program's sixth over-all—but the first under coach Paul Mainieri. LSU swept through the CWS bracket to meet Texas in the championship series, where they prevailed in three games.

runs in the bottom of the fifth, Mitchell sparked the big sixth-inning rally by working an eight-pitch walk to lead off the frame. He scored a batter later on freshman Mikie Mahtook's RBI double, and LSU never trailed again.

"I thought we were a little flat in those middle innings," Ochinko said. "I knew when Jared came up there and fought really hard for that walk that that was going to start something."

Texas righthander Brandon Workman, who came in to start the third after starter Cole Green allowed four runs in the first two innings, had retired nine straight Tigers heading into the sixth, but Longhorns coach Augie Garrido pulled him after Mahtook's double, and relievers Austin Dicharry and Austin Wood could not provide any answers.

LSU capitalized on two walks, two hit batters and a throwing error by Dicharry to score five times in the inning despite managing just two hits. Ochinko, who moved into the cleanup spot because coach Paul Mainieri liked his chances against a lefthander like Wood in a tight spot, faced the Longhorns senior and capped the rally with a two-run single through the left side of the infield.

"Answering right back, it really was devastating," Texas second baseman Travis Tucker said of LSU's sixth. "They got the momentum back; we had it our way, they chipped it back to theirs. They're a great ball club."

Garrido echoed Tucker's praise for the Tigers, who opened the season ranked No. 2 in the nation and finished it on top of the college baseball world. In between, LSU won the Southeastern Conference regular season and tournament titles.

"We've won several championships this year, but if we hadn't won this one, it probably would have left a little bit of an empty feeling," Mainieri said. "But we won't have to know that, because we did it."

# 2009 NEWSMAKERS

A talented but inexperienced **Texas** team pushed **Louisiana State** to Game 3 of the CWS finals before bowing out. It was the sixth time Texas had finished runner-up at the CWS, a record. The Longhorns won the **Big 12 Conference** regular season and tournament titles, then kept defying the odds in the postseason. During regionals, they won the longest game in NCAA history—25 innings—against Boston College, then overcame a four-run ninth-inning deficit with a walk-off grand slam against Army. Texas then compiled three dramatic wins in Omaha, winning twice in their last at-bat and also overcoming a 6-0 deficit against **Arizona State** and ace **Mike Leake**.

Making his third straight trip to Omaha, **North Carolina** first baseman **Dustin Ackley** set a CWS record with 28 career hits.

**Florida State** routed **Ohio State** 37-6 in a regionals matchup in which FSU led 32-0 in the fifth inning. The Seminoles set an NCAA postseason record with 37 runs, 38 hits and 66 total bases. Their 15 doubles are an NCAA record for any game.

The **NCAA** added a week at the start of the regular season to stretch it to 14 weeks, thus cutting down on five-game weeks.

**FINAL TOP 25 FOR 2009**

1. Louisiana State*
2. Texas*
3. Arizona State*
4. Cal State Fullerton*
5. Virginia*
6. North Carolina*
7. Arkansas*
8. Rice
9. Florida State
10. UC Irvine
11. Southern Mississippi*
12. Florida
13. Mississippi
14. Texas Christian
15. Louisville
16. Clemson
17. East Carolina
18. Oklahoma
19. Kansas State
20. Georgia Tech
21. Minnesota
22. Gonzaga
23. Western Kentucky
24. Elon
25. South Carolina

\* Reached College World Series
\# Texas A&M was preseason No. 1

# IN RETROSPECT: 2009 DRAFT

## Top 10 Draft Picks From College

With overall selection number (Ov), drafting team (Team) and rank on Baseball America draft board (BA).

| Player | Pos | School | Ov | Team | BA |
|---|---|---|---|---|---|
| Stephen Strasburg | RHP | San Diego State | 1 | Nationals | 1 |
| Dustin Ackley | OF | North Carolina | 2 | Mariners | 2 |
| Tony Sanchez | C | Boston College | 4 | Pirates | 32 |
| Mike Minor | LHP | Vanderbilt | 7 | Braves | 35 |
| Mike Leake | RHP | Arizona State | 8 | Reds | 14 |
| Drew Storen | RHP | Stanford | 10 | Nationals | 36 |
| Grant Green | SS | Southern California | 13 | Athletics | 13 |
| Alex White | RHP | North Carolina | 15 | Indians | 6 |
| A.J. Pollock | OF | Notre Dame | 17 | D-backs | 23 |
| Chad Jenkins | RHP | Kennesaw State | 20 | Blue Jays | 20 |

## Top 10 Major League Players From College Draft Class

With draft round and Baseball-Reference.com total for wins above replacement (WAR) through 2019.

| Player | Pos | School | Rd | Ov | Team | WAR |
|---|---|---|---|---|---|---|
| Paul Goldschmidt | 1B | Texas State | 8 | 246 | D-backs | 43.1 |
| Stephen Strasburg | RHP | San Diego State | 1 | 1 | Nationals | 33.9 |
| Kyle Seager | 3B | North Carolina | 3 | 82 | Mariners | 30.4 |
| Matt Carpenter | 3B | Texas Christian | 13 | 399 | Cardinals | 26.7 |
| Brian Dozier | 2B | Southern Miss. | 8 | 252 | Twins | 24.5 |
| J.D. Martinez | OF | Nova Southeastern | 20 | 611 | Astros | 23.9 |
| DJ LeMahieu | 2B | Louisiana State | 2 | 79 | Cubs | 23.5 |
| Brandon Belt | 1B | Texas | 5 | 147 | Giants | 23.2 |
| Jason Kipnis | 2B | Arizona State | 2 | 63 | Indians | 22.2 |
| Dallas Keuchel | LHP | Arkansas | 7 | 221 | Astros | 20.3 |

Mainieri shook things up to improve his defense in April, inserting freshman Austin Nola at shortstop and sliding preseason All-America shortstop DJ LeMahieu to second base, and preseason All-America second baseman Ryan Schimpf to left field. The Tigers went 28-5 from that point on, and any lingering doubt that they were the nation's best team in 2009 was erased with that 11-4 win against Texas in Game 3.

"I don't think we lost this tournament; I think that they won it," Garrido said. "It was a great effort that combined all the things that baseball is about."

The Tigers' sixth national title will require an addition to the new Alex Box Stadium. At the old stadium, which was replaced at the start of this year, a giant billboard—known as the Intimidator—stood behind the right field wall, displaying the years of all five LSU national titles alongside a fearsome photo of a Tiger.

Toward the end of LSU's postgame press conference, Mainieri called out to Alleva standing at the back of the new Hall of Fame room, "Joe, are we getting a new Intimidator with a new number on it?"

"Yeah, no doubt," Alleva called back.

For players like Mitchell, who grew up in Louisiana watching the Tigers dominate college baseball, putting a new number on that board is what it's all about.

"It's an unbelievable feeling to be put in position where, basically, you'll be remembered forever in Baton Rouge now," said Mitchell, who along with reliever Chad Jones was also a part of LSU's 2007 Bowl Championship Series football title. "To be a part of that company with guys who've done it before is unbelievable. To put LSU baseball back on top where it belongs, for years to come—to be a part of that is something special." ■

# Sky's the limit for top player Strasburg

By **AARON FITT**

As time passes, Stephen Strasburg might be remembered as the greatest pitcher in college baseball history, and his 2009 junior campaign as the most dominant season ever. Strasburg, San Diego State's 6-foot-4, 220-pound righthander, went 13-1, 1.32 with 195 strikeouts and 19 walks in 109 innings to lead the Aztecs to regionals for the first time since 1991. His 16.1 strikeouts per nine innings ranks third on the NCAA's single-season list.

With an overpowering fastball that sometimes reaches triple digits, a devastating, hard breaking ball and excellent feel for a changeup, Strasburg was a no-brainer choice for the No. 1 overall pick in the draft by the Nationals. He was also an easy selection for College Player of the Year.

San Diego State's Stephen Strasburg lived up to the hype and went No. 1 overall to the Nationals in the draft. The three-time all-star shined as a frontline starter in his first decade with Washington.

**San Diego State coach Tony Gwynn:**

"We were spoiled rotten, really. As the year went on and he got more and more attention, you would expect somewhere in there for him to have one (start) where he wasn't effective. But he did what he needed to do. There were nights where he needed to punch a bunch of guys out, and he did that. There were nights he needed to pitch to contact, and he did that. I try to downplay everything, because I know the expectations are through the roof with him. But he did what he needed to do—I think that's the best description.

"You can tell the impact he had on our program already. Our phones are ringing off the hook. I've got a stack of DVDs sitting on my desk. People are interested in San Diego State baseball again—I've got alumni coming through the roof. The impact he's had on not just San Diego State but college baseball has been tremendous."

**Texas Christian coach Jim Schlossnagle:**

"The thing that goes so underrated with him in my mind is his pitchability. I think every year in the country there's a guy—and we had one last year in Andrew Cashner— who can throw in the upper 90s. But usually those guys, their command's not great or the ball is straight or they can't throw a secondary pitch consistently for strikes. The thing with Stephen is he throws like he's an 87-89 (mph) sinker/slider guy. He pitches at the knees with movement with his fastball.

"He is obviously physically gifted, but he's the most complete package I've ever seen at the amateur level. To me, it's his pitchability that separates him from everybody else."

**San Diego coach Rich Hill:**

"It's an unbelievable story. We all knew him here in San Diego in his previous life, as we like to put it. He was out in East County, and he's just completely transformed his body. He was a little emotional, probably a little soft, a blame-game kind of guy. But he's just completely turned things around. He's in yoga classes, pilates, arm strengthening programs. To do what he did from the mental side, to me, is the story.

"Every team schemed and planned on him this year, tried to bunt on him, tried to run on him, tried to get him rattled. Every single game, he's facing an offense that's had all week to prepare, it's going to make their season if they beat him. And still there was nothing you could do. You couldn't rattle him, you couldn't short-game him, you couldn't do anything. We just have a different perspective here in San Diego because we've all seen Stephen grow up and transform into this beast that he's become. It's remarkable."

**Stephen Strasburg:**

"It was a great season, and I had a lot of fun doing it. I have a lot of great memories at San Diego State. Definitely the one moment that I remember most is—I think it was our last home game for me—pitching that no-hitter in front of my home crowd, it was unbelievable. I knew it was going to be a lot of fun, but to go out there and pitch a no-hitter, something I've never done since Little League—it still hasn't really sunk in yet." ■

# TOP PLAYERS OF 2009

## ALL-AMERICA TEAM

| Pos | Player | School | Yr | AVG | AB | R | H | HR | RBI | SB | BB | SO | OBP | SLG |
|-----|--------|--------|-----|-----|-----|-----|-----|-----|-----|-----|-----|-----|-----|-----|
| C | Tony Sanchez | Boston College | Jr | .346 | 228 | 63 | 79 | 14 | 51 | 1 | 30 | 40 | .443 | .614 |
| 1B | Dustin Ackley | North Carolina | Jr | .412 | 250 | 73 | 103 | 22 | 70 | 13 | 50 | 32 | .513 | .776 |
| 2B | Derek McCallum | Minnesota | Jr | .409 | 232 | 57 | 95 | 18 | 86 | 6 | 30 | 34 | .484 | .741 |
| 3B | Chris Dominguez | Louisville | Jr | .345 | 258 | 80 | 89 | 25 | 82 | 19 | 32 | 55 | .441 | .698 |
| SS | Stephen Cardullo | Florida State | Jr | .376 | 237 | 76 | 89 | 10 | 51 | 20 | 45 | 46 | .479 | .612 |
| OF | Jason Kipnis | Arizona State | Jr | .385 | 221 | 71 | 85 | 16 | 71 | 26 | 48 | 30 | .496 | .729 |
| OF | Marc Krauss | Ohio | Jr | .402 | 209 | 73 | 84 | 27 | 70 | 6 | 46 | 29 | .521 | .852 |
| OF | Kent Matthes | Alabama | Sr | .358 | 204 | 67 | 73 | 28 | 81 | 13 | 32 | 46 | .461 | .858 |
| DH | Rich Poythress | Georgia | Jr | .376 | 25 | 86 | 89 | 25 | 86 | 4 | 42 | 39 | .468 | .764 |
| UT | Bryce Brentz | Middle Tennessee State | So | .465 | 230 | 79 | 107 | 28 | 73 | 7 | 31 | 32 | .535 | .930 |

| Pos | Pitcher | School | Yr | W | L | ERA | G | SV | IP | H | BB | SO |
|-----|---------|--------|-----|-----|-----|-----|-----|-----|-----|-----|-----|-----|
| SP | Louis Coleman | Louisiana State | Sr | 13 | 2 | 2.76 | 21 | 0 | 114 | 92 | 19 | 124 |
| SP | Mike Leake | Arizona State | Jr | 16 | 1 | 1.36 | 17 | 0 | 133 | 79 | 21 | 150 |
| SP | A.J. Morris | Kansas State | Jr | 14 | 1 | 2.09 | 16 | 0 | 116 | 98 | 30 | 100 |
| SP | Stephen Strasburg | San Diego State | Jr | 13 | 1 | 1.32 | 15 | 0 | 109 | 65 | 19 | 195 |
| RP | Kyle Bellamy | Miami | Jr | 3 | 1 | 0.97 | 30 | 16 | 46 | 23 | 20 | 63 |
| UT | Bryce Brentz | Middle Tenn. State | So | 5 | 3 | 4.57 | 15 | 0 | 89 | 90 | 31 | 63 |

## SECOND TEAM

**C**—J.T. Wise, Oklahoma. **1B**—Troy Channing, St. Mary's. **2B**—Chris Sedon, Pittsburgh. **3B**—Anthony Rendon, Rice. **SS**—Christian Colon, Cal State Fullerton. **OF**—Tyler Holt, Florida State; Jarrett Parker, Virginia; and Tim Wheeler, Sacramento State. **DH**—Wade Gaynor, Western Kentucky. **UT**—Mike McGee, Florida State. **SP**—Eric Arnett, Indiana; Daniel Bibona, UC Irvine; Kyle Gibson, Missouri; and Deck McGuire, Georgia Tech. **RP**—Addison Reed, San Diego State.

## THIRD TEAM

**C**—Josh Phegley, Indiana. **1B**—Paul Goldschmidt, Texas State. **2B**—Ryan Wood, East Carolina. **3B**—Tom Mendonca, Fresno State. **SS**—Ryan Goins, Dallas Baptist. **OF**—Jeremy Hazelbaker, Ball State; A.J. Pollock, Notre Dame; and Tyler Townsend, Florida International. **DH**—Luke Murton, Georgia Tech. **UT**—Danny Hultzen, Virginia. **SP**—Justin Marks, Louisville; Daniel Renken, Cal State Fullerton; Josh Spence, Arizona State; and Alex Wimmers, Ohio State. **RP**—Brian Moran, North Carolina.

The College World Series shifted to TD Ameritrade in downtown Omaha in 2011. The move coincided with new bat standards that altered the complexion of the college game.

THE
**2010s**

# TOP 25 PROGRAMS OF THE 2010s

Coastal Carolina won the 2016 CWS, yet fell just outside the top 25 with 111 points.
See Introduction (Page 4) for a key to abbreviations and scoring. Category leaders in **bold**.

| No. | School | Regional | Super | CWS | Title | AA1 | AA2 | AA3 | Top 10 | MLB | Points |
|-----|--------|----------|-------|-----|-------|-----|-----|-----|--------|-----|--------|
| 1. | Florida | **10** | 7 | **7** | 1 | 6 | 2 | 4 | **43** | 14 | 290 |
| 2. | Vanderbilt | **10** | 8 | 4 | **2** | 5 | 6 | 3 | 40 | 11 | 286 |
| 3. | Florida State | **10** | 8 | 4 | 0 | 6 | 5 | 2 | 27 | 9 | 231 |
| 4. | Oregon State | 9 | 4 | 3 | 1 | **7** | 5 | 4 | 30 | 9 | 220 |
| 5. | Louisiana State | 9 | 6 | 3 | 0 | **7** | 4 | 2 | 35 | 9 | 212 |
| 6. | Louisville | 9 | 6 | 4 | 0 | 3 | 5 | 5 | 31 | 10 | 208 |
| 7. | Virginia | 8 | 5 | 3 | 1 | 4 | 3 | 1 | 38 | 8 | 202 |
| 8. | South Carolina | 7 | 6 | 3 | **2** | 2 | 1 | 3 | 25 | 8 | 199 |
| 9. | UCLA | 8 | 4 | 3 | 1 | 4 | 4 | 4 | 29 | 10 | 197 |
| 10. | Arkansas | 9 | 5 | 4 | 0 | 1 | 5 | 1 | 32 | 11 | 185 |
| 11. | Texas Christian | 8 | 6 | 5 | 0 | 0 | 3 | 4 | 24 | 6 | 179 |
| 12. | Mississippi State | 8 | 6 | 3 | 0 | 5 | 3 | 3 | 17 | 9 | 178 |
| 13. | Cal State Fullerton | 9 | 5 | 2 | 0 | 4 | 5 | 2 | 24 | 9 | 172 |
| 14. | Texas A&M | **10** | 4 | 2 | 0 | 3 | 5 | 3 | 29 | 6 | 169 |
| 15. | North Carolina | 8 | 4 | 3 | 0 | 5 | 0 | 3 | 23 | 4 | 156 |
| 16. | Texas | 6 | 4 | 3 | 0 | 3 | 2 | 1 | 23 | 9 | 143 |
| 17. | Arizona | 5 | 2 | 2 | 1 | 2 | 4 | 1 | 28 | 10 | 141 |
| 18. | Texas Tech | 5 | 4 | 4 | 0 | 1 | 4 | 1 | 23 | 3 | 138 |
| 19. | Clemson | **10** | 1 | 1 | 0 | 3 | 3 | 4 | 22 | 9 | 130 |
| 20. | Miami | 8 | 3 | 2 | 0 | 3 | 0 | 1 | 20 | 3 | 121 |
| 21. | Mississippi | 8 | 2 | 1 | 0 | 3 | 2 | 1 | 25 | 8 | 120 |
| 22. | Arizona State | 7 | 2 | 1 | 0 | 3 | 2 | 2 | 27 | 8 | 119 |
| 23. | Stanford | 7 | 4 | 0 | 0 | 1 | 4 | 1 | 28 | 6 | 116 |
| 24. | Oklahoma State | 8 | 3 | 1 | 0 | 2 | 2 | 3 | 16 | 4 | 113 |
| 25. | North Carolina State | 9 | 2 | 1 | 0 | 3 | 0 | 3 | 18 | 4 | 112 |

# SEC dominates new lower-scoring era

By **TEDDY CAHILL**

The 2010s wasted no time in announcing the dawn of a new decade—and new era in college baseball, one of Southern dominance and of lower scoring.

The Southeastern Conference's grip on the game began in 2009, when Louisiana State won the national title. It was the first time an SEC school had won the College World Series since LSU's last championship in 2000.

LSU's sixth national title foretold what was to come in the following decade, but it was South Carolina that would make it clear over the next three seasons. The Gamecocks won the 2010 national championship—their first in program history. They were back in the finals the following year and doubled up on their CWS title with a sweep of Florida. The Gamecocks made it to the finals again in 2012, becoming the first team to play for the title three years in a row since Texas in 1983-85. Arizona denied South Carolina a third straight title, but the Wildcats' championship was a rare interlude amid the South's success in Omaha.

South Carolina's success owed much to the duo of coach Ray Tanner and lefthander Michael Roth. Tanner built the Gamecocks into a power-house in his 16 years as head coach. Though he became South Carolina's athletic director following the 2012 season, his influence on the sport was felt through his presence on the Division I baseball committee. Roth finished his career as a two-time

## TOP 10 STORYLINES OF THE 2010s

**1** **NOW BATTING.** New BBCOR bat standards adopted for 2011 made bats play more like wood. It also sucked much of the offense out of the game, before a move to a baseball with lower seams in 2015.

**2** **NEW DIGS.** The home of the CWS moved from Rosenblatt Stadium to new TD Ameritrade Park in downtown Omaha in 2011.

**3** **LEVEL FIELD.** Parity at the CWS reigned throughout the decade. Six programs won their first ever national championship, including five straight from 2013-17.

**4** **ROOM FOR ALL.** The level playing field helped mid-major programs Coastal Carolina, Kent State and Stony Brook reach the CWS.

**5** **CALL IN A COMEBACK.** Indiana in 2013 became the first Big Ten Conference team to reach the CWS since 1984, and Michigan in 2019 became the first Big Ten team to play for the national championship since 1966

**6** **ALL-TIMER.** Louisville lefthander/first baseman Brendan McKay became the third player ever to be a three-time first-team All-American and the first to do so in 30 years

**7** **FOND FAREWELL.** Revered coaches such as Augie Garrido, Mike Gillespie, Wayne Graham, Mark Marquess and Jim Morris retired. Mike Martin, who retired following the 2019 season, became the first coach to win 2,000 games

**8** **CONFERENCE REALIGNMENT.** Louisville and Texas Christian were two of the winners, as they positioned themselves in the top tier of the ACC and Big 12 Conference

**9** **BUILDING BOOM.** Mississippi State's new Dudy Nobel Field, which cost $68 million, headlined ballpark boom, but programs as varied as Boston College, Coastal Carolina, Jacksonville State and Purdue all joined in.

**10** **POWER SURGE.** In the midst of a dead ball era, Kris Bryant slugged 31 home runs in 2013, the highest single-season total of the 2010s.

national champion and with a place in Omaha lore. He holds the record for CWS innings (60.1) and was one of the best pitchers in program history, going 26-6, 1.91 in four years.

LSU and South Carolina set the stage for the 2010s to be the SEC's decade. Beginning with LSU's title in 2009, the conference won six national championships and placed at least one team in the CWS finals in every year but 2016. Four different teams from the SEC won at least one title—Florida (2017), LSU (2009), South Carolina (2010, 2011) and Vanderbilt (2014, 2019)—while Arkansas (2018) and Mississippi State (2013) played for a title. Three times the conference placed a record 10 teams in the NCAA Tournament, a total that has only been matched once by any other conference.

And when the SEC wasn't dogpiling in Omaha, another team from the South typically was. Virginia won its first national championship in 2015—beating Vanderbilt—to end the Atlantic Coast Conference's title drought that began after Wake Forest won the CWS in 1955. Coastal Carolina followed with a title the following year, the lone time in the 2010s a team outside the Power Five conferences even made the CWS finals.

At no time was this more apparent than in 2016, when no regional was hosted west of Texas or north of the Ohio River. It was the first time the West Coast had been shut out of hosting regionals since 1994.

Still, the Pacific-12 Conference was a factor all decade long. Arizona won the 2012 title and fell a game short of another in 2016. After its initial disappointment, UCLA won the 2013 CWS and Oregon State returned to the pinnacle of the sport in 2018. The Beavers also authored an incredible 2017 season that saw them go 56-6 and finish with the fourth highest winning percentage in Division I history. A Pac-12 team was the No. 1 overall seed in the tournament five times, but on the biggest stage, the conference was largely unable to overcome the SEC's powerful pitching staffs.

Meanwhile, the Big 12 and Big West conferences receded from the top tier. Texas, which had played for the national championship four times in the 2000s, won just three games in three trips to Omaha in the 2010s. Cal State Fullerton, the Big West standard bearer, went winless in two trips to Omaha.

# ALL-AMERICA TEAM OF THE DECADE

| Pos, Player, School | Summary |
|---|---|
| C Adley Rutschman, Ore. State | The 2010 POY ably handled the Beavers' premium pitching staff for 3 years |
| 1B Andrew Vaughn, California | All-around hitter batted .377/.495/.695 with 50 HR during three years at Cal |
| 2B Nick Madrigal, Oregon State | Hit .361 in 3 years as one of Beavers' leaders, culminating in 2018 national title |
| 3B Kris Bryant, San Diego | Prolific power hitter hit 31 HR in 2013 POY season, a total unmatched in 2010s |
| SS Dansby Swanson, Vanderbilt | The 2014 CWS Most Outstanding Player was leader on back-to-back CWS finalists |
| OF Seth Beer, Clemson | After enrolling a semester early, went on to hit 56 HR and hit .321/.489/.648 |
| OF Jake Mangum, Miss. State | In 4-year career set SEC record for hits (383) and finished fourth all time |
| OF George Springer, Connecticut | Power-speed threat hit .348/.469/.653 with 46 HR and 76 SB |
| DH Anthony Rendon, Rice | One of most respected hitters in the country and the 2010 POY as a Soph |
| UT Brendan McKay, Louisville | First in 30 years (and third ever) to be first-team All-America for 3 straight years |
| SP Trevor Bauer, UCLA | Enrolled a semester early, went 34-8, 2.36 with 460 SO in 372 IP; won 2011 POY |
| SP Tom Eshelman, C.S. Fullerton | Ultimate control artist walked just 18 batters in 375 IP and went 28-11, 1.65 |
| SP Danny Hultzen, Virginia | Went 32-5, 2.08 with 395 SO in 319 IP to lead UVa to first two CWS trips |
| SP Aaron Nola, Louisiana State | Went 30-6, 2.09 with 345/52 SO/BB in 331 IP while pitching for hometown Tigers |
| RP David Berg, UCLA | Perhaps the best reliever in college history; went 22-6, 1.11 with a record 49 SV |

All that left the door open for the SEC to take control of the sport at a time when the conference was beginning to invest more heavily in the sport. Over the course of the decade, half the SEC would build new stadiums or renovate existing facilities. Coaching salaries also jumped over the course of the decade, with four schools pushing their coach's salary over $1 million by 2019.

Ultimately, it was Florida and Vanderbilt that truly defined the decade. Tim Corbin and Kevin O'Sullivan, who both coached under Jack Leggett at Clemson at the turn of the century, built two of the best player development pipelines in the sport and turned their programs into the models for success. Vanderbilt twice won the CWS and played for a third, and Corbin was named Coach of the Year in 2014. Florida won its first national championship in program history in 2017, and O'Sullivan was named Coach of the Year in 2011, when his Gators first played for the national championship.

The Gators were the most consistent program of the decade. They reached Omaha seven times, including a four-year streak from 2015-18.

The difference in resumes between Florida and Vanderbilt raises the question of which is the more significant accomplishment: getting to the CWS on a near annual basis or winning two national championships? Regardless, Florida and Vanderbilt stand as the 1A and 1B of the 2010s, twin pillars of success unmatched by anyone else.

The start of the new decade also ushered in a new era in Omaha. After 60 years as home of the CWS, Rosenblatt Stadium hosted the event for the final time in 2010. The tournament had grown significantly over the last 20 years, and the old ballpark on the hill was no longer able to accommodate the crowds and modern necessities of the game.

Omaha agreed to build a new ballpark downtown and the NCAA agreed to a 25-year contract to keep the CWS in the city through 2035. TD Ameritrade Park opened in 2011 and cost $131 million to construct. The opening of TD Ameritrade coincided with college baseball moving to the BBCOR bat standard, meant to deaden trampoline effect of metal bats and make them play more like wood bats. The change certainly took the charge out of the bats. While the new park had the same dimensions as Rosenblatt, it was situated differently and the prevailing wind typically blows in, instead of out, as it had at the old park. The combination of that and the new bats meant that scoring plummeted during the CWS. In 2011, the eight teams combined for a 2.66 ERA, the lowest of any CWS since 1973, the last year of the wood bat era. There were just nine home runs hit during the CWS and the teams combined for a .239 batting average, both the lowest since 1974.

The dip in offense would not be a one-year aberration. Offense around college baseball continued to stagnate until 2015, when the NCAA switched to a lower-seam baseball. The more aerodynamic ball flew farther and home runs and scoring increased across the sport. While some observers called for the fences at TD Ameritrade Park to be moved in, by the end of the decade, CWS games had become more open and the ballpark was playing more fairly than it originally did, bringing the home run back into play. ∎

## TEAM OF THE DECADE

**2019 Vanderbilt**

The Commodores made the most of their four trips to Omaha in the 2010s, three times playing for the national championship and winning a pair of titles. Their 2019 team was the best team of the decade and, perhaps, the 21st century. That team won a Southeastern Conference record 59 games and became the first team in two decades to win the national championship after it was ranked No. 1 in the preseason Top 25.

**2010**

South Carolina's Whit Merrifield celebrates after hitting the walk-off single in the 11th inning that brought the Gamecocks their first national title.

# South Carolina exhibits Palmetto pride

By **AARON FITT**

Ray Tanner stood by himself, a few paces off the dirt surrounding home plate, where his players were being introduced one by one.

He looked around, trying to process what he was seeing, trying to catch his breath. He shook his head.

"It's beautiful, isn't it?" he said. "Just a blue-collar team . . ."

Tanner's blue-collar team will be remembered as the final College World Series champion in Rosenblatt Stadium history. South Carolina won its first national title in dramatic fashion. Whit Merrifield's walk-off RBI single in the 11th gave the Gamecocks a thrilling 2-1 win against UCLA. It was the first CWS-ending walk-off hit since 2000.

**FROM THE ISSUE:**
JULY 26–AUG. 8, 2010

"This is what everyone dreams about. This," Merrifield said, nodding toward the celebration continuing on the field around him. "It hasn't sunk in yet what actually just happened. Growing up as a little kid, you dream about getting the big hit to win the World Series. I just can't believe that happened."

It was a storybook ending for the Gamecocks and for Rosenblatt Stadium, which hosted its 61st and final College World Series. The final CWS game in the venerable ballpark was a classic.

"The game was special," UCLA coach John Savage said. "The game was as good as it gets at this level . . . A national championship's supposed to be played like that."

In college baseball's modern 64-team tournament era, which dates back to 1999, only one team—Oregon State in 2006—had run through the losers' bracket to win the CWS. It's not easy to do, and heroic performances are required to pull it off. South Carolina's magical ride was chock full of heroes.

There was Michael Roth, the lefthanded specialist who threw a complete-game three-hitter in his first start of the season in the CWS bracket finals against Clemson. Roth threw 108 pitches in that one, then came back on three days' rest and gave South Carolina five strong innings in the clincher against UCLA.

## TOP TEAMS
### 2010 COLLEGE WORLD SERIES STANDINGS

| School | Conference | Record | CWS | Head Coach |
|--------|-----------|--------|-----|-----------|
| South Carolina | Southeastern | 54–16 | 6–1 | Ray Tanner |
| UCLA | Pacific-10 | 51–17 | 3–3 | John Savage |
| Texas Christian | Mountain West | 54–14 | 3–2 | Jim Schlossnagle |
| Clemson | Atlantic Coast | 45–25 | 2–2 | Jack Leggett |
| Florida State | Atlantic Coast | 48–20 | 1–2 | Mike Martin |
| Oklahoma | Big 12 | 50–18 | 1–2 | Sunny Golloway |
| Arizona State | Pacific-10 | 51–10 | 0–2 | Tim Esmay |
| Florida | Southeastern | 47–17 | 0–2 | Kevin O'Sullivan |

### NATIONAL CHAMPION
### SOUTH CAROLINA

In the final CWS played at Rosenblatt, South Carolina claimed its first national title by sweeping UCLA in the championship series. Whit Merrifield struck the 11th-inning single in Game 2 to give the Gamecocks the walk-off win.

"I was planning on going nine innings again," quipped Roth, a relative unknown who turned into a CWS media darling. "You know, never would I have ever thought that I was going to start a game here in Omaha. But it's been great."

There was closer Matt Price, the flame-throwing redshirt freshman righthander who threw 130 pitches over three dominating relief outings earlier in the CWS. Three days after he worked 2.1 strong innings to earn the win against Clemson that propelled the Gamecocks to the finals, Price worked 2.2 scoreless innings to earn the final win against the Bruins, allowing one hit and a walk while striking out three. Price went 2-0, 0.93 with 15 strikeouts and one walk in 9.2 innings over 10 appearances in Omaha.

"Matt Price and the entire bullpen have been very special for us the entire year, and toward the latter part, he's been sort of the guy that we get on his back there at the end and say, 'Either keep us alive or win it for us or save it for us,' " Tanner said.

There was Blake Cooper, who carried a one-hit shutout into the ninth inning in the CWS finals opener on Monday—in his second consecutive start on three days' rest.

There was Jackie Bradley Jr., the CWS Most Outstanding Player, who kept South Carolina's season alive with a two-out, two-strike, game-tying RBI single in the 12th inning against Oklahoma in the Gamecocks' second elimination game.

There was Brady Thomas, who delivered the game-winning hit in that 12th inning against Oklahoma. Thomas came up big again in the finale against UCLA, delivering a pinch-hit single to lead off the eighth. Robert Beary pinch-ran for him and scored the tying run on an error by first baseman Dean Espy.

There was second baseman Scott Wingo, a defensive specialist who drew a walk to lead off the 11th, then advanced to second on a passed ball, advanced to third on Evan Marzilli's sacrifice bunt, then scored the winning run on Merrifield's single to right.

# 2010 NEWSMAKERS

**Rosenblatt Stadium**, home to the CWS since 1950, hosted the event for the final time. The stadium hosted all but the first three years of the event, making for a six-decade run that captured much of the sport's history. But as the CWS grew in attendance and TV ratings, Rosenblatt's shortcomings were magnified. The city of Omaha decided to build a new downtown ballpark, with the NCAA agreeing to a 25-year contract with the city to keep the CWS in Omaha through 2035.

Florida International shortstop **Garrett Wittles** produced a 56-game hitting streak to end the season, leaving him just two games shy of the D-I record set by Oklahoma State's Robin Ventura in 1987. Wittles' streak came to an end on Opening Day in 2011, when he went 0-for-4 against Southeastern Louisiana.

**Texas Christian** was one of the more upwardly mobile programs of the 2000s, and it broke through to make its first-ever CWS appearance in 2010, beating blue-blood Texas in super regionals. It would be the first of five trips to Omaha in the decade for the Horned Frogs, who took their place as a national power under coach Jim Schlossnagle.

**FINAL TOP 25 FOR 2010**

1. South Carolina*
2. UCLA*
3. Texas Christian*
4. Arizona State*
5. Oklahoma*
6. Florida State*
7. Florida*
8. Virginia
9. #Texas
10. Clemson*
11. Cal State Fullerton
12. Coastal Carolina
13. Arkansas
14. Vanderbilt
15. Miami
16. Alabama
17. Louisville
18. Georgia Tech
19. Auburn
20. Virginia Tech
21. Rice
22. UC Irvine
23. Texas A&M
24. Washington State
25. Oregon

* Reached College World Series
# Preseason No. 1

# IN RETROSPECT: 2010 DRAFT

### Top 10 Draft Picks From College
With overall selection number (Ov), drafting team (Team) and rank on Baseball America draft board (BA).

| Player | Pos | School | Ov | Team | BA |
|---|---|---|---|---|---|
| Christian Colon | SS | Cal State Fullerton | 4 | Royals | 9 |
| Drew Pomeranz | LHP | Mississippi | 5 | Indians | 4 |
| Barret Loux* | RHP | Texas A&M | 6 | D-backs | 35 |
| Matt Harvey | RHP | North Carolina | 7 | Mets | 20 |
| Michael Choice | OF | Texas-Arlington | 10 | Athletics | 11 |
| Deck McGuire | RHP | Georgia Tech | 11 | Blue Jays | 7 |
| Yasmani Grandal | C | Miami | 12 | Reds | 13 |
| Chris Sale | LHP | Florida Gulf Coast | 13 | White Sox | 5 |
| Hayden Simpson | RHP | Southern Arkansas | 16 | Cubs | 191 |
| Kolbrin Vitek | 2B | Ball State | 20 | Red Sox | 25 |

\* Did not sign

### Top 10 Major League Players From College Draft Class
With draft round and Baseball-Reference.com total for wins above replacement (WAR) through 2019.

| Player | Pos | School | Rd | Ov | Team | WAR |
|---|---|---|---|---|---|---|
| Chris Sale | LHP | Florida Gulf Coast | 1 | 13 | White Sox | 45.3 |
| Jacob deGrom | RHP | Stetson | 9 | 272 | Mets | 34.9 |
| Adam Eaton | OF | Miami (Ohio) | 19 | 571 | D-backs | 19.0 |
| Yasmani Grandal | C | Miami | 1 | 12 | Reds | 16.1 |
| Kole Calhoun | OF | Arizona State | 8 | 264 | Angels | 15.9 |
| Whit Merrifield | 2B | South Carolina | 9 | 269 | Royals | 15.1 |
| Drew Pomeranz | LHP | Mississippi | 1 | 5 | Indians | 10.8 |
| Jedd Gyorko | 2B | West Virginia | 2 | 59 | Padres | 10.4 |
| Matt Harvey | RHP | North Carolina | 1 | 7 | Mets | 10.3 |
| Drew Smyly | LHP | Arkansas | 2 | 68 | Tigers | 9.2 |

There was Bayler Teal, the avid 7-year-old Gamecocks fan who lost his two-year battle with cancer during the CWS. The Gamecocks had visited him in the hospital, and in March he threw out the first pitch of a game in Columbia. The team dedicated its CWS run to Teal, even writing his initials on their hats.

Teal's favorite player was Merrifield—the man who delivered the final indelible image in the rich history of Rosenblatt Stadium.

Fans had been waiting for that moment since the ninth inning, when the stadium was illuminated with flashbulbs. Every pitch had a chance to be the last at Rosenblatt.

"You don't notice it until you're in the dugout," Merrifield said of the flashbulbs. "I came back in and guys were like, 'Did you not get blinded up there?' I looked around and saw all the flashbulbs going off. It's unbelievable."

Merrifield gave Rosenblatt the picture-perfect ending all those fans were dreaming of. And he gave Rosenblatt the ideal champion for its last hurrah—a gritty, blue-collar bunch that lost its CWS opener to Oklahoma and went on to become the first team in history to win six straight games in a single College World Series.

"I was sitting out by the third base line for opening ceremonies with the other teams thinking, 'What a venue, what an atmosphere, what a history,' " Tanner said. "And it dawned on me—it would be wonderful to go deep into this thing and be around at the end. And to be able to survive and win the last game is really incredible.

"I know the new stadium will be very special and a great facility. But this is history. And we'll be a part of the College World Series and Rosenblatt for a long, long time.

"It's an incredible journey and an incredible ending." ∎

# Rice's Rendon stands a cut above

By **AARON FITT**

For the first time in a decade, the College Player of the Year is an under-classman. In the 30-year history of the award, underclassmen won just three times before this year, and all three were special talents who went on to long, successful big league careers: sophomores Robin Ventura of Oklahoma State (1987), John Olerud of Washington State (1988) and Mark Teixeira of Georgia Tech (2000).

Rice sophomore third baseman Anthony Rendon fits the same mold. The early favorite to be drafted No. 1 overall in 2011, Rendon put up numbers that match his prodigious talent, hitting .394/.530/.801 with 26 home runs and 85 RBIs. That power output is even more impressive given how seldom he got good pitches to hit, as evidenced by his 65 walks and 22 strikeouts in 226 at-bats. If that weren't enough, Rendon also stole 14 bases in 18 tries and posted a .973 fielding percentage at the hot corner, where he committed just five errors all season.

Anthony Rendon was the fourth sophomore to win Player of the Year. He hit just six homers as a junior in 2011 and fell to the sixth pick, but he has been an unassuming star in seven big league seasons.

### Rice coach Wayne Graham:

"I think you get a little comfortable sometimes with how good a guy is; you expect him to do it every time. He does some phenomenal things. The thing that in my mind stood out is this year, defensively, he was absolutely wonderful. He had five errors the whole year, and that doesn't tell the whole story—he made a lot of sensational plays. And the bat is obvious.

"I remember the first time he hit on our field. I'd seen him hit a little in high school and knew he could hit. He started the second round of batting practice, I said to our coaches, 'You want to see Hank Aaron's wrists? There they are.' I said, 'Don't mess with him.' And we haven't. Him and Teixeira are the two best hitters I've seen in college base-ball. (Lance) Berkman is right up there, too, but the bat was different in those days."

### East Carolina coach Billy Godwin:

"He's a baseball player, No. 1. If you look at him, you're not going to be overwhelmingly impressed physically, but he plays the game with as much feel as anybody I've ever seen. Just his confidence at the plate . . . It's one thing to pitch around the guy and not let him beat you, but it's another for him to stand up there and take it. He could hack and go into a slump, but he doesn't do that, he takes what you give him.

"I don't think I've seen anybody better. What more would you want? He can play defense, he can hit, he's a good runner, he's instinctive. Yeah, I don't know what else you could look for in a player."

**Tulane coach Rick Jones:**

"As good as he is offensively, he's just as good defensively. You can't bunt on him, he can move laterally, and he can make throws going laterally with something on it—he's just got that body control. He can do things that big leaguers do; he's special."

**Anthony Rendon:**

"On a personal note, it's pretty crazy. I didn't think I'd be able to do it back-to-back years—even improve my numbers from last year. Last year, everything just clicked, and this year it felt like everything clicked again. I got in that groove and kept seeing the ball well the last month of the season. I know at one point earlier in the season, I dropped down to like .310 or something. I was really mad. That's the one thing I did want to do is hit at least .400; I don't care how many home runs or RBIs I have.

"I guess I learned a lot last year by being patient. I started putting up pretty good numbers at the beginning of the year last year. I knew going into this season I wasn't going to get as many pitches as I got last year. When I got the pitch, maybe one or two per at-bat, I had to make something happen. I just had to stay patient." ∎

# TOP PLAYERS OF 2010

## ALL-AMERICA TEAM

| Pos | Player | School | Yr | AVG | AB | R | H | HR | RBI | SB | BB | SO | OBP | SLG |
|-----|--------|--------|----|----|----|----|----|----|----|----|----|----|----|----|
| C | Yasmani Grandal | Miami | Jr | .401 | 222 | 56 | 89 | 15 | 60 | 1 | 57 | 35 | .527 | .721 |
| 1B | Hunter Morris | Auburn | Jr | .386 | 272 | 66 | 105 | 23 | 76 | 6 | 26 | 50 | .455 | .743 |
| 2B | Zack MacPhee | Arizona State | So | .394 | 221 | 66 | 87 | 9 | 64 | 19 | 40 | 38 | .491 | .679 |
| 3B | Anthony Rendon | Rice | So | .394 | 226 | 83 | 89 | 26 | 85 | 14 | 65 | 22 | .530 | .801 |
| SS | Christian Colon | Cal State Fullerton | Jr | .358 | 268 | 73 | 96 | 17 | 68 | 13 | 34 | 18 | .447 | .631 |
| OF | Jeremy Baltz | St. John's | Fr | .396 | 240 | 64 | 95 | 24 | 85 | 6 | 28 | 44 | .479 | .771 |
| OF | Michael Choice | Texas-Arlington | Jr | .383 | 196 | 67 | 75 | 16 | 59 | 12 | 76 | 54 | .568 | .704 |
| OF | Taylor Dugas | Alabama | So | .395 | 243 | 70 | 96 | 2 | 37 | 19 | 59 | 21 | .525 | .523 |
| DH | Chris Duffy | Central Florida | Sr | .447 | 206 | 54 | 92 | 21 | 81 | 3 | 33 | 35 | .539 | .850 |
| UT | Mike McGee | Florida State | Jr | .328 | 238 | 58 | 78 | 15 | 68 | 5 | 44 | 50 | .443 | .584 |

| Pos | Pitcher | School | Yr | W | L | ERA | G | SV | IP | H | BB | SO |
|-----|---------|--------|----|----|----|----|----|----|----|----|----|----|
| SP | Seth Blair | Arizona State | Jr | 12 | 0 | 3.35 | 17 | 0 | 102 | 105 | 24 | 104 |
| SP | Barret Loux | Texas A&M | Jr | 11 | 2 | 2.83 | 17 | 0 | 105 | 78 | 34 | 136 |
| SP | Drew Pomeranz | Mississippi | Jr | 9 | 2 | 2.24 | 16 | 0 | 101 | 71 | 49 | 139 |
| SP | Chris Sale | Florida Gulf Coast | Jr | 11 | 0 | 2.01 | 17 | 2 | 103 | 83 | 14 | 146 |
| RP | Chance Ruffin | Texas | Jr | 6 | 1 | 1.11 | 37 | 14 | 63 | 42 | 19 | 97 |
| UT | Mike McGee | Florida State | Jr | 4 | 0 | 1.37 | 18 | 12 | 26 | 11 | 16 | 33 |

## SECOND TEAM

**C**—Micah Gibbs, Louisiana State. **1B**—Ricky Oropesa, Southern California. **2B**—Ryan Wright, Louisville. **3B**—Garrett Buechele, Oklahoma. **SS**—Jedd Gyorko, West Virginia. **OF**—Gary Brown, Cal State Fullerton; Tyler Holt, Florida State; and Kyle Parker, Clemson. **DH**—Zack Cox, Arkansas. **UT**—Kolbrin Vitek, Ball State. **SP**—Trevor Bauer, UCLA; Danny Hultzen, Virginia; Taylor Jungmann, Texas; and Matt Purke, Texas Christian. **RP**—John Stilson, Texas A&M.

## THIRD TEAM

**C**—C.J. Cron, Utah. **1B**—Paul Hoilman, East Tennessee State. **2B**—Garrett Wittels, Florida International. **3B**—Phil Wunderlich, Louisville. **SS**—Derek Dietrich, Georgia Tech. **OF**—Alex Dickerson, Indiana; Rico Noel, Coastal Carolina; and Nate Roberts, High Point. **DH**—A.J. Kirby-Jones, Tennessee Tech. **UT**—Brett Eibner, Arkansas. **SP**—Kyle Blair, San Diego; Gerrit Cole, UCLA; Noe Ramirez, Cal State Fullerton; and Asher Wojciechowski, The Citadel. **RP**—Neil Holland, Louisville.

South Carolina players celebrate after winning their second straight College World Series championship, this one during the first year at new TD Ameritrade Park.

2011

# South Carolina follows formula to title repeat

By **AARON FITT**

For two years, South Carolina coach Ray Tanner has insisted his team is not "imposing" or "great" or "formidable" or—as he put in his final College World Series press conference of 2011—"awesome."

It's time to revise that position.

Maybe the Gamecocks don't score runs by the truckload or blast towering home runs. Maybe they win a lot of close games in the late innings and do it in improbable fashion. But when it comes to the business of winning, nobody is more imposing or great of formidable than South Carolina—which won its second consecutive national championship with a dominating 5-2 victory against Florida, sweeping the best-of-three CWS finals.

**FROM THE ISSUE:**
JULY 25–AUG. 7, 2011

"Our talent might not be a bunch of first-rounders," said South Carolina senior second baseman Scott Wingo, the CWS Most Outstanding Player. "But I think I'd play with these guys more than any other team. We don't give you one yard . . . and we're tough to beat."

So tough, in fact, that the Gamecocks haven't been beaten in their last 16 NCAA Tournament games, the longest postseason winning streak ever. They have not lost in the postseason since their first game at the 2010 CWS. They ran through the loser's bracket en route to a thrilling national title last year, then extended their CWS winning streak to a record 11 games with an unbeaten run to the 2011 title.

Wingo was a driving force behind his title run. He delivered a walk-off hit in South Carolina's CWS opener against Texas A&M, then provided a game-tying RBI single in the eighth inning of the finals opener. His sensational defense bailed out the Gamecocks over and over again—most notably in the first finals game against Florida, when he made two great plays to extract South Carolina from a bases-loaded, no-out jam in the ninth.

He came up huge again in the championship clincher, driving in South Carolina's first run with a sacrifice fly in the third inning against Karsten Whitson, helping key a three-run rally that put the Gamecocks in command. He added an RBI single over a drawn-in infield in the eighth to give the Gamecocks a three-run cushion.

"We wouldn't be here where we are today without that guy," South Carolina ace

## TOP TEAMS
### 2011 COLLEGE WORLD SERIES STANDINGS

| School | Conference | Record | CWS | Head Coach |
|---|---|---|---|---|
| South Carolina | Southeastern | 55–14 | 5–0 | Ray Tanner |
| Florida | Southeastern | 53–19 | 3–2 | Kevin O'Sullivan |
| Vanderbilt | Southeastern | 54–12 | 2–2 | Tim Corbin |
| Virginia | Atlantic Coast | 56–12 | 2–2 | Brian O'Connor |
| California | Pacific-10 | 38–23 | 1–2 | David Esquer |
| North Carolina | Atlantic Coast | 51–16 | 1–2 | Mike Fox |
| Texas | Big 12 | 49–19 | 0–2 | Augie Garrido |
| Texas A&M | Big 12 | 47–22 | 0–2 | Rob Childress |

## NATIONAL CHAMPION
### SOUTH CAROLINA

The CWS shifted to TD Ameritrade Park, but the champion remained the same.  Coach Ray Tanner guided South Carolina to a 5-0 record in Omaha. New BBCOR composite bats helped make this the lowest-scoring CWS in the event's aluminum bat era.

Michael Roth said of Wingo. "He's one of the most electric players on this team. I grew up playing with him, and that makes it that much more special. I can't imagine a better captain, a better second baseman. Whenever the ball's hit that way, I know he's got it."

Roth added to his own South Carolina legend, starting the CWS clincher on three days' rest for the second consecutive year. In 2010, it was just his second start of the season, and he earned a no-decision with five-innings of one-run ball. This time around, he was a first-team All-American making his third start of this CWS—and this time he earned the win, holding the Gators to two runs on five hits and two walks while striking out six.

"The thing coming into the season was the pitching staff—was it going to be good enough, was the starting rotation going to be good enough?" Roth said before the finals. "I think some of us had something to prove. And thus far I think we've done a good job."

Roth lowered his career College World Series ERA to 1.17 in 38.1 innings—the second-lowest all time among pitchers with at least 30 career innings. Only Ohio State's Steve Arlin (0.96 in 1965 and '66) has a lower ERA.

Matt Price's name is right there with Roth's. South Carolina's fearless closer appeared in all five of his team's CWS games, going 2-0, 0.00 with two saves in nine innings of work. He worked 1.1 perfect innings in the clincher, after working an inning in the first game the day before and 5.2 taxing innings two days earlier against Virginia.

The performance against the Cavaliers was an epic high-wire act. Virginia loaded the bases three times after the ninth inning—once with no outs—but failed to score a run. Price willed his way through a season-high 95-pitch outing. The two teams combined to go 3-for-25 with runners in scoring position and 0-for-21 with two outs.

The finals opener against Florida was similarly stressful. Tied 1-1 heading into the 11th, sophomore first baseman Christian Walker scored the winning run for South Carolina.

# 2011 NEWSMAKERS

The new **BBCOR bat standards** dramatically changed the complexion of the sport. The new standards were meant to make bats act more like wood and decrease the speed with which the ball came off the bat. As a result, runs dropped from 6.98 per game to 5.58, the first time scoring fell below six runs per game since 1977. Home runs were cut almost in half to 0.52 per game, their lowest level since 1975.

**TD Ameritrade Park**, which cost $131 million to build, opened April 19 with a game between Creighton and Nebraska. Nebraska won 2-1 in front of a crowd of 22,197, the largest regular season crowd of the year. The first CWS game in the ballpark was held June 18 between North Carolina and Vanderbilt. The Commodores went on to win 7-3.

**California** shocked the sport in September 2010 when it announced it would cut its 108-year-old program because of budget woes. Supporters fought to save the program, and it was reinstated in April after donors pledged $9 million. Undeterred, the Golden Bears produced a storybook run and reached the CWS for the first time since 1992.

## FINAL TOP 25 FOR 2011

1. South Carolina*
2. #Florida*
3. Virginia*
4. Vanderbilt*
5. North Carolina*
6. Texas*
7. Texas A&M*
8. Florida State
9. Arizona State
10. Oregon State
11. California*
12. Connecticut
13. Stanford
14. Cal State Fullerton
15. Rice
16. UC Irvine
17. Mississippi State
18. Dallas Baptist
19. Texas Christian
20. Georgia Tech
21. Clemson
22. UCLA
23. Miami
24. Arkansas
25. East Carolina

* Reached College World Series
# Preseason No. 1

# IN RETROSPECT: 2011 DRAFT

## Top 10 Draft Picks From College

With overall selection number (Ov), drafting team (Team) and rank on Baseball America draft board (BA).

| Player | Pos | School | Ov | Team | BA |
|---|---|---|---|---|---|
| Gerrit Cole | RHP | UCLA | 1 | Pirates | 3 |
| Danny Hultzen | LHP | Virginia | 2 | Mariners | 4 |
| Trevor Bauer | RHP | UCLA | 3 | D-backs | 5 |
| Anthony Rendon | 3B | Rice | 6 | Nationals | 1 |
| George Springer | OF | Connecticut | 11 | Astros | 11 |
| Taylor Jungmann | RHP | Texas | 12 | Brewers | 8 |
| Jed Bradley | LHP | Georgia Tech | 15 | Brewers | 14 |
| Chris Reed | LHP | Stanford | 16 | Dodgers | 60 |
| C.J. Cron | 1B | Utah | 17 | Angels | 26 |
| Sonny Gray | RHP | Vanderbilt | 18 | Athletics | 12 |

## Top 10 Major League Players From College Draft Class

With draft round and Baseball-Reference.com total for wins above replacement (WAR) through 2019.

| Player | Pos | School | Rd | Ov | Team | WAR |
|---|---|---|---|---|---|---|
| Anthony Rendon | 3B | Rice | 1 | 6 | Nationals | 27.3 |
| George Springer | OF | Connecticut | 1 | 11 | Astros | 24.6 |
| Gerrit Cole | RHP | UCLA | 1 | 1 | Pirates | 24.0 |
| Marcus Semien | SS | California | 6 | 201 | White Sox | 20.6 |
| Kyle Hendricks | RHP | Dartmouth | 8 | 264 | Rangers | 19.5 |
| Sonny Gray | RHP | Vanderbilt | 1 | 18 | Athletics | 18.3 |
| Trevor Bauer | RHP | UCLA | 1 | 3 | D-backs | 15.6 |
| Kolten Wong | 2B | Hawaii | 1 | 22 | Cardinals | 15.6 |
| Kevin Pillar | OF | Cal State Dom. Hills | 32 | 979 | Blue Jays | 15.6 |
| Jackie Bradley Jr. | OF | South Carolina | 1.5 | 40 | Red Sox | 15.0 |
| Travis Shaw | 3B | Kent State | 9 | 292 | Red Sox | 10.6 |

Just as the Gamecocks scored the winning run against UVA on back-to-back errors, they scored the winning run against Florida on back-to-back errors—on the same play.

After Walker hit a one-out single up the middle, he headed to second on a hit-and-run play, but Adam Matthews swung through the pitch. Catcher Mike Zunino's throw to second sailed into center field, so Walker bolted for third. And center fielder Bryson Smith's throw to third bounced in the dirt and out of play, allowing Walker to waltz home. Walker finished the game 2-for-5 with a double, a single and the game-winning run.

Price recorded the final three outs to save the 11-inning thriller. The next day, Price picked up a four-out save, getting pinch-hitter Ben McMahan to fly out to center field for the final out—setting off a dogpile around Price at the pitcher's mound.

"It's been phenomenal, the success that those guys have enjoyed," Tanner said of Roth and Price. "It's just like they've been almost unblemished. Ask me to bring up some days where they didn't do very well, I'd have to think long and hard, because it seems like every time the chips have been down, they've been able to perform."

In a CWS dominated by pitching, South Carolina's staff was the most dominant, posting a 0.88 ERA in five games, the fourth-lowest team ERA in CWS history and the lowest since 1972.

"We've really played some great baseball while we were here, and it's hard for me to understand it all right now," Tanner said. "I'll have to let it sink in a little bit . . .

"Our players, they've made it happen between the lines. They made plays. They made pitches. They got big hits. They always felt they had a chance to win. They believed."

And belief is a powerful thing. ∎

# Bauer transcends labels en route to POY

By **AARON FITT**

**A**fter a while, you run out of new ways to describe greatness.

When we shined the Golden Spikes spotlight on Trevor Bauer back on April 18, his dominance was already becoming old hat.

"That's kind of how it feels—the ho-hum part. It's like, 'Eh,'" Bauer said then, after he threw a complete-game, four-hit shutout of Arizona, striking out 13.

If you were expecting a different reaction after what turned out to be his final career start in the Los Angeles Regional, after Bauer struck out 14 Fresno State batters and allowed only a run on six hits in UCLA's 3-1 win, you were disappointed. Bauer does this every week—really. It was his ninth consecutive complete game, and his 14th double-digit strikeout game in 16 starts this spring. It improved him to 13-2, 1.25 on the season—tying him for the national lead in wins and moving him up to third in the

UCLA's Trevor Bauer went deep into starts and dominated with metronomic precision as a junior. As a pro, he vied for a Cy Young Award in 2018 and had gone 70-60, 4.04 record through eight seasons.

national ERA race—and cemented him as the College Player of the Year.

"The one thing Trevor is is very consistent," UCLA coach John Savage said. "He's the same guy in a lot of different situations—on the road, at home, in big games. I thought he was himself (against Fresno). That's what makes him so good. He wasn't anything spectacular beyond what he has been in the past. It was just Trevor being Trevor."

Trevor being Trevor meant Trevor blowing hitters away with a fastball that peaked repeatedly at 96 mph and sat 93-95 for all nine innings. It meant a hammer curveball in the 75-78 mph range, a putaway slider at 81-83 mph, a deceptive changeup and 84-85 mph, a "reverse slider" that runs away from lefties and even a couple of splitters.

"Right when you think the guy is going to crack or not pitch as well, he goes out and outdoes himself," Savage said. "He's as consistent as any guy I've ever been around, and he's as competitive a guy as I've ever been around. The guy just keeps coming at you and gets better as the game goes on."

In his final UCLA start against Fresno State, Bauer struck out the side in the fifth, seventh and eighth, and his final strikeout in the eighth broke the Pacific-10 Conference's single-season strikeout record. He surged past Tim Lincecum (199) and Mark Prior (202) on the list, finishing the season with 203, to go along with 36 walks in 137 innings.

Bauer is famously cerebral, of course, and it should be no surprise that he has a deep appreciation for the history of the game.

"There are certain achievements that are good, and they're a little surreal to me," Bauer said. "To get mentioned up there with the likes of Mark Prior and Tim Lincecum and Stephen Strasburg, with some of those stats, it's pretty cool."

In the preseason, Bauer confessed to harboring some apprehension that his unconventional training methods, unusual delivery and slight stature would negatively affect his draft stock. Two days after his final college start—and a day after UC Irvine ended UCLA's season in regionals—Bauer became the No. 3 overall pick in the draft by the D-backs.

"It's extremely satisfying," he said on draft day. "It's a credit to all the hard work I've put in over the years—all the hours of prep, video analysis, conditioning on days you don't really want to be conditioning. And it's a credit to the D-backs organization as well that they're willing to sit down and talk to me about why I do the things I do, and understand more about it.

"Today is a very individual day, and yesterday was a team day. I wish today was another team day. But sometimes there's room for personal accomplishment and celebration of that, and I think today is that day."

More than any other player in college baseball, Bauer has earned the right to be excited—finally—about what he has accomplished. ■

# TOP PLAYERS OF 2011

## ALL-AMERICA TEAM

| Pos | Player | School | Yr | AVG | AB | R | H | HR | RBI | SB | BB | SO | OBP | SLG |
|-----|--------|--------|----|-----|----|----|----|----|-----|----|----|----|-----|-----|
| C | Mike Zunino | Florida | So | .371 | 264 | 75 | 98 | 19 | 67 | 7 | 32 | 52 | .442 | .674 |
| 1B | C.J. Cron | Utah | Jr | .434 | 198 | 51 | 86 | 15 | 59 | 1 | 31 | 21 | .517 | .803 |
| 2B | Kolten Wong | Hawaii | Jr | .378 | 209 | 48 | 79 | 7 | 53 | 23 | 42 | 20 | .492 | .560 |
| 3B | Colin Moran | North Carolina | Fr | .335 | 248 | 46 | 83 | 9 | 71 | 2 | 47 | 33 | .442 | .540 |
| SS | Brad Miller | Clemson | Jr | .395 | 195 | 53 | 77 | 5 | 50 | 21 | 40 | 34 | .498 | .559 |
| OF | Jason Krizan | Dallas Baptist | Jr | .413 | 247 | 63 | 102 | 10 | 81 | 13 | 42 | 23 | .498 | .700 |
| OF | Mikie Mahtook | Louisiana State | Jr | .383 | 196 | 61 | 75 | 14 | 56 | 29 | 41 | 32 | .496 | .709 |
| OF | Victor Roache | Georgia Southern | So | .326 | 230 | 58 | 75 | 30 | 84 | 3 | 37 | 42 | .438 | .778 |
| DH | Jake Lowery | James Madison | Jr | .359 | 251 | 80 | 90 | 24 | 91 | 9 | 38 | 47 | .442 | .797 |
| UT | Danny Hultzen | Virginia | Jr | .309 | 136 | 18 | 42 | 1 | 35 | 6 | 18 | 12 | .396 | .441 |

| Pos | Pitcher | School | Yr | W | L | ERA | G | SV | IP | H | BB | SO |
|-----|---------|--------|----|----|----|-----|----|----|----|----|----|----|
| SP | Trevor Bauer | UCLA | Jr | 13 | 2 | 1.25 | 16 | 0 | 137 | 73 | 36 | 203 |
| SP | Sean Gilmartin | Florida State | Jr | 12 | 2 | 2.09 | 18 | 0 | 120 | 92 | 21 | 130 |
| SP | Taylor Jungmann | Texas | Jr | 13 | 3 | 1.60 | 19 | 0 | 141 | 81 | 36 | 126 |
| SP | Michael Roth | South Carolina | Jr | 14 | 3 | 1.06 | 20 | 0 | 145 | 108 | 41 | 112 |
| RP | Cody Martin | Gonzaga | Sr | 2 | 1 | 0.86 | 25 | 12 | 52 | 30 | 19 | 63 |
| UT | Danny Hultzen | Virginia | Jr | 12 | 3 | 1.37 | 18 | 0 | 118 | 76 | 23 | 165 |

## SECOND TEAM

C—Nick Rickles, Stetson. 1B—Aaron Westlake, Vanderbilt. 2B—Tommy La Stella, Coastal Carolina. 3B—Jason Esposito, Vanderbilt. SS—Joe Panik, St. John's. OF—Trever Adams, Creighton; Bryson Myles, Stephen F. Austin; and George Springer, Connecticut. DH—Adam Brett Walker, Jacksonville. UT—Nick Ramirez, Cal State Fullerton. SP—Matt Barnes, Connecticut; Grayson Garvin, Vanderbilt; Sam Gaviglio, Oregon State; and Sonny Gray, Vanderbilt. RP—Corey Knebel, Texas.

## THIRD TEAM

C—Tyler Ogle, Oklahoma. 1B—Christian Walker, South Carolina. 2B—Dan Paolini, Siena. 3B—Matt Leeds, College of Charleston. SS—Chad Zurcher, Memphis. OF—Daniel Aldrich, College of Charleston; James Ramsey, Florida State; and Dusty Robinson, Fresno State. DH—Joey DeMichele, Arizona State. UT—Bo Reeder, East Tennessee State. SP—Greg Gonzalez, Fresno State; Mark Pope, Georgia Tech; Matt Summers, UC Irvine; and Michael Wacha, Texas A&M. RP—Matt Price, South Carolina.

Arizona's Robert Refsnyder poses with the national championship trophy after the Wildcats spoiled South Carolina's bid to three-peat in Omaha.

**2012**

# Athletic Wildcats end Gamecocks' CWS reign

By **AARON FITT**

A s two of Arizona's great leaders, Alex Mejia and Robert Refsnyder, posed together for a postgame photo, Mejia grinned at the photographer and shook his head.

"Brandon Dixon—that's all you need to say," Mejia blurted. "Brandon Dixon! He saved us all."

Arizona's core veterans—led by Mejia, Refsnyder, Kurt Heyer and Konner Wade—might have carried the Wildcats to the College World Series finals, but unlikely heroes such as Dixon led them to a 4-1 win against South Carolina, clinching the fourth national championship in school history, the first since 1986.

Dixon, a sophomore first baseman, entered the game as a defensive replacement in the sixth inning, when the Wildcats led 1-0. The Gamecocks tied the game in the seventh, and the score remained 1-1 until the ninth, when Dixon doubled down the left field line against South Carolina closer Matt Price—the all-time wins leader at the CWS.

"Oh, ye of little faith—I was going to pinch-hit for him," Arizona coach Andy Lopez said of Dixon's ninth-inning at-bat. "I was going to pinch-hit for him, and coach (Matt) Siegel looked at me and shook his head no. OK, I'll go with the guy's gut. Please forgive me, Brandon—but he obviously came through."

Dixon's double put runners at second and third with one out and knocked Price out of the game. Two batters later, another less-heralded Wildcat provided crucial insurance. Freshman second baseman Trent Gilbert, the No. 9 hitter, lined a two-run single into right field against Tyler Webb to give Arizona its final margin of victory.

"I think it's no secret the juniors, they're the main contributors throughout the season," said Gilbert, a slick defender who carried a .268 average into the final game, but had come up with his share of big hits in the postseason. "But I mean, with me and some of the other younger guys, I think we feel just as confident in those situations."

James Farris was the big story on the mound for Arizona in the finale, and though he was a weekend starter all season long, he still qualified as an unlikely hero. The right-

**FROM THE ISSUE:**
JULY 24–AUG. 7, 2012

## TOP TEAMS
### 2012 COLLEGE WORLD SERIES STANDINGS

| School | Conference | Record | CWS | Head Coach |
|---|---|---|---|---|
| Arizona | Pacific-12 | 48–17 | 5–0 | Andy Lopez |
| South Carolina | Southeastern | 49–20 | 4–3 | Ray Tanner |
| Arkansas | Southeastern | 46–22 | 2–2 | Dave Van Horn |
| Florida State | Atlantic Coast | 50–17 | 2–2 | Mike Martin |
| Kent State | Mid-American | 47–20 | 1–2 | Scott Stricklin |
| UCLA | Pacific-12 | 48–16 | 1–2 | John Savage |
| Florida | Southeastern | 47–20 | 0–2 | Kevin O'Sullivan |
| Stony Brook | America East | 52–15 | 0–2 | Matt Senk |

### NATIONAL CHAMPION
### ARIZONA

The Wildcats went 10-0 in the postseason to claim their fourth national championship, while Andy Lopez joined Augie Garrido as the only coaches to win CWS titles with two different programs. Lopez previously won with Pepperdine in 1992.

hander threw only one inning as a freshman last year and entered 2012 with a career ERA of 36.00. He had a solid sophomore year, going 7–3, 4.18 in 99 innings, but his last appearance before the CWS finals came 22 days earlier in regionals.

The Wildcats hadn't needed Farris since they won their super regional in two games and their CWS bracket in three, bringing junior righthander Kurt Heyer back on five days' rest to win the bracket clincher against Florida State.

Lopez had debated bringing Heyer back again on three days' rest to start the second game of the finals, especially because South Carolina was planning to start lefthander Michael Roth—whom Lopez later called "a legend." Eventually, he decided it was wiser to get Heyer an extra day of rest for a potential third game. Lopez reasoned that Farris' bullpen sessions would have him ready to go, but he admitted that doubts lingered.

"Against Michael Roth—against Michael Roth," Lopez said, shaking his head. "Listen: someone's going to get mad at me, so go ahead and get mad at me. When I woke up this morning, I went, 'Farris against Roth. We're probably going to be playing (Game 3).' "

"Nothing against James Farris. I've just watched Michael Roth in the postseason and conference games when I get a chance to watch some TV . . . He's just a lefthander with the presence, and knows how to pitch and all the rest. So I was really hoping that Farris would match up with him until we could possibly score a run or two."

The Wildcats did scratch out a run against Roth in the third, and again it was freshmen doing the heavy lifting. Freshman first baseman Joseph Maggi led off the third with a double to left, ending a streak of 28 consecutive batters retired by Roth, dating back to his start against Kent State three days prior. The next batter, freshman Riley Moore, bunted Maggi to third, and Gilbert drove him in with a ground out to second.

That was all the scoring Arizona would do against Roth, who left the mound for the

# 2012 NEWSMAKERS

**Kent State** and **Stony Brook** both advanced to the CWS, giving the 2012 edition two compelling underdog stories. Kent State won the Gary, Ind., Regional, beating Big Ten Conference champion Purdue, before winning a super regional at Oregon. Stony Brook won a regional at Miami before stunning Louisiana State at Alex Box Stadium to advance to Omaha. Their successes gave hope to small Northern programs.

Florida righthander **Jonathon Crawford** threw a no-hitter in a 4-0 victory against Bethune-Cookman in regionals. It was the first no-hitter during the NCAA Tournament since 1991 and just the seventh ever.

**Utah Valley** put together one of the best winning streaks in college baseball history, running off 32 straight wins over 54 days. The Wolverines' streak ended two wins shy of matching the all-time record held by Texas (1977) and Florida Atlantic (1999) and is tied for third all time with Arizona State (1972) and Fresno State (1988). After a loss to Utah snapped the streak, Utah Valley ran off eight more wins to finish the season with 40 wins in its last 41 games.

| FINAL TOP 25 FOR 2012 |
| --- |
| 1. Arizona* |
| 2. South Carolina* |
| 3. #Florida* |
| 4. Florida State* |
| 5. UCLA* |
| 6. Arkansas* |
| 7. Stony Brook* |
| 8. Kent State* |
| 9. Louisiana State |
| 10. Baylor |
| 11. Oregon |
| 12. North Carolina State |
| 13. Stanford |
| 14. Oklahoma |
| 15. St. John's |
| 16. Texas Christian |
| 17. North Carolina |
| 18. Rice |
| 19. Texas A&M |
| 20. Kentucky |
| 21. Cal State Fullerton |
| 22. Mississippi State |
| 23. Purdue |
| 24. Oregon State |
| 25. Virginia |
| * Reached College World Series |
| # Preseason No. 1 |

# IN RETROSPECT: 2012 DRAFT

### Top 10 Draft Picks From College
With overall selection number (Ov), drafting team (Team) and rank on Baseball America draft board (BA).

| Player | Pos | School | Ov | Team | BA |
|---|---|---|---|---|---|
| Mike Zunino | C | Florida | 3 | Mariners | 2 |
| Kevin Gausman | RHP | Louisiana State | 4 | Orioles | 5 |
| Kyle Zimmer | RHP | San Francisco | 5 | Royals | 3 |
| Mark Appel* | RHP | Stanford | 8 | Pirates | 4 |
| Andrew Heaney | LHP | Oklahoma State | 9 | Marlins | 17 |
| Tyler Naquin | OF | Texas A&M | 15 | Indians | 25 |
| Michael Wacha | RHP | Texas A&M | 19 | Cardinals | 8 |
| Chris Stratton | RHP | Mississippi State | 20 | Giants | 18 |
| Marcus Stroman | RHP | Duke | 22 | Blue Jays | 10 |
| James Ramsey | OF | Florida State | 23 | Cardinals | 51 |

\* Did not sign

### Top 10 Major League Players From College Draft Class
With draft round and Baseball-Reference.com total for wins above replacement (WAR) through 2019.

| Player | Pos | School | Rd | Ov | Team | WAR |
|---|---|---|---|---|---|---|
| Marcus Stroman | RHP | Duke | 1 | 22 | Blue Jays | 14.6 |
| Chris Taylor | SS | Virginia | 5 | 161 | Mariners | 11.9 |
| Alex Wood | LHP | Georgia | 2 | 85 | Braves | 11.4 |
| Mitch Haniger | OF | Cal Poly | 1s | 38 | Brewers | 10.7 |
| Kevin Gausman | RHP | Louisiana State | 1 | 4 | Orioles | 10.2 |
| Max Muncy | 1B | Baylor | 5 | 169 | Athletics | 9.7 |
| Matt Duffy | 3B | Long Beach State | 18 | 568 | Giants | 8.9 |
| Stephen Piscotty | OF | Stanford | 1s | 36 | Cardinals | 8.1 |
| Michael Wacha | RHP | Texas A&M | 1 | 19 | Cardinals | 7.4 |
| Mike Zunino | C | Florida | 1 | 3 | Mariners | 7.0 |
| Devon Travis | 2B | Florida State | 13 | 424 | Tigers | 6.6 |

final time in his brilliant career to a standing ovation with two outs in the seventh.

But Farris more than matched Roth, holding the Gamecocks scoreless on one hit through the first six innings. They manufactured a run in the seventh, and Farris wound up taking a no-decision, but the Wildcats could not have asked for more from Farris, who allowed just two hits and two walks while striking out four over 7.2 innings.

"It was exactly what this program needed, and it was exactly what I'd hoped he would do. I'm really happy for him," Lopez said.

"Two or three days ago, I pointed out Farris, brought him in front of the group and I said, 'This guy's been passed over twice in the postseason, and he's ready to pitch. He'll get a chance to pitch here before everything's said and done.' And he was pretty marvelous."

A night earlier, Lopez had asked his two veteran leaders—Mejia and Refsnyder— who they thought he should start. Neither of them hesitated: Farris, they said.

"Because I know how hard Farris has worked," explained Refsnyder, who won CWS Most Outstanding Player honors by hitting .476/.542/.762 with two homers and five RBIs.

"Farris, honestly, a lot of people thought he wasn't going to be back in the program (this season). He didn't really have the maturity and poise a lot of people look for. But when he came back, he was determined. He started lifting with Kurt, and really motivated himself.

"I didn't hesitate because I knew Farris would be ready. I knew how hard he's worked."

So maybe Farris and the rest were unlikely heroes to the world.

But the men in the Arizona dugout believed in them. ■

# Zunino's all-around ability draws accolades

By **AARON FITT**

**F**ew players have had more of an impact on college baseball over the last three years than Florida's Mike Zunino.

Maybe Zunino's offensive numbers this spring weren't eye-popping, but they were plenty robust—he tied for fourth in the nation with 19 home runs, ranked 10th with 67 RBIs, third with 28 doubles, 11th with a .669 slugging percentage and fifth with 164 total bases. He finished the year hitting .322/.394/.669, and he did it while playing rock-solid defense behind the plate—baseball's most physically demanding position.

His combination of offensive production, quality defense, superb leadership and remarkable durability made Zunino the No. 3 overall pick in the draft, and it makes him the College Player of the Year.

**Florida coach Kevin O'Sullivan:**

"He's been a tremendous leader, both on and off the field. He's been a major reason why this program has taken the next step. Obviously he's improved each year, and I'm awfully proud of what he's been able to accomplish on the field, and off the field as well.

Florida's Mike Zunino shined offensively and defensively for the Gators. In seven big league seasons he has shown a well below-average bat but outstanding skill behind the plate and a strong arm.

"Offensively, he's probably improved that part of his game more than anything else. He's always been a really good defender, always been able to throw, always been able to separate offense from defense. He's learned to use the other side of the field very well. Like most young hitters, he was very pull-oriented early in his career. His balance is a lot better, he stays through the ball better, and he's learned to drive the ball the other way."

**Georgia coach David Perno:**

"He's a catcher, he doesn't miss a game, runs the show, hits three-hole. The power, the leadership—he does it all. If I'm picking first, I'm picking Zunino. Any player in our league, it's him, no-brainer. He's just a phenomenal kid. It's amazing what he's done through the years there, and the durability is probably underrated. I don't know that he's missed a game in two years.

"He's almost like a good umpire—you don't notice him, other than he hits the ball out of the yard, makes every throw, blocks every ball. It's just amazing. Through the years while he's been at Florida, you just have had to earn everything you got. You weren't getting any gifts from him. You could just tell the respect he commands. They just don't come around like him very often. He makes everybody better, no question about it."

**Mississippi State coach John Cohen:**

"I think the neat thing about that kid is, and I'm not taking anything away from his physical skills, but what makes him special to me is he is like having a coach on the field.

"He is a winner. If you take him out of that equation—I think this is the best way to say it. Florida has been knocking on the door for a national championship for a while, but if you take him out, they're done. He is the difference-maker for their club. He's been the guy. He runs the whole deal. You know a program is running on cylinders when, dadgummit, they've got a guy on the field who's running the show for them."

**Mississippi coach Mike Bianco:**

"When you look at Zunino, he plays one of the toughest positions as a position player, catcher or shortstop. They really lean on him, you can tell just from leadership, handling a great pitching staff behind the plate, he blocks balls, throws guys out. Zunino's the total package. He does it in all the phases of the game, defensively and offensively. I think he brings that intangible to the game as a great leader. You feel his presence on the field."

**Mike Zunino:**

"Without the University of Florida, without the coaching staff, I wouldn't be where I'm at. They've sculpted me as a player and helped me tremendously. I couldn't be happier with the decision I made out of high school. It's been the best three years of my life." ∎

# TOP PLAYERS OF 2012

## ALL-AMERICA TEAM

| Pos | Player | School | Yr | AVG | AB | R | H | HR | RBI | SB | BB | SO | OBP | SLG |
|-----|--------|--------|----|-----|----|---|---|----|----|----|----|----|----|----|
| C | Mike Zunino | Florida | Jr | .322 | 239 | 53 | 77 | 19 | 31 | 9 | 31 | 47 | .390 | .678 |
| 1B | Chris Serritella | Southern Illinois | Jr | .389 | 234 | 56 | 91 | 13 | 61 | 6 | 34 | 51 | .461 | .667 |
| 2B | Alex Yarbrough | Mississippi | Jr | .380 | 250 | 43 | 95 | 3 | 43 | 4 | 22 | 24 | .437 | .508 |
| 3B | Kris Bryant | San Diego | So | .366 | 213 | 59 | 78 | 14 | 57 | 9 | 39 | 38 | .483 | .671 |
| SS | Jimmy Rider | Kent State | Sr | .359 | 295 | 70 | 106 | 6 | 58 | 3 | 33 | 41 | .425 | .529 |
| OF | Jeff Gelalich | UCLA | Jr | .351 | 245 | 56 | 86 | 11 | 48 | 16 | 34 | 45 | .444 | .535 |
| OF | Travis Jankowski | Stony Brook | Jr | .414 | 266 | 79 | 110 | 5 | 46 | 36 | 24 | 22 | .475 | .620 |
| OF | James Ramsey | Florida State | Sr | .378 | 233 | 78 | 88 | 13 | 58 | 11 | 63 | 42 | .513 | .652 |
| DH | Josh Ludy | Baylor | Sr | .362 | 232 | 41 | 84 | 16 | 71 | 1 | 32 | 41 | .455 | .634 |
| UT | Marco Gonzales | Gonzaga | So | .325 | 151 | 23 | 49 | 2 | 29 | 0 | 11 | 21 | .372 | .430 |

| Pos | Pitcher | School | Yr | W | L | ERA | G | SV | IP | H | BB | SO |
|-----|---------|--------|----|----|---|-----|---|----|----|---|----|----|
| SP | Andrew Heaney | Oklahoma State | Jr | 8 | 2 | 1.60 | 15 | 0 | 118 | 74 | 22 | 140 |
| SP | Nick Petree | Missouri State | So | 10 | 4 | 1.01 | 16 | 0 | 115 | 85 | 36 | 114 |
| SP | Carlos Rodon | North Carolina State | Fr | 9 | 0 | 1.57 | 17 | 0 | 115 | 71 | 41 | 135 |
| SP | Chris Stratton | Mississippi State | Jr | 11 | 2 | 2.38 | 17 | 1 | 110 | 84 | 25 | 127 |
| RP | Robert Benincasa | Florida State | Jr | 4 | 2 | 1.32 | 32 | 16 | 41 | 24 | 7 | 58 |
| UT | Marco Gonzales | Gonzaga | So | 8 | 2 | 1.55 | 12 | 0 | 93 | 63 | 23 | 92 |

## SECOND TEAM

**C**—Kevin Plawecki, Purdue. **1B**—D.J. Hicks, Central Florida. **2B**—Jamodrick McGruder, Texas Tech. **3B**—D.J. Peterson, New Mexico. **SS**—Alex Mejia, Arizona. **OF**—Michael Conforto, Oregon State; Mitch Haniger, Cal Poly; and Brandon Miller, Samford. **DH**—William Carmona, Stony Brook. **UT**—Brian Johnson, Florida. **SP**—Mark Appel, Stanford; Kevin Gausman, Louisiana State; Kurt Heyer, Arizona; and Michael Wacha, Texas A&M. **RP**—Jimmie Sherfy, Oregon.

## THIRD TEAM

**C**—Mitchell Garver, New Mexico. **1B**—Goose Kallunki, Utah Valley. **2B**—Brock Hebert, Southeastern Louisiana. **3B**—Trenton Moses, Southeast Missouri State. **SS**—Matt Wessinger, St. John's. **OF**—Tyler Naquin, Texas A&M; Danny Poma, Hofstra; and Raph Rhymes, Louisiana State. **DH**—Patrick Kivlehan, Rutgers. **UT**—Stephen Piscotty, Stanford. **SP**—Tyler Johnson, Stony Brook; Adam Plutko, UCLA; Marcus Stroman, Duke; and Josh Turley, Baylor. **RP**—Michael Morin, North Carolina.

College World Series Most Outstanding Player Adam Plutko of UCLA went 2-0, 1.38 in a pair of starts in which his Bruins defeated Louisiana State and Mississippi State.

2013

# UCLA wins first national title its own way

By **AARON FITT**

U CLA head coach John Savage stood off to the side of the makeshift stage that had been erected around home plate, cradling the national championship trophy in both hands, a huge grin plastered across his face.

"Can you believe we did it?" Savage said, as his grin turned sly. "And the way we did it!"

UCLA won its first national championship with an 8-0 victory against Mississippi State in Game 2 of the College World Series finals. The way the Bruins marched unbeaten through the post-season wasn't quite like any champion that came before them.

**FROM THE ISSUE:**
JULY 23–AUG. 6, 2013

UCLA scored just 19 runs in its five games in the College World Series—the fewest ever for a national champion. The Bruins slugged .193 in Omaha—the lowest ever for a national champion by a wide margin. UCLA hit .227 in Omaha, the lowest of any champion in the metal-bat era. The Bruins did not hit a home run in Omaha—they didn't even come close—making them the first homerless champion since 1966.

But in becoming the seventh Pacific-12 Conference member to win the CWS, UCLA also became the first team to allow one run or fewer in every CWS game en route to the national championship. The Bruins, who allowed just 14 runs total during their 10-0 run through the NCAA Tournament, pitched historically well in the postseason.

The title-clinching victory featured yet another dominating performance by a UCLA starter. Righthander Nick Vander Tuig allowed just five hits over eight shutout innings.

Back on March 16, after Vander Tuig threw his first career shutout against Washington, Savage sat in his office at UCLA's Jackie Robinson Stadium, leaned back in his chair and tried to assess his team, which was off to a 14-3 start.

"We haven't swung the bats very well—it's no secret—but we think we have some good, young, capable players," Savage said. "We feel like we are deep. We don't have that star power right now, certainly on offense. We have a bunch of guys who are blue-collar guys on the mound, with good stuff. It's not crazy stuff, but it's guys who are pounding the zone with multiple pitches. They're good enough."

## TOP TEAMS
### 2013 COLLEGE WORLD SERIES STANDINGS

| School | Conference | Record | CWS | Head Coach |
|---|---|---|---|---|
| UCLA | Pacific-12 | 49–17 | 5–0 | John Savage |
| Mississippi State | Southeastern | 51–20 | 3–2 | John Cohen |
| North Carolina | Atlantic Coast | 59–12 | 2–2 | Mike Fox |
| Oregon State | Pacific-12 | 52–13 | 2–2 | Pat Casey |
| Indiana | Big Ten | 49–16 | 1–2 | Tracy Smith |
| North Carolina State | Atlantic Coast | 50–16 | 1–2 | Elliott Avent |
| Louisiana State | Southeastern | 57–11 | 0–2 | Paul Mainieri |
| Louisville | Big East | 51–14 | 0–2 | Dan McDonnell |

### NATIONAL CHAMPION
**UCLA**

The Bruins went 10-0 in the post-season, and looked especially sharp in Omaha by allowing no more than one run in any CWS game, on their way to the program's first national title. UCLA swept Mississippi State in the championship series.

**225**

As it turned out, Savage knew exactly what he had, because his assessment in mid-March rang truer than ever in late June. UCLA might have lacked star power on offense, but its pitching was most definitely good enough. Vander Tuig and fellow junior right-hander Adam Plutko will go down as one of the great pitching tandems in CWS history.

Each of them started twice in Omaha, and each of them won twice; they allowed a combined three runs in 28 innings (0.96 ERA). Plutko, who won UCLA's CWS opener against Mississippi State, was named CWS Most Outstanding Player.

Before the season started, Vander Tuig said, the Bruins visited the school's Hall of Champions on the day of their first weightlifting session.

"(Savage) took us to the national championships, and there were so many," Vander Tuig said, referencing the school's 108 trophies for NCAA team championships. "Then we went to baseball, and there were none. And I remember coach was saying, 'We've got to get our name on that board.' So I think we worked hard from day one."

Sophomore closer David Berg, who broke the NCAA single-season saves record in the CWS finals opener, harkened back to another team meeting, in early April after the Bruins had dropped a home series against Oregon State—their second straight series loss.

"We all sat in the locker room and looked at each other . . . we had gone through a little bit of a rough patch," Berg said. "The bats weren't going and it felt like, 'Hey, we're not achieving what we could,' and we weren't sure we were putting our all into everything we did. So we sat in that meeting and looked each other in the eyes and made that commitment to each other that, hey, we have a chance to do something special here."

After that meeting, Berg said, "You could really just see a spark where every single detail, we really put 100 percent into everything we did." From weightlifting to practice to cleaning the bus, the Bruins became dedicated to getting every little detail better.

# 2013 NEWSMAKERS

**North Carolina** ranked No. 1 in the preseason and largely lived up to expectations with a banner season. The Tar Heels won a program-record 59 games and advanced to the CWS, where they lost to eventual champion UCLA. UNC won the ACC Tournament and entered the NCAA Tournament as the No. 1 overall seed. In super regionals they knocked out South Carolina, which had played for the title the last three years.

Behind a powerful lineup led by **Kyle Schwarber**, Indiana became the first Big Ten team to reach the CWS since 1984, when Michigan made it. It was the Hoosiers' first-ever appearance in the CWS and they went 1-2, eliminating Louisville. They also won their first Big Ten championship outright since 1932 and claimed the conference tournament title.

Led by sophomores and future first-round picks in lefthander **Carlos Rodon** and shortstop **Trea Turner**, **North Carolina State** put together its best season in more than four decades and snapped its 45-year College World Series drought. The Wolfpack won a program-record 50 games and advanced to the CWS for just the second time in school history.

**FINAL TOP 25 FOR 2013**

1. UCLA*
2. Mississippi State*
3. #North Carolina*
4. Oregon State*
5. Louisiana State*
6. North Carolina State*
7. Indiana*
8. Louisville*
9. Vanderbilt
10. Cal State Fullerton
11. Virginia
12. Florida State
13. Kansas State
14. South Carolina
15. Oklahoma
16. Rice
17. Oregon
18. Arkansas
19. Virginia Tech
20. Florida Atlantic
21. Austin Peay State
22. Arizona State
23. San Diego
24. Oklahoma State
25. Troy

\* Reached College World Series
\# Preseason No. 1

# IN RETROSPECT: 2013 DRAFT

**Top 10 Draft Picks From College**
With overall selection number (Ov), drafting team (Team) and rank on Baseball America draft board (BA).

| Player | Pos | School | Ov | Team | BA |
|---|---|---|---|---|---|
| Mark Appel | RHP | Stanford | 1 | Astros | 2 |
| Kris Bryant | 3B | San Diego | 2 | Cubs | 3 |
| Jon Gray | RHP | Oklahoma | 3 | Rockies | 1 |
| Colin Moran | 3B | North Carolina | 6 | Marlins | 7 |
| Hunter Dozier | SS | Stephen F. Austin | 8 | Royals | 39 |
| D.J. Peterson | 3B | New Mexico | 12 | Mariners | 12 |
| Hunter Renfroe | OF | Mississippi State | 13 | Padres | 11 |
| Braden Shipley | RHP | Nevada | 15 | D-backs | 8 |
| Chris Anderson | RHP | Jacksonville | 18 | Dodgers | 45 |
| Marco Gonzales | LHP | Gonzaga | 19 | Cardinals | 28 |

**Top 10 Major League Players From College Draft Class**
With draft round and Baseball-Reference.com total for wins above replacement (WAR) through 2019.

| Player | Pos | School | Rd | Ov | Team | WAR |
|---|---|---|---|---|---|---|
| Kris Bryant | 3B | San Diego | 1 | 2 | Cubs | 25.1 |
| Aaron Judge | OF | Fresno State | 1 | 32 | Yankees | 18.6 |
| Jon Gray | RHP | Oklahoma | 1 | 3 | Rockies | 10.6 |
| Sean Manaea | LHP | Indiana State | 1s | 34 | Royals | 8.6 |
| Adam Frazier | 2B | Mississippi State | 6 | 179 | Pirates | 7.8 |
| Jeff McNeil | 2B | Long Beach State | 12 | 356 | Mets | 7.4 |
| Matthew Boyd | LHP | Oregon State | 6 | 175 | Blue Jays | 6.7 |
| Hunter Renfroe | OF | Mississippi State | 1 | 13 | Padres | 6.2 |
| Michael Lorenzen | RHP | Cal State Fullerton | 1s | 38 | Reds | 6.0 |
| Trey Mancini | 1B | Notre Dame | 8 | 249 | Orioles | 5.9 |
| Marco Gonzales | LHP | Gonzaga | 1 | 19 | Cardinals | 5.8 |

That unwavering focus was critical in Omaha, where UCLA played superb defense and consistently took advantage when its opponents made mistakes. The Bruins cobbled together just enough offense to win for most of the CWS, moving runners over when they reached via walks, errors, wild pitches or even hits.

In fact, UCLA tied the CWS record with 12 sacrifice bunts, matching Santa Clara in 1962. And when the Bruins needed a timely hit in the postseason, they generally got one.

In the end, it was a team effort. UCLA's pitching and defense were its biggest strengths, but the Bruins were simply sharper, more focused and more cohesive than every other team they played in the postseason.

That is how they vanquished one juggernaut after another, from Cal State Fullerton in super regionals to Louisiana State, North Carolina State, North Carolina and Mississippi State in Omaha. All five were No. 1 regional seeds, while UNC (No. 1), LSU (No. 4) and Fullerton (No. 5) were national seeds.

Now, with three CWS trips in four years capped by an undefeated postseason run to a national championship, UCLA can count itself among college baseball's truly elite.

"I'm just so proud of these guys. They did it on the field," Savage said. "I don't think any of the experts thought we would be here at this stage, and we did it the right way. We played good baseball. We pitched, we defended. We had quality offense, opportunistic offense for sure, and at the end of the day, I think we outlasted everybody."

It wasn't the same way Arizona dominated during its unbeaten run to last year's national title. It was different from South Carolina's 10-0 run to the 2011 title.

It was UCLA's way, all the way. ∎

# Bryant leaves legacy of tall tales in his wake

By **AARON FITT**

Everyone has a favorite Kris Bryant story. The 2013 College Player of the Year left a trail of gaping mouths and shaking heads this spring on his way to 31 home runs—the most by a college player since 2003. So naturally, the most common story about San Diego's third baseman involves a massive display of power.

Longtime USD radio play-by-play man Jack Murray can't stop talking about the ball Bryant hit over the light tower against Saint Louis on a cool night back in March. Murray swears the ball traveled 600 feet

Bryant's father Mike won't argue with that estimate.

"It was 20 feet above the light tower, and it was going up," Mike Bryant said, his voice rising in pitch like the flight of his son's home run. "Look—I get goose bumps talking about it. It was legendary."

Bryant's total package—not just his top-of-the-charts power—makes him the kind

In college baseball's dead ball era, Kris Bryant slammed 31 homers as a junior and 54 in his career. His major league career already includes a Rookie of the Year award, an MVP and a World Series ring.

of player that San Diego coach Rich Hill said "comes along once in a coach's career."

Bryant hasn't always been such a complete, polished player, of course. While fellow Las Vegas native Bryce Harper was widely regarded as a can't-miss superstar since he was 15, scouts had doubts about Bryant during his high school days.

Those doubts and Bryant's strong commitment to USD caused him to slip to the Blue Jays in the 18th round of the 2010 draft, and he was an instant star for the Toreros, hitting .365/.482/.599 with nine home runs, 36 RBIs and 18 stolen bases in 21 tries. He was a freshman All-American in 2011, but he was just scratching the surface of his potential.

"The maturity I've seen in him as a player, it's been leaps and bounds," Hill said. "His freshman year, he was kind of a 6-foot-5, wiry, gangly kid coming in with some holes in his swing. He really had work to do on his defense. To his sophomore year, he kept getting better. To this year, he just blossomed.

"I mean, 31 home runs with a BBCOR bat is ridiculous. The fact that he can play third base like a major leaguer now is ridiculous. The fact that he can go first to third, second to home in the blink of an eye is ridiculous. If you put him on the warning track and told him to throw this ball as hard as you can to home plate, it would be Ichiro-esque."

Bryant's offensive numbers have escalated steadily each season. He hit .366/.483/.671 with 14 homers and 57 RBIs as a sophomore, increasing his walk total from 33 to 39 while decreasing his strikeout total from 55 to 38.

This spring, Bryant took another leap forward, hitting .329/.493/.820 with 31 homers and 62 RBIs. By the end of the season, Bryant led the nation in homers, slugging, runs (80), total bases (187) and walks (66). He did an admirable job maintaining his disciplined approach even while opponents constantly pitched around him. The Toreros got creative in an effort to get him as many opportunities as possible, often using him in the leadoff or No. 2 spots in the lineup. And when he got pitches to hit, he rarely missed.

It is fun to contemplate Bryant's future, because as Hill put it, if he's this good now, "What's it going to be three years from now, when he really fills that uniform out, when he shaves more than once every two weeks?"

But it's also fun to contemplate what is now the past—Bryant's remarkable college career. After the Los Angeles Regional ended, Bryant and the USD seniors got to address their teammates in an emotional postgame huddle on the field. He greeted reporters with glassy eyes and halting but heartfelt words

"Tonight was more than just a baseball game to me," Bryant said. "Just looking back on the three years that I've had at USD, I can't even put into words how special it was . . . I just had a lot of good memories here."

And he left a lot of other people with stories they will always remember. ■

# TOP PLAYERS OF 2013

## ALL-AMERICA TEAM

| Pos | Player | School | Yr | AVG | AB | R | H | HR | RBI | SB | BB | SO | OBP | SLG |
|-----|--------|--------|----|----|----|----|----|----|----|----|----|----|----|----|
| C | Stuart Turner | Mississippi | Jr | .374 | 222 | 44 | 83 | 5 | 51 | 2 | 28 | 37 | .444 | .518 |
| 1B | D.J. Peterson | New Mexico | Jr | .408 | 218 | 68 | 89 | 18 | 72 | 5 | 46 | 35 | .520 | .807 |
| 2B | Tony Kemp | Vanderbilt | Jr | .391 | 266 | 64 | 104 | 0 | 33 | 34 | 35 | 32 | .471 | .485 |
| 3B | Kris Bryant | San Diego | Jr | .329 | 228 | 80 | 75 | 31 | 62 | 7 | 66 | 44 | .493 | .820 |
| SS | Alex Bregman | Louisiana State | Fr | .369 | 282 | 59 | 104 | 6 | 52 | 16 | 24 | 35 | .417 | .546 |
| OF | Daniel Palka | Georgia Tech | Jr | .342 | 237 | 55 | 81 | 17 | 66 | 6 | 31 | 60 | .436 | .637 |
| OF | Mike Papi | Virginia | So | .281 | 176 | 57 | 67 | 7 | 57 | 6 | 45 | 25 | .517 | .619 |
| OF | Hunter Renfroe | Mississippi State | Jr | .345 | 255 | 56 | 88 | 16 | 65 | 9 | 35 | 43 | .431 | .620 |
| DH | Colin Moran | North Carolina | Jr | .357 | 235 | 69 | 84 | 13 | 84 | 1 | 55 | 20 | .485 | .579 |
| UT | Michael Lorenzen | Cal State Fullerton | Jr | .335 | 227 | 40 | 54 | 7 | 54 | 12 | 19 | 39 | .412 | .515 |

| Pos | Pitcher | School | Yr | W | L | ERA | G | SV | IP | H | BB | SO |
|-----|---------|--------|----|----|----|----|----|----|----|----|----|----|
| SP | Tom Eshelman | Cal State Fullerton | Fr | 12 | 3 | 1.48 | 17 | 0 | 116 | 86 | 3 | 83 |
| SP | Jonathan Gray | Oklahoma | Jr | 10 | 3 | 1.64 | 17 | 0 | 126 | 83 | 24 | 147 |
| SP | Andrew Moore | Oregon State | Fr | 14 | 2 | 1.79 | 19 | 1 | 131 | 93 | 28 | 72 |
| SP | Aaron Nola | Louisiana State | So | 12 | 1 | 1.57 | 17 | 0 | 126 | 83 | 18 | 122 |
| RP | David Berg | UCLA | So | 7 | 0 | 0.92 | 51 | 24 | 78 | 55 | 11 | 78 |
| UT | Michael Lorenzen | Cal State Fullerton | Jr | 3 | 0 | 1.99 | 22 | 19 | 23 | 17 | 4 | 20 |

## SECOND TEAM

**C**—Kyle Schwarber, Indiana. **1B**—Ryan Kinsella, Elon. **2B**—Michael Bass, UNC Wilmington. **3B**—Eric Jagielo, Notre Dame. **SS**—Hunter Dozier, Stephen F. Austin. **OF**—Philip Ervin, Samford; Justin Parr, Illinois; and Mike Tauchman, Bradley. **DH**—Matt Oberste, Oklahoma. **UT**—Marco Gonzales, Gonzaga. **SP**—Mark Appel, Stanford; Tyler Beede, Vanderbilt; Justin Garza, Cal State Fullerton; and Ryne Stanek, Arkansas. **RP**—Jonathan Holder, Mississippi State.

## THIRD TEAM

**C**—Zane Evans, Georgia Tech. **1B**—Jimmy Yezzo, Delaware. **2B**—Ross Kivett, Kansas State. **3B**—Dustin DeMuth, Indiana. **SS**—Trea Turner, North Carolina State. **OF**—Forrestt Allday, Central Arkansas; Danny Collins, Troy; and Ben McQuown, Campbell. **DH**—L.B. Dantzler, South Carolina. **UT**—C.K. Irby, Samford. **SP**—Matt Boyd, Oregon State; Nick Petree, Missouri State; Carlos Rodon, North Carolina State; and Kevin Ziomek, Vanderbilt. **RP**—Zech Lemond, Rice.

Vanderbilt players dogpile in Omaha after winning the program's first ever national title, courtesy of a pair of one-run victories against Virginia.

2014

# Norwood's homer lifts Vanderbilt to CWS title

By **AARON FITT**

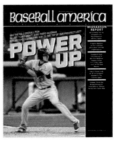

**FROM THE ISSUE:**
JULY 18–AUG. 1, 2014

**S**ometimes, immortality comes to those who wait. John Norwood waited two seasons for a chance to play every day at Vanderbilt. He earned that chance in 2014, and on the last day of the season, he ensured that his name will be remembered forever, like Warren Morris and Whit Merrifield and the other select few who have provided some of the most indelible moments in College World Series lore.

Norwood blasted a tie-breaking home run in the eighth inning of the decisive third game of the CWS finals, propelling Vanderbilt to a 3-2 win against Virginia.

But if Norwood had his way, the names of Carson Fulmer and Dansby Swanson, Vince Conde, Hayden Stone, Rhett Wiseman and so many others would go down in history right there with his. All of them will be remembered as part of the team that brought Vanderbilt its first national championship.

"I didn't bring it to them," Norwood insisted on the field after the game. "It was the people way before us, and they caused us to be here. Coach (Tim) Corbin did a great job getting a bunch of great guys year-in and year-out, and he finally got one. So it's an amazing feeling to do that for the university."

As the Commodores celebrated on the field, their alumni celebrated from afar. One Vanderbilt big leaguer after another rejoiced on Twitter, sending out heartfelt expressions of gratitude and joy for Corbin, a man they love like another father.

Corbin and his coaching staff have been a model program in part through their incredible ability to recruiting marquee players with winning makeup. The current groups of sophomores and juniors both rated as the No. 1 recruiting classes in college baseball when they showed up on campus in the falls of 2011 and 2012.

Vanderbilt has gotten plenty of meaningful contributions from talented freshmen in recent years, but Norwood and righthander Adam Ravenelle were raw talents when they arrived in Nashville in 2011, and both played sparingly over their first two seasons.

But they kept working hard, they stayed patient and waited for their opportunities.

## TOP TEAMS
### 2014 COLLEGE WORLD SERIES STANDINGS

| School | Conference | Record | CWS | Head Coach |
|---|---|---|---|---|
| Vanderbilt | Southeastern | 51–21 | 5–2 | Tim Corbin |
| Virginia | Atlantic Coast | 53–16 | 4–2 | Brian O'Connor |
| Texas | Big 12 | 46–21 | 3–2 | Augie Garrido |
| Mississippi | Southeastern | 48–21 | 2–2 | Mike Bianco |
| Texas Christian | Big 12 | 48–18 | 1–2 | Jim Schlossnagle |
| UC Irvine | Big West | 41–25 | 1–2 | Mike Gillespie |
| Louisville | American Athletic | 50–17 | 0–2 | Dan McDonnell |
| Texas Tech | Big 12 | 45–21 | 0–2 | Tim Tadlock |

## NATIONAL CHAMPION
### VANDERBILT

Vanderbilt coach Tim Corbin's pursuit of players with winning makeup paid off with the program's first national title, courtesy of a pair of one-run wins against Virginia in the championship series. John Norwood supplied the series-clinching homer.

The coaching staff stayed patient, too, helping them develop into key cogs on a championship team. With a national title hanging in the balance, it was Norwood who gave Vanderbilt the lead, and Ravenelle who preserved it, working two scoreless innings of relief for his second save of the finals, and third of the CWS.

He had no saves in his career before Omaha.

Norwood, who finished 3-for-3 with two of Vandy's three runs, came to the plate with one out in the top of the eighth and tomahawked a 97 mph fastball from Virginia closer Nick Howard into the left field bullpen. It was just the third home run of the CWS, and the first for Vanderbilt since May 16. It was the first home run allowed all season by Howard, a Reds first-round pick who had been dominant in his two previous CWS appearances, allowing just two hits over five shutout innings.

"I was just hoping that it didn't have enough topspin that it would hit the fence," Corbin said. "But Johnny's strength and bat speed, with the velocity of Howard—that doesn't happen to that kid. A 97 mph fastball and someone to turn it around like that takes a great amount of ability.

"I'm just happy for Johnny . . . the kid that grown so much as a person and as a player, even in the last four weeks. You can talk to the players about his approach at the plate, his calmness, and just his overall offensive productivity. So just a big moment."

Ravenelle then worked a 1-2-3 ninth inning, striking out Branden Cogswell and Daniel Pinero to end the game and trigger a dogpile around Ravenelle on the mound.

"Coming into the College World Series, I couldn't tell you that I was going to be closing games out here," Ravenelle said. "But it's just an opportunity, and I was just trying to take it pitch by pitch, and let my defense work, and I've trusted these guys all year. These guys are the best defense in the country, so that's all I was trying to do."

# 2014 NEWSMAKERS

Long considered one of the best programs that had not reached the CWS, **Texas Tech** broke through in 2014 in Tim Tadlock's second season as head coach. The Red Raiders went 45-19, won the Coral Gables Regional, upsetting Miami in the process, and then swept the College of Charleston in super regionals. Texas Tech would go on to make three more Omaha appearances during the decade.

**Mississippi** put together its best season in more than four decades. The Rebels went 46-19 and won the SEC West Division title. They swept through the Oxford Regional and went on the road to defeat Louisiana-Lafayette in super regionals to advance to Omaha for the first time since 1972. They reached the bracket final before losing to Virginia.

Hall of Fame outfielder **Tony Gwynn** died June 16 after a battle with cancer. He returned to San Diego State, his alma mater, as head coach before the 2003 season and remained in that role until taking a medical leave of absence two months before his death. He went 321-342 as head coach and led the Aztecs to three regional appearances, including 2014.

## FINAL TOP 25 FOR 2014

1. Vanderbilt*
2. #Virginia*
3. Mississippi*
4. Texas*
5. Texas Christian*
6. Louisville*
7. Louisiana-Lafayette
8. UC Irvine*
9. Texas Tech*
10. Oklahoma State
11. Houston
12. Pepperdine
13. Oregon State
14. Maryland
15. Stanford
16. Kennesaw State
17. College of Charleston
18. Florida
19. Florida State
20. Cal Poly
21. Indiana
22. Louisiana State
23. Miami
24. Washington
25. South Carolina

* Reached College World Series
# Preseason No. 1

# IN RETROSPECT: 2014 DRAFT

**Top 10 Draft Picks From College**
With overall selection number (Ov), drafting team (Team) and rank on Baseball America draft board (BA).

| Player | Pos | School | Ov | Team | BA |
|---|---|---|---|---|---|
| Carlos Rodon | LHP | North Carolina State | 3 | White Sox | 3 |
| Kyle Schwarber | C | Indiana | 4 | Cubs | 17 |
| Aaron Nola | RHP | Louisiana State | 7 | Phillies | 7 |
| Kyle Freeland | LHP | Evansville | 8 | Rockies | 5 |
| Jeff Hoffman | RHP | East Carolina | 9 | Blue Jays | 13 |
| Michael Conforto | OF | Oregon State | 10 | Mets | 8 |
| Max Pentecost | C | Kennesaw State | 11 | Blue Jays | 10 |
| Trea Turner | SS | North Carolina State | 13 | Padres | 9 |
| Tyler Beede | RHP | Vanderbilt | 14 | Giants | 15 |
| Sean Newcomb | LHP | Hartford | 15 | Angels | 11 |

**Top 10 Major League Players From College Draft Class**
With draft round and Baseball-Reference.com total for wins above replacement (WAR) through 2019.

| Player | Pos | School | Rd | Ov | Team | WAR |
|---|---|---|---|---|---|---|
| Aaron Nola | RHP | Louisiana State | 1 | 7 | Phillies | 19.6 |
| Matt Chapman | 3B | Cal State Fullerton | 1 | 25 | Athletics | 18.5 |
| Michael Conforto | OF | Oregon State | 1 | 10 | Mets | 12.8 |
| Trea Turner | SS | N.C. State | 1 | 13 | Padres | 12.8 |
| Kyle Freeland | LHP | Evansville | 1 | 8 | Rockies | 10.8 |
| Brian Anderson | 3B | Arkansas | 3 | 76 | Marlins | 7.6 |
| Carlos Rodon | LHP | N.C. State | 1 | 3 | White Sox | 6.6 |
| Kyle Schwarber | OF | Indiana | 1 | 4 | Cubs | 4.9 |
| John Means | LHP | West Virginia | 11 | 331 | Orioles | 4.5 |
| Brandon Woodruff | RHP | Mississippi State | 11 | 326 | Brewers | 4.3 |

As talented as the Commodores were, they were the clear underdogs heading into the finals. Virginia was the older club, with six upperclassmen in its lineup compared with just two for Vanderbilt. Tyler Beede was the lone upperclassman in Vandy's rotation, while Brian Miller and Ravenelle were juniors in the bullpen.

But by this point in the season, freshmen aren't freshmen anymore; both teams were battle-tested, tough and confident. Virginia, the preseason No. 1, had been a bit more consistent from start to finish this year. The Cavaliers had played like a veteran team on a mission, and their focus had never really wavered.

Vanderbilt had more growing pains with its younger team. After all, the Commodores had to replace six everyday stalwarts and the ace from their 2013 team that won a record 26 games in Southeastern Conference play, earned the No. 2 national seed and lost in a super regional to Louisville.

"This season, from the beginning to the middle part, it's certainly a progression," Corbin said. "There's maturity issues you work through . . . But as the season has progressed, we've come across experiences that have enabled us and moved us forward, and we've gained confidence through it. Last year, it was like flying a plane that was on autopilot. And you'd come to the ballpark, and your sons, who are now 21, 22 years old, have everything in order for you . . . We just ran out of gas at the wrong time.

"This team has gained energy as the season progressed. It's two completely different units, which is great, because they're always different. We find ourselves in a spot that we may have been last year. Not that either team didn't earn their way here—we have. We've just done it in a different way." ■

# Kentucky's Reed starred at plate, on mound

By **AARON FITT**

**N**ot since John Olerud has a college player had the kind of two-way impact A.J. Reed did for Kentucky this year.

Olerud, the 1988 College Player of the Year for Washington State, has been the gold standard for two-way brilliance since hitting .464 with 23 homers and going 15-0, 2.49 on the mound. But in a number of ways, Reed raised the bar this spring, earning him the College Player of the Year award.

Using deadened BBCOR bats, Reed smacked 23 home runs, matching Olerud's total with supercharged bats. Reed led the nation in homers, slugging percentage (.735) and OPS (1.211), while ranking second in total bases (164) and third in RBIs (73). He hit .336 with a .476 on-base percentage, walking (49) more than he struck out (48).

That offensive season alone would make him worthy of the Player of the Year award,

Not since John Olerud had the college game seen a two-way star like A.J. Reed, who slammed 23 homers and served as Kentucky's Friday night starter. He had yet to make an impact in the big leagues.

but Reed also went 12-2, 2.09 in 112 innings as Kentucky's Friday night ace in the rugged Southeastern Conference. He ranked only one win shy of the national lead and topped the SEC.

### Kentucky Coach Gary Henderson:

"A.J. is a genuine kid. He's smart, he's got great baseball instincts, he treats people well, he's got a good sense of humor, he's a very good student, he's a hard worker, he's done a great job of doing everything we've asked him to do.

"Look at what he did at Harwich (in the Cape Cod League) over the summer offensively; (he hit .218 in) 55 at-bats or something. He didn't get to hit. So you have the conversations that you have with kids, and some of them are pretty pointed. And the relationships are close. When you have those conversations with kids, they either buy in or not, make the adjustments or not. Kids don't always make the right adjustments. But he did."

### Tennessee Coach Dave Serrano:

"The numbers he's put up in this conference, it's unbelievable to be honest with you.

"And not only what he's done at the plate, but what he's done on the mound . . . I think he should walk away with almost all the awards, except for the just pure pitching awards. You don't put up those type of numbers in what I feel like is the best conference in America, especially in today's era where the bats have changed."

**Texas A&M Coach Rob Childress:**

"I don't think there's any question as to who the national Player of the Year is. It's A.J. Reed. When you consider him doing both in this league, at the highest level, and being consistent week in and week out, offensively and on the mound, it was unbelievable. And to watch him take BP and to watch him in the games, a lot of different teams played the shift on him and tried a lot of different things and obviously pitched around him every chance they got—I know we did—and it didn't matter. He still made a difference."

**Vanderbilt Coach Tim Corbin:**

"You certainly have to look at his numbers and you're astonished by them. I mean, even two-way players like John Olerud didn't put up those types of numbers. I think he's an outstanding player; he really is in a lot of ways. He's got a good way about him. He's got great presence."

**South Carolina Coach Chad Holbrook:**

"Oh, I think he's the national Player of the Year. I don't think there's any doubt about it, at least from me. I mean, that's crazy what he's done, leading the conference in home runs and being a Friday night starter. I don't think anybody's come close to doing the things on the field that he's done, and I'm sure he's obviously the most important player to Kentucky's team." ■

# TOP PLAYERS OF 2014

## ALL-AMERICA TEAM

| Pos | Player | School | Yr | AVG | AB | R | H | HR | RBI | SB | BB | SO | OBP | SLG |
|-----|--------|--------|----|-----|----|----|----|----|-----|----|----|----|-----|-----|
| C | Max Pentecost | Kennesaw State | Jr | .422 | 268 | 59 | 113 | 9 | 61 | 17 | 30 | 26 | .482 | .627 |
| 1B | Casey Gillaspie | Wichita State | Jr | .389 | 211 | 50 | 82 | 15 | 50 | 8 | 58 | 28 | .520 | .682 |
| 2B | Jace Conrad | Louisiana-Lafayette | Jr | .364 | 264 | 63 | 96 | 9 | 65 | 22 | 18 | 27 | .438 | .564 |
| 3B | Dustin DeMuth | Indiana | Sr | .374 | 211 | 40 | 79 | 5 | 40 | 4 | 20 | 40 | .449 | .531 |
| SS | Trea Turner | North Carolina State | Jr | .321 | 215 | 65 | 69 | 8 | 36 | 26 | 37 | 25 | .418 | .516 |
| OF | Caleb Adams | Louisiana-Lafayette | Jr | .381 | 223 | 67 | 85 | 11 | 42 | 7 | 46 | 60 | .502 | .673 |
| OF | Michael Conforto | Oregon State | Jr | .345 | 203 | 52 | 70 | 7 | 56 | 4 | 55 | 38 | .504 | .547 |
| OF | Bradley Zimmer | San Francisco | Jr | .368 | 220 | 45 | 81 | 7 | 31 | 21 | 31 | 34 | .461 | .573 |
| DH | Kyle Schwarber | Indiana | Jr | .358 | 232 | 66 | 83 | 14 | 48 | 10 | 44 | 30 | .464 | .659 |
| UT | A.J. Reed | Kentucky | Jr | .336 | 223 | 60 | 75 | 23 | 73 | 0 | 49 | 48 | .476 | .735 |

| Pos | Pitcher | School | Yr | W | L | ERA | G | SV | IP | H | BB | SO |
|-----|---------|--------|----|----|----|-----|----|----|----|----|----|----|
| SP | Kyle Freeland | Evansville | Jr | 10 | 2 | 1.90 | 14 | 0 | 100 | 79 | 13 | 128 |
| SP | Nathan Kirby | Virginia | So | 9 | 3 | 2.06 | 18 | 0 | 113 | 68 | 33 | 112 |
| SP | Aaron Nola | Louisiana State | Jr | 11 | 1 | 1.47 | 16 | 0 | 116 | 69 | 27 | 134 |
| SP | Ben Wetzler | Oregon State | Sr | 12 | 1 | 0.78 | 14 | 0 | 104 | 49 | 31 | 83 |
| RP | Jacob Lindgren | Mississippi State | Jr | 6 | 1 | 0.88 | 25 | 3 | 51 | 20 | 21 | 93 |
| UT | A.J. Reed | Kentucky | Jr | 12 | 2 | 2.09 | 16 | 0 | 112 | 98 | 29 | 71 |

## SECOND TEAM

**C**—Grayson Greiner, South Carolina. **1B**—Sam Travis, Indiana. **2B**—Mark Mathias, Cal Poly. **3B**—Alex Blandino, Stanford. **SS**—Blake Trahan, Louisiana-Lafayette. **OF**—Jordan Luplow, Fresno State; D.J. Stewart, Florida State; and Drew Weeks, North Florida. **DH**—Michael Katz, William & Mary. **UT**—Aaron Brown, Pepperdine. **SP**—Tom Eshelman, Cal State Fullerton; Jace Fry, Oregon State; Andrew Morales, UC Irvine; and Preston Morrison, Texas Christian. **RP**—Brendan McCurry, Oklahoma State.

## THIRD TEAM

**C**—Brett Austin, N.C. State. **1B**—Connor Jones, San Diego. **2B**—Dansby Swanson, Vanderbilt. **3B**—Matt Chapman, Cal State Fullerton. **SS**—Michael Russell, North Carolina. **OF**—Austin Bousfield, Mississippi; Zach Fish, Oklahoma State; and Mark Payton, Texas. **DH**—Ty France, San Diego State. **UT**—Louie Lechich, San Diego. **SP**—Brandon Finnegan, Texas Christian; Kyle Funkhouser, Louisville; Sean Newcomb, Hartford; and Josh Prevost, Seton Hall. **RP**—Ryan Thompson, Campbell.

Virginia coach Brian O'Connor poses with the championship trophy after his Cavaliers captured the first College World Series title for the ACC in 60 years.

2015

# Virginia stuns Vandy to win first national title

By **JIM SHONERD**

FROM THE ISSUE:
JULY 17-31, 2015

**R**ight to the very end, Virginia was still a long shot.

"I think my brother told me this afternoon the odds in Vegas today were 310-to-1 that we'd win this thing," head coach Brian O'Connor said, after it was over.

Yet here they are. A team besieged by injuries. A team that scrambled to make the NCAA Tournament, then flew cross-country for regionals. A team that had to piece together its pitching against two of the nation's best lineups in the College World Series. No amount of odds stacked against them were too great to overcome, even if 310-to-1 sounds like hyperbole.

A tournament run that defied expectations at almost every turn culminated in Virginia's first-ever national title, the Cavaliers taking the decisive third game of the CWS finals 4-2 to dethrone reigning champion Vanderbilt.

"I think every step of the way, everybody was predicting somebody else to win," O'Connor said. "It's just amazing what you can accomplish in whatever it is if you put your mind to it, hang in there and stay together. It's a very, very special group."

It started with a special arm on the mound.

The Cavaliers weren't expecting too much out of Brandon Waddell. With the junior lefty starting on three days' rest, the hope was that he could give them three innings. Instead, Waddell solidified his place as one of the best big-game pitchers in recent history. He worked seven innings and allowed just two runs on four hits. In five career CWS starts, it was the fourth time he'd gone at least that deep and allowed that many runs or fewer.

"First of all, coming into this game I knew we'd get his best," O'Connor said. "How he's pitched in this championship two years in a row is pretty special and doesn't really happen."

Things didn't start out according to script, though. Waddell came out in the first inning and was leaving balls up in the zone—balls the Commodores jumped on for a pair of runs on doubles by Rhett Wiseman and Zander Wiel. Waddell said later that he knew he wouldn't have his best stuff. His fastball operated around 89-90 mph, the short rest

## TOP TEAMS

### 2015 COLLEGE WORLD SERIES STANDINGS

| School | Conference | Record | CWS | Head Coach |
|---|---|---|---|---|
| Virginia | Atlantic Coast | 44-24 | 5-2 | Brian O'Connor |
| Vanderbilt | Southeastern | 51-21 | 4-2 | Tim Corbin |
| Florida | Southeastern | 52-18 | 3-2 | Kevin O'Sullivan |
| Texas Christian | Big 12 | 51-15 | 2-2 | Jim Schlossnagle |
| Louisiana State | Southeastern | 54-12 | 1-2 | Paul Mainieri |
| Miami | Atlantic Coast | 50-17 | 1-2 | Jim Morris |
| Arkansas | Southeastern | 40-25 | 0-2 | Dave Van Horn |
| Cal State Fullerton | Big West | 39-25 | 0-2 | Rick Vanderhook |

## NATIONAL CHAMPION
### VIRGINIA

The Cavaliers avenged their loss to Vanderbilt the year before by winning Games 2 and 3 of the championship series by margins of 3-0 and 4-2. Virginia was the first Atlantic Coast Conference team to win the CWS since Wake Forest in 1955.

knocking down his velocity from the low 90s he'd shown earlier in the CWS.

Getting out of the first inning with a couple ground outs to strand Wiel at second, Waddell was able to get back to the dugout and refocus—keep that ball down. He came back in the second and retired Vanderbilt in order, and the momentum kept carrying from there, one inning to the next. Waddell finally came to pitching coach Karl Kuhn at the end of the seventh and admitted he was out of gas after throwing 104 pitches. By that time, he'd just retired 11 straight and allowed two hits and one walk over his final six frames.

That three-innings idea was nothing more than a speck in the rear view mirror.

"It's just a matter of taking a breath, getting your mind right," Waddell said. "I knew 2-0 wasn't going to be the final score. I knew our offense was going to score."

Pavin Smith took care of that part.

There's a reason the Cavaliers' coaches kept running him out there in the middle of their order, even though Smith was just 5-for-24 through Virginia's first six games in Omaha. The Cavaliers first baseman enjoyed a Freshman All-America season this spring, hitting .307/.373/.467. Whatever struggles he might have had over the previous two weeks, it only took one swing to wipe them away.

The fact Vanderbilt was getting to start a first-round pick on the mound in Walker Buehler opposite Waddell was one of the big reasons Vandy was such a strong favorite. But Buehler struggled with his command, walking four in three-plus innings of work. After giving a free pass to Kenny Towns to lead off the fourth, Buehler fell behind Smith 1-0, then left an 87 mph changeup over the middle of the plate. Smith drilled it just over the right-center field wall, tying the game and giving the Cavs a jolt of momentum.

"I wasn't thinking about trying to hit a home run," Smith said. "I was just trying to get on base, trying to extend the inning, trying to keep the rally going. When I hit it, I knew

# 2015 NEWSMAKERS

In an effort to recalibrate the offensive environment following the introduction of the BBCOR bat standard in 2011, the NCAA switched to a **lower-seamed baseball** in 2015. The change restored balance to the game after teams had become overly reliant on small ball in the lower-scoring environment. Scoring ticked up with the new balls, as did home runs, which increased by 43.5 percent. Scoring and home runs were also up during the CWS, with the event setting highs for runs and home runs in TD Ameritrade Park, which opened in 2011.

**Illinois** won a program-record 50 games, reached super regionals and set a Big Ten Conference record with a 27-game winning streak. The Illini lost only once during conference play and won their first regional in program history but fell short of their first trip to Omaha after being swept by Vanderbilt in supers.

**Virginia Commonwealth** went on a Cinderella run, winning 11 straight games to finish the regular season and win the Atlantic-10 Conference Tournament to reach the NCAA Tournament. There, the Rams upset host Dallas Baptist to advance to super regionals for the first time in program history.

## FINAL TOP 25 FOR 2015

1. Virginia*
2. #Vanderbilt*
3. Florida*
4. Texas Christian*
5. Louisiana State*
6. Miami*
7. UCLA
8. Illinois
9. Cal State Fullerton*
10. Louisville
11. Arkansas*
12. Missouri State
13. Texas A&M
14. Maryland
15. Florida State
16. Louisiana-Lafayette
17. Virginia Commonwealth
18. Houston
19. Oklahoma State
20. Southern California
21. Dallas Baptist
22. California
23. College of Charleston
24. Radford
25. Iowa

* Reached College World Series
# Preseason No. 1

# IN RETROSPECT: 2015 DRAFT

**Top 10 Draft Picks From College**

With overall selection number (Ov), drafting team (Team) and rank on Baseball America draft board (BA).

| Player | Pos | School | Ov | Team | BA |
|---|---|---|---|---|---|
| Dansby Swanson | SS | Vanderbilt | 1 | D-backs | 2 |
| Alex Bregman | SS | Louisiana State | 2 | Astros | 4 |
| Dillon Tate | RHP | UC Santa Barbara | 4 | Rangers | 3 |
| Tyler Jay | LHP | Illinois | 6 | Twins | 13 |
| Andrew Benintendi | OF | Arkansas | 7 | Red Sox | 9 |
| Carson Fulmer | RHP | Vanderbilt | 8 | White Sox | 6 |
| Ian Happ | OF | Cincinnati | 9 | Cubs | 24 |
| James Kaprelian | RHP | UCLA | 16 | Yankees | 19 |
| Kevin Newman | SS | Arizona | 19 | Pirates | 29 |
| Richie Martin | SS | Florida | 20 | Athletics | 31 |

**Top 10 Major League Players From College Draft Class**

With draft round and Baseball-Reference.com total for wins above replacement (WAR) through 2019.

| Player | Pos | School | Rd | Ov | Team | WAR |
|---|---|---|---|---|---|---|
| Alex Bregman | 3B | Louisiana State | 1 | 2 | Astros | 20.8 |
| Paul DeJong | SS | Illinois State | 4 | 131 | Cardinals | 10.6 |
| Andrew Benintendi | OF | Arkansas | 1 | 7 | Red Sox | 8.7 |
| Harrison Bader | OF | Florida | 3 | 100 | Cardinals | 5.9 |
| David Fletcher | 2B | Loyola Marymount | 6 | 195 | Angels | 5.7 |
| Walker Buehler | RHP | Vanderbilt | 1 | 24 | Dodgers | 5.5 |
| Dansby Swanson | SS | Vanderbilt | 1 | 1 | D-backs | 3.7 |
| Brandon Lowe | 2B | Maryland | 3 | 87 | Rays | 3.6 |
| Ian Happ | OF | Cincinnati | 1 | 9 | Cubs | 3.5 |
| Kevin Newman | SS | Arizona | 1 | 19 | Pirates | 2.2 |
| Trent Thornton | RHP | North Carolina | 5 | 139 | Astros | 1.8 |

the wind was blowing out and I was just, like, telling it to go."

The Cavs got contributions up and down the roster throughout their run, right through to the second game of the CWS finals when they were sparked by unlikely heroes Ernie Clement and Thomas Woodruff. But on Wednesday, it was season-long leading lights Waddell, Smith and Towns that delivered. Smith added the go-ahead RBI single in the fifth, and Towns made the defensive play of the night with a diving stop that saved a run in the fourth and then drove in an insurance run with an RBI single in the seventh.

Last but not least came Nathan Kirby. The junior lefthander who was supposed to be the Cavs' ace, Kirby had been relegated to the sidelines for eight weeks, dealing with a lat strain and bout of mono. He returned for an ineffective start against Florida earlier in the CWS, but he finally got to put his own stamp on the title run in the finale. With closer—and CWS Most Outstanding Player—Josh Sborz unavailable after working four innings in Game 2, the Cavs summoned Kirby to pitch the final two innings.

A year after infamously falling apart against Vandy in the 2014 CWS finals, Kirby dominated the Commodores with his slider, striking out five over the last two frames. It was with one final slider that Kirby caught pinch-hitter Kyle Smith looking for the final out, flinging his cap and glove into the air before leaping into the arms of catcher Matt Thaiss.

"It was a very, very gutty performance by their team, their pitching staff, to allow them to get to this point and be successful," Vanderbilt coach Tim Corbin said.

"I thought Waddell, in a lot of ways, was left for dead, but he just got himself up in the fifth, sixth and seventh. He turned the game around. And when they brought Kirby out, he pitched with a lot of adrenaline and . . . just shut us down." ■

# Benintendi swings into spotlight

By **MICHAEL LANANNA**

Every mythic hero grapples with some sort of adversity or flaw before his meteoric rise.

True to form, Andrew Benintendi had surgery to remove the hamate bone in his right hand before he even began his college career. As a result, he hit .276/.368/.333 with one home run and 17 steals as an Arkansas freshman. Certainly, those numbers didn't hint at the type of season the center fielder would have this year.

In 226 at-bats Benintendi hit .376/.488/.717 with 20 homers, 57 RBIs and 24 steals in 28 attempts. For that tremendous sophomore season, he is the College Player of the Year.

"Andrew has just made an incredible jump, just night and day as far as confidence-wise and just the way he plays the game," said Arkansas head coach Dave Van Horn, who on the recruiting trail witnessed Benintendi hit a 390-foot home run using

A breakout sophomore year at Arkansas launched Andrew Benintendi's draft prospect into orbit. He ranked as the No. 1 prospect in baseball heading into 2017, the year he became a Red Sox regular.

a wood bat. "Last year was probably the first time ever in his life that he failed a little bit. He took it to heart and went home and worked his butt off."

Both Benintendi and Van Horn point to three reasons for his sophomore surge. There's health, obviously. Mechanically, Benintendi closed up his open stance in early April last season. Almost immediately, the ball jumped off his bat better, so much so that Van Horn moved him from leadoff to the No. 3 hole. Thirdly, ailed by a strained quad, Benintendi took time off from summer ball and committed himself in the weight room, packing on about 10 pounds of good weight.

"I approached it like a job this summer, really," Benintendi said. "I just dedicated myself to getting bigger and stronger. I think that's definitely helped me this year."

In the eyes of scouts, Benintendi has become a mythic figure, too. An enigma.

"People have fallen in love with him," said one area scout. "He's the kind of guy where your scouting director calls you and goes, 'Hey, what do you have on this guy? This guy is going off.' "

Standing in at 5-foot-10, 180 pounds, Benintendi's 20 homers came as a surprise to some. Benintendi himself said he was a bit surprised at that total.

His compact package of power and speed in center field is a unique one, and scouts have struggled to put a major league comp on him—from Shane Robinson to Adam Eaton to Darren Bragg and more. They haven't had much time to figure it out, either, with Benintendi being a draft-eligible sophomore.

"I think probably half the teams didn't realize he was sophomore eligible coming into the year," another scout said. "So much of it is you just don't expect it. He's 5-10, 180, not selling out for power. He just hits balls out of the park easy."

Van Horn said some of the recognition might have gotten to Benintendi during the Southeastern Conference tournament, where he went hitless until the ninth inning of the second game. His first hit was a jaw-dropper of a home run that clanked off of the Hoover Metropolitan Stadium scoreboard in right field.

"I think that was just a lot of frustration coming out of him," Van Horn said, laughing.

Since then, Benintendi has seemingly come to terms with it all. More relaxed at the plate, he helped lead the Razorbacks back to the College World Series. And after his electric four months in Fayetteville, he soared up draft boards, eventually sticking as the seventh overall pick, to the Red Sox. His draft worries are over.

"It's been a lot, especially with all these awards and things like that, but I just try to take it in," Benintendi said. "It's exciting, though. I get a lot of texts from people that I know and people from back home (in Cincinnati), and it sounds like they're excited, almost more excited than I am." ∎

# TOP PLAYERS OF 2015

## ALL-AMERICA TEAM

| Pos | Player | School | Yr | AVG | AB | R | H | HR | RBI | SB | BB | SO | OBP | SLG |
|-----|--------|--------|----|-----|----|---|---|----|-----|----|----|----|-----|-----|
| C | Garrett Stubbs | Southern California | Sr | .346 | 228 | 51 | 79 | 1 | 25 | 20 | 27 | 31 | .435 | .434 |
| 1B | Kyle Martin | South Carolina | Sr | .350 | 203 | 50 | 71 | 14 | 56 | 11 | 39 | 27 | .455 | .635 |
| 2B | Scott Kingery | Arizona | Jr | .392 | 237 | 53 | 93 | 5 | 36 | 11 | 9 | 18 | .423 | .561 |
| 3B | David Thompson | Miami | Jr | .328 | 253 | 59 | 83 | 19 | 90 | 1 | 43 | 29 | .434 | .640 |
| SS | Dansby Swanson | Vanderbilt | Jr | .335 | 281 | 76 | 94 | 15 | 64 | 16 | 43 | 54 | .423 | .623 |
| OF | Andrew Benintendi | Arkansas | So | .376 | 226 | 62 | 85 | 20 | 57 | 24 | 50 | 32 | .488 | .717 |
| OF | Donnie Dewees | North Florida | So | .422 | 251 | 88 | 106 | 18 | 68 | 23 | 30 | 16 | .483 | .749 |
| OF | D.J. Stewart | Florida State | Jr | .318 | 214 | 62 | 68 | 15 | 59 | 12 | 69 | 47 | .550 | .593 |
| DH | Alex Bregman | Louisiana State | Jr | .323 | 260 | 59 | 84 | 9 | 49 | 38 | 36 | 22 | .412 | .535 |
| UT | Brendan McKay | Louisville | Fr | .308 | 211 | 32 | 65 | 4 | 34 | 4 | 38 | 42 | .418 | .431 |

| Pos | Pitcher | School | Yr | W | L | ERA | G | SV | IP | H | BB | SO |
|-----|---------|--------|----|---|---|-----|---|----|----|----|----|----|
| SP | Tom Eshelman | Cal State Fullerton | Jr | 8 | 5 | 1.58 | 19 | 1 | 137 | 105 | 7 | 139 |
| SP | Carson Fulmer | Vanderbilt | Jr | 14 | 2 | 1.83 | 19 | 0 | 128 | 81 | 50 | 167 |
| SP | Michael Freeman | Oklahoma State | Sr | 10 | 3 | 1.31 | 15 | 0 | 109 | 72 | 29 | 97 |
| SP | Alex Lange | Louisiana State | Fr | 12 | 0 | 1.97 | 17 | 0 | 114 | 87 | 46 | 131 |
| RP | Tyler Jay | Illinois | Jr | 5 | 2 | 1.08 | 30 | 14 | 67 | 40 | 7 | 76 |
| UT | Brendan McKay | Louisville | Fr | 9 | 3 | 1.77 | 20 | 4 | 97 | 53 | 34 | 117 |

### SECOND TEAM
C—Kade Scivicque, Louisiana State. 1B—David Kerian, Illinois. 2B—Mike Garzillo, Lehigh. 3B—Bobby Dalbec, Arizona. SS—Kevin Kramer, UCLA. OF—Ian Happ, Cincinnati; Kevin Kaczmarski, Evansville; and Corey Ray, Louisville. DH—Will Craig, Wake Forest. UT—Corbin Olmstead, North Florida. SP—Mike Shawaryn, Maryland; Taylor Clarke, College of Charleston; Kevin Duchene, Illinois; and Matt Hall, Missouri State. RP—David Berg, UCLA.

### THIRD TEAM
C—Chris Okey, Clemson. 1B—Austin Byler, Nevada. 2B—George Iskenderian, Miami. 3B—Josh Tobias, Florida. SS—Kevin Newman, Arizona. OF—Cody Jones, Texas Christian; Andrew Stevenson, Louisiana State; and Christin Stewart, Tennessee. DH—J.J. Schwarz, Florida. UT—Reid Love, East Carolina. SP—Matthew Crownover, Clemson; Jon Harris, Missouri State; James Kaprielian, UCLA; and Andrew Moore, Oregon State. RP—Logan Cozart, Ohio.

Mid-major Coastal Carolina stunned the college baseball world with a dramatic run through the postseason that culminated in a national title.

2016

# Chants of a lifetime: Coastal wins it

By **TEDDY CAHILL**

Nothing about Coastal Carolina's journey was easy, so it was only fitting that the final out of the decisive third game of the College World Series finals was stressful.

With two outs in the bottom of the ninth, Arizona had the tying run on third base and the winning run on second. It was as close as the Wildcats could get to completing the comeback. Righthander Alex Cunningham blew a fastball by Ryan Haug to strike out the sophomore and clinch a 4-3 victory and the national championship.

For Coastal Carolina, a school of 10,000 students in suburban Myrtle Beach, S.C., that wasn't even a four-year college until 1974, and didn't become autonomous under its current name until 1993.

Righthander Andrew Beckwith, who won Game 3 and was named CWS Most Outstanding Player, said the victory was just the culmination of a long journey.

"Just the hard work we put in," he said. "The hard work the alumni have put in to get us to have these great facilities, and this coaching staff is just unbelievable. And the senior class pushed everyone from the start when they got back in the fall, and just one goal was to get to Omaha and win it all."

Coastal's run to that national championship was improbable not because of its lack of pedigree—the Chanticleers won 55 games and have been to super regionals three times—but rather because of the road it faced to get here.

The Chanticleers had hoped to host a regional, and went into Selection Monday ranked No. 12 in RPI. The selection committee followed RPI almost exactly when picking the 16 host sites. The only team ranked in the RPI's top 16 not to host: Coastal Carolina.

So the Chanticleers began a monthlong road trip that took them from North Carolina State to Louisiana State to Omaha. In the Raleigh Regional, they were pushed to the brink by the host Wolfpack. In the second regional final game, rain forced the game to be suspended with one out in the ninth inning and Coastal trailing by two runs. The Chanticleers came back the next day and found a way to win.

**FROM THE ISSUE:**
JULY 15-29, 2016

## TOP TEAMS
### 2016 COLLEGE WORLD SERIES STANDINGS

| School | Conference | Record | CWS | Head Coach |
|---|---|---|---|---|
| Coastal Carolina | Big South | 55–18 | 6–2 | Gary Gilmore |
| Arizona | Pacific-12 | 49–24 | 5–3 | Jay Johnson |
| Oklahoma State | Big 12 | 41–22 | 2–2 | Josh Holliday |
| Texas Christian | Big 12 | 49–18 | 2–2 | Jim Schlossnagle |
| Texas Tech | Big 12 | 45–18 | 1–2 | Tim Tadlock |
| UC Santa Barbara | Big West | 43–20–1 | 1–2 | Andrew Checketts |
| Florida | Southeastern | 52–16 | 0–2 | Kevin O'Sullivan |
| Miami | Atlantic Coast | 50–14 | 0–2 | Jim Morris |

## NATIONAL CHAMPION
### COASTAL CAROLINA

The Chanticleers became the first team to win the CWS in their first appearance since Minnesota in 1956. A rainout allowed Coastal Carolina to throw ace Andrew Beckwith in Game 3 of the championship series to key a 4-3 victory against Arizona.

Emboldened, they went into Alex Box Stadium, one of the toughest venues for a visiting team, and swept LSU, the No. 8 national seed.

In Omaha, Coastal found itself in the tougher bracket and opened its first CWS with Florida, the No. 1 national seed. Led by Beckwith, the Chanticleers knocked off the Gators, then fell into the loser's bracket with a loss to TCU. Coastal fought its way out, eliminating Texas Tech, the No. 5 national seed, and then beating TCU twice to reach the finals.

After losing the first game to Arizona, Coastal's back was again against the wall. But the Chanticleers again wouldn't be denied. They won Game 2, pushed through a rainout the next day, and again led by Beckwith, found a way to win the decisive third game.

"To do this is an incredible feat. I don't care what team you are," Coastal Carolina coach Gary Gilmore said. "To go through LSU and then come here, Florida, TCU, Texas Tech, TCU twice and (Arizona) three times, it's an incredible journey for any program."

At the CWS, Coastal leaned heavily on Beckwith. The junior flummoxed hitters with his ability to mix arm slots, pitches and velocities, maxing out at 87 mph but consistently beating hitters with sink to get ground balls.

When hitters moved up in the box to beat the sink, he jammed them or ran pitches away for weak fly balls. Beckwith started the CWS by holding Florida to one run in a complete game. He matched that effort five days later against TCU.

In the finale, Beckwith held Arizona to two runs (zero earned) on six hits and three walks in 5.2 innings. He finished the year 15-1, 1.85 and set a program record for wins.

Bobby Holmes and Cunningham followed him out of the bullpen. Holmes got the Chanticleers out of a jam with an inning-ending strikeout in the sixth. Cunningham, who had been slated to start the finale before the rainout, followed with three innings to earn his first save of the season.

# 2016 NEWSMAKERS

On the eve of the first day of regionals, Vanderbilt freshman righthander **Donny Everett** died in a drowning accident. Everett and several of his teammates were out fishing when the accident happened. Everett died just nine days after touching 101 mph during an appearance at the SEC Tournament, a moment that has been memorialized on the Hoover Metropolitan Stadium outfield wall just below the radar gun.

College baseball's epicenter had long been migrating to the **Southeast**, and that development was plainly illustrated in 2016. No regionals were hosted west of Texas or north of the Ohio River. The **West Coast** was shut out of hosting regionals for the first time since 1994, and the ACC and SEC combined to host 13 of the 16 regionals. The SEC set a record with seven.

Texas coach **Augie Garrido** stepped down from his position following a disappointing season, ending a historic coaching career. He finished with a career record of 1,975-952 in 48 seasons and won five national championships. His retirement was the first of many by longtime head coaches over the next few years, as the profession began a generational turnover.

## FINAL TOP 25 FOR 2016

1. Coastal Carolina*
2. Arizona*
3. Texas Christian*
4. Oklahoma State*
5. #Florida*
6. Miami*
7. Texas Tech*
8. Texas A&M
9. UC Santa Barbara*
10. Mississippi State
11. Louisville
12. Louisiana State
13. Florida State
14. South Carolina
15. East Carolina
16. Boston College
17. Clemson
18. Mississippi
19. Tulane
20. Vanderbilt
21. Virginia
22. Louisiana-Lafayette
23. Florida Atlantic
24. Southern Mississippi
25. North Carolina State

\* Reached College World Series
\# Preseason No. 1

# IN RETROSPECT: 2016 DRAFT

**Top 10 Draft Picks From College**
With overall selection number (Ov), drafting team (Team) and rank on Baseball America draft board (BA).

| Player | Pos | School | Ov | Team | BA |
|---|---|---|---|---|---|
| Nick Senzel | 3B | Tennessee | 2 | Reds | 6 |
| Corey Ray | OF | Louisville | 5 | Brewers | 7 |
| A.J. Puk | LHP | Florida | 6 | Athletics | 1 |
| Cal Quantrill | RHP | Stanford | 8 | Padres | 38 |
| Zack Collins | C | Miami | 10 | White Sox | 16 |
| Kyle Lewis | OF | Mercer | 11 | Mariners | 4 |
| Matt Thaiss | C | Virginia | 16 | Angels | 28 |
| Justin Dunn | RHP | Boston College | 19 | Mets | 22 |
| T.J. Zeuch | RHP | Pittsburgh | 21 | Blue Jays | 20 |
| Will Craig | 3B | Wake Forest | 22 | Pirates | 45 |

**Top 10 Major League Players From College Draft Class**
With draft round and Baseball-Reference.com total for wins above replacement (WAR) through 2019.

| Player | Pos | School | Rd | Ov | Team | WAR |
|---|---|---|---|---|---|---|
| Shane Bieber | RHP | UC Santa Barbara | 4 | 122 | Indians | 6.0 |
| Pete Alonso | 1B | Florida | 2 | 64 | Mets | 5.0 |
| Bryan Reynolds | OF | Vanderbilt | 2 | 59 | Giants | 3.9 |
| Tommy Edman | 3B | Stanford | 6 | 196 | Cardinals | 3.8 |
| Cavan Biggio | 2B | Notre Dame | 5 | 162 | Blue Jays | 2.8 |
| Zac Gallen | RHP | North Carolina | 3 | 106 | Cardinals | 2.5 |
| Dakota Hudson | RHP | Mississippi State | 1 | 34 | Cardinals | 2.4 |
| Joey Lucchesi | LHP | SE Missouri State | 4 | 114 | Padres | 2.1 |
| Zach Plesac | RHP | Ball State | 12 | 362 | Indians | 1.9 |
| Will Smith | C | Louisville | 1 | 32 | Dodgers | 1.6 |
| Aaron Civale | RHP | Northeastern | 3 | 92 | Indians | 1.6 |

Gilmore said he decided after the rainout that Beckwith would start Game 3.

"I told (pitching coach Drew Thomas), 'Since this thing got rained out, I just feel like, for me, the way Beckwith has pitched, he deserves the opportunity to go out,' " Gilmore said. "And if we get beat, we get beat with our guy on the mound."

Beckwith would not be denied. After Arizona righthander Bobby Dalbec shut Coastal out for five innings, the Chanticleers broke through with four runs in the top of the sixth. They took advantage of two walks by Dalbec and two errors by second baseman Cody Ramer to score two runs. G.K. Young, the DH, then doubled his team's score with a two-run homer to right field.

Beckwith, Holmes and Cunningham made that advantage stand up, even as Arizona refused to let its season end quietly. In the end, though, the Chanticleers ended their incredible postseason with a dogpile in the middle of TD Ameritrade Park.

It was a national championship a long time coming for Gilmore, who has been the head coach at his alma mater since 1996. The final win marked the 1,100th in his career, and he became the first coach to win the national championship in his first CWS appearance since 2008, when Mike Batesole led Fresno State to the title.

Batesole's Bulldogs did it at Rosenblatt Stadium in an offensive era. Gilmore's Chanticleers did it by grinding through TD Ameritrade Park in a challenging offensive atmosphere, where the teams combined to hit .232 with 10 home runs. They did it by beating teams from the Southeastern, Big 12 and Pacific-12 conferences.

"Whenever I die, I'll know that this group of guys here, they willed themselves to be national champions," Gilmore said. ■

# Lewis powers away from field

By **JIM SHONERD**

A s a recruit, Kyle Lewis didn't exactly fit Mercer's mold.

The Bears look for players ready to contribute quickly. Lewis wasn't going to be that guy, his attention always having been divided between baseball and basketball. Still, between his athleticism, his intelligence and his tools—even if he only showed them in flashes—Mercer coaches decided he was worth bringing in.

"He was just an athletic piece and his skill level wasn't there (as a high schooler)," Mercer head coach Craig Gibson said. "So he's generally not what we sign. We like more guys who are a little more skilled, who can come in and play immediately. But he was a guy we took a chance on—who we thought if his skill level ever caught up with his athleticism, he's going to be a good player."

Lewis' skill level did catch up. Three years later, he will leave as the program's new gold standard. "He's the best player in school history," Gibson said.

Kyle Lewis began his career at Mercer as a raw talent and exited as the program's new gold standard. Waylaid by a knee injury in his pro debut, Lewis reached to the majors late in 2019—and mashed.

Lewis' statistics read like something out of another era. He hit .395/.535/.731 in 61 games. Though Mercer's season ended in the finals of the Southern Conference Tournament, Lewis ranked among the top five nationally in total bases (163), slugging (.731) and on-base percentage (.535). Mercer's coaches are quick to point out his 66 walks, which ranked second in the nation, cost him roughly 15 games of at-bats, meaning he did his greatest damage—his 20 homers and 72 RBIs—as if he played in 45 games.

With that level of domination, on top of being one of college baseball's premier talents, Lewis is the College Player of the Year.

Even though the thunderous power in his bat is usually the first thing mentioned in any Lewis scouting report, he doesn't think of himself as a home run hitter. For Lewis, home runs are just a byproduct of trying to hit balls on a line, a mentality that would make any hitting coach proud.

"I'm not trying to go up there and just slug home runs and swing for the fences. I'm trying to put hard line drives in play consistently," Lewis said. "I think that if you try to hit low line drives consistently that you'll get the elevation and you'll get some balls out of the park, and I've been able to do that. But I think that as an overall hitter, I try to just be a hitter for average."

TOM PRIDDY

Lewis hit a 461-foot moon shot over the batter's eye at Fluor Field in the SoCon tournament that was as majestic as a home run can be. The blast elicited "oohs" and "aahs" from the crowd and the video of it spread quickly on Twitter. In the Bears' dugout, though, it wasn't anything they hadn't seen before. Just Kyle doing his thing.

"That's nothing abnormal," teammate Trey Truitt said. "Kyle does that all the time."

After not playing every day as a freshman, Lewis took off as a sophomore last year. He hit .367/.423/.677 with 17 homers for Mercer, then tore up the prestigious Cape Cod League over the summer, hitting .300/.344/.500 and ranking as the Cape's No. 3 prospect.

Scouts have followed Lewis ever since. But even with his hometown team, the Braves, owning the No. 3 overall pick, Lewis doesn't let his mind wander. Sure, he's thought about the draft, but as he was wearing a Mercer uniform, the Bears were his priority.

"We'll have 15-30 or more scouts at each game," Mercer assistant coach Brent Shade said. "He knows that they're there, but he puts it out of his mind and just goes about his business and lets his play do the talking for him. He's a team guy, I will tell you that. He's all about Mercer first and Kyle second. That's hard to find guys like that."

Lewis led the Bears to back-to-back SoCon regular season titles in 2015 and 2016, winning conference player of the year honors in both. Suffice to say that chance the Bears took paid off. "I don't know what's to come," Lewis said, "but it's going to be fun." ∎

# TOP PLAYERS OF 2016

## ALL-AMERICA TEAM

| Pos | Player | School | Yr | AVG | AB | R | H | HR | RBI | SB | BB | SO | OBP | SLG |
|---|---|---|---|---|---|---|---|---|---|---|---|---|---|---|
| C | Zack Collins | Miami | Jr | .357 | 185 | 53 | 66 | 15 | 57 | 1 | 75 | 51 | .538 | .649 |
| 1B | Eric Gutierrez | Texas Tech | Sr | .333 | 234 | 54 | 78 | 13 | 60 | 3 | 42 | 37 | .465 | .581 |
| 2B | Ryne Birk | Texas A&M | Jr | .310 | 255 | 52 | 79 | 7 | 45 | 9 | 29 | 34 | .378 | .478 |
| 3B | Boomer White | Texas A&M | R-Jr | .386 | 259 | 49 | 100 | 5 | 46 | 10 | 33 | 16 | .462 | .517 |
| SS | Taylor Walls | Florida State | So | .355 | 248 | 72 | 88 | 6 | 46 | 14 | 59 | 45 | .479 | .516 |
| OF | Seth Beer | Clemson | Fr | .369 | 203 | 57 | 75 | 18 | 70 | 1 | 62 | 27 | .535 | .700 |
| OF | Kyle Lewis | Mercer | Jr | .395 | 223 | 70 | 88 | 20 | 72 | 6 | 66 | 48 | .535 | .731 |
| OF | Anfernee Grier | Auburn | Jr | .366 | 238 | 56 | 87 | 12 | 41 | 19 | 32 | 55 | .457 | .576 |
| DH | Will Craig | Wake Forest | Jr | .379 | 182 | 53 | 69 | 16 | 66 | 0 | 47 | 35 | .520 | .731 |
| UT | Brendan McKay | Louisville | So | .333 | 228 | 43 | 76 | 6 | 41 | 0 | 24 | 33 | .414 | .513 |

| Pos | Pitcher | School | Yr | W | L | ERA | G | SV | IP | H | BB | SO |
|---|---|---|---|---|---|---|---|---|---|---|---|---|
| SP | Eric Lauer | Kent State | Jr | 10 | 2 | 0.69 | 15 | 0 | 104 | 49 | 28 | 125 |
| SP | A.J. Puckett | Pepperdine | Jr | 9 | 3 | 1.27 | 14 | 0 | 99 | 65 | 26 | 95 |
| SP | Cody Sedlock | Illinois | Jr | 5 | 3 | 2.49 | 14 | 0 | 101 | 80 | 31 | 116 |
| SP | Logan Shore | Florida | Jr | 12 | 1 | 2.31 | 18 | 0 | 105 | 82 | 19 | 96 |
| RP | Troy Rallings | Washington | Sr | 4 | 1 | 0.89 | 28 | 16 | 61 | 32 | 12 | 60 |
| UT | Brendan McKay | Louisville | So | 12 | 4 | 2.30 | 17 | 0 | 110 | 89 | 42 | 128 |

## SECOND TEAM

C—Chris Okey, Clemson. 1B—Jameson Fisher, Southeastern Louisiana. 2B—Jake Noll, Florida Gulf Coast. 3B—Nick Senzel, Tennessee. SS—C.J. Chatham, Florida Atlantic. OF—Heath Quinn, Samford; Corey Ray, Louisville; and J.B. Woodman, Mississippi. DH—Matt Thaiss, Virginia. UT—Luken Baker, Texas Christian. SP—Corbin Burnes, St. Mary's; Connor Jones, Virginia; Brigham Hill, Texas A&M; and Dakota Hudson, Mississippi State. RP—Mark Ecker, Texas A&M.

## THIRD TEAM

C—Nick Feight, UNC Wilmington. 1B—Pete Alonso, Florida. 2B—Nick Solak, Louisville. 3B—Jake Burger, Mississippi State. SS—Donnie Walton, Oklahoma State. OF—Ronnie Dawson, Ohio State; Jake Mangum, Miss. State; and David Oppenheim, USC. DH—Brett Cumberland, California. UT—Adam Haseley, Virginia. SP—Keegan Akin, Western Michigan; Justin Dunn, Boston College; Joey Lucchesi, Southeast Missouri State; and Thomas Hatch, Oklahoma State. RP—Pat Krall, Clemson.

Florida players celebrate the Gators'
first ever national championship,
a hard-earned sweep of SEC rival
Louisiana State. The Tigers had never
before lost in the finals.

2017

# Gators claim first CWS title, fulfilling promise

By **TEDDY CAHILL**

**FROM THE ISSUE:**
JULY 21–AUG. 4, 2017

**A**s fireworks lit up the Omaha skyline above TD Ameritrade Park and blue and orange streamers soared over the infield, Florida fell into a raucous dogpile.

Florida had just defeated Louisiana State 6-1 on June 27 in Game 2 of the College World Series finals to complete a sweep and win the first national championship in program history. Righthander Alex Faedo was named Most Outstanding Player after two dominant starts in the first week of the tournament carried the Gators to the finals.

"You never know how you're going to feel when you get the last out in the College World Series, and I'm still kind of numb," Florida coach Kevin O'Sullivan said. "Just overwhelmed with emotions for our players."

Florida relied on its elite rotation all spring and throughout the CWS. But because of how the schedule fell, the Gators were unable to start any of their trio of Faedo, Brady Singer and Jackson Kowar in Game 2 against LSU. Instead, Florida called on freshman righthander Tyler Dyson, typically its setup man, to make just his second career start against LSU lefthander Jared Poché, the winningest pitcher in program history.

Dyson outdueled Poché, holding the Tigers to one run on three hits and two walks in six innings. He turned a lead over to closer Michael Byrne as he had done so many times.

"I didn't get much sleep last night, thinking about this game," Dyson said. "I just went out there and executed the pitch call."

LSU, however, didn't make anything easy for Florida. The Gators grabbed an early lead with one run in both of the first two innings, but they were unable to expand it against Poché. And the Tigers' potent offense threatened late in the game.

After scoring once in the seventh, LSU got runners on first and third with no outs to start the eighth. Byrne struck out Antoine Duplantis, the Tigers' three-hole hitter, before O'Sullivan called on Kowar, who was slated to start if the series went to three games. Kowar got All-American Greg Deichmann to hit a grounder to first baseman J.J. Schwarz, who threw home to get Kramer Robertson, who had taken off from third base on contact.

## TOP TEAMS
### 2017 COLLEGE WORLD SERIES STANDINGS

| School | Conference | Record | CWS | Head Coach |
|---|---|---|---|---|
| Florida | Southeastern | 52–19 | 5–1 | Kevin O'Sullivan |
| Louisiana State | Southeastern | 52–20 | 4–3 | Paul Mainieri |
| Texas Christian | Big 12 | 50–18 | 3–2 | Jim Schlossnagle |
| Oregon State | Pacific-12 | 56–6 | 2–2 | Pat Casey |
| Florida State | Atlantic Coast | 46–23 | 1–2 | Mike Martin |
| Louisville | Atlantic Coast | 53–12 | 1–2 | Dan McDonnell |
| Cal State Fullerton | Big West | 39–24 | 0–2 | Rick Vanderhook |
| Texas A&M | Southeastern | 41–23 | 0–2 | Rob Childresss |

## NATIONAL CHAMPION
### FLORIDA

Making their sixth trip to Omaha in the past eight seasons under coach Kevin O'Sullivan, the Gators broke through for their first national title. Florida swept LSU in the championship series, led by a surprising turn buy freshman Tyler Dyson.

"It was a heads-up play," O'Sullivan said. "He made a perfect throw. Quick feet. Probably saved the game, to be honest with you."

Florida scored four insurance runs in the bottom of the eighth against electric LSU freshman righthander Zack Hess. Deacon Liput drove in two runs in the inning and finished the night 2-for-5 with a run and three RBIs to celebrate his 21st birthday in style.

Kowar returned to the mound in the ninth and got the final three outs with little drama. He had last pitched June 23 against Texas Christian. Though he was in line to start Game 3, he went to O'Sullivan before the final game and told his coach that he had a few innings in him if he was needed. O'Sullivan said before that conversation, he had not thought about using Kowar, but he wanted to do anything he could to wrap up the series in two games to avoid LSU ace Alex Lange, who was also in line to start Game 3.

"Sometimes you make these decisions and they don't work out, and you look like a fool," O'Sullivan said. "And sometimes you make them and the players make you look like you're smart."

O'Sullivan has looked smart far more often than not in his 10 years at Florida. He has led the Gators to the CWS six times in the last eight years and turned the program into a powerhouse both for on-field production and player development.

But despite the parade of All-Americans and first-round draft picks that have come through Gainesville, including Gators stars such as Brian Johnson, Logan Shore and Mike Zunino, O'Sullivan had not been able to break through to win the program's first title. That changed a year after Florida went 0-2 in Omaha with a team that was the No. 1 national seed and had eight players drafted in the top 10 rounds.

All eight of those players signed, leaving several holes for the Gators to replace this year. They lacked the depth many of O'Sullivan's teams have had, with injuries through-

# 2017 NEWSMAKERS

**Oregon State** fell short in the CWS, losing in the bracket final to Louisiana State, but the Beavers put together an all-time season. They went 56-6 and their .903 winning percentage is the fourth-best in D-I history. Their 27-3 Pac-12 Conference mark set a record, and they twice went on 23-game winning streaks. But they lost twice to LSU in Omaha—their first back-to-back losses of the year—and instead will go down in history as one of the best teams not to win the national championship.

Mississippi State first baseman **Brent Rooker** became the second player ever to win the SEC triple crown, joining fellow Bulldogs slugger Rafael Palmeiro, who claimed it in 1984. Rooker hit .387 with 23 home runs and 82 RBIs.

**Davidson** dramatically reached super regionals for the first time in program history. The Wildcats upset top-seeded Virginia Commonwealth in the Atlantic-10 Conference Tournament to reach the NCAA Tournament for the first time in program history. Then, they swept through the Chapel Hill Regional, stunning No. 2 overall seed North Carolina. Davidson's run came to an end in the super regionals with a sweep at Texas A&M.

## FINAL TOP 25 FOR 2017

1. Florida*
2. Louisiana State*
3. Oregon State*
4. #Texas Christian*
5. Louisville*
6. Florida State*
7. Cal State Fullerton*
8. Long Beach State
9. Kentucky
10. Texas A&M*
11. North Carolina
12. Texas Tech
13. Wake Forest
14. Mississippi State
15. Stanford
16. Southern Mississippi
17. Missouri State
18. Vanderbilt
19. Arkansas
20. Sam Houston State
21. Virginia
22. Houston
23. Clemson
24. Texas
25. Auburn

* Reached College World Series
# Preseason No. 1

# IN RETROSPECT: 2017 DRAFT

### Top 10 Draft Picks From College
With overall selection number (Ov), drafting team (Team) and rank on Baseball America draft board (BA).

| Player | Pos | School | Ov | Team | BA |
|---|---|---|---|---|---|
| Brendan McKay | LHP | Louisville | 4 | Rays | 3 |
| Kyle Wright | RHP | Vanderbilt | 5 | Braves | 2 |
| Pavin Smith | 1B | Virginia | 7 | D-backs | 15 |
| Adam Haseley | OF | Virginia | 8 | Philllies | 8 |
| Keston Hiura | 2B | UC Irvine | 9 | Brewers | 14 |
| Jake Burger | 3B | Missouri State | 11 | White Sox | 20 |
| J.B. Bukauskas | RHP | North Carolina | 15 | Astros | 6 |
| Clarke Schmidt | RHP | South Carolina | 16 | Yankees | 32 |
| Evan White | 1B | Kentucky | 17 | Mariners | 12 |
| Alex Faedo | RHP | Florida | 18 | Tigers | 10 |

### Top 9 Major League Players From College Draft Class
With draft round and Baseball-Reference.com total for wins above replacement (WAR) through 2019.

| Player | Pos | School | Rd | Ov | Team | WAR |
|---|---|---|---|---|---|---|
| Keston Hiura | 2B | UC Irvine | 1 | 9 | Brewers | 2.1 |
| Adam Haseley | OF | Virginia | 1 | 8 | Phillies | 1.7 |
| Griffin Canning | RHP | UCLA | 2 | 47 | Angels | 1.1 |
| James Karinchak | RHP | Bryant | 9 | 282 | Indians | 0.1 |
| Josh Rojas | 2B | Hawaii | 26 | 781 | Astros | 0.0 |
| Brendan McKay | LHP | Louisville | 1 | 4 | Rays | -0.1 |
| Corbin Martin | RHP | Texas A&M | 2 | 56 | Astros | -0.2 |
| Kyle Wright | RHP | Vanderbilt | 1 | 5 | Braves | -0.6 |
| Nick Margevicius | LHP | Rider | 7 | 189 | Padres | -0.9 |

out the spring testing their depth even further. Florida's offense never truly clicked, and it ended the season without a .300 hitter. As a team, the Gators hit .259/.355/.378.

Through it all, Florida found a way to win. The Gators won 19 one-run games, the most in the nation, thanks in large part to its defense and Byrne, who set a program record with 19 saves. Most importantly, Florida was always able to rely on its rotation.

Faedo went 9-2, 2.26, earned All-America honors and was drafted 18th overall by the Tigers. Singer, a sophomore who is an early favorite to be the No. 1 overall pick in next year's draft, went 9-5, 3.21, while Kowar, his classmate, went 12-1, 4.08.

Faedo and Singer found another level during the postseason. The righthanders combined to go 4-0, 1.27 with 43 strikeouts and nine walks in 28.1 innings in the CWS.

Singer won Game 1 of the finals, striking out 12 batters in seven innings. Faedo was so good in the first half of the CWS that he didn't need to appear in the finals to win Most Outstanding Player. He struck out 22 batters in 14.1 scoreless innings over two starts against TCU, and he won the game that clinched Florida's spot in the finals.

For years, particularly in recent seasons once Florida got rolling under O'Sullivan, many have expected the Gators to break through for a national championship.

To finally win it all says a lot about O'Sullivan, athletic director Scott Stricklin said.

"We've had 10 sports win national titles and as good as baseball's been, it has not done that before now," he said. "To be able to put that banner up at the baseball facility— 'national champions'—it's really special."

The Gators will be able to hang that banner at McKethan Stadium, fulfilling the program's ultimate promise. ∎

# Two-way McKay excels on all fronts

By **TEDDY CAHILL**

Even after Brendan McKay dyed his hair blond along with his teammates before Louisville began the Atlantic Coast Conference Tournament, nobody would confuse the lefthander/first baseman with Robert Redford. But Redford's Hollywood looks are about the only thing separating McKay from becoming "The Natural."

Baseball appears to come so easily to McKay. In his senior year at his Pittsburgh-area high school, he had a 72-inning scoreless streak. At Louisville, he has been a staple of the rotation and the middle of the lineup throughout his career.

He spent the last two summers playing for USA Baseball's Collegiate National Team. He was Freshman of the Year in 2015 and has earned first-team All-America honors for three straight seasons. He's just the third player to do so in Baseball America's 37-year history, joining Texas' Greg Swindell (1984-86) and Oklahoma State's Robin Ventura (1986-88).

One of the most valuable players in college history, Brendan McKay was a three-year first-team All-American as a two-way star. As a junior he went 9-3, 2.31 while hitting .357 with 17 home runs.

McKay's junior season was his best yet. He went 11-3, 2.56 with 146 strikeouts in 109 innings on the mound and hit .341/.457/.659 with 18 home runs. He helped lead Louisville to the ACC regular season title and the No. 7 national seed. For his sensational season and two-way talent, McKay is the College Player of the Year.

McKay has considerable physical talents, but his mental capabilities play a big role in his success as well. He shoulders a hefty burden for the Cardinals but never allows the pressure to overwhelm him.

"Baseball's hard as it is, just being a regular player," McKay said. "If you put any extra pressure on yourself, it can take even more of a toll. That's when you play your best, when you're free and you've got a clear mind and you're just doing your thing out there."

While Louisville had high hopes for McKay, he first had to prove he belonged in the mix on the mound and in the lineup. He quickly did both. He opened his freshman year in the bullpen and earned four saves before moving into the rotation about a month into the season. He became a regular in the lineup in the first few weeks of the spring.

McKay went 9-3, 1.77 in 96.2 innings. At the plate, he hit .308/.418/.431 with four home runs. Just a year after Kentucky's A.J. Reed won the College Player of the Year award, college baseball had found its next two-way superstar.

"If you put Brendan the pitcher on one side and Brendan the hitter on the other side, they could almost have their own competition to see who's better at that craft," Louisville coach Dan McDonnell said.

McKay has always been a two-way player, but pitching was long considered his forte and likely long-term position. His development at the plate this spring, however, led evaluators to seriously consider drafting him as a hitter. If pitching wins out, it will be the allure of a lefthander throwing 91-93 mph with a hammer curveball and solid changeup. Many also believe his stuff will play up a tick when he stops hitting every day.

Managing McKay's workload has not been easy, but after three seasons of splitting his time, he said he has found a good routine. He does everything his position player team-mates do, with the small concession of serving as the DH the day after he pitches. He has also condensed his post-start weightlifting into one session to minimize his soreness.

McDonnell is not shy about declaring McKay the best player in program history. He is a transformative talent and has played a critical role in Louisville winning the ACC title in two of its first three years in the league.

Winning drives McKay more than any individual records, awards or his draft position.

"He just wants to win," McDonnell said.

"He loves to compete. We're so blessed to have him." ■

# TOP PLAYERS OF 2017

## ALL-AMERICA TEAM

| Pos | Player | School | Yr | AVG | AB | R | H | HR | RBI | SB | BB | SO | OBP | SLG |
|-----|--------|--------|----|-----|----|----|----|----|-----|----|----|----|-----|-----|
| C | David Banuelos | Long Beach State | Jr | .289 | 201 | 31 | 58 | 7 | 29 | 5 | 17 | 45 | .368 | .468 |
| 1B | Brent Rooker | Mississippi State | R-Jr | .387 | 248 | 60 | 96 | 23 | 82 | 18 | 48 | 58 | .495 | .810 |
| 2B | Nick Madrigal | Oregon State | So | .380 | 237 | 53 | 90 | 4 | 40 | 16 | 27 | 16 | .449 | .532 |
| 3B | Jake Burger | Missouri State | Jr | .328 | 247 | 69 | 81 | 22 | 65 | 3 | 43 | 38 | .443 | .648 |
| SS | Logan Warmoth | North Carolina | Jr | .336 | 271 | 60 | 91 | 10 | 49 | 18 | 28 | 47 | .404 | .554 |
| OF | Greg Deichmann | Louisiana State | Jr | .308 | 266 | 54 | 82 | 19 | 73 | 7 | 51 | 62 | .417 | .579 |
| OF | Stuart Fairchild | Wake Forest | Jr | .360 | 261 | 65 | 94 | 17 | 67 | 21 | 31 | 54 | .439 | .636 |
| OF | Adam Haseley | Virginia | Jr | .390 | 223 | 68 | 87 | 14 | 56 | 10 | 44 | 21 | .491 | .659 |
| DH | Keston Hiura | UC Irvine | Jr | .442 | 199 | 48 | 88 | 8 | 42 | 9 | 50 | 38 | .567 | .693 |
| UT | Brendan McKay | Louisville | Jr | .341 | 223 | 57 | 76 | 18 | 57 | 2 | 45 | 39 | .457 | .659 |

| Pos | Pitcher | School | Yr | W | L | ERA | G | SV | IP | H | BB | SO |
|-----|---------|--------|----|----|----|-----|----|----|----|----|----|----|
| SP | J.B. Bukauskas | North Carolina | Jr | 9 | 1 | 2.53 | 15 | 0 | 93 | 62 | 37 | 116 |
| SP | Steven Gingery | Texas Tech | So | 10 | 1 | 1.58 | 15 | 0 | 91 | 60 | 29 | 107 |
| SP | Cory Abbott | Loyola Marymount | Jr | 11 | 2 | 1.74 | 15 | 0 | 98 | 61 | 28 | 130 |
| SP | Jake Thompson | Oregon State | R-Jr | 14 | 1 | 1.96 | 20 | 0 | 128 | 85 | 40 | 119 |
| RP | Josh Hiatt | North Carolina | R-Fr | 4 | 2 | 1.90 | 32 | 13 | 52 | 31 | 20 | 64 |
| RP | Wyatt Marks | Louisiana-Lafayette | Jr | 2 | 1 | 2.28 | 30 | 7 | 59 | 29 | 25 | 100 |
| UT | Brendan McKay | Louisville | Jr | 11 | 3 | 2.56 | 17 | 0 | 109 | 77 | 35 | 146 |

## SECOND TEAM

**C**—Joey Morgan, Washington. **1B**—Evan White, Kentucky. **2B**—Braden Shewmake, Texas A&M. **3B**—Drew Ellis, Louisville. **SS**—Kevin Merrell, South Florida. **OF**—Garrett McCain, Oklahoma State; Will Robertson, Davidson; and Matt Wallner, Southern Mississippi. **DH**—J.J. Matijevic, Arizona. **UT**—Taylor Braley, Southern Mississippi. **SP**—Tyler Holton, Florida State; Alex Faedo, Florida; Alex Lange, Louisiana State; and Kyle Wright, Vanderbilt. **RP**—Lincoln Henzman, Louisville; and Colton Hock, Stanford.

## THIRD TEAM

**C**—Daulton Varsho, Wisconsin-Milwaukee. **1B**—Gavin Sheets, Wake Forest. **2B**—Riley Mahan, Kentucky. **3B**—Jake Scheiner, Houston. **SS**—Jeremy Eierman, Missouri State. **OF**—D.J. Artis, Liberty; Jeren Kendall, Vanderbilt; and Tristan Pompey, Kentucky. **DH**—Jake Adams, Iowa. **UT**—Jake Meyers, Nebraska. **SP**—Griffin Canning, UCLA; David Peterson, Oregon; J.P Sears, The Citadel; and Casey Mize, Auburn. **RP**—Michael Byrne, Florida; and Nate Harris, Louisiana Tech.

Oregon State's Pat Casey cemented his place in coaching history with his third national title. The victory was especially sweet after the Beavers' bitter defeat in 2017.

2018

# Oregon State 'finishes' off CWS title

By **TEDDY CAHILL**

**STORY APPEARED ONLINE:**
JUNE 29, 2018

**A**ll year long, Oregon State has broken its huddles to one word: finish. The word, repeated so many times after practices and games and any time the Beavers were together, was a reminder of the disappointing end to the 2017 season and a goal for the 2018 season.

Oregon State last year entered the NCAA Tournament as the No. 1 overall seed and one of the favorites at the College World Series. But its season came to disappointing end when it lost back-to-back games against Louisiana State in the CWS semifinals. A team that had a chance to be one of the greatest of all time instead was knocked out before it even had a chance to play for the national title.

That loss fueled the Beavers this year. Second baseman Nick Madrigal said as soon as LSU eliminated Oregon State, he flipped a switch mentally to the 2018 season and did everything he could to get the Beavers back to Omaha. Shortstop Cadyn Grenier said the feeling at the end of last year's CWS was one that none of the Beavers wanted to experience again. Right fielder Trevor Larnach said it left a salty taste in their mouths.

That taste was washed away on June 28. Oregon State defeated Arkansas 5–0 in Game 3 of the CWS finals to claim the national championship. It is the third national title in program history and first since the Beavers went back-to-back in 2006 and '07.

Freshman righthander Kevin Abel threw a two-hit shutout and All-American catcher Adley Rutschman powered the offense with three hits and two RBIs. The victory saw Oregon State complete a comeback that started the night before, when it was one strike away from being swept in the best-of-three series before ultimately forcing Game 3.

Above all, the Beavers had finished.

"All offseason long, from the first day, this has been our goal," Madrigal said. "We've said we've got to finish this year and we did exactly that. It took a total team effort. Not one guy could have won this by themselves. From top to bottom, we needed every single guy on this team."

## TOP TEAMS

### 2018 COLLEGE WORLD SERIES STANDINGS

| School | Conference | Record | CWS | Head Coach |
|---|---|---|---|---|
| Oregon State | Pacific-12 | 55–12–1 | 6–2 | Pat Casey |
| Arkansas | Southeastern | 48–21 | 4–2 | Dave Van Horn |
| Florida | Southeastern | 49–21 | 2–2 | Kevin O'Sullivan |
| Mississippi State | Southeastern | 39–29 | 2–2 | Gary Henderson |
| North Carolina | Atlantic Coast | 44–20 | 1–2 | Mike Fox |
| Texas Tech | Big 12 | 45–18 | 1–2 | Tim Tadlock |
| Texas | Big 12 | 42–23 | 0–2 | David Pierce |
| Washington | Pacific-12 | 35–26 | 0–2 | Lindsay Meggs |

### NATIONAL CHAMPION
### OREGON STATE

The Beavers claim their third national title by defeating Arkansas in three games in the championship series. OSU catcher Adley Rutschman sets a CWS record with 17 hits, and coach Pat Casey claims his third title following wins in 2006-07.

Oregon State really did need just about its whole roster in Omaha. It lost its opening game of the CWS against North Carolina, dropping it into the losers' bracket. But Oregon State fought through four straight elimination games, knocking out Washington, North Carolina and Mississippi State to get to the finals. Arkansas beat Oregon State in the first game of the finals, putting the Beavers' backs against the walls again.

But, again, the Beavers found a way. Oregon State trailed Arkansas 3-2 in the ninth inning of Game 2 and nearly saw its dream crushed again. Grenier lofted a pop-up into foul ground up the first base line, a ball that he thought was going to be caught for the final out. Instead, it fell, and Grenier took advantage of his newfound life to drive in the game-tying run. Larnach followed with a two-run home run to send the series to a decisive Game 3, where the Beavers wouldn't be denied.

Grenier said the only time he ever doubted that Oregon State would win the championship was in the moment Wednesday night when his pop-up was in the air.

"I thought for sure it was going to get caught," he said. "After I got that hit and Trevor hit that home run, we came into today and I knew there was no way we were going to let that get away from us again."

Rutschman and Larnach led the way offensively for Oregon State. Rutschman set a CWS record with 17 hits in the tournament and was named Most Outstanding Player. Larnach had 15 hits of his own, including that game-winning home run in Game 2.

On the mound, Abel won four games during the CWS—another record. Lefthander Brandon Eisert, deployed as a longman, often looked like Oregon State's best pitcher. All up and down Oregon State's roster, players found a way to contribute.

The depth of Oregon State's roster and the elite talent in its junior class—Madrigal, Larnach and Grenier were all drafted earlier in June among the top 40 picks—made it one

# 2018 NEWSMAKERS

With a 3-2 victory in 11 innings at Clemson on May 5, Florida State coach **Mike Martin** won his 1,976th game and broke Augie Garrido's record to become the all-time winningest coach in college baseball history. He achieved the mark in about 250 fewer games than Garrido and reached the record total over 39 years at his alma mater. The Seminoles were again unable to deliver Martin's elusive national championship as they would be upset in the Tallahassee Regional a month later.

**Augie Garrido**, the historic coach who won five CWS titles, died March 15 after suffering a stroke. He was 79. Garrido had retired after the 2016 season after a 48-year career as head coach, most notably at Cal State Fullerton and Texas. He was the winningest coach of all-time when he retired.

Arizona State freshman first baseman **Spencer Torkelson** hit 25 home runs to lead the nation. It took him just 25 games to break the Sun Devils' freshman home run record of 11 set by Barry Bonds in 1983, and he finished two shy of the school's single-season record. He also became the sixth player to reach 25 home runs since the BBCOR bat regulations went into effect.

## FINAL TOP 25 FOR 2018

1. Oregon State*
2. Arkansas*
3. #Florida*
4. North Carolina*
5. Texas Tech*
6. Mississippi State*
7. Texas*
8. Minnesota
9. Washington*
10. Duke
11. Tennessee Tech
12. Stetson
13. Auburn
14. Stanford
15. Mississippi
16. South Carolina
17. Vanderbilt
18. Cal State Fullerton
19. Clemson
20. Fresno State
21. Georgia
22. North Carolina State
23. East Carolina
24. Coastal Carolina
25. Houston

* Reached College World Series
# Preseason No. 1

# IN RETROSPECT: 2018 DRAFT

**Top 10 Draft Picks From College**
With overall selection number (Ov), drafting team (Team) and rank on Baseball America draft board (BA).

| Player | Pos | School | Ov | Team | BA |
|---|---|---|---|---|---|
| Casey Mize | RHP | Auburn | 1 | Tigers | 1 |
| Joey Bart | C | Georgia Tech | 2 | Giants | 5 |
| Alec Bohm | 3B | Wichita State | 3 | Phillies | 7 |
| Nick Madrigal | SS | Oregon State | 4 | White Sox | 3 |
| Jonathan India | 3B | Florida | 5 | Reds | 6 |
| Kyler Murray | OF | Oklahoma | 9 | Athletics | 77 |
| Travis Swaggerty | OF | South Alabama | 10 | Pirates | 11 |
| Logan Gilbert | RHP | Stetson | 14 | Mariners | 19 |
| Brady Singer | RHP | Florida | 18 | Royals | 4 |
| Trevor Larnach | OF | Oregon State | 20 | Twins | 27 |

of the dominant forces in college baseball over the last two years. The Beavers won 111 games, twice reached the final four of the CWS and produced six All-Americans.

As much talent as the Beavers have had the last two years, coach Pat Casey said the makeup and mentality of the team has been the real key to their success.

"We've won a lot of games in the last two years," Casey said. "I know it's a cliché people use all the time about their character and their guys. But it's really true. There's nothing that's going to come from anything if everybody isn't invested in on another."

Oregon State has been tested on the field over the last few years. In 2016, it was perhaps the biggest snub from the NCAA Tournament. That slight fueled the Beavers during their magical 2017 run. The disappointment of last year then fed into this year's fire.

But this year wasn't easy for Oregon State. Madrigal, the 2017 Pacific-12 Conference player of the year, broke his hand in February and was sidelined for six weeks. During that time, the Beavers lost back-to-back conference series. Those losses ultimately cost them a chance at back-to-back conference titles and forced a reckoning within the team.

"We stubbed our toe pretty good there," Casey said. "We just didn't buy into the fact that we weren't going to be great. We came out and worked every day, talked about getting better. Everybody had to get better. I had to get better. The coaching staff had to get better. The players had to get better. We just weren't going to take no for an answer."

Oregon State has also been the subject of a harsh spotlight over the last year after "The Oregonian" reported last year that ace lefthander Luke Heimlich pled guilty to a sex crime he committed as a teenager. The report came last year following regionals and Heimlich did not pitch the rest of the year, removing himself from the team before the CWS. He returned to the mound this year and went 16-3, 2.92. Heimlich was not drafted in either of the last two years following the report.

This Beavers team, unlike last year's, didn't come to Omaha with the chance to go down as one of the best ever. Their winning percentage isn't one of the four best of all time, and they didn't rewrite the Pac-12 record book.

But they have something the 2017 team doesn't—a national championship, the goal they have all held since committing to Oregon State.

"This is the reason you come (to Oregon State)," Grenier said. "And that's aside of making a lot of lifetime friends and playing with some of the best players in the nation and getting some real good coaching. I can't explain this feeling."

In the end, the Beavers did what they came to Omaha to do. They finished. ■

# POY Singer lives up to the hype

By **TEDDY CAHILL**

Looking back on his remarkable regular season, Florida righthander Brady Singer is drawn all the way back to facing Siena on Opening Day. The junior took over as the Gators' ace and came into the year regarded as the top prospect in this year's draft class. The Gators were the defending national champions and all eyes were on Singer to get the season off to a strong start.

Singer did just that. He threw 89 pitches in seven innings and struck out eight batters while holding Siena to one run (unearned) on two hits and a walk.

"Walking out there for the first time my junior year with all the pressure—you know the draft stuff and people are watching with the No. 1 tag on me," Singer said. "To go into that start and get it started on the right foot going into the next weekend with Miami, I think that was the toughest one."

Singer has carried that momen-

Brady Singer helped pitch Florida to the College World Series in each of his three years in Gainesville. That stretch included the Gators' first national championship team in 2017.

tum through the rest of the season. As Florida's ace, he helped lead the Gators to the Southeastern Conference title and the top seed in the NCAA Tournament. He went 10-1, 2.25 with a 92-to-18 strikeout-to-walk ratio and held opposing hitters to a .186 average in 88 innings.

He carried the mantle of being the early favorite to be the No. 1 draft pick.

For his exemplary season and premium talent, Singer is the College Player of the Year.

Singer has long been regarded as a high-level prospect. He ranked No. 54 on the BA 500 pre-draft rankings in 2015, when he was coming out of Eustis (Fla.) High and was drafted No. 56 overall by the Blue Jays that June. He was the top-ranked prospect in the Cape Cod League after his freshman season. Through it all, he has lived up to the high expectations and now joins Mike Zunino as the only Gators to be named POY.

Singer has impressive physical tools and some of the best stuff in the country. He gets a lot of sinking action on his low-90s fastball and his sharp slider can be an out pitch.

After watching him pitch, those tools are readily apparent. What's more difficult to see is the hard work he puts in between starts to prepare. Coach Kevin O'Sullivan said Singer has completely changed his body over his three years at Florida, filling out his lanky frame and getting stronger.

Beyond physical gains, Singer also spends a lot of time on the mental side of the game.

"He's a tremendously hard worker between starts," O'Sullivan said. "Forget just the weight room but the watching of video and preparation and understanding the game."

Singer's competitiveness is also a part of what makes him an elite college pitcher. That competitive fire famously spilled over last year in super regionals when his appearance was interrupted by the umpteenth rain delay of the weekend in Gainesville.

Singer's mentality on the mound helps him excel on big stages. He last year was at his best in the College World Series. This year he rose to the occasion time after time when facing the SEC's best pitchers, including outdueling Auburn's Casey Mize in front of more than 60 scouts.

Singer said his competitive spirit comes from his parents, especially his mother.

"Even when we play board games, we can't lose," he said. "She's a huge competitor and I get it from her."

All those pieces have come together for Singer to make him a true college ace and the leader of the best pitching staff in the country. And they should enable him to sustain that success for years to come.

"This guy's going to pitch forever," O'Sullivan said.

"It's not just ability. He's extremely talented, and he has a competitive spirit. He's just different. That's hard to come by." ■

# TOP PLAYERS OF 2018

## ALL-AMERICA TEAM

| Pos | Player | School | Yr | AVG | AB | R | H | HR | RBI | SB | BB | SO | OBP | SLG |
|-----|--------|--------|----|----|----|---|---|----|----|----|----|----|-----|-----|
| C | Joey Bart | Georgia Tech | Jr | .359 | 220 | 55 | 79 | 16 | 38 | 3 | 41 | 56 | .471 | .632 |
| 1B | Bren Spillane | Illinois | Jr | .389 | 175 | 57 | 68 | 23 | 60 | 16 | 36 | 57 | .498 | .903 |
| 2B | Kody Clemens | Texas | Jr | .344 | 209 | 53 | 72 | 19 | 61 | 4 | 34 | 37 | .437 | .703 |
| 3B | Jonathan India | Florida | Jr | .362 | 188 | 57 | 68 | 17 | 42 | 11 | 47 | 47 | .502 | .723 |
| SS | Terrin Vavra | Minnesota | Jr | .405 | 163 | 43 | 66 | 7 | 42 | 6 | 23 | 13 | .477 | .620 |
| OF | Seth Beer | Clemson | Jr | .316 | 209 | 60 | 66 | 20 | 52 | 1 | 52 | 31 | .471 | .656 |
| OF | Trevor Larnach | Oregon State | Jr | .324 | 204 | 52 | 66 | 17 | 64 | 3 | 64 | 50 | .447 | .637 |
| OF | Bryant Packard | East Carolina | So | .403 | 206 | 47 | 83 | 14 | 50 | 5 | 50 | 42 | .460 | .680 |
| DH | Andrew Vaughn | California | So | .402 | 199 | 59 | 80 | 23 | 63 | 4 | 63 | 18 | .531 | .819 |
| UT | Brooks Wilson | Stetson | Sr | .287 | 167 | 28 | 48 | 3 | 26 | 8 | 26 | 39 | .399 | .437 |

| Pos | Pitcher | School | Yr | W | L | ERA | G | SV | IP | H | BB | SO |
|-----|---------|--------|----|----|----|-----|---|----|----|----|----|----|
| SP | Logan Gilbert | Stetson | Jr | 10 | 1 | 2.52 | 14 | 0 | 100 | 60 | 20 | 143 |
| SP | Casey Mize | Auburn | Jr | 9 | 5 | 3.07 | 15 | 0 | 103 | 73 | 10 | 140 |
| SP | Nick Sandlin | Southern Mississippi | Jr | 9 | 0 | 1.13 | 14 | 0 | 95 | 51 | 15 | 134 |
| SP | Brady Singer | Florida | Jr | 10 | 1 | 2.25 | 13 | 0 | 88 | 59 | 18 | 92 |
| RP | Michael Byrne | Florida | Jr | 2 | 1 | 1.99 | 29 | 13 | 45 | 33 | 4 | 46 |
| RP | Jack Little | Stanford | So | 3 | 0 | 0.66 | 23 | 15 | 41 | 24 | 7 | 54 |
| UT | Brooks Wilson | Stetson | Sr | 6 | 0 | 2.13 | 31 | 20 | 55 | 40 | 19 | 68 |

## SECOND TEAM

**C**—Adley Rutschman, Oregon State. **1B**—Spencer Torkelson, Arizona State. **2B**—Nick Dunn, Maryland. **3B**—Josh Jung, Texas Tech. **SS**—Cadyn Grenier, Oregon State. **OF**—Delvin Granberg, Dallas Baptist; Grant Little, Texas Tech; and Steele Walker, Oklahoma. **DH**—Alec Bohm, Wichita State. **UT**—Tanner Dodson, California. **SP**—Kyle Brnovich, Elon; Colton Eastman, Cal State Fullerton; Blaine Knight, Arkansas; and John Rooney, Jofstra. **RP**—Parker Caracci, Mississippi; and Ryley Gilliam, Clemson.

## THIRD TEAM

**C**—Cal Raleigh, Florida State. **1B**—Chase Chambers, Tenn. Tech. **2B**—Nick Madrigal, Oregon State. **3B**—Luke Reynolds, Southern Miss. **SS**—Logan Davidson, Clemson. **OF**—Gage Canning, Arizona State; Keegan McGovern, Georgia; and Andrew Moritz, UNC Greensboro. **DH**—Kevin Strohschein, Tenn. Tech. **UT**—Jack Labosky, Duke. **SP**—Mason Feole, UConn; Joey Murray, Kent State; Andre Pallente, UC Irvine; and Adam Wolf, Louisville. **RP**—Robert Broom, Mercer; and Durbin Feltman, TCU.

Vanderbilt claimed two national titles in the decade, with the 2019 edition staking a claim as single-season team of the decade after winning an SEC-record 59 games.

**2019**

# Vanderbilt begins and ends season at No. 1

By **TEDDY CAHILL**

**V**anderbilt wore its gold uniforms for Game 3 of the College World Series finals. It wasn't a coronation, not with Michigan on a magical postseason run in the opposite dugout, but the Commodores were dressed for success.

Vanderbilt started the season No. 1, and that's where it was going to finish. The Commodores played like the best team in the country throughout the second half of the season, and while they had been pushed during the NCAA Tournament, losing the first game of super regionals to Duke and the first game of the CWS finals to Michigan, they never buckled.

**STORY APPEARED ONLINE:**
JUNE 27, 2019

Vanderbilt had the nation's home run king in JJ Bleday. It had a catalyst at the top of the lineup in Austin Martin, a freshman ace in Kumar Rocker, a premium closer in Tyler Brown and a committed, experienced senior class that has stuck together through a trying four years. It led the nation in wins, won the Southeastern Conference regular season and SEC Tournament championships and beaten every other SEC team.

Vanderbilt wasn't going to be denied in Omaha. It was too deep, too talented, too well built for this stage. Vanderbilt, which had been unstoppable for the last three months, cruised to an 8-2 victory against Michigan to claim the national championship.

Vanderbilt won everything it possibly could have this season, but coach Tim Corbin said the team hadn't talked much about championships. That approach led to a trophy case full of them, including the Commodores' second national championship in program history and first since 2014. They finished 59-12, setting an SEC record for wins and won more games than any national champion since 1989 Wichita State won 68 games.

Vanderbilt came into the season ranked No. 1, but it has evolved as a team over the last five months. Its pitching staff, in particular, made big strides. Through many parts of the season, its offense led the way.

Bleday's power surge made him the No. 4 overall pick in the draft. Martin has established himself as a premium prospect in the 2020 draft. Seniors Ethan Paul and Stephen

## TOP TEAMS

### 2019 COLLEGE WORLD SERIES STANDINGS

| School | Conference | Record | CWS | Head Coach |
|---|---|---|---|---|
| Vanderbilt | Southeastern | 59–12 | 5–1 | Tim Corbin |
| Michigan | Big Ten | 50–22 | 4–2 | Erik Bakich |
| Louisville | Atlantic Coast | 51–18 | 2–2 | Dan McDonnell |
| Texas Tech | Big 12 | 46–20 | 2–2 | Tim Tadlock |
| Florida State | Atlantic Coast | 42–23 | 1–2 | Mike Martin |
| Mississippi State | Southeastern | 52–15 | 1–2 | Chris Lemonis |
| Arkansas | Southeastern | 46–20 | 0–2 | Dave Van Horn |
| Auburn | Southeastern | 38–28 | 0–2 | Butch Thompson |

### NATIONAL CHAMPION
### VANDERBILT

The Commodores won their second national title in a storybook season in which they entered and exited the year ranked No. 1 in the nation. Along the way, Vanderbilt established a Southeastern Conference record with 59 wins.

Scott anchored the lineup, and the Commodores averaged more than eight runs per game.

But in Omaha, the Commodores' bats weren't as strong. They hit just .221 as a team, the lowest batting average for a national champion since 1972 Southern California—two years before college baseball switched to metal bats.

As a result, the Commodores leaned more heavily on their pitching staff, which was up to the challenge. In six games at the CWS, they allowed just 16 runs, nearly half of which came in a loss to Michigan in Game 1 of the finals.

Rocker twice delivered outstanding starts to finish off a spectacular freshman season that lived up to the considerable hype that preceded him. He became the first freshman since Oregon State's Jorge Reyes in 2007 to be named Most Outstanding Player.

With Vanderbilt needing a win in Game 2 to extend the series, Rocker struck out 11 batters in 6.1 innings. It was the second time he starred for Vanderbilt with its season on the line. In super regionals he struck out 19 batters in a no-hitter against Duke.

"Handing him the ball, I didn't feel at any time that that was above him," Corbin said. "That's what he wanted. That's something that he could do. He pitches for Vanderbilt. He loves to pitch for his team, and it's pure, and it's raw, and it's not manufactured."

But Vanderbilt's pitching went far beyond Rocker, the early favorite to be the No. 1 overall pick in the 2021 draft. Righthander Mason Hickman delivered two quality starts in Omaha, including winning the national championship clincher when he held Michigan to one run in six innings. Lefthander Jake Eder closed out the clincher, the second time he delivered a strong relief performance in the CWS. Brown was lights out at the end of games, throwing 7.2 scoreless innings in Omaha. Righthander Drake Fellows opened Vanderbilt's CWS with an excellent start against Louisville.

Pitching coach Scott Brown said this Commodores' staff has been steadily improving all

# 2019 NEWSMAKERS

Florida State's **Mike Martin** became the first coach to reach 2,000 victories, setting the mark in his 40th and final season as head coach of his alma mater. He again led the Seminoles to the NCAA Tournament and, after an up-and-down year, they got hot in the postseason and made a run to the CWS, knocking out Georgia and Louisiana State, the Nos. 4 and 13 overall seeds, along the way. FSU's run and Martin's career came to an end in Omaha with a loss to Texas Tech. He finished his career with 2,029 victories and was named 2019 Coach of the Year.

Vanderbilt righthander **Kumar Rocker** made history in super regionals when he threw a no-hitter against Duke, striking out 19 batters. It was the eighth no-hitter in NCAA Tournament history and the first in super regionals. Rocker continued his dominance in the CWS, where he was named Most Outstanding Player after two strong starts. He was named Freshman of the Year after going 12-5, 3.25 with 114 strikeouts in 99.2 innings.

Mississippi State center fielder **Jake Mangum** broke the SEC hits record, which had long been held by LSU's Eddy Furniss. He ended his career with 383 hits, the fourth most in D-I history.

| FINAL TOP 25 FOR 2019 |
| --- |
| 1. #Vanderbilt* |
| 2. Michigan* |
| 3. Louisville* |
| 4. Texas Tech* |
| 5. Mississippi State* |
| 6. UCLA |
| 7. Florida State* |
| 8. Arkansas* |
| 9. Auburn* |
| 10. Stanford |
| 11. Oklahoma State |
| 12. East Carolina |
| 13. Mississippi |
| 14. North Carolina |
| 15. Louisiana State |
| 16. Georgia |
| 17. Georgia Tech |
| 18. Duke |
| 19. Oregon State |
| 20. West Virginia |
| 21. Fresno State |
| 22. Miami |
| 23. Texas A&M |
| 24. UC Santa Barbara |
| 25. Creighton |
| * Reached College World Series |
| # Preseason No. 1 |

# IN RETROSPECT: 2019 DRAFT

**Top 10 Draft Picks From College**
With overall selection number (Ov), drafting team (Team) and rank on Baseball America draft board (BA).

| Player | Pos | School | Ov | Team | BA |
|---|---|---|---|---|---|
| Adley Rutschman | C | Oregon State | 1 | Orioles | 1 |
| Andrew Vaughn | 1B | California | 3 | White Sox | 3 |
| JJ Bleday | OF | Vanderbilt | 4 | Marlins | 6 |
| Nick Lodolo | LHP | Texas Christian | 7 | Reds | 8 |
| Josh Jung | 3B | Texas Tech | 8 | Rangers | 17 |
| Shea Langeliers | C | Baylor | 9 | Braves | 9 |
| Hunter Bishop | OF | Arizona State | 10 | Giants | 7 |
| Alek Manoah | RHP | West Virginia | 11 | Blue Jays | 13 |
| Bryson Stott | SS | Nevada-Las Vegas | 14 | Phillies | 10 |
| Will Wilson | SS | N.C. State | 15 | Angels | 22 |

season and was then ready when called upon at the CWS.

"Our offense has been outstanding, and our offense has afforded us throughout the year to get guys into roles they could grow into without the pressure of this is a huge, huge pitch," Brown said. "We've stayed steady and done our thing."

Vanderbilt's experience helped it develop that approach. The Commodores last season nearly reached the CWS, falling just short in a back-and-forth super regional against Mississippi State. Nearly that entire team returned this season, including five seniors, a luxury Vanderbilt doesn't usually have.

But that group, including Paul, Scott, infielder Julian Infante, righthander Patrick Raby and outfielder Walker Grisanti, stuck together and were rewarded with a championship.

Paul said while the national title made his decision to return easier in retrospect, it wasn't their sole aim when they chose to return for his senior year.

"Our No. 1 reason to come back to school wasn't to have this outlandish season or anything like that," he said. "I think that we all wanted to just be a part of something special.

"It's great to win a national championship, it's great to do all those things, but the program means so much more to us than just winning."

Paul and the rest of Vanderbilt's four-year players have been through a lot during their college careers. When the class of 2015 came to Nashville, Vanderbilt was coming off back-to-back College World Series finals appearances against Virginia, winning in 2014 and losing in 2015. They were the top-ranked recruiting class in the country, loaded with premium talent. At the heart of it all, was Donny Everett, a powerful righthander from Tennessee who was a first-round talent but chose to instead play for Vanderbilt.

The Commodores were getting ready for regionals the next spring when Everett tragically drowned while he and some teammates were fishing. Everett's memory has been kept alive in the program in the years since. His parents, Teddy and Susan, are often around the team and were on the field at TD Ameritrade Park for the celebration, even joining the team for the trophy presentation. Several Commodores gave them hugs.

"Those two mean so much to this program and all the players and the seniors," Paul said. "To this day, every time I look at Teddy, I think of Donny. Just being able to share that moment with them was something that I think—I can speak for the seniors, but probably the whole team—is something that we've all really wanted to do."

In so many ways, it was an emotional night for the Commodores. It was cathartic, it was the fulfillment of promise, it was pure joy.

And in the end, Vanderbilt was back on top, steady and unflinching as a champion. ■

# Rutschman offers complete package

By **TEDDY CAHILL**

**A**dley Rutschman knew he had to fix his swing, but Oregon State coach Pat Casey asked the freshman catcher to focus on defense in 2016 so he could manage the Beavers' elite pitching staff.

That's just what he did, guiding OSU pitchers to a 1.93 ERA, the best in the nation. But Rutschman hit just .234 and knew something had to change if he was going to play in the big leagues.

So after Oregon State's season ended with a pair of disappointing losses to Louisiana State in the College World Series, Rutschman got to work overhauling his swing. It was work that he hadn't had time to do before because he had always played football, including the previous fall when he was the Beavers' kickoff specialist.

Rutschman started the overhaul in the Cape Cod League, where he continued to struggle. He hit .164 with two doubles in 20 games, and his struggles extended into the

As a switch-hitting catcher lauded for both his bat and glove, Adley Rutschman rode a distinguished college career, which included a CWS title in 2018, to the No. 1 overall selection in the 2019 draft.

fall and winter. He was trying to improve his load so that he could see the ball better and create more explosive separation with his hips.

It was a long, gradual process, but eventually Rutschman found his swing while hitting in the batting cage during winter break.

"It took summer, fall and finally over winter break, it clicked for me as far as, 'Wow it feels comfortable,' " Rutschman said. "It was at least a six-month deal for me."

The results have been undeniable. Rutschman transformed from a light-hitting freshman into the most productive player in the country the last two years. He hit .408/.505/.628 as a sophomore and was named Most Outstanding Player at the CWS after guiding Oregon State to a national championship and setting a CWS record with 17 hits.

He took another step forward as a junior, making his mark on the Oregon State record book previously dominated by Michael Conforto, Jacoby Ellsbury and Nick Madrigal.

Rutschman's offensive ability combined with his premium defensive skills and athleticism made him not just the top player in the 2019 draft class, but now the College Player of the Year. It is, as much as anything, a testament to his focus, determination and competitiveness, traits that those around him have long seen.

Now with a reworked swing, Rutschman is a switch-hitter who works hard to maintain his swings from both sides of the plate and continues to improve it. The scouting report used to say that you wanted to turn him around from his natural lefthanded swing and make him hit righthanded. That wasn't true in 2019.

This season, Rutschman had gotten to his power more consistently and hit prodigious home runs all spring. He did so without compromising too much contact. His strikeout rate rose roughly two percentage points since 2018, when he also had greater lineup protection from Cadyn Grenier, Trevor Larnach and Madrigal, all top 40 picks in 2018.

Rutschman has never strayed this year from his disciplined approach, even as he is pitched around, subtly and not so subtly. He was averaging 1.28 walks per game, the most since Florida's Brad Wilkerson averaged 1.33 in 1998, the height of the gorilla ball era.

Part of Rutschman's plate discipline is a sheer force of will, a determination to not expand his strike zone and wait for a pitcher to come to him. But he also attributes it to the tracking drills he does when he spends a round of batting practice taking pitches so he can track their flight out of the pitcher's hand.

"Some guys have better eyes than others, but it's something you can work on," he said. "The beautiful part of baseball is you can improve on everything."

That might as well be Rutschman's mantra. It helped him through a difficult offseason that began with a desire to clean up his swing and ultimately turned him into one of college baseball's biggest offensive threats in just two years. ■

# TOP PLAYERS OF 2019

## ALL-AMERICA TEAM

| Pos | Player | School | Yr | AVG | AB | R | H | HR | RBI | SB | BB | SO | OBP | SLG |
|---|---|---|---|---|---|---|---|---|---|---|---|---|---|---|
| C | Adley Rutschman | Oregon State | Jr. | .411 | 185 | 57 | 76 | 17 | 58 | 0 | 76 | 38 | .575 | .751 |
| 1B | Andrew Vaughn | California | Jr. | .374 | 179 | 50 | 67 | 15 | 50 | 2 | 60 | 33 | .539 | .704 |
| 2B | Cameron Cannon | Arizona | Jr. | .397 | 232 | 71 | 92 | 8 | 56 | 0 | 35 | 29 | .478 | .651 |
| 3B | Kody Hoese | Tulane | Jr. | .391 | 235 | 72 | 92 | 23 | 61 | 4 | 39 | 34 | .486 | .779 |
| SS | Will Wilson | North Carolina State | Jr. | .339 | 221 | 55 | 75 | 16 | 57 | 1 | 22 | 46 | .429 | .665 |
| OF | Hunter Bishop | Arizona State | Jr. | .344 | 218 | 66 | 75 | 22 | 63 | 12 | 50 | 59 | .482 | .757 |
| OF | JJ Bleday | Vanderbilt | Jr. | .347 | 274 | 82 | 95 | 27 | 72 | 1 | 61 | 58 | .465 | .701 |
| OF | Matt Wallner | Southern Mississippi | Jr. | .323 | 226 | 58 | 73 | 23 | 60 | 2 | 48 | 50 | .446 | .681 |
| DH | Austin Martin | Vanderbilt | So. | .392 | 268 | 87 | 105 | 10 | 46 | 18 | 40 | 34 | .486 | .604 |
| UT | Aaron Schunk | Georgia | Jr. | .336 | 226 | 47 | 76 | 13 | 52 | 3 | 13 | 28 | .368 | .580 |

| Pos | Pitcher | School | Yr | W | L | ERA | G | SV | IP | H | BB | SO |
|---|---|---|---|---|---|---|---|---|---|---|---|---|
| SP | Ryan Garcia | UCLA | Jr. | 10 | 1 | 1.44 | 16 | 0 | 94 | 52 | 26 | 117 |
| SP | Alek Manoah | West Virginia | Jr. | 9 | 4 | 2.08 | 16 | 0 | 108.1 | 71 | 27 | 144 |
| SP | Ethan Small | Mississippi State | R-Jr. | 10 | 2 | 1.94 | 18 | 0 | 107 | 61 | 32 | 176 |
| SP | Noah Song | Navy | Sr. | 11 | 1 | 1.44 | 14 | 0 | 94 | 55 | 31 | 161 |
| RP | Kyle Hill | Baylor | Sr. | 6 | 0 | 0.00 | 23 | 7 | 29.1 | 10 | 10 | 35 |
| RP | Jacob Wallace | Connecticut | Jr. | 3 | 1 | 0.64 | 30 | 16 | 42 | 20 | 10 | 68 |
| UT | Aaron Schunk | Georgia | Jr. | 1 | 2 | 2.49 | 17 | 12 | 21.2 | 15 | 7 | 18 |

## SECOND TEAM

C—Eric Yang, UC Santa Barbara. 1B—Spencer Torkelson, Arizona State. 2B—Nick Gonzales, New Mexico State. 3B—Drew Mendoza, Florida State. SS—Josh Jung, Texas Tech. OF—Peyton Burdick, Wright State; Jake Mangum, Mississippi State; and Jake Sanford, Western Kentucky. DH—Kyle McCann, Georgia Tech. UT—J.C. Flowers, Florida State. SP—Jake Agnos, East Carolina; Isaiah Campbell, Arkansas; Emerson Hancock, Georgia; and TJ Sikkema, Missouri. RP—Matt Cronin, Arkansas; and Holden Powell, UCLA.

## THIRD TEAM

C—Korey Lee, California. 1B—Aaron Sabato, UNC. 2B—Justin Foscue, Miss. State. 3B—Davis Wendzel, Baylor. SS—Bryson Stott, UNLV. OF—Zach Ashford, Fresno State; Jordan Brewer, Michigan; and Kevin Strohschein, Tennessee Tech. DH—Cameron Warren, Texas Tech. UT—Tristin English, Georgia Tech. SP—John Doxakis, Texas A&M; George Kirby, Elon; Nick Lodolo, Texas Christian; and Zack Thompson, Kentucky. RP—Brandon Eisert, Oregon State; and Andrew Magno, Ohio State.

Skip
Bertman

# EARNING
# THEIR
# STRIPES

*Paced by six national titles
and 22 first-team All-Americans,
Louisiana State is No. 1 in the BA era*

Ben McDonald

Alex Bregman

Aaron N

# EPILOGUE: TOP 25 PROGRAMS FROM 1981-2019

To tie 39 seasons and four decades of college baseball history together, we determined the top 25 programs of the Baseball American era, as determined by cumulative totals in our college program scoring system.

Who else but Louisiana State could rank as the No. 1 program of the BA era, which stretches back to 1981? Led by coach Skip Bertman, the Tigers won four College World Series titles in the 1990s and a fifth in 2000. Coach Paul Mainieri guided LSU to another CWS championship in 2009 and a runner-up finish in 2017.

Louisiana State made it to Omaha 18 times since 1981, more than any team except Miami (21), and the program also ranks third with 22 first-team All-Americans, including two-time first-teamers Ben McDonald (1988-89), Todd Walker (1993-94), Eddy Furniss (1996, 1998), Aaron Nola (2013-14) and Alex Bregman (2013, 2015).

| No. | Team | 1980s | 1990s | 2000s | 2010s | Total |
|-----|------|-------|-------|-------|-------|-------|
| 1. | Louisiana State | 94 | **309** | 255 | 212 | 870 |
| 2. | Florida State | 153 | 230 | 216 | 231 | 830 |
| 3. | Miami | 213 | 233 | 260 | 121 | 827 |
| 4. | Texas | **257** | 121 | 277 | 143 | 798 |
| 5. | Cal State Fullerton | 155 | 187 | 265 | 172 | 779 |
| 6. | Stanford | 191 | 196 | 234 | 116 | 737 |
| 7. | Arizona State | 208 | 155 | 225 | 119 | 707 |
| 8. | Florida | 60 | 105 | 112 | **290** | 567 |
| 9. | Clemson | 49 | 164 | 191 | 130 | 534 |
| 10. | Oklahoma State | 202 | 136 | 82 | 113 | 533 |
| 11. | South Carolina | 83 | 37 | 209 | 199 | 528 |
| 12. | Rice | 17 | 108 | **283** | 73 | 481 |
| 13. | Wichita State | 170 | 176 | 98 | 25 | 469 |
| 14. | Mississippi State | 102 | 102 | 82 | 178 | 464 |
| 15. | North Carolina | 65 | 35 | 204 | 156 | 460 |
| 16. | Arkansas | 104 | 48 | 107 | 185 | 444 |
| 17. | UCLA | 63 | 110 | 73 | 197 | 443 |
| 18. | Texas A&M | 67 | 123 | 79 | 169 | 438 |
| 19. | Georgia Tech | 47 | 122 | 180 | 78 | 427 |
| 20. | Oregon State | 27 | 13 | 156 | 220 | 416 |
| 21. | Southern California | 56 | 198 | 128 | 29 | 411 |
| 22. | Arizona | 110 | 40 | 115 | 141 | 406 |
| 23. | Vanderbilt | 8 | 16 | 77 | 286 | 387 |
| 24. | Oklahoma | 69 | 130 | 68 | 102 | 369 |
| 25. | Fresno State | 119 | 88 | 92 | 44 | 343 |

## FOR THE RECORD

*The most distinguished college programs for the 39 seasons encompassing 1981 to 2019.*

**MOST REGIONALS:** Florida State, 39; Miami, 37; and Cal State Fullerton, 34.

**MOST SUPER REGIONALS:** Florida State, 17; and Cal State Fullerton and Louisiana State, 14.

**MOST COLLEGE WORLD SERIES:** Miami, 21; and Louisiana State and Texas, 18.

**MOST NATIONAL TITLES:** Louisiana State, 6; Miami, 4; and Cal State Fullerton, Oregon State and Texas, 3.

**MOST FIRST-TEAM ALL-AMERICANS:** Florida State, 27; Arizona State, 23; and Louisiana State, 22.

**MOST TOTAL ALL-AMERICANS:** Florida State, 61; Arizona State, 50; and Texas, 46.

**MOST DRAFT PICKS SIGNED FROM TOP 10 ROUNDS:** Arizona State, 122; Stanford, 113; and Texas, 100.

**MOST MAJOR LEAGUERS:** Stanford, 63; Arizona State, 59; and Cal State Fullerton, 56.

# TOP 25 PROGRAMS FROM 1981-2019

All information presented here refers only to the years 1981 to 2019, the Baseball America era.

**Top Five Big Leaguers** are ranked by Baseball-Reference.com wins above replacement (WAR), rounded to the nearest integer. An asterisk (*) denotes a player active in 2019.

**Draft Top 10 Rounds** includes signed players only. **All-Americans** who reached the major leagues are denoted with an pound sign (#). The utility position (**UT**) signifies a two-way player.

### 1. LOUISIANA STATE

**Record:** 1,748–770–7 (.694).

**Coaches:** Jack Lamabe (1979–83), Skip Bertman (1984–2001), Smoke Laval (2002–06) and Paul Mainieri (2007–).

**National Champion (6x):** 1991, 1993, 1996, 1997, 2000, 2009. **Runner-Up (1x):** 2017.

**NCAA Tournament:** 31. **College World Series:** 18. **All-Americans:** 44.

**First-Team All-Americans: SP**—Ben McDonald# (1988-89), Lloyd Peever (1992), Ed Yarnall# (1996), Kurt Ainsworth# (1999), Louis Coleman# (2009) Aaron Nola# (2013-14) and Alex Lange (2015). **C**—Brad Cresse (2000). **1B**—Eddy Furniss (1996, 98). **2B**—Todd Walker# (1993-94). **SS**—Brandon Larson# (1997), Aaron Hill# (2003) and Alex Bregman# (2013, 15). **OF**—Wes Grisham (1990), Blake Dean (2008), Mikie Mahtook# (2011) and Greg Deichmann (2017).

**Draft Top 10 Rounds:** 94. **Top Pick:** 1st—Ben McDonald, RHP (1989/Orioles).

**Annual Award Winners: Player**—Ben McDonald, RHP, 1989. **Coach**—Skip Bertman, 1986 and 1996; and Paul Mainieri, 2009. **Freshman**—Todd Walker, 2B, 1992; Brett Laxton, RHP, 1993; and Alex Bregman, SS, 2013.

**Top Five Big Leaguers: 1.** Albert Belle, OF, 1987 (2), 40 WAR. **2.** Aaron Hill, 2B, 2003 (1), 24 WAR; **3.** *DJ LeMahieu, 2B, 2009 (2), 24 WAR. **4.** Ben McDonald, RHP, 1989 (1), 21 WAR. **5.** *Alex Bregman, 3B, 2015 (1), 21 WAR. **Others:** *Aaron Nola, RHP, 2014 (1), 20 WAR; and *Kevin Gausman, RHP, 2012 (1), 10 WAR.

### 2. FLORIDA STATE

**Record:** 1923–695–4 (.734).

**Coach:** Mike Martin (1980–2019).

**National Champion:** None. **Runner-Up (2x):** 1986, 1999.

**NCAA Tournament:** 39. **College World Series:** 16. **All-Americans:** 61.

**First-Team All-Americans: SP**—Mike Loynd# (1986), Richie Lewis# (1986-87), Paul Wilson# (1994), Jonathan Johnson# (1995) and Sean Gilmartin# (2011). **RP**—Robert Benincasa (2012). **C**—Pedro Grifol (1991), Tony Ritchie (2002) and Buster Posey# (2008). **2B**—Luis Alicea# (1986), Marshall McDougall# (1999) and Tony Thomas (2007). **SS**—Stephen Cardullo# (2009) and Taylor Walls (2016). **OF**—Jeff Ledbetter (1982), Frank Fazzini (1985), J.D. Drew# (1996-97), Jeremy Morris (1997), John-Ford Griffin# (2001), Eddy Martinez-Esteve (2004), Shane Robinson# (2005), James Ramsey (2012) and D.J. Stewart# (2015). **UT**—Mike McGee (2010).

**Draft Top 10 Rounds:** 85. **Top Pick:** 1st—Paul Wilson, RHP (1994/Mets).

**Annual Award Winners: Player**—Jeff Ledbetter, OF, 1982; J.D. Drew, OF, 1997; and Buster Posey, C, 2008. **Coach**—Mike Martin, 2012 and 2019. **Freshman**—Stephen Drew, SS, 2002.

**Top Five Big Leaguers: 1.** J.D. Drew, OF, 1998 (1), 45 WAR. **2.** *Buster Posey, C, 2008 (1), 42 WAR. **3.** Stephen Drew, SS, 2004 (1), 17 WAR. **4.** Jody Reed, 2B, 1984 (8), 16 WAR. **5.** Doug Mientkiewicz, 1B, 1995 (5), 12 WAR.

Led by Mike Martin, Florida State is the only program to reach the NCAA Tournament in all 39 seasons of the BA era. While FSU never won it all, the Seminoles' consistency and high-profile big leaguers, including Buster Posey and J.D. Drew, are remarkable.

### 3. MIAMI

**Record:** 1,795–719–6 (.713).

**Coaches:** Ron Fraser (1963–1992), Brad Kelley (1993), Jim Morris (1994–2018) and Gino DiMare (2019–).

**National Champion (4x):** 1982, 1985, 1999, 2001. **Runner-Up (1x):** 1996.

**NCAA Tournament:** 37. **College World Series:** 21. **All-Americans:** 41.

**First-Team All-Americans: SP**—Neal Heaton# (1981), Alex Fernandez# (1989), Oscar Munoz# (1990), Jeff Alkire (1992) and Alex Santos (1998). **RP**—Rick Raether (1985-86), Danny Graves# (1994) and Kyle Bellamy (2009). **C**—Yasmani Grandal# (2010) and Zack Collins# (2016). **1B**—Yonder Alonso# (2008). **3B**—Pat Burrell# (1996-97), Aubrey Huff# (1998), Ryan Braun# (2005) and David Thompson (2015). **OF**—Mike Fiore (1988).

**Draft Top 10 Rounds:** 88. **Top Pick:** 1st—Pat Burrell, 3B (1998/Phillies).

**Annual Award Winners: Coach**—Ron Fraser, 1981; and Jim Morris, 1994. **Freshman**—Alex Fernandez, RHP, 1989; Pat Burrell, 3B, 1996; Kevin Howard, 3B/SS, 2000; Ryan Braun, SS, 2003; Chris Hernandez, LHP, 2008; and Zack Collins, C, 2014.

Top Five Big Leaguers: **1.** *Ryan Braun, OF, 2005 (1), 48 WAR. **2.** Charles Johnson, C, 1992 (1), 23 WAR. **3.** Aubrey Huff, 3B, 1998 (5), 20 WAR. **4.** Pat Burrell, OF, 1998 (1), 19 WAR. **5.** *Yasmani Grandal, C, 2010 (1), 16 WAR.

## 4. TEXAS

**Record:** 1,790–744–4 (.706).

**Coaches:** Cliff Gustafson (1968–1996), Augie Garrido (1997–2016) and David Pierce (2016–).

**National Champion (3x):** 1983, 2002, 2005. **Runner-Up (5x):** 1984, 1985, 1989, 2004, 2009.

**NCAA Tournament:** 33. **College World Series:** 18. **All-Americans:** 46.

    **First-Team All-Americans: SP**—Tony Arnold# (1981), Calvin Schiraldi# (1983), Greg Swindell# (1984-86), Curt Krippner (1987), Kirk Dressendorfer# (1988, 90), J.P. Howell# (2004) and Taylor Jungmann# (2011). **RP**—Charlie Thames (2000) and Chance Ruffin# (2010). **2B**—Bill Bates (1985) and Kody Clemens (2018). **3B**—David Denny (1984). **OF**—Brian Cisarik (1987), Scott Bryant (1989), Calvin Murray# (1992), Brooks Kieschnick# (1993), Dustin Majewski (2003) and Kyle Russell (2007).

    **Draft Top 10 Rounds:** 100. **Top Pick:** 2nd—Greg Swindell, LHP (1986/Indians).

    **Annual Award Winners: Player**—Brooks Kieschnick, RHP/DH, 1993. **Coach**—Augie Garrido, 2002; and David Pierce, 2018. **Freshman**—Greg Swindell, LHP, 1984; Kirk Dressendorfer, RHP, 1988; and Brooks Kieschnick, RHP/DH, 1991.

    Top Five Big Leaguers: **1.** Roger Clemens, RHP, 1983 (1), 140 WAR. **2.** Greg Swindell, LHP, 1986 (1), 31 WAR. **3.** *Brandon Belt, 1B, 2009 (5), 23 WAR. **4.** Shane Reynolds, RHP, 1989 (3), 18 WAR. **5.** Huston Street, RHP, 2004 (1s), 14 WAR.

## 5. CAL STATE FULLERTON

**Record:** 1,668–781–3 (.681).

**Coaches:** Augie Garrido (1975–1987, 1991–1996), Larry Cochell (1988–1990), George Horton (1997–2007), Dave Serrano (2008–2011) and Rick Vanderhook (2012–).

**National Champion (3x):** 1984, 1995, 2004. **Runner-Up (1x):** 1992.

**NCAA Tournament:** 34. **College World Series:** 16. **All-Americans:** 45.

    **First-Team All-Americans: SP**—Ted Silva (1995), Wes Roemer (2006) and Tom Eshelman# (2013, 15). **RP**—Scott Wright (1984). **C**—Kurt Suzuki# (2004). **3B**—Phil Nevin# (1992). **SS**—Christian Colon# (2010). **OF**—John Christensen# (1981) and Mark Kotsay# (1995-96). **UT**—Michael Lorenzen# (2013).

    **Draft Top 10 Rounds:** 90. **Top Pick:** 1st—Phil Nevin, 3B (19929/Astros).

    **Annual Award Winners: Player**—Phil Nevin, 3B, 1992. **Coach**—Augie Garrido, 1984; and George Horton, 2003. **Assistant Coach**—Dave Serrano, 2004.

    Top Five Big Leaguers: **1.** *Justin Turner, 3B, 2006 (7), 28 WAR. **2.** Mark Kotsay, OF, 1996 (1), 21 WAR. **3.** Aaron Rowand, OF, 1998 (1s), 21 WAR. **4.** *Kurt Suzuki, C, 2004 (2), 20 WAR. **5.** *Matt Chapman, 3B, 2014 (1), 18 WAR. **Others:** Phil Nevin, 3B, 1992 (1), 16 WAR; and *Khris Davis, OF, 2009 (7), 12 WAR.

## 6. STANFORD

**Record:** 1,576–813–6 (.659).

**Coaches:** Mark Marquess (1977–2017) and David Esquer (2018–).

**National Champion (2x):** 1987, 1988. **Runner-Up (3x):** 2000, 2001, 2003.

**NCAA Tournament:** 32. **College World Series:** 14. **All-Americans:** 41.

    **First-Team All-Americans: SP**—Stan Spencer# (1990), Kyle Peterson# (1995, 97), Jeff Austin# (1998), Justin Wayne# (2000) and Jeremy Guthrie# (2002). **RP**—Jack Little (2018). **C**—A.J. Hinch# (1995) and Ryan Garko# (2003). **1B**—David McCarty# (1991). **2B**—Jed Lowrie# (2004). **OF**—Jeffrey Hammonds# (1990, 92), Sam Fuld# (2002) and Danny Putnam# (2004).

    **Draft Top 10 Rounds:** 113. **Top Pick:** 1st—Mark Appel, RHP (2013/Astros).

    **Annual Award Winners: Player**—David McCarty, 1B, 1991; and Jeff Austin, RHP, 1998. **Coach**—Mark Marquess, 1987. **Assistant Coach**—Dean Stotz, 1999. **Freshman**—Jack McDowell, RHP, 1985; Paul Carey, OF, 1987; Jeffrey Hammonds, OF, 1990; and Kyle Peterson, RHP, 1995.

    Top Five Big Leaguers: **1.** Mike Mussina, RHP, 1990 (1), 83 WAR. **2.** Jack McDowell, RHP, 1987 (1), 28

WAR. **3.** Rick Helling, RHP, 1992 (1), 20 WAR. **4.** Jeremy Guthrie, RHP, 2002 (1), 18 WAR. **5.** *Jed Lowrie, 2B, 2005 (1s), 18 WAR. **Other:** *Jason Castro, C, 2008 (1), 12 WAR.

## 7. ARIZONA STATE

**Record:** 1,613–796–1 (.670).
**Coaches:** Jim Brock (1972–1994), Pat Murphy (1995–2009), Tim Esmay (2010–2014) and Tracy Smith (2015–).
**National Champion (1x):** 1981. **Runner-Up (2x):** 1988, 1998.
**NCAA Tournament:** 30. **College World Series:** 12. **All-Americans:** 50.

**First-Team All-Americans: SP**—Kendall Carter (1981), Sean Rees (1990), Mike Leake# (2009) and Seth Blair (2010). **C**—Paul Lo Duca# (1993). **2B**—Kevin Higgins# (1988), Anthony Manahan (1990) and Zach MacPhee (2010). **3B**—Mike Sodders (1981), Antone Williamson# (1993-94) and Brett Wallace# (2007-08). **SS**—Mike Benjamin# (1987), Willie Bloomquist# (1999) and Dustin Pedroia# (2004). **OF**—Oddibe McDowell# (1984), Mike Kelly# (1990-91), Mitch Jones# (2000), Jason Kipnis# (2009) and Hunter Bishop (2019). **UT**—Ike Davis# (2008).

**Draft Top 10 Rounds:** 122. **Top Pick:** 2nd—Mike Kelly, OF (1991/Braves).
**Annual Award Winners: Player**—Mike Sodders, 3B, 1981; Oddibe McDowell, OF, 1984; and Mike Kelly, OF, 1990. **Coach**—Jim Brock, 1988; and Pat Murphy, 1998.

Top Five Big Leaguers: **1.** Barry Bonds, OF, 1985 (1), 163 WAR. **2.** *Dustin Pedroia, 2B, 2004 (2), 52 WAR. **3.** *Jason Kipnis, 2B, 2009 (2), 22 WAR. **4.** Andre Ethier, OF, 2003 (2), 21 WAR. **5.** Alvin Davis, 1B, 1982 (6), 20 WAR. Others: Paul Lo Duca, C, 1993 (25), 18 WAR; and *Mike Leake, RHP, 2009 (1), 17 WAR.

## 8. FLORIDA

**Record:** 1,588–857–5 (.649).
**Coaches:** Jay Bergman (1976–1981), Jack Rhine (1982–1983), Joe Arnold (1984–1994), Andy Lopez (1995–2001), Pat McMahon (2002–2007) and Kevin O'Sullivan (2008–).
**National Champion (1x):** 2017. **Runner-Up (2x):** 2005, 2011.
**NCAA Tournament:** 30. **College World Series:** 12. **All-Americans:** 24.

**First-Team All-Americans: SP**—John Burke# (1991), Logan Shore (2016) and Brady Singer (2018). **RP**—Josh Fogg# (1998) and Michael Byrne (2018). **C**—Mike Zunino# (2011-12). **1B**—Matt LaPorta# (2005, 07). **3B**—Jonathan Indian (2018). **OF/UT**—Brad Wilkerson# (1997-98)

**Draft Top 10 Rounds:** 81. **Top Pick:** 3rd—Mike Zunino, C (2012/Mariners).
**Annual Award Winners: Player**—Mike Zunino, C, 2012; and Brady Singer, RHP, 2018. **Coach**—Kevin O'Sullivan, 2011.

Top Five Big Leaguers: **1.** Mark Ellis, 2B, 1999 (9), 34 WAR. **2.** Mike Stanley, C, 1985 (16), 21 WAR. **3.** David Eckstein, SS, 1997 (19), 21 WAR. **4.** Brad Wilkerson, OF, 1998 (1s), 11 WAR. **5.** David Ross, C, 1998 (7), 10 WAR.

## 9. CLEMSON

**Record:** 1,696–812–4 (.676).
**Coaches:** Bill Wilhelm (1958–1993), Jack Leggett (1994–2015) and Monte Lee (2016–).
**National Champion:** None. **Runner-Up:** None.
**NCAA Tournament:** 33. **College World Series:** 7. **All-Americans:** 33.

**First-Team All-Americans: SP**—Brian Barnes# (1989) and Kris Benson# (1996). **C**—Matt LeCroy# (1997). **3B**—Jeff Baker# (2001-02). **SS**—Khalil Greene# (2002) and Brad Miller# (2011). **OF**—Shane Monahan# (1994), Tyler Colvin# (2006) and Seth Beer (2016, 18).

**Draft Top 10 Rounds:** 85. **Top Pick:** 1st—Kris Benson, RHP (1996/Pirates).
**Annual Award Winners: Player**—Kris Benson, RHP, 1996; and Khalil Greene, SS, 2002. **Assistant Coach**—Tim Corbin, 2000. **Freshman**—Seth Beer, OF, 2016.

Top Five Big Leaguers: **1.** Jimmy Key, LHP, 1982 (3), 49 WAR. **2.** Kris Benson, RHP, 1996 (1), 13 WAR. **3.** Bill Spiers, SS, 1987 (1), 10 WAR. **4.** Khalil Greene, SS, 2002 (1), 9 WAR. **5.** Brad Miller, SS, 2011 (2), 7 WAR.

### 10. OKLAHOMA STATE

**Record:** 1,718–773–2 (.690).

**Coaches:** Gary Ward (1978–1996), Tom Holliday (1997–2003), Frank Anderson (2004–2012) and Josh Holliday (2013–).

**National Champion:** None. **Runner-Up (3x):** 1981, 1987, 1990.

**NCAA Tournament:** 33. **College World Series:** 12. **All-Americans:** 32.

**First-Team All-Americans: SP**—Dennis Livingston (1983), Jason Bell (1994), Andrew Heaney# (2012) and Michael Freeman (2015). **C**—Mike Daniel (1991). **3B**—Robin Ventura# (1986-88). **SS**—Monty Fariss# (1988). **OF**—Pete Incaviglia# (1984-85).

**Draft Top 10 Rounds:** 69. **Top Pick:** 6th—Monty Fariss, SS (1988/Rangers).

**Annual Award Winners: Player**—Pete Incaviglia, OF, 1985; and Robin Ventura, 3B, 1987. **Assistant Coach**—Rob Walton, 2016. **Freshman**—Robin Ventura, 3B, 1986.

**Top Five Big Leaguers: 1.** Robin Ventura, 3B, 1988 (1), 56 WAR. **2.** Mickey Tettleton, C, 1981 (5), 29 WAR. **3.** Jeromy Burnitz, OF, 1990 (1), 20 WAR. **4.** Scott Baker, RHP, 2003 (2), 16 WAR. **5.** Mike Henneman, RHP, 1984 (4), 13 WAR.

### 11. SOUTH CAROLINA

**Record:** 1,622–803–1 (.669).

**Coaches:** June Raines (1977–1996), Ray Tanner (1997–2012), Chad Holbrook (2013–2017) and Mark Kingston (2018–).

**National Champion (2x):** 2010, 2011. **Runner-Up (2x):** 2002, 2012.

**NCAA Tournament:** 27. **College World Series:** 9. **All-Americans:** 26.

**First-Team All-Americans: SP**—Mike Cook# (1985), Kip Bouknight (2000), David Marchbanks (2003) and Michael Roth# (2011). **1B**—Yaron Peters (2002), Justin Smoak# (2008) and Kyle Martin (2015). **SS**—Adam Everett# (1998). **OF**—Mike Curry (1998).

**Draft Top 10 Rounds:** 62. **Top Pick:** 10th—Drew Meyer, SS (2002/Rangers).

**Annual Award Winners: Coach**—Ray Tanner, 2000 and 2010. **Assistant Coach**—Jim Toman, 2002; and Chad Hollbrook, 2011.

**Top Five Big Leaguers: 1.** Brian Roberts, 2B, 1999 (1s), 30 WAR. **2.** Dave Hollins, 3B, 1987 (6), 18 WAR. **3.** *Jackie Bradley Jr., OF, 2011 (1s), 15 WAR. **4.** *Whit Merrifield, 2B, 2010 (9), 15 WAR. **5.** Adam Everett, SS, 1998 (1), 13 WAR.

### 12. RICE

**Record:** 1,529–817–0 (.652).

**Coaches:** David Hall (1981–1991), Wayne Graham (1992–2018) and Matt Bragga (2019–).

**National Champion (1x):** 2003. **Runner-Up:** None.

**NCAA Tournament:** 24. **College World Series:** 7. **All-Americans:** 29.

**First-Team All-Americans: SP**—Jeff Niemann# (2003), Wade Townsend (2003-04) and Eddie Degerman (2006). **RP**—Matt Anderson# (1997) and Cole St. Clair (2006). **1B**—Lance Berkman# (1997). **3B**—Anthony Rendon# (2010). **SS**—Damon Thames (1998) and Brian Friday (2006). **OF**—Jose Cruz Jr.# (1994-95) and Bubba Crosby# (1998). **UT**—Joe Savery# (2007).

**Draft Top 10 Rounds:** 69. **Top Pick:** 1st—Matt Anderson, RHP (1997/Tigers).

**Annual Award Winners: Player**—Anthony Rendon, 3B, 2010. **Coach**—Wayne Graham, 1999. **Freshman**—Joe Savery, LHP/1B, 2005; and Anthony Rendon, 3B, 2009.

**Top Five Big Leaguers: 1.** Lance Berkman, OF, 1997 (1), 52 WAR. **2.** *Anthony Rendon, 3B, 2011 (1), 28 WAR. **3.** Jose Cruz Jr., OF, 1995 (1), 20 WAR. **4.** Norm Charlton, LHP, 1984 (1s), 8 WAR. **5.** *Brock Holt, 2B, 2009 (9), 8 WAR.

### 13. WICHITA STATE

**Record:** 1,857–794–1 (.700).

**Coaches:** Gene Stephenson (1978–2013) and Todd Butler (2014–2019).

**National Champion (1x):** 1989. **Runner-Up (3x):** 1982, 1991, 1993.

**NCAA Tournament:** 27. **College World Series:** 7. **All-Americans:** 42.

    **First-Team All-Americans: SP**—Don Heinkel# (1982), Bryan Oelkers# (1982), Kennie Steenstra# (1991) and Rob Musgrave (2008). **RP**—Darren Dreifort# (1992-93) and Braden Looper# (1996). **C**—Charlie O'Brien# (1982). **1B**—Phil Stephenson# (1981-82), Russ Morman# (1983) and Casey Gillaspie (2014). **OF**—Joe Carter# (1981).

    **Draft Top 10 Rounds:** 65. **Top Pick:** 2nd—Joe Carter, OF (1981/Cubs); and Darren Dreifort, RHP (1993/Dodgers).

    **Annual Award Winners: Coach**—Gene Stephenson, 1982 and 1993.

    Top Five Big Leaguers: **1.** Casey Blake, 3B, 1996 (7), 25 WAR. **2.** Joe Carter, OF, 1981 (1), 20 WAR. **3.** Mike Lansing, 2B, 1990 (6), 10 WAR. **4.** Charlie O'Brien, C, 1982 (5), 10 WAR. **5.** Braden Looper, RHP, 1996 (1), 8 WAR.

### 14. MISSISSIPPI STATE

**Record:** 1,424–738–3 (.658).

**Coaches:** Ron Polk (1976–1997, 2002–2008), Pat McMahon (1998–2001), John Cohen (2009–2016), Andy Cannizaro (2017–2018), Gary Henderson (2018) and Chris Lemonis (2019–).

**National Champion:** None. **Runner-Up (1x):** 2013.

**NCAA Tournament:** 30. **College World Series:** 9. **All-Americans:** 24.

    **First-Team All-Americans: SP**—Jeff Brantley# (1985), Gary Rath# (1994), Chris Stratton# (2012) and Ethan Small (2019). **RP**—Jacob Lindgren# (2014). **1B**—Will Clark# (1985) and Brent Rooker (2017). **OF**—Rafael Palmeiro# (1983-84), Brad Corley (2004) and Hunter Renfroe# (2013).

    **Draft Top 10 Rounds:** 50. **Top Pick:** 2nd—Will Clark, 1B (1985/Giants).

    **Annual Award Winners: Coach**—Ron Polk, 1985. **Assistant Coach**—Butch Thompson, 2014. **Freshman**—Rafael Palmeiro, 1983.

    Top Five Big Leaguers: **1.** Rafael Palmeiro, 1B, 1985 (1), 72 WAR. **2.** Will Clark, 1B, 1985 (1), 57 WAR. **3.** Jonathan Papelbon, RHP, 2003 (4), 24 WAR. **4.** Paul Maholm, LHP, 2003 (1), 12 WAR. **5.** Jeff Brantley, RHP, 1985 (6), 11 WAR.

### 15. NORTH CAROLINA

**Record:** 1,606–777–3 (.674).

**Coaches:** Mike Roberts (1978–1998) and Mike Fox (1999–).

**National Champion:** None. **Runner-Up (2x):** 2006, 2007.

**NCAA Tournament:** 26. **College World Series:** 8. **All-Americans:** 29.

    **First-Team All-Americans: SP**—Scott Bankhead# (1984), Andrew Miller# (2006) and J.B. Bukauskas (2017). **RP**—Josh Hiatt (2017). **C**—B.J. Surhoff# (1985). **1B**—Dustin Ackley# (2009). **2B**—Russ Adams# (2002). **3B**—Colin Moran# (2011, 13). **SS**—Logan Warmoth (2017).

    **Draft Top 10 Rounds:** 68. **Top Pick:** 1st—B.J. Surhoff, C (1985/Brewers).

    **Annual Award Winners: Player**—Andrew Miller, LHP, 2006. **Coach**—Mike Fox, 2008. **Freshman**—Brian Roberts, SS, 1997; Dustin Ackley, 1B, 2007; and Colin Moran, 3B, 2011.

    Top Five Big Leaguers: **1.** B.J. Surhoff, OF, 1985 (1), 34 WAR. **2.** *Kyle Seager, 3B, 2009 (2), 30 WAR. **3.** Walt Weiss, SS, 1985 (1), 17 WAR. **4.** *Chris Iannetta, C, 2004 (4), 16 WAR. **5.** Scott Bankhead, RHP, 1984 (1), 11 WAR. **Others:** *Matt Harvey, RHP, 2010 (1), 10 WAR; and *Andrew Miller, LHP, 2006 (1), 8 WAR.

## 16. ARKANSAS

**Record:** 1,539–854–3 (.643).
**Coaches:** Norm DeBriyn (1970–2002) and Dave Van Horn (2003–).
**National Champion:** None. **Runner-Up (1x):** 2018.
**NCAA Tournament:** 28. **College World Series:** 9. **All-Americans:** 16.
**Draft Top 10 Rounds:** 81. **Top Pick:** 1st—Jeff King, 3B (1986/Pirates).

First-Team All-Americans: 3B—Jeff King# (1985) and Greg D'Alexander (1990). OF—Andrew Benintendi# (2015).

Annual Award Winners: Player—Andrew Benintendi, OF, 2015.

Top Five Big Leaguers: **1.** Cliff Lee, LHP, 2000 (4), 44 WAR. **2.** Kevin McReynolds, OF, 1981 (1), 30 WAR. **3.** *Dallas Keuchel, LHP, 2009 (7), 20 WAR. **4.** Jeff King, 3B, 1986 (1), 17 WAR. **5.** *Logan Forsythe, 2B, 2008 (1s), 13 WAR. **Others:** *Andrew Benintendi, OF, 2015 (1), 9 WAR; and *Brian Anderson, 3B, 2014 (3), 8 WAR.

## 17. UCLA

**Record:** 1,313–1,046–5 (.556).
**Coaches:** Gary Adams (1975–2004) and John Savage (2005—).
**National Champion (1x):** 2013. **Runner-Up (1x):** 2010.
**NCAA Tournament:** 21. **College World Series:** 4. **All-Americans:** 32.
First-Team All-Americans: SP—Alex Sanchez# (1986), Jim Parque# (1997), Trevor Bauer# (2011) and Ryan Garcia (2019). RP—David Berg (2013). C—Paul Ellis (1990). 1B—Ryan McGuire# (1993). 2B—Torey Lovullo# (1987) and Chase Utley# (2000). 3B—Troy Glaus# (1997). OF—Shane Mack# (1983), Eric Valent# (1998), Bill Scott (2000), Jeff Gelalich (2012).

Draft Top 10 Rounds: 88. Top Pick: 1st—Gerrit Cole, RHP (2011/Pirates).

Annual Award Winners: Player—Trevor Bauer, RHP, 2011. Coach—John Savage, 2013.

Top Five Big Leaguers: **1.** Chase Utley, 2B, 2000 (1), 65 WAR. **2.** Troy Glaus, 3B, 1997 (1), 38 WAR. **3.** *Gerrit Cole, RHP, 2011 (1), 24 WAR. **4.** *Brandon Crawford, SS, 2008 (5), 23 WAR. **5.** Shane Mack, OF, 1984 (1), 22 WAR. **Others:** Jeff Conine, OF, 1987 (58), 20 WAR; Todd Zeile, 3B, 1986 (2s), 19 WAR; Mike Gallego, 2B, 1981 (2), 17 WAR; *Trevor Bauer, RHP, 2011 (1), 16 WAR; and Eric Karros, 1B, 1988 (6), 10 WAR.

## 18. TEXAS A&M

**Record:** 1,543–786–7 (.662).
**Coaches:** Tom Chandler (1959–1984), Mark Johnson (1985–2005) and Rob Childress (2006–).
**National Champion:** None. **Runner-Up:** None.
**NCAA Tournament:** 27. **College World Series:** 4. **All-Americans:** 32.

First-Team All-Americans: SP—Jeff Granger# (1993) and Barret Loux (2010). 2B—Terry Taylor (1989) and Ryne Birk (2016). 3B—Scott Livingston# (1987), John Blyington (1989) and Boomer White (2016). OF—Daylan Holt (1999). UT—Scott Beerer (2003).

Draft Top 10 Rounds: 82. Top Pick: 5th—Jeff Granger, LHP (1993/Royals).

Annual Award Winners: Assistant Coach—Jim Lawler, 2003.

Top Five Big Leaguers: **1.** Chuck Knoblauch, 2B, 1989 (1), 45 WAR. **2.** Cliff Pennington, SS, 2005 (1), 10 WAR. **3.** *Michael Wacha, RHP, 2012 (1), 8 WAR. **4.** *Alex Wilson, RHP, 2009 (2), 5 WAR. **5.** *Ross Stripling, RHP, 2012 (5), 5 WAR.

## 19. GEORGIA TECH

**Record:** 1,576–816–1 (.659).

**Coaches:** Jim Luck (1962–1981), Jim Morris (1982–1993) and Danny Hall (1994–).

**National Champion:** None. **Runner-Up (1x):** 1994.

**NCAA Tournament:** 30. **College World Series:** 3. **All-Americans:** 35.

First-Team All-Americans: **C**—Jason Varitek# (1992-94), Matt Wieters# (2006-07) and Joey Bart (2018). **3B**—Mark Teixeira# (2000). **SS**—Nomar Garciaparra# (1994) and Tyler Greene# (2005). **OF**—Riccardo Ingram# (1987), Jay Payton# (1994) and Daniel Palka# (2013).

**Draft Top 10 Rounds:** 76. **Top Pick:** 2nd—Joey Bart, C (2018/Giants).

**Annual Award Winners: Player**—Jason Varitek, C, 1994; and Mark Teixeira, 3B, 2000.

Top Five Big Leaguers: **1.** Kevin Brown, RHP, 1986 (1), 68 WAR. **2.** Mark Teixeira, 1B, 2001 (1), 52 WAR. **3.** Nomar Garciaparra, SS, 1994 (1), 44 WAR. **4.** Jason Varitek, C, 1994 (1), 24 WAR. **5.** *Matt Wieters, C, 2007 (1), 19 WAR. **Others:** *Charlie Blackmon, OF, 2008 (2), 18 WAR; and Jay Payton, OF, 1994 (1s), 15 WAR.

## 20. OREGON STATE

**Record:** 1,347–739–8 (.645).

**Coaches:** Jack Riley (1973–1994), Pat Casey (1995–2018) and Pat Bailey (2019).

**National Champion (3x):** 2006, 2007, 2018. **Runner-Up:** None.

**NCAA Tournament:** 16. **College World Series:** 6. **All-Americans:** 24.

First-Team All-Americans: **SP**—Dallas Buck (2005), Andrew Moore# (2013), Ben Wetzler (2014) and Jake Thompson (2017). **C**—Adley Rutschman (2019). **2B**—Nick Madrigal (2017). **OF**—Jacoby Ellsbury# (2005), Cole Gillespie# (2006), Michael Conforto# (2014) and Trevor Larnach (2018).

**Draft Top 10 Rounds:** 62. **Top Pick:** 1st—Adley Rutschman, C (2019/Orioles).

**Annual Award Winners: Player**—Adley Rutschman, C, 2019. **Coach**—Pat Casey, 2006. **Freshman**—Kevin Abel, RHP, 2018.

Top Five Big Leaguers: **1.** *Jacoby Ellsbury, OF, 2005 (1), 31 WAR. **2.** *Michael Conforto, OF, 2014 (1), 13 WAR. **3.** Darwin Barney, 2B, 2007 (4), 9 WAR. **4.** *Matt Boyd, LHP, 2013 (6), 7 WAR. **5.** *Sam Gaviglio, RHP, 2011 (5), 2 WAR.

## 21. SOUTHERN CALIFORNIA

**Record:** 1,261–996–4 (.559).

**Coaches:** Rod Dedeaux (1943–1945, 1951–1986), Mike Gillespie (1987–2006), Chad Kreuter (2007–2010), Frank Cruz (2011–2012) and Dan Hubbs (2013–2019).

**National Champion (1x):** 1998. **Runner-Up (1x):** 1995.

**NCAA Tournament:** 17. **College World Series:** 4. **All-Americans:** 32.

First-Team All-Americans: **SP**—Seth Etherton# (1998), Barry Zito# (1999), Mark Prior# (2001) and Ian Kennedy# (2005). **C**—Jim Campanis (1988), Jeff Clement# (2005) and Garrett Stubbs# (2015). **1B**—Mark McGwire# (1984). **OF**—Mark Smith# (1991) and Geoff Jenkins# (1995).

**Draft Top 10 Rounds:** 85. **Top Pick:** 2nd—Mark Prior, RHP (2001/Cubs).

**Annual Award Winners: Player**—Mark Prior, RHP, 2001.

Top Five Big Leaguers: **1.** Randy Johnson, LHP, 1985 (2), 101 WAR. **2.** Mark McGwire, 1B, 1984 (1), 62 WAR. **3.** Jeff Cirillo, 3B, 1991 (11), 35 WAR. **4.** Barry Zito, LHP, 1999 (1), 32 WAR. **5.** Bret Boone, 2B, 1990 (5), 23 WAR. **Others:** Geoff Jenkins, OF, 1995 (1), 22 WAR; Mark Prior, RHP, 2001 (1), 17 WAR; and *Ian Kennedy, RHP, 2006 (1), 17 WAR.

## 22. ARIZONA

**Record:** 1,295–978–2 (.570).

**Coaches:** Jerry Kindall (1972–1995), Jerry Stitt (1995–2001), Andy Lopez (2002–2015) and Jay Johnson (2016–).

**National Champion (2x):** 1986, 2012. **Runner-Up (1x):** 2016.

**NCAA Tournament:** 17. **College World Series:** 5. **All-Americans:** 24.

**First-Team All-Americans: SP**—Scott Erickson# (1989) and Preston Guilmet# (2007). **C**—Alan Zinter# (1989). **2B**—Bob Ralston (1984), Scott Kingery# (2015) and Cameron Cannon (2019). **OF**—Shelley Duncan# (2001) and Trevor Crowe# (2005). **UT**—Ben Diggins# (2000).

**Draft Top 10 Rounds:** 79. **Top Pick:** 14th—Trevor Crowe, OF (2005/Indians).

**Annual Award Winners:** None.

Top Five Big Leaguers: **1.** Kenny Lofton, OF, 1988 (17), 68 WAR. **2.** Trevor Hoffman, RHP, 1989 (11), 28 WAR. **3.** Scott Erickson, RHP, 1989 (4), 25 WAR. **4.** Joe Magrane, LHP, 1985 (1), 12 WAR. **5.** J.T. Snow, 1B, 1989 (5), 11 WAR. **Others:** *Mark Melancon, RHP, 2006 (9), 11 WAR; *Kevin Newman, SS, 2015 (1), 2 WAR; and *Scott Kingery, 3B, 2015 (3), 2 WAR.

## 23. VANDERBILT

**Record:** 1,339–915–9 (.594).

**Coaches:** Roy Mewbourne (1979–2002) and Tim Corbin (2003–).

**National Champion (2x):** 2014, 2019. **Runner-Up (1x):** 2015.

**NCAA Tournament:** 15. **College World Series:** 4. **All-Americans:** 24.

**First-Team All-Americans: SP**—David Price# (2007), Carson Fulmer# (2015). **RP**—Casey Weathers (2007). **2B**—Warner Jones (2004) and Tony Kemp# (2013). **3B**—Pedro Alvarez# (2006-07) and Austin Martin (2019). **SS**—Dansby Swanson# (2015). **OF**—J.J. Bleday (2019).

**Draft Top 10 Rounds:** 71. **Top Pick:** 1st—David Price, LHP (2007/Rays); and Dansby Swanson, SS (2015/D-backs).

**Annual Award Winners: Player**—David Price, LHP, 2007. **Coach**—Tim Corbin, 2014. **Assistant Coach**—Derek Johnson, 2010. **Freshman**—Pedro Alvarez, 3B, 2006; and Kumar Rocker, RHP, 2019.

Top Five Big Leaguers: **1.** *David Price, LHP, 2007 (1), 40 WAR. **2.** *Sonny Gray, RHP, 2011 (1), 18 WAR. **3.** *Mike Minor, LHP, 2009 (1), 18 WAR. **4.** Joey Cora, 2B, 1985 (1), 8 WAR. **5.** Pedro Alvarez, 3B, 2008 (1), 6 WAR. **Others:** *Walker Buehler, RHP, 2015 (1), 6 WAR; and *Dansby Swanson, SS, 2015 (1), 4 WAR.

## 24. OKLAHOMA

**Record:** 1,496–888–3 (.627).

**Coaches:** Enos Semore (1968–1989), Stan Meek (1990), Larry Cochell (1991–2005), Sunny Golloway (2005–2013), Pete Hughes (2014–2017) and Skip Johnson (2018–).

**National Champion (1x):** 1994. **Runner-Up (x):** None.

**NCAA Tournament:** 26. **College World Series:** 4. **All-Americans:** 19.

**First-Team All-Americans: SP**—Mark Redman# (1995) and Jon Gray# (2013). **2B**—Brian Eldridge (1992).

**Draft Top 10 Rounds:** 66. **Top Pick:** 3rd—Bobby Witt, RHP (1985/Rangers); and Jon Gray, RHP (2013/Rockies).

**Annual Award Winners:** None.

Top Five Big Leaguers: **1.** Jason Bartlett, SS, 2001 (13), 18 WAR. **2.** Bobby Witt, RHP, 1985 (1), 15 WAR. **3.** Russ Ortiz, RHP, 1995 (4), 13 WAR. **4.** *Jon Gray, RHP, 2013 (1), 11 WAR. **5.** Mark Redman, LHP, 1995 (1), 9 WAR. **Others:** *Chase Anderson, RHP, 2009 (9), 8 WAR; and *Garrett Richards, RHP, 2009 (1s), 7 WAR.

## 25. FRESNO STATE

**Record:** 1,461–930–5 (.611).

**Coaches:** Bob Bennett (1970–2002) and Mike Batesole (2003–).

**National Champion (1x):** 2008. **Runner-Up:** None.

**NCAA Tournament:** 24. **College World Series:** 3. **All-Americans:** 24.

    **First-Team All-Americans: SP**—Randy Graham (1982), John Hoover# (1984), Bobby Jones# (1991) and Jeff Weaver# (1997). **1B**—Lance Shebelut (1988). **SS**—Eddie Zosky# (1989). **OF**—Tom Goodwin# (1988-89).

    **Draft Top 10 Rounds:** 67. **Top Pick:** 6th—Steve Soderstrom, RHP (1993/Giants).

**Annual Award Winners:** None.

    Top Five Big Leaguers: **1.** Terry Pendleton, 3B, 1982 (7), 29 WAR. **2.** Doug Fister, RHP, 2006 (7), 20 WAR. **3.** *Aaron Judge, OF, 2013 (1), 19 WAR. **4.** Jeff Weaver, RHP, 1998 (1), 15 WAR. **5.** Matt Garza, RHP, 2005 (1), 12 WAR.

# HOW THE COLLEGE GAME HAS CHANGED

### Rates For Scoring And Home Runs In Division 1, 1970–2019

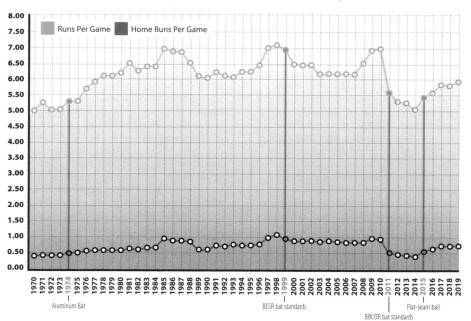

# PHOTO CREDITS

**PAGE 5:** Reggie Jackson by Arizona State/Collegiate Images via Getty Images. **PAGE 13:** Tom Seaver by Southern California/Collegiate Images via Getty Images. **PAGE 20:** Mike Moore by B Bennett/Getty Images. **PAGE 23:** Mike Moore by Focus on Sport/Getty Images. **PAGE 23:** Tony Gwynn by Diamond Images/Getty Images. **PAGE 26:** Charlie O'Brien by Otto Greule/Allsport. **PAGE 29:** Spike Owen by Ronald C. Modra/Getty Images. **PAGE 29:** Jmmy Key by David Cooper/Toronto Star via Getty Images. **PAGE 35:** Jeff Kunkel by Sporting News via Getty Images. **PAGE 35:** Roger Clemens by John Reid III/MLB Photos via Getty Images. **PAGE 36:** Dave Magadan by Focus on Sport/Getty Images. **PAGE 41:** Bill Swift by Steve Dunn/Allsport. **PAGE 41:** Mark McGwire by Focus on Sport/Getty Images. **PAGE 42:** Oddibe McDowell by B Bennett/Getty Images. **PAGE 44:** Ron Fraser by Miami/Collegiate Images/Getty images. BA cover photo by Mike Janes. **PAGE 47:** BJ Surhoff by Focus on Sport/Getty Images. **PAGE 47:** Barry Bonds by Focus on Sport/Getty Images. **PAGE 50:** Gil Heredia by Jeff Hixon/Allsport. BA cover photo by Morris Fostoff. **PAGE 53:** Jeff King by Jonathan Daniel/Getty Images. **PAGE 53:** Kevin Brown by Bernstein Associates/Getty Images. **PAGE 59:** Mike Harkey by Otto Greule Jr/Getty Images. **PAGE 59:** Craig Biggio by Owen C. Shaw/Getty Images. **PAGE 62:** Lee Plemel by Tim Davis. BA cover photo by Tom DiPace. **PAGE 65:** Andy Benes by Scott Halleran/Getty Images. **PAGE 65:** Kenny Lofton by Mitchell Layton/Getty Images. **PAGE 71:** Ben McDonald by Focus on Sport/Getty Images. **PAGE 71:** Jeff Bagwell by Jonathan Daniel/Getty Images. **PAGE 72:** Ben McDonald by Ronald C. Modra/Getty Images. **PAGE 81:** Dan Wilson by Mitchell Layton/Getty Images. **PAGE 81:** Mike Mussina by Focus on Sport/Getty Images. **PAGE 82:** Mike Kelly by Jonathan Kirn/Allsport. **PAGE 87:** Mike Kelly by Jonathan Kirn/Al **PAGE 87:** Jeff Cirillo by Don Bartletti/Los Angeles Times via Getty Images. **PAGE 93:** Phil Nevin by Mitchell Layton/Getty Images. **PAGE 93:** Jason Giambi by Jeff Carlick/MLB Photos via Getty Images. **PAGE 99:** Darren Dreifort by Tom Hauck/Allsport. **PAGE 99:** Billy Wagner by Sporting News via Getty Images. **PAGE 105:** Paul Wilson by Mitchell Layton/Getty Images. **PAGE 105:** Nomar Garciaparra by Mitchell Layton/Getty Images. **PAGE 106:** Jason Varitek by Georgia Tech/Collegiate Images via Getty Images. **PAGE 108:** Mark Kotasy by Andy Lyons/Getty Images. BA cover photo by Bill Nichols. **PAGE 111:** Darin Erstad by Jeff Carlick/Allsport. **PAGE 111:** Todd Helton by John Williamson/MLB Photos via Getty Images. **PAGE 114:** LSU CWS by Jed Jacobsohn. **PAGE 117:** Kris Benson by David Seelig/Allsport. **PAGE 117:** Casey Blake by Andy Lyons/Allsport. **PAGE 121:** BA cover photo by Tom DiPace. **PAGE 123:** Matt Anderson by Craig Melvin/Allsport. **PAGE 123:** Tim Hudson by Jed Jacobsohn/Allsport. **PAGE 127:** BA cover photo by Tom DiPace. **PAGE 129:** Pat Burrell by Rick Stewart/Allsport. **PAGE 129:** JD Drew by Ezra Shaw. **PAGE 130:** Jeff Austin by Larry Goren/Four Seam Images. **PAGE 132:** Jon Lester by J. Meric/Getty Images. BA cover photo by Dennis Wolverton. **PAGE 135:** Barry Zito by Tom Hauck/Allsport. **PAGE 135:** Mark Ellis by Harry How/Getty Images. **PAGE 138:** Augie Garrido by Jamie Schwaberow/NCAA Photos via Getty Images. **PAGE 142:** Brad Hawpe by Andy Lyons/Allsport. BA cover photo by Carl Kline. **PAGE 145:** Adam Johnson by Elsa/Allsport. **PAGE 145:** Chase Utley by Rick Stewart/Allsport. **PAGE 146:** Mark Teixeira by Georgia Tech/Collegiate Images via Getty Images. **PAGE 148:** 2001 Miami Hurricanes Men's College World Series by Jamie Schwaberow/NCAA Photos via Getty Images. **PAGE 151:** Mark Prior by Jonathan Daniel/Getty Images. **PAGE 151:** Mark Teixeira by Rick Stewart/Getty Images. **PAGE 152:** Mark Prior by Larry Goren. **PAGE 154:** Huston Street and Michael Hollimon by Jamie Schwaberow/NCAA Photos via Getty Images. BA cover photo by George Gojkovich. **PAGE 157:** Bryan Bullington by Marc Serota/Getty Images. **PAGE 157:** Curtis Granderson by John Reid III/MLB via Getty Images. **PAGE 158:** Khalil Greene by Clemson/Collegiate Images via Getty Images. **PAGE 160:** Jeff Niemann and Philip Humber by Jamie Schwaberow/NCAA Photos via Getty Images. BA cover photo courtesy Oakland Athletics. **PAGE 163:** Rickie Weeks by Brian Bahr/Getty Images. **PAGE 163:** Ian Kinsler by Jed Jacobsohn/Getty Images. **PAGE 164:** Rickie Weeks by David Schofield. **PAGE 166:** Cal State Fullerton 2004 Division I Men's Baseball Championship by Jamie Schwaberow/NCAA

Photos via Getty Images. BA cover photo by Larry Goren. **PAGE 169:** Jeff Niemann by Jamie Squire/Getty Images. **PAGE 169:** Justin Verlander by Andy Altenburger/Icon SMI/Icon Sport Media via Getty Images. **PAGE 170:** Jered Weaver by Kirby Lee/WireImage. **PAGE 172:** Augie Garrido by Jamie Schwaberow/NCAA Photos via Getty Images. BA cover photo by Larry Goren. **PAGE 175:** Alex Gordon by Jonathan Ferrey/Getty Images. **PAGE 175:** Ryan Braun by Mark Cunningham/MLB Photos via Getty Images. **PAGE 176:** Alex Gordon by Peter Aiken/WireImage. **PAGE 178:** Oregon State CWS by Doug Pensinger/Getty Images. BA cover photo by David L. Greene. **PAGE 181:** Greg Reynolds by Lisa Blumenfeld/Getty Images. **PAGE 181:** Max Scherzer by Jonathan Willey/Arizona Diamondbacks/MLB via Getty Images. **PAGE 182:** Andrew Miller Douglas Jones/Icon SMI/Icon Sport Media via Getty Images. **PAGE 184:** Oregon State CWS by Kevin C. Cox/Getty Images. BA cover photo by Ron Vesely. **PAGE 187:** David Price by Cliff Welch/Icon SMI/Corbis via Getty Images. **PAGE 187:** Josh Donaldson by Ezra Shaw/Getty Images. **PAGE 188:** David Price by Matthew Sharpe/WireImage. **PAGE 190:** Douglas Jones/Icon SMI/Icon Sport Media via Getty Images. BA cover photo by Ron Vesley. **PAGE 193:** Pedro Alvarez by Michael Zagaris/Getty Images. **PAGE 193:** Buster Posey by Harry How/Getty Images. **PAGE 194:** Buster Poseyy by Brian Westerholt. **PAGE 196:** LSU CWS by Elsa/Getty Images. BA cover photo by Tom DiPace. **PAGE 199:** Stephen Strasburg by Scott Cunningham/Getty Images. **PAGE 199:** Paul Goldschmidt by Ezra Shaw/Getty Images. **PAGE 202:** Ameritrade by Justin Tafoya/NCAA Photos via Getty Images. **PAGE 206:** Whit Merrifield by Christian Petersen/Getty Images. BA cover photo by Jesse Soll. **PAGE 209:** Christian Colon by Jason Miller/Getty Images. **PAGE 209:** Chris Sale by Ron Vesely/MLB via Getty Images. **PAGE 210:** Anthony Rendon by Bob Levey/Getty Images. **PAGE 212:** South Carolina CWS by Ronald Martinez/Getty Images. **PAGE 215:** Gerrit Cole by J. Meric/Getty Images. **PAGE 215:** Anthony Rendon by Mitchell Layton/Getty Images. **PAGE 216:** Trevor Bauer by Bill Mitchell. **PAGE 218:** Arizona CWS by Harry How/Getty Images. BA cover photo by David Stoner. **PAGE 221:**

Mike Zunino by Otto Greule Jr/Getty Images. **PAGE 221:** Marcus Stroman by Leon Halip/Getty Images. **PAGE 222:** Mike Zunino by Jamie Schwaberow/NCAA Photos via Getty Images. **PAGE 224:** Adam Plutko by Stephen Dunn/Getty Images. **PAGE 227:** Mark Appel by Kevin C. Cox/Getty Images. **PAGE 227:** Kris Bryant by Rob Tringali/MLB via Getty Images. **PAGE 228:** Kris Bryant by Robert Gurganus. **PAGE 230:** Vanderbilt CWS by John S. Peterson-Icon SMI/Corbis/Icon Sportswire via Getty Images. BA cover photo by Michael Ponzini. **PAGE 233:** Carlos Rodon by Ric Tapia/Icon Sportswire/Corbis/Icon Sportswire via Getty Images. **PAGE 233:** Aaron Nola by Rich Schultz/Getty Images. **PAGE 234:** AJ Reed by Bobby McDuffie/Icon SMI/Corbis/Icon Sportswire via Getty Images. **PAGE 236:** Virginia CWS by Peter Aiken/Getty Images. BA cover photo by David Schofield. **PAGE 239:** Dansby Swanson by Norm Hall/Getty Images. **PAGE 239:** Alex Bregman by Mark Cunningham/MLB Photos via Getty Images. **PAGE 240:** Andrew Benintendi by John Korduner/Icon SMI/Corbis/Icon Sportswire via Getty Images. **PAGE 242:** Coastal Carolina CWS by Peter Aiken/Getty Images. **PAGE 245:** Nick Senzel by Joe Robbins/Getty Images). **PAGE 245:** Pete Alonso by Jim McIsaac/Getty Images. **PAGE 246:** Tom Priddy. **PAGE 248:** Florida CWS by Jamie Schwaberow/NCAA Photos via Getty Images. **PAGE 251:** Brendan McKay by Denis Poroy/Getty Images. **PAGE 251:** Keston Hiura by Quinn Harris/MLB Photos via Getty Images. **PAGE 252:** Brendan McKay by Brian westerholt. **PAGE 254:** Pat Casey by Peter Aiken-Getty Images. **PAGE 257:** Casey Mize by Mark Cunningham/MLB Photos via Getty Images. **PAGE 258:** Brady Singer by Jamie Schwaberow/NCAA Photos via Getty Images. **PAGE 260:** Vanderbilt CWS by Corey Solotorovsky/NCAA Photos via Getty Images. **PAGE 263:** Adley Rutschman by Cliff Welch/Icon Sportswire via Getty Images. **PAGE 264:** Adley Rutschman by Peter Aiken/Getty Images. **PAGE 266:** Skip Bertman by Vincent Laforet/Allsport. **PAGE 266:** Ben McDonald by Ronald C. Modra/Getty Images. **PAGE 266:** Alex Bregman by Stacy Revere/Getty Images. **PAGE 266:** Aaron Nola by John Korduner/Icon SMI/Corbis/Icon Sportswire via Getty Images. **PAGE 269:** Mike Martin by Don Juan Moore/Getty Images.